The Who's Who of
IPSWICH TOWN

The Who's Who of
IPSWICH TOWN

The Football League Years

Dean Hayes

First published in Great Britain in 2006 by

The Breedon Books Publishing Company Limited

Breedon House, 3 The Parker Centre,

Derby, DE21 4SZ.

© Dean Hayes 2006

All Rights Reserved. No part of this publication may be reproduced, stored in a retrieval system, or transmitted in any form, or by any means, electronic, mechanical, photocopying, recording or otherwise without the prior permission in writing of the copyright holders, nor be otherwise circulated in any form or binding or cover other than in which it is published and without a similar condition being imposed on the subsequent publisher.

ISBN 1 85983 515 5

Printed and bound by Cromwell Press, Trowbridge, Wiltshire.

Contents

Introduction	7
The Who's Who of Ipswich Town A–Z	8
Football League Managers	170
Ipswich Town Internationals	177
Individual Scoring Feats	179
Ipswich Town Career Records	185

Introduction

The Who's Who of Ipswich Town – The Football League Years revisits the many contrasting experiences of the Tractor Boys through its life blood – the players. Some have been great, some good, some others, all with one thing in common – all have pulled on an Ipswich shirt and taken to the field to represent the club in a Football League game. A total of 396 Ipswich players have taken to the field during the Blues' League matches.

This book features not only the well-known names in Town's past, but also those less famous players to have appeared for the club, researched down to the last man, whether they played four or 400 matches.

Piecing together information from numerous sources and slowly identifying a career from birth to death (where applicable) is in many ways like a huge jigsaw. Gathering information on Ipswich's stars past and present is a lifetime's work; players will come and go and facts will continue to be unearthed in an attempt to obtain a comprehensive biography.

In a text with such a huge amount of data, I have tried hard to eradicate mistakes. Football writing in the past has been prone to error, many carried through the years from volume to volume. While every care has been taken, it is maybe inevitable in a work containing so much material that errors have slipped the net. This book is a text that will give nostalgic pleasure, reviving memories. It is also a historical research document for present and future generations – a history of the men who made the Town!

Dean P. Hayes
Pembrokeshire
August 2006

The Who's Who of Ipswich Town A–Z

ABIDALLAH Nabil

Midfield

Born: Amsterdam, Holland, 5 August 1982.
Career: Ajax (Holland) 1999; IPSWICH TOWN 2000; Northampton Town (loan) 2004; Clacton Town; Heerenveen (Holland).

■ A Moroccan Youth international, Nabil Abidallah joined Ipswich Town from Ajax's youth programme and

made steady progress in the reserves during his first season at Portman Road. He stepped up for his first-team debut when he came on for the final 11 minutes at home to Everton in February 2001, and also featured in the closing stages of the home game with Bradford City the following month. Predominantly a right-footed creative midfield player, with a style similar to Kieron Dyer, he was only on the fringes of the Ipswich side in 2002–03 and his only appearance was as a substitute in the FA Cup tie with Morecambe. Unable to establish himself, he had a spell on loan with Northampton Town but had made just two appearances from the bench for the Cobblers before suffering an injury. He then played non-League football for Clacton Town before spending the remainder of the campaign on trial with clubs in Holland before signing for Heerenveen.

ABOU Samassi

Forward

Born: Gabnoa, Ivory Coast, 4 August 1973.
Career: Lyon (France) 1995; Cannes (France) 1995; West Ham United 1997; IPSWICH TOWN (loan) 1998; Walsall (loan) 1999; Kilmarnock (loan) 2000; Lorient (France).

■ Joining West Ham United from French League side Cannes in November 1997, the Ivory Coast international striker quickly became a cult hero at Upton Park. Having made his Premiership debut at Chelsea, he opened his scoring account in a brilliant game against Barnsley, when he set up two goals and scored twice himself in a 6–0 rout. A further two goals against Leicester on the final day of the season brought the 'Aboooo' chant ringing round the ground. Surprisingly, in 1998–99 he was used sparingly up front and in December 1998 he was loaned to Ipswich as cover for David Johnson, who was having a knee operation. He scored for Town in a 2–1 win at Sheffield United and then combined well with Richard Naylor for his two goals at Portsmouth before returning to Upton Park. Still out of the running for a first-team place, he had loan spells with Walsall and Kilmarnock before being released by the Hammers, when he returned to France to play for Lorient.

ACRES Basil Derek John

Full-back

Born: Samford, 27 October 1926.
Career: Brantham; IPSWICH TOWN 1951.

■ Basil Acres was a regular member of the Suffolk County FA side before joining Ipswich as an amateur from Brantham in the summer of 1951. He made his debut in a disastrous 5–1 defeat at Brighton & Hove Albion in September of that year, a team which Town had beaten 5–0 at home a week earlier! Acres developed into a strong-tackling defender with good distributional skills and in 1953–54, when the club won the Third Division South Championship, he was one of five players to appear in all 53 League and Cup games. His

only goal during that campaign, in which he was part of a solid Town defence consisting of Feeney, Myles, Rees and Parker, was the winner on the ground where he made his debut as Brighton were beaten 2–1. When the club won the Third Division South Championship again in 1956–57, Acres lost his place to Larry Carberry halfway through the season and, when he did return, he showed his versatility by playing in a variety of positions. In fact, in the last game of the season, which Town had to win to overtake Torquay United while hoping the Devon club did not win their game at Crystal Palace, Acres played centre-forward and scored one of the goals in a 2–0 win at Southampton. He went on to score six goals in 232 League and Cup games but at the end of the 1960–61 season he was forced to quit the game as a result of a troublesome ankle injury. On hanging up his boots, he remained at Portman Road, working in the club's Development Office.

ALSOP Gilbert Arthur

Centre-forward

Born: Bristol, 10 September 1908.
Died: April 1992.
Career: Bath City; Coventry City 1929; Walsall 1931; West Bromwich Albion 1935; IPSWICH TOWN 1937; Walsall 1938.

■ After playing non-League football for Bath City, centre-forward Gilbert Alsop joined Coventry City, but in two seasons with the club he failed to establish himself as a first-team regular. In October 1931 he started the first of two spells with Walsall, which lasted four years and during which he made 160 appearances and scored 126 times. From there he moved to nearby West Bromwich Albion in November 1935 for two seasons before signing for Ipswich Town in the summer of 1937. Alsop played a season of Southern League football for Ipswich, scoring 24 goals in 24 games, a total that included four in a 7–0 defeat of Aldershot reserves and a hat-trick in an 8–2 demolition of Newport County reserves. Alsop made his Football League debut for the Blues in the club's first-ever game in the competition, scoring in a 4–2 win over Southend United. He ended his career with a second spell at Walsall, making 35 League appearances and scoring 25 times. Alsop is remembered perhaps most fondly by Walsall fans. He was part of one of the greatest FA Cup upsets of all time when the Saddlers defeated the mighty Arsenal 2–0 in January 1933. After retiring, Alsop stayed in the Walsall area, becoming groundsman and trainer at Fellows Park. A stand was named after him at Walsall's Bescot Stadium.

AMBROSE Darren Paul

Midfield

Born: Harlow, 29 February 1984.
Career: IPSWICH TOWN 2001; Newcastle United 2003; Charlton Athletic 2005.

■ An England Under-16 international, attacking midfielder Darren Ambrose joined Ipswich's School of Excellence at the age of 11 and progressed through the age

Darren Ambrose

groups until he was offered a scholarship and joined the Academy full-time in the summer of 2000. An integral member of the Under-17 League-winning team and the successful FA Youth Cup team that reached the semi-finals in 2001, he made his first-team debut when he came on as a late substitute against Arsenal at Highbury in April 2002. He scored on his first League start against Walsall on the opening day of the 2002–03 season, but was unable to celebrate his success afterwards because he took the full force of the ball in the face later on in the game and needed 11 stitches in his mouth. Able to play on either flank, he contributed more than his fair share of goals and was used effectively by Joe Royle as a second-half substitute to run at tired defences. In March 2003 he was sold to Newcastle United for £1 million, but a troublesome knee injury prevented him making his Magpie debut until the last game of the season, when he came off the bench at West Bromwich Albion. Injuries hampered his progress at St James' Park at the start of the following season but after scoring as a substitute in the UEFA Cup tie against NAC Breda, he became a regular on the club's bench. He scored his first Premiership goal against Leicester City and, following Nobby Solano's departure to Aston Villa, he began to appear in the starting line up. An England Under-21 international, he appeared only sporadically in 2004–05, and of his 56 appearances at the time of his transfer to Charlton Athletic, more than half had been made from the bench.

APPLEBY Richard Dean

Right-back/Midfield

Born: Middlesbrough, 18 September 1975. Career: Newcastle United 1993; IPSWICH TOWN 1995; Swansea City 1996; Kidderminster Harriers 2001; Hull City 2002; Kidderminster Harriers 2004; Forest Green 2004; Llanelli 2006.

■ The younger brother of former Darlington player Matty Appleby, the left-sided midfielder, Richard made a couple of first-team appearances for Newcastle United before arriving at Portman Road in December 1995. Possessing the ability to dribble past defenders, he appeared in the Anglo-Italian Cup victory over Salernitana and then made three League appearances from the bench, never finishing on the losing side, before being released at the end of the season. He then joined Swansea City, but in his first season at the Vetch he suffered from knee problems before a horrific head injury in a reserve game ended his campaign. In 1997–98, his over-enthusiastic approach saw him sent off in two consecutive matches, though when he was in the team he was the Swans' most creative player. He was sent off at Southend in March 1999 – a likely lengthy ban was overruled by the Welsh FA during an appeal. He went on to win a Third Division Championship medal the following season, but was then placed on the transfer list, although he continued to turn out for the Welsh club. In November 2001 he rejoined his former boss Jan Molby at Kidderminster Harriers, later following the former Liverpool star to Hull City prior to rejoining Kidderminster. He only spent two months there before joining Forest Green of the Conference. Appleby is now back in Wales, playing for Welsh Premier League full-timers Llanelli FC.

ARMSTRONG Alun

Forward

Born: Gateshead, 22 February 1975. Career: Newcastle United 1993; Stockport County 1994; Middlesbrough 1998; Huddersfield Town (loan) 2000; IPSWICH TOWN 2000; Bradford City (loan) 2003; Darlington 2004.

■ Alun Armstrong was one of Stockport County manager Danny Bergara's many clever signings when he snapped up the Geordie striker for a nominal fee from Newcastle United in June 1994. Although he had failed to break into the first-team set up at St James' Park, he scored on his debut in a 4–1 defeat of Cardiff City. He ended the season as County's top scorer, with 15 goals in all competitions, and he started to show real potential with some superb displays leading the line. An FA Cup tie against holders Everton the following season gave him the chance to really put his name in lights. He scored in the first game at Goodison as County held the Cup-holders to a 2–2 draw and then, in the replay at Edgeley Park, netted the equaliser with only seconds remaining. Unfortunately, the Toffees responded immediately to grab a dramatic winner. In 1996–97, the Hatters enjoyed a remarkable campaign, regaining First Division status after an absence of 60 years and reaching the Coca-Cola Cup semi-final. Armstrong had scored 62 goals in 200 games when, in February 1998, Middlesbrough paid £1.6 million for his services. He scored a number of important goals to help the Teesside club win promotion. While at the Riverside he was loaned out to

Huddersfield Town before, still out of favour, he signed for Ipswich for £500,000. He made his debut from the bench in a tremendous win over Liverpool at Anfield and his first goal followed a week later when he sealed another win against Southampton. His partnership up front with Marcus Stewart flourished so much that George Burley allowed David Johnson to join Nottingham Forest. In that 2000–01 season he scored eight goals, but none were sweeter than the two he scored on his return to the Riverside, which enabled Town to beat his former team. His first full season at Portman Road was disrupted by a niggling back injury, though the undoubted highlight has to be scoring in both legs of the UEFA Cup tie with Inter Milan. His powerful header sealed a famous home win, while his penalty conversion in the San Siro proved to be just a consolation. The 2002–03 season was much the same, but he did help the club maintain its unbeaten home European record when he notched the equaliser against Sartid. A loan spell with Bradford City followed before, in September 2004, having scored 19 goals in 94 games, he joined Darlington, where injuries again hampered his progress.

ASHCROFT Charles Thomas

Goalkeeper

Born: Croston, 3 July 1926.
Career: Eccleston; Liverpool 1946; IPSWICH TOWN 1955; Coventry City 1957.

■ Goalkeeper Charlie Ashcroft joined Liverpool midway through World War Two but had to wait until September 1946 before making his League debut – the same day as Bob Paisley – when Liverpool beat Chelsea 7–4 at Anfield. Though never a regular in the Liverpool side, he did enough to win England B international honours during his time at Anfield. Latterly understudying Cyril Sidlow, Ashcroft left Liverpool in 1955 to sign for Ipswich Town, making his debut in a 2–0 defeat at home to Torquay United on the opening day of the 1955–56 season. In fact, Ashcroft conceded two goals in each of his first six games, but then, after helping Town to a 1–1 draw against Queen's Park Rangers, lost his place to George McMillan. His performances were such that Ashcroft was confined to the club's reserve side, for whom he was playing when he broke his arm in the match against Coventry in March 1956. He never regained his first-team place and moved on to Coventry City, where he ended his playing days.

ATKINS Ian Leslie

Defender/Midfield

Born: Birmingham, 16 January 1957.
Career: Shrewsbury Town 1975; Sunderland 1982; Everton 1984; IPSWICH TOWN 1985; Birmingham City 1988; Colchester United; Birmingham City 1991; Cambridge United 1992; Sunderland 1993; Doncaster Rovers 1994.

■ Ian Atkins started out with Shrewsbury Town where, in seven seasons with the club, he scored 58 goals in 279 appearances. In 1978–79 he was instrumental in the Shrews winning the Third Division Championship and it came as no surprise that in August 1982 he followed manager Alan Durban to Sunderland. After two seasons in the top flight with the Wearsiders he moved to Everton, but never really commanded a first-team place at Goodison. He arrived at Portman Road in September 1985, lending considerable experience to a young Town team. Even so, at the end of his first season with the club, he was unable to prevent them slipping out of the top flight for the first time in 18 years. The following season, despite massive injury problems, Atkins led

the club to the Play-offs, where they lost over two legs in the semi-final to Charlton Athletic. This resulted in Bobby Ferguson being deposed as manager, but Atkins then did not see eye to eye with his replacement John Duncan and, after losing the captaincy to Ian Cranson, a parting of the ways was inevitable. In March 1988 he joined and left Birmingham City, going from there to Colchester United. After three years at Layer Road he again joined Birmingham, staying for a year before signing for Cambridge United. After a short spell at Sunderland he ended his playing days at Doncaster Rovers. Appointed manager of Northampton Town, he helped them to promotion by winning the Division Three Play-offs in 1996–97 and then led the club to the Division Two Play-offs the following season. Following the club's relegation he managed Chester City, but quit after six months when they were relegated to the Conference after 69 years in the Football League. After a spell as a assistant at Cardiff, he managed Oxford United before subsequently taking over the reins at Bristol Rovers.

ATKINSON Dalian Robert
Forward

Born: Shrewsbury, 21 March 1968. Career: IPSWICH TOWN 1985; Sheffield Wednesday 1989; Real Sociedad (Spain); Aston Villa 1991; Fenerbahce (Turkey); Metz (France) (loan); Manchester City (loan) 1997.

■ Dalian Atkinson made an impressive League debut for Ipswich as a substitute at Newcastle United in March 1986. After only occasional appearances for the Blues, he finally established a first-team place in February 1988, scoring eight goals in only 13 full appearances to the end of the season, including a magnificent hat-trick of 'solo' goals against promotion-bound Middlesbrough and the maturing Gary Pallister. Atkinson was top marksman with 13 goals the following season, but manager John Duncan found him hard to handle and in the summer of 1989 he was transferred to Sheffield Wednesday for a fee of £450,000. He immediately became a great favourite with the Hillsborough faithful, but he only stayed in Yorkshire for 12 months before being sold to Real Sociedad, with the Owls pocketing well over £1 million in the transaction. After one year in Spain, where he scored 12 goals in 29 games in partnership with John Aldridge, he was re-signed by his former boss at Hillsborough, Ron Atkinson, who had now taken charge at Aston Villa. He scored on his Villa debut in a 3–2 victory at Wednesday before being laid low by injuries, but in 1992–93 he struck up a good partnership with Dean Saunders, the pair netting 19 goals between them from 15 games. It was during this period that he scored the goal that will remain etched in the memory by all

who were either there or who saw it on television. Playing against Wimbledon, his 70-yard run from his own half, which ended with a chip over the 'keeper, won the *Match of the Day* 'Goal of the Season' competition. Unfortunately his goals then dried up and with them went Villa's Championship-winning hopes. In the summer of 1995 the partnership was broken up when Saunders went to Galatasaray and Atkinson to Fenerbahce. Atkinson failed to settle in Turkey and had loan spells with Metz and Manchester City before leaving in 1997.

AUSTIN Terence Willis
Forward

Born: Isleworth, 1 February 1954. Career: Crystal Palace 1972; IPSWICH TOWN 1973; Plymouth Argyle 1976; Walsall 1978; Mansfield Town 1979; Huddersfield Town 1980; Doncaster Rovers 1982; Northampton Town 1983.

■ Unable to make the grade with Crystal Palace, Terry Austin joined Ipswich Town and, after some good displays for the club's reserve side, made his first-team debut in a 2–1 home win over Leicester City in March 1975. An understudy to both David Johnson and Trevor Whymark, he appeared on a more regular basis in 1975–76. He scored his only goal for the club when he came off the bench in a 2–0 defeat of eventual First Division champions Liverpool. Allowed to leave Portman Road, Austin joined Plymouth Argyle but, following the Devon club's relegation to the Third Division, he moved on to Walsall. It was a similar story at Fellows Park as the Saddlers dropped into the Fourth Division. Austin completed an unwanted treble when his next club, Mansfield Town, also suffered relegation! Austin then moved to Huddersfield Town and he remained in Yorkshire when, in the summer of 1982, he signed for Doncaster Rovers. The Belle Vue club were relegated from the Third Division before the much-travelled Austin joined his eighth and final club, Northampton Town. He had scored 94 League goals in 327 games when he decided to leave the first-class scene in the summer of 1984.

AXELDAHL Jonas Michael
Forward

Born: Holm, Sweden, 2 September 1970. Career: Halmstad (Sweden); Malmo FF (Sweden); Osters IF (Sweden); Foggia (Italy); IPSWICH TOWN 1999; Cambridge United 2000.

■ Jonas Axeldahl guested for Ipswich Town during the club's pre-season tour of Sweden in 1999 and returned to England with the team for an official trial. As a result the striker was offered and accepted a one-year contract. Seen as a player who could cover for the club's existing strikers, he seemed to suit playing as a foil for a big target man. At first-team level he was used mainly as a substitute, but, despite notching 20 goals for Town's reserve side and topping the Avon Insurance Combination scoring charts, he failed to find the net for the first team. Axeldahl was released in the close season and moved to Second Division Cambridge United. He featured regularly for the U's until he was sidelined by knee ligament trouble in the New Year. The injury required corrective surgery, after which he struggled to win back his place in the side and parted company with the club.

BAILEY Roy Norman

Goalkeeper

Born: Epsom, 26 May 1932.
Died: April 1993.
Career: Crystal Palace 1949; IPSWICH TOWN 1956.

■ Goalkeeper Roy Bailey first made a name for himself with Crystal Palace. Playing for the Selhurst Park club's reserve side he saved three penalties in a match. He was waiting to begin his National Service when Palace called him up for his League debut against Torquay United in March 1950. Bailey, who was then 17, did not play regular League football until his Army service was completed. He played in 119 League and Cup games for Palace before Alf Ramsey signed him for Ipswich just prior to the transfer deadline in March 1956. Bailey went straight into the Ipswich side for the East Anglian derby against Norwich City. He conceded two goals in the first three minutes but, despite such a disastrous start – the Canaries eventually winning 3–2 – he soon displaced George McMillan as the club's regular 'keeper. The following season, Bailey was the only ever present as the club swept to the Third Division Championship, his displays being rated as on a par with Mick Burns, Town's custodian either side of World War Two. After missing just four games in 1957–58, he was ever present again for the next two seasons, appearing in 88 consecutive League games. In the 1959–60 season, he gained something of a reputation for saving penalties, doing so in four League games. Bailey was one of five players – the others being Carberry, Elsworthy, Phillips and Leadbetter – to have won First, Second and Third Division Championship medals with the same club. After playing in 346 League and Cup games during his nine seasons with Ipswich, Bailey was given a free transfer and emigrated to South Africa, where he became national coach. He later took up media work with such success that he became as well known in his adopted country as Jimmy Hill in England. His son Gary Bailey kept goal for Manchester United and won full international honours for England.

BAIRD Henry

Wing-half/Inside-forward

Born: Belfast, 17 August 1913.
Died: 1973.
Career: Linfield; Manchester United 1937; Huddersfield Town 1938; IPSWICH TOWN 1946.

■ Wing-half Harry Baird arrived at Old Trafford from Irish League side Linfield in January 1937 and made his debut against Sheffield Wednesday. He appeared in 14 games that season as the Red Devils were relegated to Division Two. In 1937–38, as United won promotion at the first time of asking, Baird scored 12 goals in 35 games including braces in the wins over Nottingham Forest and West Ham United. He left Old Trafford in September 1938 to spend a season with Huddersfield Town prior to the outbreak of World War Two. While with the Yorkshire club, Baird won full international honours for Northern Ireland when he played against England. He initially appeared for Ipswich as a guest player during the latter stages of hostilities, signing professional forms for the Portman Road club after demobilisation. He made his League debut for Town in a 2–2 draw against Leyton Orient on the opening day of the 1946–47 season, missing just a couple of games as the club finished sixth in the Third Division South. Baird was ever present the following season as Town moved up to fourth place and kept his place in the side for a further three seasons until, after appearing in 227 League and Cup games, he hung up his boots.

BAKER Clive Edward

Goalkeeper

Born: North Walsham, 14 March 1959.
Career: Norwich City 1977; Barnsley 1984; Coventry City 1991; IPSWICH TOWN 1992; Sudbury Town.

■ Clive Baker started out with Norwich City and, with both Kevin Keelan and Roger Hansbury unavailable, he got a first-team opportunity earlier than expected, making his debut in a 2–2 draw against Newcastle United in April 1978. However, despite spending seven years as a professional at Carrow Road, his first-team opportunities were limited and, following the signing of Chris Woods, he did not get a look in until his free transfer to Barnsley in 1984. After displacing Andy Rhodes as the Tykes' first-choice

'keeper, he was ever present in 1985–86, 1987–88, 1988–89 and 1990–91. He had made 291 appearances and twice won the Player of the Year award when, after surprisingly being released on the eve of the 1991–92 season, he was offered a one-year contract by Coventry City as short-term cover for Steve Ogrizovic. On being freed in the summer of 1992, he seemed a forgotten man until Ipswich Town signed him as cover for Craig Forrest. Baker became the first substitute goalkeeper under the new Premier League rules when he replaced the injured Forrest in only the third minute of the game against Sheffield United in September 1992, and he kept a clean sheet. Three weeks later, when Forrest suffered a recurrence of his previous injury, he started his first match in the top flight since 1991 away to Chelsea and subsequently performed with such safety and consistency that he held his place even when Forrest was available again. After signing a new contract, he became the first Town 'keeper to keep a clean sheet at Anfield. Knee injuries forced his first-class retirement, but he was then signed by Sudbury Town of the Jewson Eastern Counties League as non-contract cover for their goalkeepers.

BAKER Gerard Austin

Centre-forward

Born: New York, United States, 11 April 1938.
Career: Larkhall Thistle; Chelsea 1955; Motherwell; St Mirren; Manchester City 1960; Hibernian; IPSWICH TOWN 1963; Coventry City 1967; Brentford (loan) 1969; Margate; Nuneaton Borough.

■ The brother of England international forward Joe Baker, Gerry played junior football for Larkhall Thistle before joining Chelsea. Unable to win a first-team place at Stamford

Bridge, he returned north of the border to sign for St Mirren. At Love Street he wrote himself into the record books when he scored 10 of his club's goals in a 15–0 Scottish Cup win over Glasgow University. His prolific goalscoring for the Scottish club led to him joining Manchester City but, after netting 14 goals in 37 games, he returned to Scotland to play for Hibernian. Although he was brought up in Scotland, he had been born in New York and played international football for the United States. He left Easter Road in December 1963 to join Ipswich Town for a fee of £17,000 and so became the club's most expensive signing. After making his debut in a goalless home draw against Blackburn Rovers, he scored in each of his next five appearances before netting League hat-tricks against Tottenham Hotspur and Blackpool and in the FA Cup against Oldham Athletic. His three goals at White Hart Lane represent the only occasion on which an Ipswich player has scored a hat-trick and been on the losing side. He ended the season as the club's top scorer, with 18 goals in 22 appearances. Baker was the club's top scorer in seasons 1964–65 (16 goals in 37 games) and 1965–66

(15 in 43 games) before becoming unsettled and going on the transfer list. He continued to find the net on a regular basis, but in November 1967, after scoring 66 goals in 151 games, he left to join First Division Coventry City. Injuries hampered his career at Highfield Road and, although he tried valiantly to continue playing, he finally had to admit defeat and quit League football. He later became player-manager of Margate and then had a spell playing for Nuneaton Borough. Following a spell working for Jaguar in Coventry, Gerry Baker has more recently taken up landscape gardening.

BAKER William George

Left-half

Born: Penrhiwceiber, 3 October 1920.
Died: March 2005.
Career: Troedyrhiw; Cardiff City 1938; IPSWICH TOWN 1955; Ton Pentre.

■ A former coal miner, Billy Baker had trials with a number of clubs including Arsenal and Wolverhampton Wanderers before joining Cardiff City in the summer of 1938. However, he had only made three appearances for the Bluebirds when World War Two intervened. After appearing in 22 wartime fixtures in 1940–41, Baker went to fight for his country but was captured by the Japanese and was a prisoner of war for almost four years. When League football resumed in 1946–47, Baker was converted from a winger to a wing-half and, over the next nine seasons, went on to make 324 first-team appearances. In 1948 he was capped by Wales in the match against Northern Ireland and in 1951–52 was instrumental in helping the Bluebirds win promotion to the First Division. His only goal in that campaign came in the 3–0 home win over South Wales rivals Swansea Town. Baker was the only Cardiff City player to have played before World War Two and enjoyed a lengthy career after it. He severed his ties with the Ninian Park club in June 1955 when he signed for Ipswich Town. An Achilles injury delayed his debut until midway through the season, but he had an outstanding game in a 3–3 draw at Colchester United, laying on Town's opening goal for Tommy Parker. Baker played in 20 consecutive games, of which only three were lost, to help the club finish third in Division Three South. In the close season he returned to Wales to play non-League football for Ton Pentre.

BALL Joseph Howard

Winger

Born: Walsall, 4 April 1931.
Died: 1974.
Career: Banbury Spencer; IPSWICH TOWN 1951; Aldershot 1954.

■ Winger Joe Ball made his Ipswich debut in a 3–1 defeat at Crystal Palace in October 1951, keeping his place in the side for the next game at home to Swindon Town. The result was a disastrous 5–1 win for the Robins and Ball did not appear again until the final two games of the season when he wore the number-11 shirt in two further defeats, including a 5–0 mauling at the hands of Southend United. In 1952–53 Ball played in 28 games and scored two goals – in each of the matches against his home-town club Walsall. Unable to force his way into the Town side that won the 1953–54 Third Division South Championship, he joined Aldershot and spent a couple of seasons at the Recreation Ground before deciding to retire.

BALTACHA Sergei

Midfield

Born: Ukraine, 17 February 1958.
Career: Metallist Kharkov (Russia); Dynamo Kiev (Russia); IPSWICH TOWN 1989; St Johnstone; Inverness Caledonian Thistle.

■ Sergei Baltacha was the first-ever Soviet player to appear in the Football League. He had been an outstanding sweeper for the USSR national side long before Town manager John Duncan signed him from Dynamo Kiev in January 1989. With him being unable to speak a word of English, it was considered risky to play him in defence, so he made his debut against Stoke City on the right of midfield. Baltacha brought the house down when he opened the scoring early in the second half – in doing so, he opened the floodgates as Town went on to win 5–1. Over the ensuing months, Baltacha found himself in and out of the Ipswich side and because he was not very strong in the air, he struggled as a member of an orthodox back four. On leaving Portman Road, he played Scottish League football for St Johnstone and Inverness Caledonian Thistle. His son Sergei played for St Mirren and won Under-21 honours for Scotland.

BARBER Frederick

Goalkeeper

Born: Ferryhill, 26 August 1963.
Career: Darlington 1981; Everton 1986; Walsall 1986; Peterborough United (loan) 1989; Chester City (loan) 1990; Blackpool (loan) 1990; Chester City (loan) 1991; Peterborough United 1991; Colchester United (loan) 1993; Luton Town 1994; Peterborough United (loan) 1994; IPSWICH TOWN (loan) 1995; Blackpool (loan) 1995; Birmingham City 1996.

■ Much-travelled goalkeeper Fred Barber came through the apprentice ranks at Darlington and made his debut at Feethams against Stockport County in March 1983 when only 19 years old. After that he made the goalkeeping position his own for the next three seasons before being transferred to Everton in April 1986 as understudy to Welsh international Neville Southall. He never made a first-team appearance at Goodison before moving on to Walsall just six months later. In 1987–88 he helped the Saddlers win promotion to Division Two, but after five seasons in the Midlands he signed for Peterborough United, one of a number of clubs he had been on loan at during his time with Walsall. In 1992–93, Posh won promotion via the Play-offs but Barber later left the London Road club to join Luton Town. While he was at Kenilworth Road, Barber joined Ipswich on loan and made his only appearance in a 2–2 draw at Wolverhampton Wanderers. Barber finally ended his playing days with Birmingham City.

BARNARD Christopher Leslie

Midfield

Born: Cardiff, 1 August 1947.
Career: Southend United 1965; IPSWICH TOWN 1966; Torquay United 1970; Charlton Athletic 1972.

■ Having started his career with Southend United, midfielder Chris Barnard joined Ipswich Town in the summer of 1966, but had to wait until December of that year before making his League debut in a 2–1 defeat at Charlton Athletic. With Town pushing for a promotion spot, Barnard found it difficult to win a regular place in the side, though he did get a run of five consecutive games – none of which were lost – towards the end of the campaign. Over the next few seasons, Barnard appeared in only a handful of games, and in October 1970 he moved to Torquay United. Here he appeared on a more regular basis, but with the Devon club struggling in the lower reaches of the Third Division, he moved to Charlton Athletic where he later ended his first-class playing career.

BARNES David

Left-back

Born: Paddington, 16 November 1961.
Career: Coventry City 1979; IPSWICH TOWN 1982; Wolverhampton Wanderers 1984; Aldershot 1987; Sheffield United 1989; Watford 1994; Colchester United 1996.

■ A player who helped England to win the UEFA International Youth Tournament in 1980, David Barnes began his career with Coventry City but, after only playing in the odd match, he opted for a move to Ipswich Town. He made his debut for the Blues in a 3–1 defeat of Swansea in November 1982 but, over the next two seasons of First Division football, infrequent appearances were again the order of the day. On moving to Wolverhampton Wanderers, he managed to hold down a regular place, but the team were struggling and during his three years at Molineux they dropped from the Second to the Fourth Division. Following that he had a spell with Aldershot, but after two years at the foot of Division Four, Dave Bassett surprisingly took him to Sheffield United. In his first season at Bramall Lane, the club were promoted from the Second Division as runners-up and he certainly did not look out of place when playing 28 First Division matches in 1990–91. Injuries, including a dislocated shoulder, limited his appearances and in January 1994 he moved to Watford. At Vicarage Road, Barnes was handicapped by persistent stomach problems following a hernia operation and also suffered an Achilles injury before being given a free transfer in the summer of 1996. He then joined Colchester United, having previously played alongside U's manager Steve Wignall at Aldershot, but again injuries ruined his chances and his contract was cancelled by mutual consent.

BARRON Scott

Defender

Born: Preston, 2 September 1985.
Career: IPSWICH TOWN 2004.

■ A product of Ipswich Town's youth set-up, the tough-tackling defender has been at Portman Road since the age of 11 and, after making great strides in the club's reserve side, he got his first taste of senior football when he was an unused substitute in the win at Walsall in March 2004. He made his senior debut at right-back in the Carling Cup tie at home to Brentford and was on the bench for the first month of League football. However, a series of groin and back injuries left him sidelined for the remainder of that campaign. Also able to play in midfield, he made his League debut as a substitute against Wolves and his first League start in a 2–2 draw at Stoke City.

BART-WILLIAMS Christopher Gerald

Midfield

Born: Freetown, Sierra Leone, 16 June 1974.
Career: Leyton Orient 1991; Sheffield Wednesday 1991; Nottingham Forest 1995; Charlton Athletic 2001; IPSWICH TOWN 2003; Apoel Nicosia (Cyprus).

■ A teenage footballing prodigy, Bart-Williams made his Football League debut for Leyton Orient at the age of 16 years and four months at Grimsby Town in October 1990 and later scored for the O's after only 10 minutes of his full League debut at home to Tranmere Rovers. Thereafter he was established in Orient's midfield. First Division clubs became alerted to his talent and in November 1991 Sheffield Wednesday manager Trevor Francis paid £275,000 for his services. He soon settled into the Wednesday side and, though most of his games were in midfield, when he was asked to play up front he responded with a hat-trick in a 5–2 home victory over Southampton. He played a vital role for England in the World Youth Cup in Australia, having earlier broken into the Under-21 side. Not selected for the Owls' League Cup Final side, he came on as a substitute in both FA Cup Final games at Wembley before having to settle for a losers' medal following a 2–1 defeat at the hands of Arsenal. Bart-Williams

left Hillsborough to sign for Nottingham Forest for a fee of £2.5 million in the summer of 1995. Much of his early time at the City Ground was spent on the treatment table, but on making a full recovery he was instrumental in Forest returning to the Premiership at the first time of asking, winning a First Division Championship medal along the way. Back in the top flight, his stamina and commitment were again in evidence and he showed his versatility by playing in five different positions for the club. Appointed club captain by manager David Platt, he was Forest's top scorer with 15 goals in 2000–01 but then asked to go on the transfer list. He eventually joined Charlton on loan before the move was made permanent. Much of his time at The Valley was spent on the bench and in September 2003 he joined Ipswich, initially on a three-month loan. However, he eventually ended up signing for the whole season. When he arrived at the club, Town were struggling near the foot of the table, but his steadying influence saw them climb towards a Play-off place. He was then troubled by a back injury, but returned to the side for the first leg of the Play-off semi-final against West Ham United. On leaving Portman Road he went to play for Apoel Nicosia of Cyprus.

BAXTER William Alexander

Centre-half

Born: Edinburgh, 23 April 1939.
Career: Broxburn Athletic; IPSWICH TOWN 1960; Hull City 1971; Watford (loan) 1971; Northampton Town 1972.

■ Bill Baxter, who signed for Town from Broxburn Athletic at the age of 21, had just completed an engineering apprenticeship and was preparing for National Service. Signed with the intention of being cover for the club's first-team regulars, he combined the

start of his Town career with normal army duties in the Royal Engineers at Aldershot and a hectic travel schedule between the barracks, Portman Road and his home in Edinburgh. He found himself pressed into service after an injury to Reg Pickett and made his debut in a 4–1 home win over Norwich City on 27 December 1960. He then played in the remaining 19 games of the campaign as Town went on to win the Second Division Championship. In 1961–62 Baxter missed just two games as the club swept to the League Championship. His form that campaign led to him representing the Army team on several occasions and, in the close season, he toured the Far East with them. He was ever present in 1962–63 and scored his first League goal for the Blues in a 1–1 draw at Fulham. Although Town finished bottom of the First Division in 1963–64, Baxter was the club's only ever present, an achievement he repeated in seasons 1965–66 and 1966–67. In 1967–68 he missed just one game as Town won the Second Division Championship, appearing in

131 consecutive League games during this period of his Portman Road career. Baxter went on to appear in 459 games for the club before leaving in sad circumstances. Following Town's exit from the League Cup at the hands of West Bromwich Albion, an article attributed to him appeared in a Sunday newspaper, berating the club. Unable to give a satisfactory explanation of this to manager Bobby Robson, he was suspended and relieved of the captaincy. In March 1971 he left the club to join fellow Second Division promotion challengers Hull City and went on to appear in 20 games for the Yorkshire club before, following a loan spell with Watford, he ended his first-class career with Northampton Town.

BEATTIE Thomas Kevin

Centre-half

Born: Carlisle, 18 December 1953.
Career: IPSWICH TOWN 1971; Colchester United 1982; Middlesbrough 1982.

■ A product of the Ipswich Town youth policy masterminded by Bobby Robson, Kevin Beattie made his League debut for the club on the opening day of the 1972–73 season in a 2–1 victory over Manchester United at Old Trafford. Two weeks later Ipswich travelled to Leeds United, where Beattie scored his first League goal in an exciting 3–3 draw. The Portman Road club ended the 1972–73 season in fourth place, their best showing since they won the League Championship 11 years earlier. Beattie had played 38 League games at the heart of the Ipswich defence and had scored five goals. He was by now one of the game's greatest creative forces and was a huge favourite with the Ipswich crowd. In the early part of the following season, Beattie turned in some outstanding performances in an Ipswich side that hovered in mid-table before ending the campaign in fourth place. Along with captain Mick Mills, he was one of only two players who had started in all 42 games for the club. His fellow professionals were so impressed with his play that they selected him as the first PFA Young Player of the Year, an award presented to him by Leeds United manager Don Revie. The following season the Leeds boss was appointed manager of England in succession to Joe Mercer. In his fourth match in charge, Revie selected Beattie in the centre of England's defence for their European Championship qualifier against Cyprus at Wembley. It was a game England won 5–0, with Malcolm Macdonald creating a post-war record by scoring all England's goals. The Ipswich player almost got his name on the scoresheet, but in the process of scoring he was adjudged to have fouled the goalkeeper. He went on to win nine caps for his country, all but one under Revie's management. In 1978 Beattie was a member of the Ipswich team that beat Arsenal in the FA Cup Final. He could have become one of the all-time greats, but he had to undergo five operations in four years on his right knee and, after scoring 32 goals for Ipswich in 307 first-team games, he played briefly for Colchester United and Middlesbrough before the injury brought his first-class playing career to a premature end in 1982. He had a spell in Scandinavia, but since hanging up his boots he has had health problems and in March 1991 underwent an emergency stomach operation. Beattie has now taken up media work.

Allan Hunter and Kevin Beattie (right)

BELCHER James Alfred

Wing-half

Born: Stepney, 31 October 1932.
Career: Leyton Orient 1950; Snowdown Colliery; West Ham United 1952; Crystal Palace 1954; IPSWICH TOWN 1958; Brentford 1961.

■ Unable to make the grade with either of his first two League clubs, Leyton Orient and West Ham United, wing-half Jimmy Belcher signed for Crystal Palace in the summer of 1954. Over the next four seasons, Belcher was a virtual ever present in the Selhurst Park club's side and in 1954–55, his first season with the Third Division South club, he was the leading scorer with 12 goals. Belcher had scored 20 goals in 138 games when, in the summer of 1958, he signed for Ipswich Town. Belcher had to wait until January 1959 before playing his first game for the club in a 3–1 defeat at Lincoln City. He got more of a look-in the following season, appearing in 24 games as Town finished the Division Two campaign in mid-table. Though he never got on the scoresheet himself he did make a number of goalscoring opportunities for Phillips and Leadbetter, but in the close season he was allowed to join Brentford. His only season at Griffin Park ended with the Bees being relegated to the Fourth Division.

BELFITT Roderick Michael

Centre-forward

Born: Bournemouth, 30 October 1945.
Career: Retford Town; Leeds United 1963; IPSWICH TOWN 1971; Everton 1972; Sunderland 1973; Fulham (loan) 1974; Huddersfield Town 1975; Worksop Town; Frickley Athletic; Bentley Victoria.

■ Rod Belfitt was an intelligent front-runner who served his apprenticeship as a draughtsman and played for Retford Town before Leeds United signed him in July 1963. He provided excellent cover as United battled on several fronts and his greatest triumph came in the 1967 Inter Cities Fairs Cup semi-final first leg against Kilmarnock, when he netted a hat-trick. In November 1971 a £55,000 transfer to Ipswich Town saw the start of a nomadic career in which he moved to a further four League clubs. Belfitt made a goalscoring debut for Town in a 2–1 home win over Wolves. He scored on his next appearance to secure a point against Crystal Palace and ended the campaign with seven goals in 26 games, including both goals in the return game with Wolves at Molineux. The following season he scored six goals in 14 appearances before moving on to Everton as a key part of the deal that brought England international David Johnson to Portman Road. Town fans were sorry to see him go, and his time at Everton was not fruitful as Joe Royle suffered a long-term injury and he was paired up front with a variety of strikers. He moved on to Sunderland but achieved little on Wearside or with his subsequent clubs. On retiring he returned to his former occupation of draughtsman before becoming a financial planning consultant for Allied Dunbar in Doncaster.

BELL David

Full-back

Born: Edinburgh, 24 December 1909. Died: Monkseaton, April 1986. Career: Wallyford Bluebell; Newcastle United 1930; Derby County 1934; IPSWICH TOWN 1938.

■ Always known as Daniel, Bell began his career with Newcastle United, where he was deputy to the tenacious Roddie Mackenzie in the Magpies squad. Bell proved to have lots of promise both at full-back and in midfield when called upon. He was, however, a victim of fate. When performing well and impressing United's team selection committee and manager Andy Cunningham, he seriously injured an ankle and then cartilage which left him sidelined for a long period. Following United's relegation from the First Division, he joined Derby County. After four seasons at the Baseball Ground, he moved on to Ipswich Town and made his debut in a 1–0 win over Torquay United in October 1938 – this after the club had gone nine games without a win. There followed an upturn in the club's fortunes and Bell went on to appear in 25 games in that first season of League football, scoring goals against Exeter City and Reading. Bell's career was then interrupted by World War Two, but when League football resumed in 1946–47, he played in 40 games as Town finished in sixth place in the Third Division South. He was a virtual ever present in the Town side for the next three seasons, playing on until he was more than 40 years old and taking his total of first-team appearances to 183 before retiring at the end of the 1949–50 season. He then worked for a period at crane manufacturers Ransome & Rapier in Ipswich, where his immense strength was renowned.

BELL Robert Charles

Centre-half

Born: Cambridge, 26 October 1950. Career: Tottenham Hotspur; IPSWICH TOWN 1968; Blackburn Rovers 1971; Crystal Palace 1971; Norwich City (loan) 1972; Hellenic (South Africa); York City 1977.

■ Signed by Bill McGarry as back-up for Ipswich Town's legendary centre-half Bill Baxter, Bobby Bell made his debut for the Portman Road club in a 2–2 draw at Southampton in September 1968, after the club had been two goals down at half-time. Bell was unable to displace the Scot and, in three seasons with the club, made just 37 League and Cup appearances. He did find the net on one occasion during his last season with the club when, in the middle of a run of 18 consecutive appearances, he rescued a point at West Ham United. Not figuring in the plans of new manager Bobby Robson, he was transferred to Blackburn Rovers as part of the deal that saw Allan Hunter move in the opposite direction. His stay at Ewood Park was short-lived and he moved on to Crystal Palace. He later had a one-month loan spell at Carrow Road where he made three appearances. After a period in South Africa, Bell ended his career with York City.

BENT Darren Ashley

Forward

Born: Wandsworth, 6 February 1984. Career: IPSWICH TOWN 2001; Charlton Athletic 2005.

■ Darren Bent was a member of the Ipswich Town Under-17 side that won the Academy League and progressed to the semi-finals of the FA Youth Cup in 2001. At the age of 17 he made his first-team debut at Helsingborg in the UEFA Cup in November 2001 and scored his first senior goal at

THE WHO'S WHO OF IPSWICH TOWN

Darren Bent

Newcastle United the same month in the League Cup. His only Premiership goal for the Blues was the winner against Middlesbrough – just 20 seconds after coming off the bench. He celebrated his first full season in the Ipswich side by finishing as the club's second highest scorer with 18 goals in all competitions. One of the memorable ones came in the game with Sheffield United when 10-man Town came back from 2–0 down to win 3–2. Good in the air and with a strong right foot, his best asset is his pace and this was used to maximum effect by occasionally playing him wide on the right of midfield. Despite only playing for two-thirds of the 2003–04 season because of injury, Darren Bent was still able to notch enough goals to finish up as leading scorer for the Portman Road club. The highlight of his season was his first senior hat-trick against Walsall in March 2004. He also scored the goal that gave Ipswich a slender Play-off semi-final first-leg advantage. He only missed one game during the 2004–05 season when he established an excellent strike partnership with Shefki Kuqi that accounted for 38 League goals. A regular member of the England Under-21 side, he became the third Tractor Boy to join Charlton Athletic in recent times after the Portman Road club finished third in the Coca-Cola Championship and failed to make the top flight via the Play-offs. Addicks manager Alan Curbishley had been tracking the youngster for two years and finally secured his services for £2.5 million, though this figure could rise by a further £500,000 depending upon appearances and international recognition. Reproducing his consistent goalscoring record in the Premiership, with a goal every other game, Bent has won full international honours but failed to make the England World Cup squad in Germany.

BENT Marcus Nathan

Forward

Born: Hammersmith, 19 May 1978.
Career: Brentford 1995; Crystal Palace 1998; Port Vale 1999; Sheffield United 1999; Blackburn Rovers 2000; IPSWICH TOWN 2001; Leicester City (loan) 2003; Everton 2004; Charlton Athletic 2006.

■ Having graduated through the ranks at Brentford, Marcus Bent played his first senior game at Bury in August 1996 and scored his first senior goal the following month in a 3–2 win over Blackpool. He was a virtual ever present in a successful season that saw Brentford reach the Second Division Play-offs in May 1997, only to be beaten by Crewe Alexandra. In January 1998, Bent moved to Crystal Palace for £300,000. Almost exactly a year later he became a Port Vale player, but only stayed for nine months before being released and joining Sheffield United. Flourishing under the guidance of new manager Neil Warnock, he netted the first senior hat-trick of his career in a 6–0 defeat of West Bromwich Albion. He also scored the winning goal in the penalty shoot-out against Rushden & Diamonds. He began the 2000–01 season on top form, netting another treble in the Worthington Cup tie against Lincoln City. Then the goals began to dry up and in November 2000 he joined Blackburn Rovers for a fee of £1.3 million. His chances at Ewood Park were few and far between, so in November 2001 he moved to Ipswich for £3 million. Initially signed as cover for Marcus Stewart, he had to wait until Boxing Day to open his account against Leicester City and then proceeded to score six goals in six games. Possessing the ability to do the unexpected, he had a mixed 2002–03 season, missing the middle part of the campaign and struggling to regain his form when he did return to first-team duty. However, he still managed to score 12 goals. Early the following campaign he joined Leicester City on loan and, though the Foxes lost their Premiership status, he could look back on his time with the club with a degree of personal satisfaction. A few eyebrows were raised when Everton paid £450,000 for him prior to the start of the 2004–05 season, but his displays soon won over the doubters. He missed just one Premiership game before losing his place early the next season. In January 2006, Bent signed for Charlton Athletic in a deal worth £2 million, reuniting him with his former Ipswich teammate and namesake Darren Bent. He then proceeded to score on his Addicks debut as a substitute against League champions Chelsea in a 1–1 draw.

Marcus Bent

BERNAL Andrew

Defender

Born: Canberra, Australia, 16 May 1966.
Career: Sporting Gijon (Spain); IPSWICH TOWN 1987; Sydney Olympic (Australia) 1990; Reading 1994.

■ Australian international defender Andy Bernal had spent a season with Sporting Gijon before joining Ipswich in September 1987. He made his first-team debut from the bench in a 1–0 defeat at Birmingham and went on to appear in nine League games that season, though he only started four of them. Unable to command a regular place, he returned to his native Australia to play for Sydney Olympic. In July 1994, Reading paid £30,000 for his signature and in his first season of a second spell in English football he helped the Royals reach the Play-offs.

Keith Bertschin

A strong yet stylish defender, he scored a number of vital goals for Reading and on occasions captained the side. The 1996–97 season was a memorable one for Bernal for a number of reasons. He was sent off on three occasions and produced an acrobatic display as a substitute goalkeeper after Bobby Mihailov had received his marching orders. His enthusiasm was not dampened in either of the following two campaigns when he took his tally of dismissals to eight in five seasons with the club. His 1999–2000 season was hampered by a persistent foot injury and, after making 226 appearances in his time with the club, he was not offered a new contract.

BERRY Peter

Outside-right

Born: Aldershot, 20 September 1933.
Career: Crystal Palace 1951; IPSWICH TOWN 1958.

■ The brother of John Berry, the Manchester United and England winger whose career ended after he was severely injured in the Munich air disaster, Peter Berry signed professional forms for Crystal Palace. Though he preferred to play on the right-wing, Peter Berry was versatile enough to occupy any of the forward line positions. After completing his National Service, he made his League debut for Palace in a 4–0 defeat at Bristol City in August 1951. Berry played well for Palace during the difficult years of the 1950s and had scored 27 goals in 161 games when Alf Ramsey signed him, together with Palace's Jimmy Belcher, in May 1958. He made his debut in a 1–1 draw with Scunthorpe United on the opening day of the 1958–59 season, going on to appear in 33 games that season. He started the following season off in fine style and in the game against Lincoln City had scored two of Town's goals in a 3–0 win when an injury put him out of the game. He valiantly tried to make a comeback, to no avail, and in the summer of 1961 he was forced into premature retirement.

BERTSCHIN Keith Edwin

Forward

Born: Enfield, 25 August 1956.
Career: Barnet; IPSWICH TOWN 1973; Birmingham City 1977; Norwich City 1981; Stoke City 1984; Sunderland 1987; Walsall 1988; Chester City 1990; Aldershot Town; Solihull Borough; Evesham Town; Barry Town; Worcester City; Hednesford Town; Stafford Rangers.

■ Keith Bertschin represented England at Youth and Under-21 level and was a member of Town's 1975 FA Youth Cup-winning side. He came off the bench to score with his first touch of the ball on his Ipswich debut in a 2–1 win against Arsenal at Highbury in April 1976. He then scored on his first full start a week later in a 4–0 defeat of West Ham United. Despite this promising start, he could not hold down a regular place in the Portman Road club's side and was allowed to join Birmingham City for a fee of £100,000. Forming a prolific scoring partnership with Trevor Francis, Bertschin was ever present in 1977–78, scoring 11 goals and making many more for his strike partner. He broke the same leg twice while at St Andrew's but bounced back each time before helping the club win promotion to the First Division in 1979–80. He was the club's leading scorer during their first season back in the top flight, his total of 12 goals including hat-tricks against Luton Town and Orient. Having scored 41 goals in 141 games he joined Norwich City and in his first season at Carrow Road helped the Canaries win promotion to Division One. A regular in the City forward line, he formed a powerful partnership up front with John Deehan before moving on to Stoke City. Here he added another 29 goals in 88 appearances to his career record before moving north to Sunderland. He never really settled at Roker Park and there followed spells with Walsall, Chester City and Aldershot before their bankruptcy led to the termination of his contract and his professional career. He then had spells in non-League football with a number of clubs, announcing his retirement while with the fifth, Stafford Rangers, in February 1998. After working as a licensed player's agent, he returned to St Andrew's to become Birmingham's reserve-team coach.

BEST David

Goalkeeper

Born: Wareham, 6 September 1943.
Career: Bournemouth 1960; Oldham Athletic 1966; IPSWICH TOWN 1968; Portsmouth 1974; Bournemouth 1975.

■ Goalkeeper David Best began his career with his local club Bournemouth and, in six seasons at Dean Court, made 230 League appearances and helped the Cherries finish in the top five of the Third Division in three consecutive seasons. In September 1966 he joined Oldham Athletic and had played in two League games short of a hundred when, in

October 1968, he signed for Ipswich Town. He made his debut for the Blues in a 2–1 win over Nottingham Forest in a game played at Notts County's Meadow Lane ground. He soon established himself as the club's first-choice 'keeper and in 1969–70 kept 11 clean sheets in 40 games as the club struggled to avoid relegation from the First Division. The following season, Best was in goal when Ipswich visited Stamford Bridge to play Chelsea and conceded 'the goal that never was' in a 2–1 win for the home side. Later in that 1970–71 season, Best lost his place to Laurie Sivell and asked for a transfer because he wanted to play first-team

football. Surprisingly, no realistic offers were received and Best stayed at Portman Road until 1974 when, after making 199 League and Cup appearances, he left to join Portsmouth. After two seasons of Second Division football with the Fratton Park club he returned to Dean Court to end his Football League career with his first club, Bournemouth.

BEVIS David Roger

Goalkeeper

Born: Southampton, 27 June 1942.
Career: IPSWICH TOWN 1959; Cambridge City.

■ Understudy to Roy Bailey and later Ken Hancocks, goalkeeper Dave Bevis was never on the winning side in any of the six League games he played during his time at Portman Road. Having made his debut in a 3–1 defeat at Sheffield United in October 1963, he played in five consecutive games before appearing in his final League game for the club in February 1966. Though he did not make any League appearances in 1964–65 he did play in two FA Cup games. After helping beat Swindon 2–1 he was between the posts when Town were beaten 5–0 by Spurs. On leaving Portman Road, Bevis went to play non-League football for Cambridge City.

BLACKMAN Ronald Henry

Centre-forward

Born: Portsmouth, 2 April 1925.
Career: Gosport Borough; Reading 1947; Nottingham Forest 1954; IPSWICH TOWN 1955; Tonbridge.

■ Ronnie Blackman began his career with Reading, where he still holds two club records: the most League goals in a season, 39 in the Third Division South season of 1951–52, when the club finished runners-up for the second time in three years, and the most League goals in total, 158 in the seven seasons he spent at Elm Park. Nottingham Forest secured his services in the summer of 1954 but he never really settled at the City Ground and a year later he joined Ipswich Town. He made a goalscoring debut for the Blues, netting in a 5–1 win over his first club Reading. Despite not winning a regular place due to the fine form of Grant, Parker and Garneys, he scored in each of his first three games and ended the season with eight goals in 13 games. He found himself in and out of the side over the next couple of seasons and he later left to play non-League football for Tonbridge.

BLACKWOOD Robert Rankin

Wing-half

Born: Edinburgh, 20 August 1934.
Died: 25 June 1997.

Career: Heart of Midlothian; IPSWICH TOWN 1962; Colchester United 1965.

■ Bobby Blackwood started out with Hearts in the early fifties and played in the Tynecastle club's title-winning team of 1957–58. A year later he helped the Jam Tarts win the Scottish League Cup and in 1960 he played a starring role up front, hitting 12 goals as Hearts won the League once again. His form led to him winning representative honours for the Scottish League XI against the Football League. In June 1962 he came south to join Alf Ramsey's Ipswich Town side and made his debut in a 2–1 defeat at Sheffield United in the third game of the 1962–63 season, going on to score four goals – two in a 5–3 defeat by Manchester United – in 19 games. He appeared on a more regular basis the following season and scored some spectacular goals, but could not prevent the club from being relegated to Division Two. After another season of being on the fringes of the first team, Blackwood left Portman Road to continue his career with Colchester United. In his first season at Layer

Road he helped the club win promotion to the Third Division, going on to appear in 105 League games in his three seasons with the club.

BOLTON John McCaig

Defender

Born: Lesmahagow, 26 October 1941. Career: Raith Rovers; IPSWICH TOWN 1963; Morton.

■ Defender Jack Bolton started out with Raith Rovers, but when the Stark's Park club lost their top-flight status he joined Ipswich and made his debut in a 3–1 win over Burnley on the opening day of the 1963–64 season. In a campaign when the club were relegated from the First Division, Bolton was probably Town's most consistent defender and, despite suffering from a number of injuries, appeared in 32 games. Injuries took their toll over the next couple of seasons, but in 1965–66 he did manage to get on the scoresheet a couple of times when asked to play up front in the games against Carlisle and Bury. At the end of that season, Bolton returned north of the border to play for Morton and in his first season at Cappielow Park helped the Greenock club win the Second Division Championship. He remained with Morton as they consolidated their position in the Scottish First Division over the next few seasons.

BOLTON Ronald

Midfield

Born: Golborne, 21 January 1938. Career: Crompton Rovers; Bournemouth 1958; IPSWICH TOWN 1965; Bournemouth 1967.

■ Midfielder Ron Bolton was a member of the Bournemouth side that finished in the top five of the Third Division for three consecutive seasons in the early sixties before joining Ipswich Town in October 1965. Bolton played his first game in Town colours against Southampton at The Dell. In a game in which the Saints led 1–0 at half-time, Bolton laid on second-half goals for Brogan and Hegan in a 2–1 win for Town. Even so, he could not hold down a regular place in the Ipswich side and in just short of two seasons at Portman Road he made just 22 League appearances. Allowed to rejoin Bournemouth, Ron Bolton proved himself a more than useful player in the Third Division and in 1968–69 helped the Cherries to fourth place. He had taken his tally of goals to 48 in 260 League games when he parted company with the Dean Court club.

BOWDITCH Dean Peter

Midfield/Forward

Born: Bishops Stortford, 15 June 1986. Career: IPSWICH TOWN 2002; Burnley (loan) 2004; Wycombe Wanderers (loan) 2005.

■ Dean Bowditch became one of the youngest players to represent Ipswich Town when he came off the bench as a second-half substitute in the derby game with Norwich City in March

2003. Within 30 seconds of arriving on the pitch, his cross from the left led to Fabian Wilnis scoring the opening goal of the game. It was also the young midfielder's through ball that sent Darren Bent away near the end to seal the win. A product of the Ipswich Academy, he made further appearances from the bench as the season drew to a close. The following season he scored his first goal for Ipswich in extra-time of the Carling Cup match against Kidderminster Harriers and made his first start in the next round of the competition at Notts County. Bowditch, who picked up the Dale Roberts Award as the star performer from the Academy in 2003–04, was capped by England at Under-19 level and created club history when he became the youngest player to score a hat-trick, achieving the feat against Watford at Portman Road. The following season he did not make the progress expected of him, mainly because of the success of the partnership of Darren Bent and Shefki Kuqi. After making just six starts, he spent the last two months of the season on loan with Burnley. In 2005–06, Bowditch went on loan to

Wycombe Wanderers to gain experience for what Ipswich Town fans hope will be a long and successful career at Portman Road. He returned to the club for the closing stages of the campaign and signed a new deal that will keep him at the club until 2008.

BOZINOSKI Vlado

Midfield

Born: Macedonia, 30 March 1964.
Career: Sporting Lisbon (Portugal); Beira Mar (loan) (Portugal); IPSWICH TOWN 1992; Beira Mar.

■ Although born in Macedonia, midfielder Vlado Bozinoski twice represented Australia at full international level, having represented the Under-23 side at the 1988 Seoul Olympic Games. He was recommended to Ipswich Town by former Ipswich and England manager Bobby Robson, then manager of Sporting Lisbon, along with Bulgarian Bontcho Guentchev. In fact, Bozinoski was not a regular performer for the Lisbon club, making only 11 appearances in 1990–91 and then spending the following season on loan to SC Beira Mar. He made his Ipswich debut as a substitute away to Coventry City in December 1992, but was unable to break into the first team on a regular basis, although he was a regular on the substitutes' bench in 1992–93. Though he did his level best to settle into the pace of the English game, he left Portman Road in May 1994 and returned to Portugal to play for Beira Mar. Bozinoski now co-runs the 'Canadian 2–for-1 Pizza Soccer Academy' in Singapore.

BRAMBLE Titus Malachi

Centre-half

Born: Ipswich, 21 July 1981
Career: IPSWICH TOWN 1998; Colchester United (loan) 1999; Newcastle United 2002.

Titus Bramble

■ Titus Bramble broke into the Ipswich side just before Christmas 1998 after producing some good performances in the reserve and academy sides, making his debut in the televised game at Sheffield United. Impressing everyone with his apparent lack of nerves and general coolness, he was ruled out of the second half of the season with a foot injury. In fact, he picked up the 'Academy Player of the Year' award complete with plaster cast! The following season saw him hampered by a series of niggling injuries and he went on loan to Colchester United to gain some much-needed match fitness, his arrival coinciding with the run that took United clear of relegation danger. An England Under-21 international, he won a regular place in the Ipswich side in 2000–01 and scored his first senior goal against Sunderland when he surged upfield, exchanging passes with Marcus Stewart before firing the ball into the net. Displaying great strength and power, some of the best strikers in the Premiership found him a difficult opponent. There was talk of him being included in England's World Cup squad, but Town's poor start to the 2001–02 season affected his confidence and this, together with a niggling heel injury, added up to a disappointing season for him. His only goal that season came in the club's UEFA Cup campaign against Torpedo Moscow and preserved Town's unbeaten European record at Portman Road. In July 2002, Town accepted a bid of £5 million from Newcastle United as the Magpies sought to strengthen their defence. Bramble took time to settle at St James' Park and, after only half-a-dozen games, found himself on the bench. He had become a regular by the time the season ended and in 2003–04 scored his first goal for the club in the UEFA Cup tie against NAC Breda, following it up with further strikes against Basle and Mallorca. Despite occasional lapses in concentration, Bramble remains an important member of the Newcastle side. His good touch and long accurate passes out of defence have become features of his game.

BRANAGAN Keith Graham

Goalkeeper

Born: Fulham, 10 July 1966.
Career: Cambridge United 1983; Millwall 1988; Brentford (loan) 1989; Gillingham (loan) 1991; Bolton Wanderers 1992; IPSWICH TOWN 2000.

■ Beginning his career with Cambridge United, goalkeeper Keith

Branagan progressed to become the club's number-one and in 1986–87 was an ever present as the Abbey Stadium club reached the fourth round of the League Cup. In March 1988, Millwall paid £100,000 to take him to The Den, but he could not force his way into the side that did well in their first season in the top flight. After a loan spell with Brentford, he helped Millwall reach the Play-offs in 1991. At the end of the following season, Millwall had six 'keepers on their books and Branagan was snapped up by his former manager Bruce Rioch, who was now in charge of Bolton Wanderers. He was an ever present in the Trotters' 1992–93 Second Division promotion-winning side and, although injury kept him out of the side the following season, he was back in 1994–95 when his penalty save in the Play-off Final against Reading turned the game Bolton's way. International recognition came his way and, after playing for the Republic of Ireland B side, he made his full international debut against Wales in February 1997 when he kept a clean sheet. In 1996–97 he was outstanding as the Wanderers won the First Division Championship, but then found himself one of three very strong 'keepers on Bolton's books. Eventually losing his place to Jussi Jaaskelainen,

Branagan, who had made 263 appearances for Bolton, left to join Ipswich as cover for Richard Wright. He made his debut against Coventry in the Worthington Cup and kept his place for the home defeat by Derby County. He made another Premiership appearance later in the season against Coventry after Wright was injured in the warm-up. The following season he found himself third in line for the 'keeper's role at Portman Road after the arrival of Andy Marshall and Matteo Sereni: his only appearance came at Leicester after Sereni had been sent off. Following an operation on his shoulder, Branagan decided to retire.

BRAZIL Alan Bernard

Forward

Born: Glasgow, 15 June 1959.
Career: IPSWICH TOWN 1977; Tottenham Hotspur 1983; Manchester United 1984; Coventry City 1986; Queen's Park Rangers 1986.

■ Although the famous Celtic Boys Club was not officially linked with the Glasgow giants, the Parkhead club were usually quick to spot any available talent. However, they overlooked Alan Brazil, who joined Ipswich Town. A Scottish Youth international, he made his League debut in a 2–1 defeat at Manchester United in January 1978. He was a member of the entertaining and highly successful side built by Bobby Robson that challenged for major honours and won the UEFA Cup in 1981. Having played for the Scotland Under-21 team, Brazil made his full international debut against Poland in May 1980 and, during his stay at Portman Road, won eight Under-21 and 11 full caps, although he won a further two caps while at White Hart Lane. A consistent goalscorer, his best season was 1981–82, when he scored 28 goals in 44 League and Cup games. On 16 February 1982, Southampton visited Portman Road as the League

Alan Brazil

leaders and had suffered only one defeat in their last 13 matches. Brazil scored a hat-trick within the space of five minutes in the first half and went on to net all five goals in Town's 5–2 win. He had scored 80 goals in 210 first-team games when in March 1983 he joined Tottenham Hotspur for a fee of £450,000. Finding that his style of play did not really fit in with that of Spurs, he was allowed to move on for £750,000 to Manchester United, who had been keen to sign him before he left East Anglia. Again Brazil was unable to recapture his outstanding form of Portman Road or adapt his play to the pattern of his club, and after an unhappy time at Old Trafford he joined Coventry City. At Highfield Road he began to rediscover his old touch but after five months he returned to London, this time signing for Queen's Park Rangers. However, he played in only four League games before suffering a serious back injury that forced him to retire from League football. He ran the Black Adder pub in Ipswich for a while but then took to media work and has made quite a name for himself on Talk Sport Radio.

BREKKE-SKARD Vemund

Midfield
Born: Norway, 11 September 1981.
Career: Brumunddal (Norway); IPSWICH TOWN 2005.

■ Vemund Brekke-Skard was training to be a teacher in Norway before being spotted by Town. He signed for the Portman Road club in November 2005 after impressing on trial the previous month. Though he agreed an 18-month contract with Town, he had to await clearance from the FA before he officially became an Ipswich player. He eventually made his debut as a substitute for Jim Magilton in a 2–2 draw with Crystal Palace before finally making his first start against Play-off hopefuls Watford towards the end of the season.

BRENNAN Mark Robert

Midfield

*Born: Rossendale, 4 October 1965.
Career: IPSWICH TOWN 1983; Middlesbrough 1988; Manchester City 1990; Oldham Athletic 1992; Sydney Olympic (Australia); Dagenham & Redbridge.*

■ A talented midfielder with a sweet left foot, Brennan was introduced to the Ipswich side by manager Bobby Ferguson, making his debut in an FA Cup tie against Queen's Park Rangers in November 1983. By the end of the season he had won a regular spot in the Town midfield and over the next four years was one of the first names on the team sheet. In the game against Manchester United at Old Trafford in May 1984, Brennan dominated the central midfield against England international Bryan Robson, helping Town to a 2–1 victory that ensured the club's top-flight survival. An England Under-21 international, his hopes of full international football were ended when he was one of the 'Toulon Four' who broke a curfew imposed by coach Dave Sexton and as a result found themselves in trouble with the FA. The long-ball game introduced at Portman Road by new manager John Duncan did not suit Brennan's style of play and after appearing in 212 games he joined Middlesbrough during the 1988 close season. He settled well on Teesside but, after two seasons in which the club struggled in the lower reaches, he moved on to Manchester City. He found it difficult to win a regular place in the Maine Road club's midfield and joined Oldham Athletic. He was never a prolific goalscorer, but he did achieve one memorable goal in the Premiership match against Chelsea, which the Latics won 3–1. Kevin Hitchcock came to the edge of the penalty area to clear a poor back pass and only succeeded in hacking the ball as far as the halfway line. The ball dropped at Brennan's feet and he lifted the ball over the goalkeeper from fully 60 yards for Oldham's third goal. After dropping out of League football, he played in Sydney and then moved on to the mainland of China. On his return to these shores he played for Dagenham & Redbridge and worked in a sports hall in that area.

BROADFOOT Joseph James

Outside-right

*Born: Lewisham, 4 March 1940.
Career: Millwall 1958; IPSWICH TOWN 1963; Northampton Town 1965; Millwall 1966; IPSWICH TOWN 1967.*

■ Winger Joe Broadfoot started out with Millwall, whom he helped win the Fourth Division Championship in 1961–62 following a few seasons of near-misses. Bill McGarry bought Broadfoot from the Lions in October 1963 and he made his Ipswich debut in a 2–2 draw against Blackpool. He was unable to prevent Town from losing their First Division status, though he did score twice in a 4–3 defeat of Aston Villa towards the end of the season. An exciting player to watch when in full flight, he had terrific pace and a powerful shot. In 1964–65, when Town finished fifth in Division Two, he scored 12 goals in 36 games. Early the following season he signed for Northampton Town and played for the Cobblers in their only season of First Division football. He then rejoined Millwall before returning to Portman Road for a second spell. He took his tally of goals for Ipswich in all competitions to 21 in 115 games before retiring.

BROGAN Frank Anthony

Winger

*Born: Glasgow, 3 August 1942.
Career: Glasgow Celtic; IPSWICH TOWN 1964; Halifax Town 1971.*

■ Beginning his career with Celtic, winger Frank Brogan was rated one of the best in Scotland when he joined the Blues in the summer of 1964. He had been selected as a reserve for the full Scotland team, but was unable to win a regular place in the Parkhead club's first team because of the form of John Hughes. Brogan made his Ipswich debut in a goalless draw at Cardiff City on the opening day of the 1964–65 season and by the end of the campaign had played in 43 League and Cup games – more than anyone else. He also netted his first hat-trick for the club in a 7–0 win over Portsmouth in November 1964. His second hat-trick for the Blues came two years later in a 6–1 defeat of Northampton Town. Two of his goals were from the penalty spot and this was the first occasion on

which the club had scored from two penalties in a Football League match. The Cobblers had been Ipswich's opponents in September 1964 when Brogan missed his first attempt at a penalty for Town. He did not try again for almost two years, when he cracked the ball home against Huddersfield Town. This was the first of 16 successful spot-kicks for Brogan. When Ipswich won the Second Division Championship in 1967–68, Brogan was the Blues' leading scorer in the League with 17 goals in 36 games, including his third hat-trick for the club in a 5–0 win over Bristol City. This followed on from a 7–0 victory over La Gantoise of Ghent in a pre-season friendly when Brogan netted five of his side's goals. He continued to be an important member of the side in the top flight but the goal output diminished. After playing the last of his 223 League and Cup games, in which he scored 69 goals, he left Portman Road to join Halifax Town where he ended his League career.

BROWN John

Outside-right

*Born: Belfast, 8 November 1914.
Career: Belfast Celtic; Wolverhampton Wanderers 1934; Coventry City 1936; Birmingham City 1938; Barry Town; IPSWICH TOWN 1948.*

■ Jackie Brown sprang to fame as a teenager in Ireland with Belfast Celtic while serving his apprenticeship in the linen trade. Transferred to Wolverhampton Wanderers, he failed to impress at Molineux, although he did gain the first of 10 full caps for Northern Ireland and made a couple of appearances for the Republic of Ireland after moving to Coventry City. On leaving Highfield Road he signed for Birmingham and, on arriving at St Andrew's, his direct approach created a favourable impression, but try as he might he was unable to inject much life into a poor attack. Brown had drifted into non-League football with Barry Town when Ipswich signed him in the summer of 1948. He made his Town debut at Bristol Rovers on the opening day of the 1948–49 season, creating chances for both Dempsey and Jennings in a 6–1 win. He went on to score 10 goals that season, including a hat-trick in a 4–1 defeat of Port Vale. The following season he endeared himself to all Town fans when he netted another treble in a 3–0 East Anglian derby win over Norwich City. Brown went on to play for another season, taking his tally of goals to 27 in 103 first-team outings before deciding to hang up his boots.

BROWN Thomas

Goalkeeper

*Born: Troon, 26 October 1919.
Career: Glenathon Rovers; IPSWICH TOWN 1938; Bury Town.*

■ Spotted playing Scottish junior football, goalkeeper Tom Brown joined Ipswich in October 1938 but had to wait until after World War Two before making his Football League debut in a 1–1 draw at Southend United in the fourth match of the 1946–47 season. It proved his only appearance that season, but midway through the 1947–48 campaign he became the club's first-choice 'keeper. Despite conceding 10 goals in the final three games of the season, all of which were defeats, Brown was between the posts when the 1948–49 season got underway. In fact, he was the club's only ever present that season as they finished seventh in the Third Division South. Brown played in every game again the following season but then lost his place to Mick Burns and, in the summer of 1951, moved into non-League football with Bury Town.

BROWN Thomas

Inside-forward

*Born: Galashiels, 7 June 1929.
Career: Annbank Juniors; IPSWICH TOWN 1952; Walsall 1956.*

■ Another player from north of the border, scheming inside-forward Thomas Brown joined the Portman Road club from Scottish junior club

Annbanks and played his first game in Town colours against Colchester United on the first day of the 1952–53 season. After appearing in the opening five games, he was injured against Bournemouth and did not return to action until the second half of the season. Over the next three seasons, Brown found himself in and out of the Ipswich side and, after scoring 21 goals in 95 games, he left Portman Road to join Walsall. Unable to propel the Saddlers away from the foot of the Third Division South, Brown parted company with the club.

BROWN Wayne Lawrence

Defender

Born: Barking, 20 August 1977.
Career: IPSWICH TOWN 1996; Colchester United (loan) 1997; Queen's Park Rangers (loan) 2001; Wimbledon (loan) 2001; Watford 2002; Gillingham (loan) 2003; Colchester United (loan) 2004.

■ Having turned professional at Ipswich in May 1996, central defender Wayne Brown progressed through the youth and reserve sides to make his

first-team debut at Middlesbrough in January 1998. Playing alongside Tony Mowbray and Adam Tanner in a three-man central defence, he helped Town to a 1–1 draw. Strong in the air, he had earlier made two appearances for Colchester United on loan. Despite the promise shown, he was unable to force his way into Ipswich's 1998–99 record-equalling defence and indeed found himself further down in the ranking, with Titus Bramble given priority. However, the following season he found himself back in favour, mainly as a deputy for Mark Venus on the left of a three-man central defensive unit. Bolstering the attack at set-pieces, he registered some near misses without getting on the scoresheet. He was the player who made way for Hermann Hreidarsson and eventually he went on loan to Queen's Park Rangers. Unfortunately he then suffered injury problems and returned to Portman Road early. Further loan spells followed in 2001–02 as both Wimbledon and Watford availed themselves of his services. Brown scored his first goal for Ipswich in the home leg of the UEFA Cup tie with Avenir Beggen at the start of the 2002–03 season, but soon afterwards left to join Watford. Though a valuable squad member, he had further loans at Gillingham and Colchester United before returning to Vicarage Road.

BROWNLOW John Martin

Winger

Born: Belfast, 18 June 1916.
Died: 1989.
Career: Gravesend & Northfleet; IPSWICH TOWN 1947; Hartlepool United 1948.

■ Belfast-born winger Jackie Brownlow joined Ipswich from non-League side Gravesend and Northfleet in May 1947 and made his only League appearance for the club in the penultimate game of the 1946–47 campaign against Aldershot. It was Brownlow's pin-point cross that allowed Tommy Parker to score what proved to be the only goal of the game. After a season playing reserve-team football, Brownlow left East Anglia to join Hartlepool United, where he made three appearances prior to returning to his native Ireland.

BUGG Alec Alfred

Goalkeeper

Born: Needham Market, 27 November 1948.
Career: IPSWICH TOWN 1967; Bournemouth (loan) 1970.

■ Following a knee injury to Ken Hancock on the opening day of the 1968–69 season, Alec Bugg made his League debut at Sunderland four days later. Powerless to prevent the Wearsiders winning 3–0, he then helped Town win 3–1 at Leicester City. A mistake in his next game gifted Leeds United the points in a 3–2 win for the Yorkshire club at Portman Road. Bugg's only other first-team outing came midway through the following season when Ipswich came from behind to draw 3–3 with Stoke City at the Victoria Ground. Bugg later had a spell on loan with Bournemouth before, following his retirement from football, he joined the local police force.

BURCHILL Mark James

Forward

Born: Broxburn, 18 August 1980.
Career: Glasgow Celtic 1997; Birmingham City (loan) 2000; IPSWICH TOWN (loan) 2001; Portsmouth 2001; Dundee (loan) 2003; Wigan Athletic (loan) 2003; Sheffield Wednesday (loan) 2003; Rotherham United (loan) 2004; Heart of Midlothian 2005.

■ A member of Celtic's Premier League Championship-winning side of 1999–2000, Burchill got off to an

■ THE WHO'S WHO OF IPSWICH TOWN

on his debut. He had netted four goals in five matches when a freak training-ground accident resulted in damage to a cruciate ligament. Capped six times by Scotland, he had loan spells with a number of clubs north and south of the border before moving permanently to Hearts, where he enjoyed better fortune.

BURLEY George Elder

Right-back

Born: Cumnock, 3 June 1956.
Career: IPSWICH TOWN 1973; Sunderland 1985; Gillingham 1988; Motherwell; Ayr United; Falkirk; Colchester United 1994.

■ An adventurous defender, George Burley was a product of Ipswich Town's prolific youth system and made a memorable debut at the age of 17 years 209 days when he completely marked George Best out of the game in a 2–0 defeat against Manchester United at Old Trafford in December 1973. Over the next 12 seasons, Burley missed very few games and in 1975–76, when the club finished sixth in Division One, he was ever present. In 1976–77 he was voted the club's Player of the Year and in 1978 won an FA Cup-winners' medal as a Roger Osborne goal was enough to beat Arsenal in the Wembley Final. Burley, who had won international honours

explosive start at Parkhead the following term, netting a hat-trick within four minutes in the 7–0 thrashing of Luxembourg's Jeunesse Esch in a UEFA Cup qualifying round tie. However, he failed to win a regular place in Martin O'Neill's team and was soon on his way to Birmingham City in a loan deal. An effective striker blessed with blinding pace, the ability to kick with either foot and the knack of being in the right place at the right time, he did well at St Andrew's, netting five goals from seven starts. He became a huge crowd favourite, so much so that the fans raised a petition to pressure the club into signing him permanently. However, the transfer fell through and in January 2001 he joined Ipswich Town on loan for the remainder of the season. He was not as successful at Portman Road. His only goal in seven outings – five of which were from the bench – came in a 3–1 win over Bradford City. Towards the end of the season he joined Portsmouth for £600,000 and scored twice in a 4–2 defeat of Grimsby Town

George Burley

for Scotland at Schoolboy and Under-21 level, won the first of 11 full caps for his country in 1979 when he played against Wales. Sadly, he was not in the Ipswich side that beat AZ67 Alkmaar to win the UEFA Cup in 1980–81, having severely damaged his knee ligaments in an FA Cup tie at Shrewsbury Town. Burley went on to appear in exactly 500 first-team games for Ipswich before leaving Portman Road in September 1985 to join Lawrie McMenemy's Sunderland, where he linked up with Eric Gates. After McMenemy was sacked less than two years later and Sunderland were relegated to the Third Division for the first time in their history, Burley joined Gillingham, the club that had put the Wearsiders out in the Play-offs. He returned to Scotland in 1989 to join Motherwell and the following year became player-manager of Ayr United. After three years he moved to Falkirk as a player before rejoining Motherwell as player-coach. In the summer of 1994 he was appointed player-coach at Colchester United, but by Christmas he had left to take over the reins at Ipswich Town. He took the club into the Premiership and achieved a fifth-place finish to qualify for UEFA Cup football, but he was sacked after eight years when the club were later relegated. He then managed Derby County and Hearts, whom he took to the top of the Premier League before a parting of the ways. Burley then became manager of Championship club Southampton.

BURNS Michael Thomas

Goalkeeper

Born: Coundon, 7 June 1908.
Died: 1982.
Career: Chilton Colliery; Newcastle United 1927; Preston North End 1936; IPSWICH TOWN 1938.

■ After once being converted to a forward for conceding too many goals, Mick Burns developed into a steady goalkeeper and served his first club Newcastle United for nine seasons. At a time when the Magpies had three or four senior 'keepers on their books, Burns was never recognised as first-choice. When he joined Preston he quickly found himself thrust into the biggest game of his life, as stand-in for Harry Holdcroft in the 1937 FA Cup Final against Sunderland. He joined Ipswich in the summer of 1938 and went straight into the side, making his debut in the Suffolk club's inaugural match, a 4–2 defeat of Southend United. He went on to be one of only two ever presents in that 1938–39 season, keeping 16 clean sheets as the club finished seventh in the Third Division South. After starring in the 2–1 Jubilee Fund match victory over Norwich City, Burns guested for the Canaries during the war years before returning to Portman Road for the start of the 1946–47 season. He missed just one game that season as Town finished sixth in the Third Division South, but midway through the following season he lost his place to Tom Brown and did not play another first-team game until 1950–51, when he returned as the club's first-choice 'keeper. He played the last of his 168 games against Gateshead in January 1952 at the age of 43 years 219 days. For the record, Town drew 2–2, with Neil Myles scoring a last-minute penalty. Burns later lived on Tyneside and became caretaker of a Roman Catholic school in Newcastle.

BUTCHER Terence Ian

Centre-half

Born: Singapore, 28 December 1958.
Career: IPSWICH TOWN 1976; Glasgow Rangers; Coventry City 1990; Sunderland 1992.

■ Terry Butcher was born in Singapore, where his father was in the Royal Navy. A competitive and commanding central defender, he made his Ipswich Town debut at Everton in April 1978 before establishing himself as a first-team regular the following season. In 1980 Butcher won his first full cap for England when he played against Australia after winning honours at Under-21 and B international level. Later that season, he helped Ipswich to a UEFA Cup Final victory over AZ67 Alkmaar and to runners'-up spot in the First Division behind Aston Villa. Butcher, who went on to win 77 England caps and become a lion-hearted lynchpin at the heart of the nation's defence for the next decade, captained his country on seven occasions and played in three consecutive World Cups. He was ever present during England's unbeaten 1982 World Cup campaign in Spain and in Mexico four years later. At that tournament he is best remembered for the despairing lunge that so very nearly prevented Diego Maradona from scoring the greatest goal in World Cup history. Butcher was a mainstay of the Ipswich defence and in 1982–83 was ever present. When Mick Mills left Portman Road to join Southampton, Butcher, who was Player of the Year in 1984–85, became captain. In the summer of 1986, after the club had been relegated, he left Portman Road after making 350 appearances. He joined Glasgow Rangers for a fee of £725,000 and at Ibrox Park he won three Scottish Premier League Championship medals, three Scottish League Cup-winners' medals and a Scottish Cup runners'-up medal. In November 1990, following a training ground bust-up with manager Graeme Souness, Butcher was transferred to Coventry City for £400,000, taking on the role of player-manager. He spent just over a year at the helm and was forced to sack his one-time Ipswich teammate Mick Mills before he too lost his job when he refused to negotiate a new 'manager only' contract after the club chairman felt he should take a cut in salary as he was suffering from a

Terry Butcher

long-term injury. Butcher later became player-manager of Sunderland but, after narrowly avoiding relegation and with the club lying bottom of the Premiership, he was sacked. During an eight-year sabbatical, Butcher ran the Old Manor Hotel in Bridge of Allan near Stirling and became a pundit for the BBC. He moved back into the game when he was appointed manager of Motherwell in 2002 and then Sydney in Australia in 2006.

CALLAGHAN Henry William

Outside-left

Born: Glasgow, 20 March 1929.
Career: Kirkintilloch Rob Roy; IPSWICH TOWN 1954.

■ Winger Harry Callaghan joined Ipswich in the summer of 1954 after impressing for Scottish junior outfit Kirkintilloch Rob Roy. Despite some impressive performances for the club's reserves, he made just one League appearance during his time at Portman Road. That came in a disastrous 6–1 defeat at Swansea midway through the 1954–55 season, the club's first in Division Two following their promotion the previous season as champions of the Third Division South.

CALLAGHAN William

Inside-right

Born: Glasgow, 7 February 1930.
Career: Great Perth Juniors; IPSWICH TOWN 1952; Sudbury Town.

■ Willie Callaghan was a scheming inside-forward who also had an eye for goal. Like his namesake Harry, he joined Town from Scottish junior football, arriving at Portman Road from Great Perth Juniors in July 1952. Despite making both Ipswich's goals on his debut, Town lost 4–2 at Bristol City, but Callaghan played in 13 successive games before losing his place. Having scored his first goal in a 2–0 defeat of Crystal Palace, he went back to the reserves and scored prolifically for the remainder of the season. When Ipswich won the Third Division South title in 1953–54, Callaghan played in six games towards the end of the campaign, all of which were won, scoring three goals. He made just a couple of appearances in Division Two, scoring his customary goal before leaving to play non-League football for Sudbury Town.

CARBERRY Lawrence James

Right-back

Born: Liverpool, 18 January 1936.
Career: Bootle; IPSWICH TOWN 1956; Barrow 1965; Burscough.

■ Liverpool-born full-back Larry Carberry had an unusual entry into the world of professional football. His father was employed at Liverpool Docks and insisted that his son was apprenticed as a sheet-metal worker. He signed amateur forms for Everton but then was called up to do his National Service. After being posted to Trieste with the Lancashire Fusiliers he was transferred to the King's Regiment and was later stationed at Bury St Edmunds. Alf Ramsey spotted him playing in a match against Bury Town and persuaded him to join Ipswich. He made his first-team debut in a 4–0 home win over Queen's Park Rangers and went on to appear in 25 games as the club won the Third Division South Championship. The following season he represented the FA XI against the RAF at Meadow Lane and against the Army at Old Trafford. He was also selected as a travelling reserve for the England Under-23 side against Romania. Over the next few seasons, Carberry established himself as one of the top defenders outside the top flight and in 1960–61 was ever present as the club won the Second Division Championship. The Ipswich defender played in all the games in 1961–62 as the club won the First Division Championship and was one of five players to win Championship medals for all three divisions with the Portman Road club. At the start of the following season, Carberry hurt his ankle in the FA Charity Shield match against Tottenham Hotspur at Portman Road and was forced to miss a number of games. Carberry, who damaged his ribs in a car accident, had played in 285 games for Town when he left to join Barrow. He appeared in just 17 League games for the Holker Street club before playing non-League football for Burscough.

CARROLL Thomas Roger

Right-back

Born: Dublin, 18 August 1942.
Career: Shelbourne; Cambridge City;

IPSWICH TOWN 1966; Birmingham City 1971.

■ Beginning his career with League of Ireland side Shelbourne, Tommy Carroll spent seven years at Tolka Park, winning a League of Ireland Championship medal, an FAI Cup-winners' medal and a President's Cup-winners' medal. He popped up in every position for the club including goalkeeper, though he was an experienced 20-year-old before he appeared in the right-back position in which he was to make his name in the Football League. Carroll left his native Dublin to join Cambridge City in August 1964. He had two seasons with the club and had the rare distinction of winning an Ireland Under-23 cap while playing Southern League football. In July 1966 he left Cambridge for Ipswich and, although it took him a few months to acclimatise to full-time League football, he eventually established himself in both the Ipswich and Republic of Ireland side. Capped 17 times by his country, his chance at Portman Road came when Mick McNeil, so unlucky with injuries, was ruled out by a car accident. During seven seasons at Portman Road, Carroll made 126 League and Cup appearances and won a Second Division Championship medal in 1967–68. Competition for defensive places at the club became acute in the late 1960s and Tommy Carroll had to vie with English internationals Mills and McNeil as well as home-grown defender Colin Harper for his place. In the end, following a disagreement with manager Bobby Robson, Carroll lost out and in November 1971, after impressing on a month's trial, he joined Birmingham City. He helped the Blues win promotion to Division One in his first season at St Andrew's, but after just 38 appearances he was forced out of the game through injury.

CARSON Thomas
Goalkeeper
Born: Dumbarton, 26 March 1959.
Career: Dumbarton 1978; Dundee 1984; Hibernian (loan) 1986; Partick Thistle (loan) 1987; Queen of the South (loan) 1987; Dunfermline Athletic (loan) 1987; IPSWICH TOWN (loan) 1988; Dunfermline Athletic (loan) 1988; Dundee 1988.

■ Goalkeeper Tom Carson began his career with his local club Dumbarton, and in five seasons at the then Boghead Park club he made 149 League appearances and helped the club win promotion to the Scottish Premier League in 1983–84. He then joined Dundee but, after an outstanding first season with the club, lost his place. In January 1988 he joined Ipswich on loan. His only League appearance for Town came at home to Leicester City when the Foxes ran out 2–0 winners. Carson later returned north of the border and won back his place in the Dundee side.

CASEMENT Christopher
Defender
Born: Belfast, 12 January 1988.
Career: IPSWICH TOWN 2005.

■ A key member of the Ipswich Town side that lifted the FA Youth Cup in 2005, Chris Casement is a central defender who is equally at home at full-back. Capped by Northern Ireland at Youth level, he was selected for the Under-19 side in February 2006. His performances for the club's reserves led to him making his first start off the bench against Play-off hopefuls Crystal Palace in a 2–2 draw in March 2006. Casement later made his full debut at right-back in an Ipswich side beaten 4–1 at Portman Road by Stoke City.

CHADWICK Frederick William
Centre-forward
Born: Manchester, 8 November 1913.
Died: 1987.
Career: British Dyes; Wolverhampton Wanderers 1935; Newport County 1936; IPSWICH TOWN 1938; Bristol Rovers 1947.

■ A prolific goalscoring centre-forward, Fred Chadwick scored 72 goals for British Dyes in the First Division of the Manchester Amateur League and signed amateur forms for Manchester City. He moved on to Wolverhampton Wanderers, but was unable to make the grade at Molineux and a year later joined Newport County. Though the Welsh club were struggling near the foot of the Third Division South, Chadwick was their leading scorer and this prompted Ipswich Town to offer him terms prior to the start of their first season of League football. Chadwick scored on his Town debut in a 2–1 defeat at Reading and went on to top the club's scoring charts with 17 goals. He also netted four of Town's goals in the FA Cup first round 7–0 defeat of non-League Street, finishing the campaign with 23 goals in 40 games in all competitions. During World War Two, Chadwick was held as a prisoner of war in Singapore by the Japanese, but still took his place in the Ipswich side when League football resumed in 1946–47. Unable to repeat his scoring feats of the 1938–39 season, he was allowed to join Bristol Rovers, where he made a handful of appearances before hanging up his boots.

CHAPMAN Lee Roy
Forward
Born: Lincoln, 5 December 1959.
Career: Stoke City 1978; Plymouth Argyle (loan) 1978; Arsenal 1982; Sunderland 1983; Sheffield Wednesday 1984; Niort (France); Nottingham Forest 1988; Leeds United 1990; Portsmouth 1993; West Ham United 1993; Southend United (loan) 1995; IPSWICH TOWN 1995; Leeds United (loan) 1996; Swansea City 1996.

■ Lee Chapman, whose father Roy played for Aston Villa and Port Vale, began his career with Stoke City and showed enough early promise to win an England Under-21 cap. He was loaned to Plymouth as a youngster but, after establishing himself at Stoke, his career faltered after two big money moves to Arsenal and Sunderland. It was Howard Wilkinson who got the best out of him at Sheffield Wednesday, Chapman scoring 69 goals in 149 appearances before trying his luck in France with Niort. The move was a disaster, and in October 1988 he joined Nottingham Forest for £300,000. He played in Forest's 1989 Littlewoods Cup and Zenith Data Systems Cup successes at Wembley before linking up with former boss Howard Wilkinson at Leeds United. Feeding off some great crosses, Chapman's goal tally continued to mount and two goals against his old club, Forest, in the final game of the 1990–91 season took his seasonal tally to 31 – the best by a striker in the First Division – and his career total to 200. The arrival of Brian Deane heralded the departure of Chapman to Portsmouth, but after only a handful of games he was back in the top flight with West Ham United. Past his prime, Chapman was loaned to Southend before being sold to Ipswich Town for a cut-price £70,000 in January 1995. Bought in the hope that his goals would prevent the club being relegated, he had his best game on his debut against Chelsea when he came on as a substitute and created both goals. Chapman scored his only goal for the club against Southampton with his head but failed to capture the fans' hearts at Portman Road and rejoined Leeds on loan. After being sent off against West Ham and playing in a 5–0 drubbing at Liverpool, he returned to Portman Road prior to finishing his career with Swansea City.

CHEETHAM Michael Martin

Midfield

Born: Nijmegen, Holland, 30 June 1967. Career: Basingstoke Town; IPSWICH TOWN 1988; Cambridge United 1989; Chesterfield 1994; Colchester United 1995; Sudbury Town; Cambridge City; AFC Sudbury.

■ Midfielder Michael Cheetham played his early football for Basingstoke Town and was recommended to Ipswich by former boss and then England manager Bobby Robson, after he had watched Cheetham represent his regiment in the Dorset Army Centenary Cup Final. A player who could add width and pace to the attack as well as posing a goal threat, his chances at Portman Road were few and far between and, after just one start and a few appearances off the bench, he left to join Cambridge United. He was an important member of the U's side, helping them win the Third Division Championship in 1990–91 and playing in the first ever Play-off Final at Wembley in their 1–0 defeat of Chesterfield. Cheetham had played in 171 games for Cambridge when he left to join Chesterfield but, unable to hold down a regular place, soon left to play for Colchester United. At the end of the 1995–96 season, following a series of injuries and a loss of form, he left Layer Road to play non-League football for Sudbury Town.

CLAPHAM James Richard

Left-back

Born: Lincoln, 7 December 1975. Career: Tottenham Hotspur 1994; Leyton Orient (loan) 1997; Bristol Rovers (loan) 1997; IPSWICH TOWN 1998; Birmingham City 2003.

■ Beginning his career with Tottenham Hotspur, Jamie Clapham had loan spells with both Leyton Orient and Bristol Rovers before making his Premiership debut for the North London club in the final game of the 1996–97 season as a replacement for the injured Colin Calderwood. After failing to add to his solitary appearance, he joined Ipswich initially on loan to provide left-sided cover at a time when injuries and suspensions left Town weak in this area. He made his debut in a goalless draw against Queen's Park Rangers and, apart from FA Cup games when he was ineligible, he played in every game. He grew in confidence and developed in an attacking role. In 1998–99 he played in every game for Ipswich though he was not quite an ever present, having been dropped for the trip to Watford and coming on as a substitute. He ended the season as the supporter's Player of the Year and fans also voted his effort against Port Vale as the Goal of the Season. He appeared in every game the following season, but again made a number of appearances from the bench. He continued to score vital goals, none more so than in extra-time in the Play-off second leg against Bolton Wanderers when he took responsibility for the third penalty of the evening and gave his side the lead for the first time in the tie. The son of former Shrewsbury Town and Chester player Graham Clapham, he continued to be an important member of the Town side, netting vital goals in the club's UEFA Cup games. He had appeared in 252 games for Town when in January 2003 he joined Birmingham City for £1 million – a move necessitated by the club's financial position. He slotted in well in the Birmingham back four before losing his place following a bout of shingles. Clever at reading the game and able to deliver an accurate pass, a knee injury then limited his appearances, but he remains an important member of the St Andrew's club's squad.

CLARKE Frank James

Forward

Born: Willenhall, 15 July 1942.
Career: Willenhall; Shrewsbury Town 1961; Queen's Park Rangers 1968; IPSWICH TOWN 1970; Carlisle United 1973.

■ Frank Clarke was the eldest of four footballing brothers: Allan, nicknamed 'Sniffer', played for Leeds United and England, while the other brothers were Derek and Wayne. Frank Clarke played his early football for his hometown club Willenhall before signing for Shrewsbury Town in November 1961. He stayed at Gay Meadow for six and a half seasons, scoring 77 goals in 188 League games and helping the Shrews to a best finish of third in Division Three in 1967–68. Clarke had left Shrewsbury just before the end of this season to sign for Queen's Park Rangers and his goals helped the Loftus Road club win promotion to the top flight. Relegated after just one season, Clarke then teamed up well with Rodney Marsh, but in March 1970 he left Rangers to join Ipswich Town for a fee of £40,000. Clarke made his Town debut in a 2–0 home win over Sunderland and his seven appearances at the end of that 1969–70 season helped to lift the club clear of relegation. On the final day of the season, he scored one of the goals in the 3–2 defeat of runners-up Leeds United that kept Town in the First Division. The following season he netted four goals in the space of five games, but thereafter he struggled to find his best form and hardly appeared at all in his last season at Portman Road. Clarke left to play for Carlisle United and in his first season at Brunton Park helped the Cumbrian club win promotion to the First Division. The club were relegated after just one season in the top flight, but Clarke remained with Carlisle for four seasons, scoring 30 goals in 126 League games.

CLARKE George Edmund

Centre-half

Born: Ipswich, 27 April 1921.
Career: IPSWICH TOWN 1946.

■ Centre-half George Clarke joined Ipswich as an amateur in November 1946 and made a goalscoring debut wearing the number-nine shirt on the final day of the 1946–47 season as Town drew 2–2 with Northampton. Clarke's only appearance the following season was again at centre-forward, and though he only played in one game in 1948–49, he had by now been converted to centre-half. The 1949–50 season saw him appear on a more regular basis and, over the next couple of seasons, he found himself in and out of the Ipswich side. Clarke was at Portman Road for seven seasons, but in that time he made just 37 League appearances before deciding to retire.

CLARKE William Arthur

Wing-half

Born: Newport, 17 April 1923.
Died: 1994.
Career: IPSWICH TOWN 1947.

■ The brother of Manchester City and Wales winger Roy Clarke, William was stationed locally with the RAF when signed by Ipswich in February 1947. A Welsh amateur international, the tough-tackling wing-half made his Ipswich debut in a 2–1 win over Bournemouth, after the Cherries had led 1–0 at half-time. He kept his place for the next game back in his native south Wales at Cardiff but, despite creating goalscoring opportunities for both Jackie Little and Stan Parker, the Bluebirds won 3–2. Clarke's third and final appearance for Town was in a 1–1 draw at Bristol Rovers and in the close season he returned to Wales, where he saw out his career.

CLARKE William

Forward

Born: Dublin, 13 December 1987.
Career: IPSWICH TOWN 2005; Colchester United (loan) 2006.

■ A Republic of Ireland Youth international, Billy Clarke was knocking on the door of the first-team squad throughout the 2004–05 season after signing his first professional contract on his 17th birthday in December 2004. His goals played a big part in the club's FA Youth Cup success, although he missed both legs of the Final after sustaining medial knee ligament damage in the closing stages of the semi-final win at Tottenham Hotspur. Voted the Dale Roberts Academy Player of the Year for 2005, he made his debut for the Tractor Boys from the bench in the 2–1 reversal at Cardiff City. Shortly afterwards, due to injuries, Clarke was given his first start, partnering Nicky Forster in the 2–2 home draw with Queen's Park Rangers. Allowed to join League One promotion chasers Colchester United on loan, he made three substitute appearances before making his full start.

CLEGG Michael Jamie

Full-back

Born: Ashton-under-Lyne, 3 July 1977.
Career: Manchester United 1995; IPSWICH TOWN (loan) 2000; Wigan Athletic (loan) 2000; Oldham Athletic 2002.

■ England B and Under-21 international Michael Clegg had a tough start to his professional career, having been seen as an average player among the stars of Manchester United's youth team. His perseverance finally paid off when he made his League debut against Middlesbrough in November 1996 in a match in which he earned rave reviews. Voted the Pontin's League Player of the Year, Clegg appeared for United in both FA Cup and European Cup matches, where his positional play earned plaudits for its maturity. Owing to the form of Gary Neville and Dennis Irwin, his first-team opportunities were limited and in February 2000 he went to Ipswich Town on a month's loan as cover for Gary Croft. He made three appearances for Town, making his debut at Crewe, where he got off to a steady start. He liked to support the attack and seemed happier when attacking than when performing his defensive duties. Croft's recovery meant that his loan stay was not extended and he joined Wigan on a similar basis. Finding it difficult to adjust to the pace of Second Division football he returned to Old Trafford but, being confined to reserve-team football, joined Oldham on a free transfer. Again struggling to adjust to the requirements of lower division football, and under Brian Talbot's managership, he lost his first-team place.

COLE Michael Washington

Forward

Born: Hillingdon, 3 September 1966.
Career: IPSWICH TOWN 1983; Port Vale (loan) 1988; Fulham 1988.

■ Having worked his way up through the ranks, Michael Cole made his first-team debut for Ipswich as a substitute in a 2–0 win at Stoke City in December 1984. With Town struggling to retain their place in the First Division – they were relegated in 1984–85 – Cole found first-team opportunities hard to come by and, after a loan spell with Port Vale, he left Portman Road in March 1988 to join Fulham. Almost half of Cole's 38 League appearances for Town had been made from the bench, but at Craven Cottage he started most of his games and appeared on a much more regular basis.

COLLARD Ian

Midfield

Born: Hetton-le-Hole, 31 August 1947.
Career: West Bromwich Albion 1964; IPSWICH TOWN 1969; Portsmouth (loan) 1975.

■ Midfielder Ian Collard began his career with West Bromwich Albion, having joined the Baggies as an apprentice. His impressive displays for the club's youth and reserve teams led to him winning a regular place in the Albion side and in 1967 he played in the first Wembley League Cup Final as the Hawthorns club lost 3–2 to Queen's Park Rangers. The following year, Collard was back at Wembley as part of the Albion team that won the FA Cup, beating Everton 1–0. He had appeared in 69 League games for West Brom when he joined Ipswich in the summer of 1969 as part of the deal that saw Danny Hegan move to the

Hawthorns. Collard made his Ipswich debut in the goalless draw with Nottingham Forest on the opening day of the 1969–70 season and played his part in the club retaining their top-flight status. Over the next four seasons, Collard struggled with a number of niggling injuries and he never really established himself as a first-team regular in that time. He had a one-match loan spell with Portsmouth, but on his return to Portman Road he was forced to retire with a hip injury.

COLLINS Aidan
Defender
Born: Chelmsford, 18 October 1986.
Career: IPSWICH TOWN 2002; Wycombe Wanderers (loan) 2005; Stockport County (loan) 2006.

■ A tall central defender, Aidan Collins is a product of the Ipswich Town youth set-up. He stepped up to make his senior debut at the age of 16 when he came on as a second-half substitute in the last match of the 2002–03 season against Derby County and had the task of marking Fabrizio Ravanelli in a 4–1 win. Injury and illness then hindered his progress, but in 2004–05 he was a regular in the first-team squad and was named on the bench 10 times without seeing action. He was outstanding in the club's FA Youth Cup Final success against Southampton. One for the future, he had loan spells with both Wycombe Wanderers and Stockport County in an effort to gain more experience.

COLRAIN John James
Forward
Born: Glasgow, 4 February 1937.
Died: 14 July 1984.
Career: Glasgow Celtic; Clyde; IPSWICH TOWN 1963; Glentoran; St Patrick's Athletic.

■ With his height and weight, John Colrain, who began his career with Celtic, was hailed as the new Hooky McPhail and was one of the best young prospects ever seen at Parkhead. Unsure as to his best position, Colrain had scored 23 goals in 58 games when he was allowed to leave the club and play for Clyde. With the Bully Wee, Colrain helped the club win the Second Division Championship in 1961–62, but after another season he left Clyde to join Ipswich Town. A Scottish Under-23 international, he made his Town debut in a goalless home draw with Everton. He took time to settle at Portman Road and was unable to prevent the club being relegated to the Second Division at the end of that 1963–64 season. He had a much better season in 1964–65, netting 10 goals in 23 games, including a brace in a 4–4 draw with Rotherham United. Colrain, better known as 'Hoss', had scored 20 goals in 62 first-team outings when he left Ipswich to become player-manager of Irish League side Glentoran. Here he created one of the best teams Glentoran have ever had and with the Glens he played in midfield in a European Cup tie against Rangers at Ibrox. Having led the Glens to two Irish League titles and only losing to the mighty Benfica on away goals, he left to end his playing days with St Patrick's prior to scouting for Manchester City and later Partick Thistle.

COMPTON John Frederick
Left-back
Born: Poplar, 27 August 1937.
Career: Chelsea 1955; IPSWICH TOWN 1960; Bournemouth 1964.

■ Unable to establish himself in Chelsea's first team owing to the form of Derek Saunders and Len Casey, Compton moved on to Ipswich Town, where Alf Ramsey subsequently converted the wing-half into a full-back. He made his debut in a 3–2 defeat at Luton Town and appeared in a further two games that season as the club won promotion to the First Division. In the fourth game of the 1961–62 season, Ken Malcolm was ruled out with injury and so Alf Ramsey switched Compton from his usual position at wing-half to play left-back. His first game in that position saw him tame England winger John Connolly as Town beat Burnley 6–2. There were Ipswich fans who had their doubts about him being able to replace Malcolm on a permanent basis, but they were soon dispelled as he improved with every match. Not only did he play his part in the club winning the League Championship, but he went on to play in 55 consecutive first-team games and in doing so became an established Town defender. Though he never got on the scoresheet in 131 games for the club, he almost did in the game against Leicester City at Filbert Street towards the end of the 1963–64 season. Ted Phillips had already had a couple of spot-kicks saved by Manchester United's Harry Gregg, so when Town were awarded another, Compton volunteered to take it. Though he hit the ball well, England 'keeper Gordon Banks brought off a fine save. At the end of that season, Compton left Portman Road to play a season of Third Division football for Bournemouth.

CONNOR John Thomas

Centre-forward

Born: Todmorden, 21 December 1919. *Died:* 14 December 1998.
Career: Albion Rovers; IPSWICH TOWN 1944; Carlisle United 1946; Ards (loan); Rochdale 1948; Bradford City 1951; Stockport County 1951; Crewe Alexandra 1956; Runcorn.

■ While stationed in Carlisle, Jack Connor signed for Ipswich Town in 1944 and, on the resumption of League football, he made the first of 12 League appearances on the opening day of the 1946–47 season, scoring both Town's goals in a 2–2 draw with Leyton Orient. His other goals came in consecutive games against Southend United and Watford but, as he was still travelling back to his home in Carlisle, he needed little persuasion to join United in December 1946. However, his appearances with Carlisle were reduced by niggling injuries and in two years with the Cumbrian club he scored 12 goals in 39 games. Following a loan spell with Irish League club Ards, he joined Rochdale and suddenly, at the age of 29, his career took off – 42 goals in 88 League games attracted a host of clubs and in April 1951 Bradford City succeeded in securing his services. Shortly afterwards, Connor and his wife were sat in a Bradford cinema when a message flashed across the screen. 'Would Jack Connor Bradford City's centre-forward please go to the foyer'. There he met Stockport County manager Andy Beattie and signed on the spot! At Edgeley Park, Jack Connor was quite simply a goal machine. He scored 140 goals in just 217 appearances. He claimed a club record 17 hat-tricks, which included four goals against Bradford Park Avenue and Tranmere Rovers, and five goals against Workington and Carlisle United. In 1953 he joined an elite band of players by scoring a hat-trick of hat-tricks in consecutive games. Following a dispute with player-manager Willie Moir, Connor left Edgeley Park for Crewe in September 1956 but, on being unable to repeat his goalscoring exploits at Gresty Road, and after a season in non-League football with Runcorn, he announced his retirement.

COOPER Paul David

Goalkeeper

Born: Brierley Hill, 21 December 1953.
Career: Birmingham City 1971; IPSWICH TOWN 1974; Leicester City 1987; Manchester City 1989; Stockport County 1989.

■ 'Super Cooper' joined Ipswich Town from Birmingham City in 1974 for £23,000 – a fee which in retrospect was ridiculously small for the service and skill this goalkeeper gave to the Portman Road club. Initially signed on loan, his first match for the club was away against champions-elect Leeds United, who won 3–2. When he first arrived in Suffolk he was unable to displace Laurie Sivell, but by the start of the 1975–76 season he was the club's first-choice 'keeper, a position he held for the next 12 seasons, appearing in a total of 575 first-team games. He learned to live with the slightly embarrassing situation of being the only uncapped player in the Ipswich Town side. The biggest consolation to him for this personal disappointment was that he was plying his trade in an era when there were two of the most outstanding England goalkeepers of any age in Peter Shilton and Ray Clemence. But he did not do so badly with other honours, collecting an FA Cup-winners' medal when the Blues beat Arsenal and a UEFA Cup-winners' medal when AZ67 Alkmaar were beaten in the two-legged Final. Cooper became something of an expert at saving penalties – 19 from 49 spot-kicks over a 14-year period! He studied the technique of the leading penalty takers and weighed up the chance of which way they would shoot and the intensity of the shot. This brought him phenomenal success and succeeded in creating grave doubts among the penalty 'kings' – a serious psychological disadvantage discovered by Liam Brady, Gerry Francis, Mickey Thomas and Terry McDermott, among others, when they tried to beat Cooper. He left Portman Road in the summer of 1987 to play for Leicester City and later had a spell with Manchester City, for whom he scored an own-goal, before ending his League career with Stockport County.

COPE John James

Left-half/Outside-left

Born: Ellesmere Port, 1 August 1908. Died: 1995.
Career: Llanelly; Bury 1933; IPSWICH TOWN 1938.

■ Jack Cope was a versatile player who began his League career with Bury. He was a regular in the Shakers side for four seasons, appearing in 67 League games and almost helping them win promotion to the First Division when they finished third in Division Two in 1936–37. Cope joined Ipswich in readiness for the first season of League football in 1938–39 and made his debut in a 2–0 defeat at Northampton Town. Due to the consistency of the Ipswich side, he only made four appearances for the club, and was not on the winning side until his final appearance, when Town beat Northampton in the return game 2–0. The Cobblers also provided Cope with his only goal for the club when he salvaged a draw in the Southern Section Cup match before he laid on the only goal of the replay for Town's Fred Chadwick to fire home.

COTTERELL Leo Spencer

Right-back

Born: Cambridge, 2 September 1974.
Career: IPSWICH TOWN 1993; Bournemouth 1996.

■ An England Schoolboy international and Ipswich Town's first player from the FA School of Excellence, Cotterell made great strides with Town's youth side and in the summer of 1993 he turned professional. The strong-tackling full-back made his Premiership debut as a substitute at Southampton during 1994–95, a season in which he made two other appearances from the bench. Despite getting forward well and showing great enthusiasm, he failed to add to his tally of first-team appearances the following season and in the summer of 1996 he left Portman Road to join Bournemouth. He struggled with injuries and a loss of form at Dean Court and drifted in and out of the side before losing his place altogether. He then moved into the local non-League scene to continue his career.

COUNAGO Pablo Gonzalez

Forward

Born: Pontevedra, Spain, 9 August 1979.
Career: Numancia (Spain) 1998; Real Celta Vigo (Spain) 1998; Huelva (Spain) 1999; Real Celta Vigo 2000; IPSWICH TOWN 2001; Malaga (Spain) 2005.

■ Joining the Tractor Boys from Celta Vigo in the summer of 2001, Pablo Counago took a little time to adjust to the English game. He was used mainly as a substitute in the Premiership, making just one start at Bolton. During the course of his first season at Portman Road, Counago, who did not score for the first team, found the net regularly for the title-winning reserve side. The following season, 2002–03, saw Counago show that he could score goals in the English game. He ended the campaign as Town's leading goalscorer with 21 goals in all competitions – the total included his first hat-trick in the club's colours in the UEFA Cup tie against Avenir Beggin. By the midway point of the 2003–04 season, the Spaniard had scored 10 goals including a Boxing Day double at West Ham after he had come off the bench. However, he then picked up a groin injury and this effectively ended his campaign. A talented striker with the ability to beat opponents, he was also very unselfish, always looking to play his teammates into goalscoring positions. He had a very disappointing season in 2004–05 and, after not seeing eye to eye with the management, found himself training and playing with the reserves. Having turned down two offers of loan spells with other Championship sides, Counago, whose contract had expired, left Portman Road in the 2005 close season and returned to Spain to play for Malaga.

COWIE Charles

Centre-half

Born: Falkirk, 23 April 1907.
Died: 1971.
Career: Heart of Midlothian; Barrow 1930; Dunfermline Athletic; Barrow 1933; IPSWICH TOWN 1936.

■ Centre-half Charlie Cowie began his career in his native Scotland with Hearts before joining Third Division North club Barrow. After just one season at Holker Street he returned north of the border to play for Dunfermline Athletic, but later rejoined Barrow. He had played in 13 League games for Barrow when in July 1936 he signed for Ipswich. He made appearances for the club during the two seasons they competed in the Southern League before making his Football League debut in a disastrous 4–1 home defeat at the hands of Newport County. He went on to appear in six League games in the inaugural 1938–39 season before joining the army in 1939.

CRANSON Ian

Centre-half

Born: Easington, 2 July 1964.
Career: IPSWICH TOWN 1982; Sheffield Wednesday 1988; Stoke City 1989.

■ Strong in the air and with sound distribution, Ian Cranson was one of a number of brilliant defenders to come off the Ipswich Town production line at Portman Road. He made his Town debut in a 4–0 defeat at Aston Villa in December 1983 and over the next five seasons missed very few games. His performances led to him being capped by England at Under-21 level and though the glory years at Portman Road were over, Cranson stood out in an Ipswich side. He did not score too many goals, but in August 1985 he scored a spectacular one against Hull City in a game watched by 11,588 – the lowest crowd at Portman Road for 21 years. Cranson left Ipswich in March 1988 to join Sheffield Wednesday but, 16 months later, after just 34 League and Cup appearances, he was on his way to Stoke City. Cranson became the Potters' record signing, costing the then Victoria Ground club £450,000. He had a problem knee which reduced his pace and at the end of the 1990–91 season he was offered reduced terms, which technically entitled him to a free transfer. Despite interest from Scottish Premier League sides Hearts and Dunfermline Athletic, he stayed and went on to make 281 appearances for the club.

CRAWFORD Raymond

Centre-forward

Born: Portsmouth, 13 July 1936.
Career: Portsmouth 1954; IPSWICH TOWN 1958; Wolverhampton Wanderers 1963; West Bromwich Albion 1965; IPSWICH TOWN 1966; Charlton Athletic 1969; Kettering Town; Colchester United 1970.

■ Ray Crawford was one of the most prolific scorers of his day and a key figure in Ipswich Town becoming League Champions. Having started out with his home-town club Portsmouth, Crawford arrived at Portman Road in September 1958, although at first he was a little reluctant. He had gone to check out his potential new employers in a game against Leyton Orient and was not impressed. He informed Pompey manager Freddie Cox that he would rather stay at Fratton Park, but was told he had no future at the south coast club and was dropped until he decided to move to Ipswich. Making his debut in October 1958, he scored both Town's goals in a 4–2 defeat at Swansea and ended the season as the club's top scorer with 25 goals in 30 League games, including a hat-trick in

Ray Crawford

the return game against Swansea and another in a 5–3 win over Brighton. Crawford and Ted Phillips soon developed a fine understanding and in 1959–60 the pair scored 42 League goals, of which Crawford's share was 18. In 1960–61, when Town won the Second Division Championship, Crawford had a remarkable season, scoring 40 of the club's 100 League goals. He netted three hat-tricks in the defeats of Brighton (away 4–2), Leeds (away 5–2) and Leyton Orient (home 6–2). The following season, Crawford scored 33 goals in 41 League games as Ipswich won the League Championship and he scored the club's only hat-trick in a 5–2 home win over Chelsea. Also during this campaign, Crawford became the first Ipswich player to gain an England cap while on the club's books when he played against Ireland at Wembley. The Ipswich player provided the cross for Bobby Charlton to score in a 1–1 draw. Later that season he scored in England's 3–1 win over Austria and also played twice for the Football League against the Irish League, when he scored twice in a 6–1 win, and against the Scottish League. Crawford had another outstanding season in 1962–63, playing in every League game and scoring 25 goals, including all three in a 3–0 defeat of Sheffield Wednesday. It was also the club's first experience of European football and when they beat the Maltese champions Floriana 10–0 at home, Ray Crawford scored five of the goals to establish a scoring record for any British player in European competitions – since equalled by Chelsea's Peter Osgood. He continued to represent the Football League and netted a hat-trick against the Irish League at Carrow Road. In September 1963, Crawford was surprisingly allowed to leave Portman Road and join Wolves but, after scoring 39 goals in 57 League games, he moved on to West Bromwich Albion. In March 1966,

Ipswich boss Bill McGarry brought Crawford back to East Anglia and in 1966–67 he top scored with 21 goals, including another treble in a 5–4 win over Hull City. The following season he scored four goals in a 5–2 League Cup victory over Southampton. In March 1969, after scoring 228 goals in 354 games, Crawford left Ipswich to join Charlton Athletic before entering non-League football with Kettering Town. In 1970–71 he was brought back to the Football League by Colchester United and scored both their goals in a 3–2 FA Cup fourth-round defeat by Leeds United. In the first round against Ringmer he had scored a hat-trick to become the first player to score hat-tricks in the Football League, League Cup, FA Cup and European Cup.

CREANEY Gerard Thomas

Centre-forward

Born: Coatbridge, 13 April 1970.
Career: Glasgow Celtic; Portsmouth 1994; Manchester City 1995; Oldham Athletic (loan) 1996; IPSWICH TOWN (loan) 1996; Burnley (loan) 1997; Chesterfield (loan) 1998; St Mirren 1998; Notts County 1999.

■ Gerry Creaney began his career with Glasgow Celtic, scoring 55 goals in 142 games for the Parkhead club before a £600,000 transfer took him to Portsmouth. Jim Smith used him as an out-and-out striker and in his first season at Fratton Park he was called up to the full Scotland squad. Easily making the transition to English football, scoring a goal every other game, Creaney was surprisingly allowed to join Premiership Manchester City for a fee of £2 million. Despite showing he could forage and screen the ball under tight marking and find the net at the highest level, he was loaned out to Oldham Athletic before returning to Maine Road. In October 1996 he was loaned out to Ipswich Town and felt refreshed to play some first-team football. He appeared in half a dozen League games for the Tractor Boys, scoring in the home win over Swindon Town. On returning to Manchester City he found himself out of contention for a place in the first team and had loan spells with Burnley and Chesterfield before returning north of the border to sign for St Mirren. Capped by Scotland at both Under-21 and B international level, he later returned to the Football League for a brief spell with Notts County.

CROFT Gary

Left-back

Born: Burton upon Trent, 17 February 1974.
Career: Grimsby Town 1992; Blackburn Rovers 1996; IPSWICH TOWN 1999; Wigan Athletic (loan) 2002; Cardiff City 2002; Grimsby Town 2005.

■ Beginning his career with Grimsby Town, Gary Croft developed nominally into a defender, but with the versatility to play almost anywhere. During his early days with the Mariners he had the misfortune to miss a League representative game due to suspension, but made up for that disappointment when selected by England for the Toulon Under-21 tournament in the summer of 1995. In March 1996, Croft left Blundell Park when he was sold to Blackburn Rovers for a fee of £1.7 million. Signed predominantly as first-team cover and insurance against injury, he eventually replaced Graeme Le Saux during the 1997–98 season before suffering a spate of niggling injuries, including a dislocated shoulder. Unable to win back his place, Croft, who had made just 52 first-team appearances in three-and-a half years at Ewood Park, joined Ipswich Town in September 1999 for £800,000. Shortly after his arrival at Portman Road things started to go wrong for him. He received a custodial sentence as a result of motoring offences and became the first professional footballer to play in a League game while wearing a 'tag'. Injuries and the competition for places restricted his first-team appearances and in January 2002 he joined Wigan Athletic on loan. He later joined Cardiff City on loan before the move was made permanent and he became an integral member of the Bluebirds side that won promotion to the First Division via the Play-offs. His Ninian Park career was wrecked by a serious knee injury and he rejoined his first club, Grimsby Town, which he helped to have a most successful 2005–06 season.

CROWE Alexander Allan

Inside-forward

Born: Motherwell, 24 November 1924.
Died: 1997.
Career: St Mirren; IPSWICH TOWN 1953.

■ Scheming inside-forward Alex Crowe joined Ipswich from St Mirren in the summer of 1953 after a number of seasons playing for the Love Street club. He made his debut in a 2–0 win over Walsall on the opening day of the 1953–54 season, going on to score six goals in 32 League games as the club won the Third Division South Championship. Crowe was a great provider of chances and Tom Garneys and John Elsworthy both benefitted from his presence in the side. Crowe lined up in the Ipswich side for their first season of Second Division football, even scoring a couple of goals in a 6–1 rout of Middlesbrough, but injuries took their toll and at the end of the campaign his contract was not renewed.

CUNDY Jason Victor

Defender

Born: Wimbledon, 12 November 1969. Career: Chelsea 1988; Tottenham Hotspur 1992; Crystal Palace (loan) 1995; Bristol City (loan) 1996; IPSWICH TOWN 1996; Portsmouth 1999.

■ An England Under-21 international, capped three times, Jason Cundy started out with Chelsea, where although never a regular in the first team he gave the Blues useful service. His best season was 1990–91 when he partnered Ken Monkou at the heart of the Chelsea defence. Having lost his place to new signing Paul Elliott, he was surprisingly loaned to Spurs just before the 1992 transfer deadline and impressed enough for the move to be made permanent. While with Spurs he scored a 50-yard freak goal against Ipswich. Standing just inside Town's half, while clearing a throw-in aimed for Jason Dozzell, he was as amazed as anyone when the ball became wind assisted and flew goalwards over out-of-position 'keeper Craig Forrest's head and into the top corner of the net. Following a disastrous game against Sheffield United in March 1993, Cundy became the forgotten man at White Hart Lane. He enjoyed successful loan spells with Crystal Palace and Bristol City before Ipswich paid £200,000 for his services in October 1996. He brought much-needed stability to the Town defence before a shin injury in February turned septic and halted his career. While recovering he was diagnosed as having cancer but made a remarkable recovery. He had an outstanding 1997–98 season, despite scoring a number of own-goals, including what turned out to be the winner in the local derby at Norwich. Cundy also captained the side at the climax of the campaign in the absence of Tony Mowbray and Geraint Williams. Prior to the start of the following season he injured his ankle in a fitness exercise at home and eventually an operation was required. When he had recovered the club's back four were playing so well that he had to settle for a place on the bench. He left Ipswich in the summer of 1999 to sign for Portsmouth. Injuries again hampered his progress and, at the age of 31, the powerful defender announced his retirement.

CURRAN Patrick James

Inside-forward

Born: Sunderland, 13 November 1917. Career: Sunderland St Patrick; Sunderland 1936; IPSWICH TOWN 1938; Watford 1939; Bradford City 1947.

■ Having impressed in junior football, inside-forward Pat Curran joined his home-town team Sunderland, but made just one appearance for the Wearsiders before signing for Ipswich Town in October 1938. Curran made his Town debut in the 4–1 defeat at Portman Road by Newport County, but kept his place in the side for a run of six consecutive games, scoring in the 2–0 defeat of Port Vale. He had appeared in one more game for Town when he left to join Watford. His transfer to the Vicarage Road club took place in unusual circumstances when the Watford boss Bill Findlay travelled to the North East and secured his signature on Sunderland station. Curran's League debut for the club was nullified by the declaration of war the next day. After the hostilities, Curran joined Bradford City of the Third Division North.

CURRIE Darren Paul

Winger/Midfield

Born: Hampstead, 29 November 1974. Career: West Ham United 1993; Shrewsbury Town (loan) 1994;

Shrewsbury Town (loan) 1995; Leyton Orient (loan) 1995; Shrewsbury Town 1996; Plymouth Argyle 1998; Barnet 1998; Wycombe Wanderers 2001; Brighton & Hove Albion 2004; IPSWICH TOWN 2004.

■ A left-winger with the ability to go past defenders and cross with either foot, Darren Currie had two spells on loan with Shrewsbury Town while with West Ham, scoring on his debut for the Gay Meadow club before returning to Upton Park. Following another loan spell, this time with Leyton Orient, Currie joined the Shrews on a permanent basis, again proving to be a real crowd-pleaser. He had made 89 appearances when it became clear he was no longer part of the club's plans. Following a heel-kicking spell, he joined Plymouth Argyle on deadline day in March 1998. In the summer he moved on to Barnet and made a whirlwind start to his career at the club. He struck two magnificent goals in successive games; the second, against Wolves was later voted the club's Goal of the Season. After that he turned provider, quickly developing a marvellous rapport with the Underhill crowd. Often plagued by comparisons with his legendary uncle (Tony Currie), he had the most successful campaign of his career in 1999–2000 when his form won him inclusion in the PFA's Division Three select side. He was a key figure behind the club's most successful start to a campaign and his dismissal in the home game against Rochdale was the only blip in an otherwise impeccable year. Although not a prolific scorer, he netted the first senior hat-trick of his career while in Barnet's colours as they thrashed Blackpool 7–0. Despite Barnet's relegation, he was once again named in the PFA Third Division team of the year. In the summer of 2001, Wycombe Wanderers paid £200,000 for his services, and he figured in every League game for the Chairboys in his first season at Adams Park. He was released following Wycombe's relegation to League Two at the end of the 2003–04 season and won a year's contract with Brighton after impressing manager Mark McGhee. With Albion strapped for cash, Currie was sold to Ipswich for a fee of £250,000. He made an immediate impression for Town on his debut from the bench at Queen's Park Rangers, setting up the equaliser and then putting his team in front with a rasping drive. During the rest of the campaign, Currie was also employed as a central playmaker. In 2005–06, Currie continued to impress and ended a worrying run of 26 matches without a goal at Millwall after being set up by Jim Magilton.

CURTIS Dermot Patrick

Centre-forward

Born: Dublin, 26 August 1932.
Career: Shelbourne; Bristol City 1956; IPSWICH TOWN 1958; Exeter City 1963; Torquay United 1966; Exeter City 1967; Bideford; Elmore.

■ Republic of Ireland international centre-forward Dermot Curtis was a prolific goalscorer for Shelbourne in the League of Ireland before Bristol City manager Pat Beesley paid £5,000 for his services in November 1956 to replace Jimmy Rogers. The previous month he had made his full international debut, marking the occasion with his side's first goal in the 2–1 home victory over Denmark in a World Cup qualifying game. He eventually took his tally to eight goals in 17 appearances, including two in the 3–2 defeat of Sweden in November 1959. With Bristol City, Curtis netted 16 goals in 26 Second Division outings alongside John Atyeo, prior to joining Ipswich in September 1958. At Portman Road he successfully deputised in either inside-forward berth. Although he found the net fairly regularly, including nine in four games in 1959–60 – a sequence that saw him net a hat-trick against Sunderland and four goals against Stoke City – his overall total of 17 goals in 42 games was spread over four seasons. He moved to Exeter City in August 1963, forming a notable goalscoring partnership with Alan Banks and helping the Grecians to win promotion in 1963–64. Curtis later moved on to play for local rivals Torquay United, who had just won promotion to the Third Division, but after just a dozen games he rejoined Exeter. Subsequently with Bideford and Elmore, where he was player-manager, he later returned to his trade as a sheet-metal worker prior to working as a roofer.

DALE William

Full-back

Born: Manchester, 17 February 1905.
Died: 1987.
Career: Sandbach Ramblers; Manchester United 1928; Manchester City 1931; IPSWICH TOWN 1938

■ Billy Dale, who was equally at home in either full-back position, joined Manchester United from Sandbach Ramblers and was a regular member of the club's First Division side before moving across the city to join their Maine Road rivals. Dale missed very few games while with City, helping them win the FA Cup in 1934 when they came from behind to beat Portsmouth 2–1 with two late goals. Dale, who appeared in 237 League games for City, was also a member of the side that won the League Championship in 1936–37. However, the Maine Road club were relegated the following season and Dale left to play for Ipswich Town. He was a member of the Town side that beat Southend United 4–2 in their inaugural game in the Football League and went on to appear in 40 games during that 1938–39 season. He appeared in the three completed

League games of the following season before war was declared, but they turned out to be his final games in Ipswich colours.

DAVIES Albert Bryn

Inside-forward

Born: Cardiff 1913.
Career: Army; Cardiff City 1935; IPSWICH TOWN 1938.

■ Bryn Davies joined Cardiff City as an amateur in 1935 following army service. Most of his time at Ninian Park was spent in the reserves as he made just seven League appearances spread over three seasons. Following Ipswich Town's admission to the Football League in 1938, Davies left Cardiff to join the Portman Road club and in his only season – his career being terminated by World War Two – he scored seven goals in 32 games, including one on his debut in the club's first-ever League game – a 4–2 win over Southend United.

DAVIN Joseph James

Full-back

Born: Dumbarton, 13 February 1942.
Career: Hibernian; IPSWICH TOWN 1963; Morton.

■ Full-back Joe Davin joined Ipswich from Scottish League Division One side Hibernian in the summer of 1963 and played his first game for the club as a replacement for Larry Carberry in a 2–0 reversal at the hands of Stoke City. After that Davin appeared in the remaining 27 games of the season. He began the following season wearing the number-two shirt, but an injury against Northampton Town, who were to win promotion, forced him to miss the middle third of the campaign. He came back strongly to help the club finish fifth while in 1965–66 he again displayed his strengths of strong tackling and good distribution. He left Portman Road in the 1966 close season to return to Scotland to play for Morton and in his first season at Cappielow Park helped them win the Second Division Championship.

DAVIS Kelvin Geoffrey

Goalkeeper

Born: Bedford, 29 September 1976.
Career: Luton Town 1994; Torquay United (loan) 1994; Hartlepool United (loan) 1997; Wimbledon 1999; IPSWICH TOWN 2003; Sunderland 2005; Southampton 2006.

■ Having made his Luton first-team debut in the final match of the 1993–94 season, this goalkeeping prodigy had to wait until the home derby against Watford the following March for his next chance. He took it in style, even making a penalty save and subsequently retaining his place. Earlier he had been on loan at Torquay United and been selected as reserve for the Endsleigh Under-21 side in Italy. Having played for the England Youth team, he was called up into the England Under-21 squad at the end of the season. However, following the signing of Ian Feuer, he was in danger of becoming a forgotten figure and so, in need of first-team football, he went on loan to Hartlepool before in 1997–98 winning back his place in the Luton side. Making a number of breathtaking saves, he was voted the club's Player of the Season in 1998–99, but was then transferred to Wimbledon for £600,000. Signed as cover for Scottish international Neil Sullivan, it was 2000–01 before he won a place in the side after Sullivan had departed for Spurs. He went on to produce a string of fine performances throughout the campaign; his ability at shot stopping was hard to better in the Football League. He was ever present for the Dons in 2002–03, taking his total of appearances to 146 before joining Ipswich in the close season. He was an immediate improvement in the Tractor Boys' defence and helped the club reach the Play-offs. His effectiveness as a shot-stopper was never demonstrated better than during the last game of the season, the second leg of the Play-off at West Ham. After producing a fantastic one-handed save to keep out Bobby Zamora's point-blank header, he then stretched full length to turn a long-range effort over the bar. It was a similar story in 2004–05 as Town once again reached the Play-offs against West Ham. In the first leg of the semi-final tie he produced a stunning save to turn Anton Ferdinand's header over the bar. Not surprisingly he was selected for the PFA Championship team of the season by his fellow professionals. Eager to play at the highest level, Davis followed Tommy Miller to Sunderland in a £1.25 million deal but, despite his heroics in the Black Cats goal, he could do little to prevent the north-east club making an immediate return to the Championship. In July 2006 Davis moved from Sunderland to Southampton.

D'AVRAY Jean Michael

Forward

Born: Johannesburg, South Africa, 19 February 1962.
Career: Rangers (Johannesburg); IPSWICH TOWN 1979; Leicester City (loan) 1987; NEC Nijmegen (Holland); Moroka Swallows (South Africa); Cape Town Spurs (South Africa).

■ The South African-born forward joined Ipswich Town on the recommendation of former Town and England midfielder Colin Viljoen, and made his debut as a substitute for John Wark in a 2–1 home win over Southampton in November 1979 before making his full debut against Coventry a week later. The following season, when Town finished runners-up to Aston Villa in the First Division,

D'Avray scored his first goal for the club in a 3–1 defeat of Leicester City. In April 1983, D'Avray at last received his British passport and went on to win two Under-21 caps for England as an over-age player, scoring on his debut in a 3–1 win over Italy in the semi-final first leg of the European Under-21 Championships. It was 1984–85 before he established himself as a first-team regular at Portman Road and, although he suffered from injuries and had a loan spell with Leicester City towards the end of his career, he went on to score 45 goals in 255 games before leaving to play in Holland for NEC Nijmegen. Back in South Africa, he became a successful player-coach, taking the reins of the national Under-21 and Olympic sides in 1994.

DAY Albert

Forward

Born: Camberwell, 7 March 1918.
Died: January 1983.
Career: Hastings & St Leonards; Brighton & Hove Albion 1938; IPSWICH TOWN 1946; Watford 1949; Folkestone; Ashford; Crawley Town.

■ As a pre-war amateur, Albert Day represented Sussex and scored a hat-trick for Hastings & St Leonards in the 1938 Sussex Senior Cup Final. Unable to force his way into the Brighton side before the hostilities, he joined Ipswich prior to the resumption of League football in 1946–47, although he had 'guested' for the club the season before. Day made his Football League debut in the East Anglian derby against Norwich City, and what a debut it was! He scored a hat-trick in a 5–0 drubbing of the Canaries, going on to top the club's scoring charts with 14 goals in 25 League games. He reached double figures again the following season, netting 11 in 35 games as Town challenged for promotion from the Third Division South. Injuries limited his appearances the following season. Transferred to Watford, his only goal for the Hornets in four appearances came against Ipswich at Portman Road.

DEACON David Benjamin

Full-back

Born: Broome, 10 March 1929.
Died: 1990.
Career: Bungay; IPSWICH TOWN 1950; Cambridge United.

■ Much of full-back David Deacon's time at Portman Road was spent as cover for players of the calibre of Jim Feeney, Basil Acres, Larry Carberry and Ken Malcolm. However, when he did make his debut against Gillingham in September 1950, Deacon was still an amateur. He was at Portman Road for nine years, playing the last of his 76 games against Rotherham United in October 1959. On leaving the club he joined non-League Cambridge United and played for a couple of seasons before hanging up his boots.

DEEHAN John Matthew

Forward

*Born: Solihull, 6 August 1957.
Career: Aston Villa 1975; West Bromwich Albion 1979; Norwich City 1981; IPSWICH TOWN 1986; Manchester City 1988; Barnsley 1990.*

■ A striker who did his fair share of creating goals as well as scoring them, John Deehan began his career with Aston Villa, where he formed prolific goalscoring partnerships with both Andy Gray and Brian Little. Deehan helped Villa win the League Cup in 1977 and during his time at the club won seven caps for England at Under-21 level. During the early part of the 1979–80 season, Deehan left to join West Bromwich Albion, but the move did not work out and in December 1981 he was transferred to Norwich City for £175,000. While at Carrow Road, Deehan, who scored 70 goals in 197 games for the Canaries, won a League Cup-winners' medal in 1985 and a Second Division Championship medal the following year. On leaving Norwich, Deehan remained in East Anglia with Ipswich Town, moving to Portman Road in exchange for Trevor Putney. Deehan, who went on to score 11 goals in 49 League outings with Town, helped the club reach the Second Division Play-offs in 1986–87, scoring 10 goals in his 29 games. He later had spells playing for Manchester City and Barnsley before, after coaching the Canaries, becoming the Carrow Road club's manager. After resigning in protest at the club's policy of selling their best players, he took over the reins at Wigan Athletic. Having led the Latics to the Third Division Championship, he later worked as assistant manager to Steve Bruce at both Sheffield United and Huddersfield Town.

DEMPSEY John

Inside-forward

*Born: Cumbernauld, 22 June 1913.
Career: Queen of the South; IPSWICH TOWN 1948.*

■ John Dempsey had impressed north of the border with Queen of the South prior to moving to Portman Road in June 1948. He had been a prolific scorer for the Palmerston Park club and he carried on in the same vein on his arrival in Suffolk. Dempsey scored twice on his debut on the opening day of the 1948–49 season as Town beat Bristol Rovers 6–1. However, although he scored some spectacular goals, especially in the games against Norwich City and Leyton Orient, he struggled with injuries during the second half of the campaign and, in the close season, decided to retire.

DE VOS Jason Richard

Defender

*Born: Ontario, Canada, 2 January 1974.
Career: Montreal Impact (Canada); Darlington 1996; Dundee United 1998; Wigan Athletic 2001; IPSWICH TOWN 2004.*

■ A Canadian Olympic Games player, De Vos joined Darlington from Montreal Impact in November 1996, but shortly after establishing himself in the heart of the Quakers' defence a broken foot curtailed his season. De Vos became the first Darlington player ever to represent his country when he played for Canada against Iran in Toronto in August 1997. He then went on to play in Canada's World Cup qualifying games before another foot injury ended his domestic season. He had appeared in 52 games for Darlington when, in October 1998, he joined Dundee United for a club record fee of £400,000. De Vos appeared in 111 games for the Tannadice club before Wigan Athletic paid £500,000 for his services in the summer of 2001. Shortly after making his Wigan debut he broke two bones in his foot in the Worthington Cup tie against Blackpool and it was the turn of the year before he was back in action. He then missed most of January after playing for Canada in the Gold Cup. In 2002–03, De Vos and Matt Jackson formed an effective partnership at the heart of the Latics defence, helping the club win the Second Division Championship. An inspirational captain, he netted a number of vital goals – all scored with a broken bone in his foot! Named in the PFA Division Two side, he was voted Wigan's Player of the Season. Capped 49 times by Canada, he made a disastrous start to the following season when, on the opening day of the campaign, he broke his foot at Millwall. He returned to help the Latics reach the First Division Play-offs but, out of contract in the summer, he moved on to join Ipswich. He played in every game for the Tractor Boys in 2004–05 apart, ironically, for the away trip to Wigan, for which he was suspended. Winning most of the aerial challenges, De Vos proved a calming influence on the Ipswich defence. When Irish international Jim Magilton was rested, De Vos took over as Town captain, building up a good understanding with Richard Naylor. Deciding to retire from the international scene following Canada's failure to qualify for the World Cup Finals in Germany, De Vos remains an important member of the Ipswich side, for whom he has been rock solid at the back, even though on some occasions he has not been fully fit.

DIALLO Drissa
Centre-half

Born: Nouadhibou, Mauritania, 4 January 1973.
Career: RC Tilleur (Belgium); Sedan (France); AS Brevannes (France); KV Mechelen (Belgium); Burnley 2003; IPSWICH TOWN 2003; Sheffield Wednesday 2005.

■ When Guinea international Drissa Diallo arrived at Turf Moor in January 2003, he went straight into the Burnley side and was, along with Ian Cox, perhaps the Lancashire club's best defender. It was possibly significant that he was absent for both the Clarets' seven-goal home humiliations towards the end of the season. He also took great delight in scoring his first goal in this country in Burnley's FA Cup fifth-round victory over Fulham. In the close season he joined Ipswich Town on a free transfer and was a regular in the side during the early weeks of the 2003–04 campaign. He then suffered an injury in the home game against Wimbledon and thereafter his appearances were sporadic. Playing both at the heart of the defence and at right-back, Diallo's aerial ability was an asset at set pieces and he settled in well alongside De Vos and Richard Naylor. A hamstring injury picked up in the game against Queen's Park Rangers ruled him out until towards the end of the season when he made a few appearances from the bench. He appeared in the first leg of the Play-off semi-final but was obviously not match fit. He left Portman Road in the summer of 2005 to join Sheffield Wednesday, but after some impressive displays, he again suffered from a number of niggling injuries.

DINNING Tony
Midfield

Born: Wallsend, 12 April 1975.
Career: Newcastle United 1993; Stockport County 1994; Wolverhampton Wanderers 2000; Wigan Athletic 2001; Stoke City (loan) 2002; Walsall (loan) 2003; Blackpool (loan) 2004; IPSWICH TOWN (loan) 2004; Bristol City 2004; Port Vale (loan) 2005.

■ Unable to make the grade with Newcastle United, Tony Dinning joined Stockport County in the summer of 1994 and soon claimed a regular first-team place. After some impressive displays in the County midfield he broke his leg in the match at Sunderland in March 1998, but won back his place after making a full recovery. In 1998–99 he was called upon to fill a number of roles, from right-back to centre-half, as well as in midfield. He eventually reverted to his more customary central midfield role in 1999–2000, ending the campaign as the Hatters' leading scorer and deservedly voted Player of the Year by the Independent Supporters' Club. Early the following season Dinning, who had scored 30 goals in 227 games for County, was surprisingly sold to Wolverhampton Wanderers for a fee of £600,000. Although he made his Wolves debut at the heart of the defence, he soon switched to midfield and scored a number of spectacular goals. Yet in September 2001 he was transferred to Wigan Athletic. He was an important member of the Latics' Second Division Championship-winning side of 2002–03, but then had spells on loan at Walsall and Blackpool, for whom he played in the LDV Vans Trophy Final before arriving at Portman Road on a similar basis. At Ipswich, Dinning covered for Jim Magilton, making his debut in a 1–1 draw at Nottingham Forest. When the Irish international recovered, Dinning reverted to the bench before signing for Bristol City. After an impressive start his form dipped and he was again loaned out, this time to Port Vale.

DOBSON Robert Peter
Forward

Born: Frimley, 13 June 1925.
Career: Wisbech Town; IPSWICH TOWN 1949; Cambridge City.

■ Dobson's goalscoring exploits for non-League Wisbech Town prompted Ipswich manager Scott Duncan to sign him for the Portman Road club in October 1949. He went straight into the side for the game against Bristol City that ended goalless but then found himself unable to hold down a first-team place. In 1950–51 he appeared in just the last two games of the season, but in the first of these he scored his first goal for the club in the East Anglian derby as Town beat Norwich City 3–1. The following season he appeared in more games, but in the 1953 close season he parted company with the club when he reverted to non-League football with Cambridge City.

DONOWA Brian Louie
Winger

Born: Ipswich, 24 September 1964. Career: Norwich City 1982; Stoke City (loan) 1985; Deportivo la Coruna (Spain); Willem II (Holland); IPSWICH TOWN 1989; Bristol City 1990; Birmingham City 1991; Burnley (loan) 1993; Shrewsbury Town (loan) 1994; Walsall (loan) 1996; Peterborough United 1996; Walsall 1997; Ayr United.

■ After representing Ipswich schoolboys, winger Louie Donowa was snapped up by rivals Norwich City. He was a member of the Canaries' FA Youth Cup-winning team of 1983 and became a regular in City's First Division side during 1983–84, scoring on his full League debut against Manchester United at Carrow Road. He collected a League Cup-winners' medal in 1985 when Sunderland were defeated 1–0 at Wembley. It was a hollow victory, however, as Norwich were relegated from the top flight. It was during that season that Louie Donowa's exciting wing play won him three England Under-21 caps, the first in a 2–1 win over Israel in Tel Aviv. After a spell on loan with Stoke he spent three years on the Continent before returning to his home-town club in the summer of 1989. He spent a season at Portman Road, but could never really recapture the form that had seen him take the top flight by storm in his early days in the game. Having scored two goals in 30 League and Cup appearances, he spent a season with Bristol City before a £60,000 move took him to Birmingham, where he helped the Blues to promotion from the old Division Three in 1991–92. There followed loan spells with Burnley and Shrewsbury before he won back his place in the Birmingham side. Having helped the St Andrew's club win the Second Division Championship and the Auto Windscreens Shield at Wembley, he had spells with Peterborough and Walsall before trying his luck north of the border with Ayr United.

DOUGAN George
Wing-half

Born: Glasgow, 22 March 1939. Career: Yiewsley Town; IPSWICH TOWN 1963.

■ Signed from non-League Yiewsley Town, Glasgow-born wing-half George Dougan made his debut in the game against Arsenal at Highbury in October 1963. The first half was fairly even, with the Gunners holding a 1–0 half-time lead, but in the second half the young Town team capitulated to the extent that Arsenal ran out 6–0 winners! Dougan kept his place in the side but, following 3–1 defeats by Sheffield United and Chelsea, he returned to the club's reserve side. He was recalled into the Ipswich side in December and starred in a 3–2 defeat of West Ham United. In his next game he was a member of the Ipswich side completely demolished by Fulham, the Cottagers winning 10–1. Dougan went on to appear in 17 League games in a season in which the club were relegated before leaving to play his football in South Africa.

DOZZELL Jason Irvin Winans
Midfield/Forward

Born: Ipswich, 9 December 1967. Career: IPSWICH TOWN 1984; Tottenham Hotspur 1993; IPSWICH TOWN 1997; Northampton Town 1997; Colchester United 1998.

■ Jason Dozzell actually made his Football League debut while an Associated Schools player, coming off the bench at home to Coventry City on 4 February 1984 and scoring in a 3–1 victory. At 16 years 56 days old, he is the youngest player to have appeared in a League match for the Tractor Boys. In scoring the club's third goal that day, he became the youngest scorer for any club in top-flight history. In 1985–86 he won a regular place in the Town side, but it was not enough to save the Blues from relegation to the Second Division. He was an ever present in the Ipswich side the following season and yet again in 1989–90. At the beginning of the 1990–91 season he lost his place, but when manager John Lyall restored him to the side it was in a forward position rather than his usual midfield role. He continued to play in this spot during the club's Second Division Championship-winning season of 1991–92 when he partnered Chris Kiwomya. Dozzell scored 11 goals in 45 League games, and another four in five FA Cup games. In 1992–93, during the club's first season in the Premier League, he missed just one game, but played in a variety of positions: midfield, striker and even central defence. Despite being offered a long-term contract, Dozzell, one of only nine players to play in more than 400 first-team games for the club, left Portman Road in the summer of 1993 to join Tottenham Hotspur for £1.9 million. Often the scorer of crucial goals, his time at White Hart Lane was hampered by injuries and in five seasons in North London he only appeared in 99 League and Cup games before returning to Ipswich for a brief spell under George Burley. He then joined Northampton Town, helping the Cobblers reach the Play-off Final.

However, he began the following season without a club before winning a month-to-month contract with Colchester United. He impressed the U's and was offered a full contract. Apart from absence due to a broken arm, he missed very few games until a toe injury forced his premature retirement from League football.

DRIVER Allenby

Inside-forward

Born: Sheffield, 29 September 1918. Career: Mansfield Shoes; Sheffield Wednesday 1936; Luton Town 1946; Norwich City 1948; IPSWICH TOWN 1950; Walsall 1952.

■ After playing League football with his home-town team Sheffield Wednesday prior to the outbreak of World War Two, inside-forward Allenby Driver served for six years with the Royal Artillery before signing for Luton Town in 1946. After two seasons at Kenilworth Road he joined Norwich City, where he scored 19 goals in 49 League appearances before leaving the Canaries to join Ipswich for a fee of £3,000. Driver made his Ipswich debut in a disastrous 4–0 defeat at Leyton Orient before scoring on his home debut in a 3–1 defeat of Swindon Town. He kept his place in the Ipswich side for the remainder of the season, scoring five goals in 18 games. In 1950–51, Driver scored 11 goals in 44 games, including a couple in the 3–0 defeat of Colchester United. Having scored on the opening day of the following season in a 4–1 win over Southend, he then scored successive doubles in defeats of Millwall and Reading before, midway through the campaign, being allowed to join Walsall, for whom he played for a season before hanging up his boots.

DURRANT Lee Roger

Midfield

Born: Great Yarmouth, 18 December 1973.

Career: IPSWICH TOWN 1992; Harwich and Parkston; Lowestoft Town.

■ Lee Durrant was a right-sided midfielder with good ball skills and crossing ability. He made his Town debut at Aston Villa in a Premier League game in March 1994, a match Town won 1–0 thanks to a Gavin Johnson goal. He played in half-a-dozen matches towards the end of that 1993–94 season, but with competition for places hotting up at Portman Road, he failed to make an impact the following season. After making just one appearance from the bench, his last appearance was against Salernitana in the Anglo-Italian Cup. After spells on trial with Torquay and Northampton, for whom he did not make any appearances, he spent a season at Harwich and Parkston before signing for Lowestoft Town.

DYER Kieron Courtney

Midfield

Born: Ipswich, 29 December 1978. Career: IPSWICH TOWN 1997; Newcastle United 1999.

■ One of the players to have come through Ipswich Town's revitalised youth policy, Kieron Dyer began to blossom during the 1997–98 season, earning rave reviews from opposition managers after unexpectedly starting in the first team and playing in the majority of games, initially at right-back. Having made his England Under-21 debut against Moldova in September 1997 and scored the only goal in Italy, he was promoted to the England B team. The impact he made during the course of that campaign was shown when he was named in the PFA's First Division select team. His performances the following season saw him called up into the full England squad and nominated for the second successive year in the PFA First Division side. He fractured his leg in March but played on and scored the opening goal in the game against Watford before leaving the field on a stretcher. Returning to action near the end of the season, he scored a double in the home leg of the Play-off semi-final against Bolton, but it was not enough to save his side from a third successive Play-off exit. In the summer of 1999, Dyer became the first English signing by Newcastle United manager Ruud Gullit. His performances in the Premiership confirmed him as a footballer of exciting potential and led to him making his full England debut against Luxembourg. In his early days on Tyneside, Dyer played in a variety of positions, but wherever he appeared he always tried his best. Injuries then hampered his progress and, after experiencing pains in his shins, the problem was eventually diagnosed as being a stress fracture needing corrective surgery. He did not return to action until December 2001, but the following month he suffered a stress fracture in his left foot and was forced to sit out the remainder of the season. He made three appearances from the bench for England in the 2002 World Cup Finals and the following season had his best season for the Magpies. He was selected for the PFA Premiership team of the season and even captained the north-east club in the absence of Alan Shearer and Gary Speed. Despite a series of niggling injuries in 2003–04, he was selected by England for the 2004 European Championships. A much-publicised incident with teammate Lee Bowyer saw him receive a red card in the home game with Aston Villa, incurring a ban which excluded him from the FA Cup semi-final. Since then injuries have continued to disrupt his progress at St James' Park, but when fully fit he remains one of the most exciting players in the Premiership.

EDMONDS Darren

Left-winger
Born: Watford, 12 April 1971.
Career: Leeds United 1989; IPSWICH TOWN 1991; Scarborough 1992; Mossley 1992; Halifax Town 1992.

■ Unable to force his way into the Leeds United side, winger Darren Edmonds joined Ipswich Town in September 1991. Following some impressive displays for the club's reserve side, he made his debut off the bench, replacing Simon Milton in a goalless home draw against Millwall. His only other appearance at League level was also as a substitute, when Town again failed to score in a 1–0 home defeat at the hands of Sunderland. He left Portman Road to play for Scarborough, but after just one substitute appearance he drifted into non-League football with Mossley before returning to League action with Halifax Town. Even then his two appearances for the Shaymen were both from the bench.

ELLIOTT Matthew Stephen

Centre-half

Born: Wandsworth, 1 November 1968. Career: Epsom & Ewell; Charlton Athletic 1988; Torquay United 1989; Scunthorpe United 1992; Oxford United 1993; Leicester City 1997; IPSWICH TOWN (loan) 2004.

■ A commanding centre-back, Elliott appeared in just one game for Charlton Athletic before playing lower League football for Torquay United, Scunthorpe United and Oxford United. It was while at the Manor Ground, where he was appointed the club's captain, that he began to dominate in the air and prove his worth at set pieces. He helped Oxford win promotion to the First Division in 1995–96 when he was also voted the club's Player of the Year. Having scored 24 goals in 175 games for Oxford, he became Leicester City's record signing when he joined the Foxes in January 1997 for a fee of £1.6 million. In his first full campaign at Filbert Street, Elliott acted as club captain when Steve Walsh was out injured and scored a number of vital goals. Over the next couple of seasons he was always solid and formidable at the back, and added spot-kick responsibilities to his duties. He was also employed as an emergency striker at various points of the campaign. In 1999–2000, Matt Elliott's coolly placed header against Aston Villa sent Leicester to Wembley for the seventh time in nine seasons. Leading the Foxes out beneath the twin towers, he headed a goal in each half against Tranmere Rovers to secure the Worthington Cup for his team and the Man of the Match trophy for himself. The following season the goals at club level dried up but Elliott, who had won selection for Scotland, scored his first international goal against San Marino in October 2000 – he also managed to hit the woodwork in the return fixture at Hampden in March 2001. A red card in the match against West Ham the following season seemed to knock his confidence and he was eventually omitted from Berti Vogts's younger-looking international squad. He was back to his best in 2002–03, leading the Foxes to promotion to the Premiership as his wealth of experience clearly made up for any lack of pace and his astute reading of the game led to his masterly defensive performances throughout the campaign. In March 2004, Elliott joined Ipswich Town on loan as they made a push for promotion via the Play-offs. Making his debut in a 3–1 win at Walsall, he had a steadying effect on Town's defence, using his experience to keep one step ahead of his opponents and forging an effective partnership with John McGreal at the heart of Town's defence. The club suffered just two defeats in the 10 games in which Elliott played, but sadly could not overcome West Ham in the Play-off semi-final. Elliott returned to Leicester, but midway through the following campaign injury ended not only his season, but also his distinguished playing career.

ELLIS Kevin Edward

Left-back

Born: Tiptree, 11 May 1977. Career: IPSWICH TOWN 1995; King's Lynn.

■ After some promising displays in the club's junior and reserve sides, left-back Kevin Ellis made his Ipswich debut in a 4–1 defeat at Arsenal during

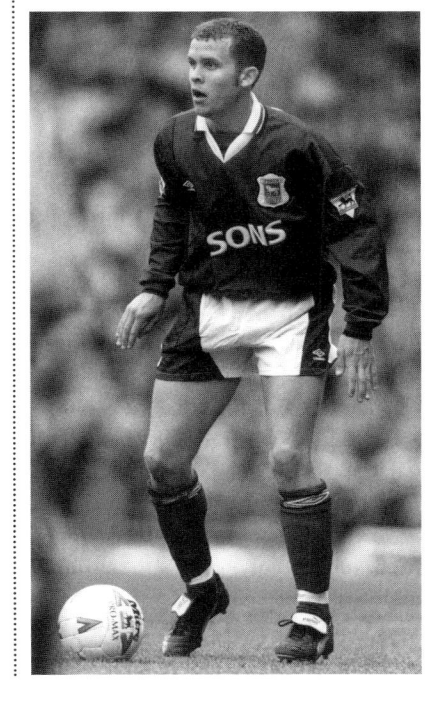

Easter 1995. However, he picked up an injury and was substituted with just 10 minutes remaining. Ellis remained on the Ipswich staff for a number of seasons without adding to his total of first-team appearances, before being released and moving into non-League football with King's Lynn.

ELSWORTHY John

Wing-half

Born: Newport, 26 July 1931.
Career: Newport County; IPSWICH TOWN 1949.

■ Only one player in the history of the Football League has won two Third Division South, one Second Division and one First Division Championship medal and that is John Elsworthy – the greatest Welsh player never to be capped by his country. Rugby was Elsworthy's first love and it was only by chance that he was spotted playing football by the ex-Manchester United player Billy Owen, who was scouting for his former boss Scott Duncan, then manager of Ipswich Town. Elsworthy made his Ipswich debut in December 1949 at Portman Road against Notts County – a match Town lost 4–0. National Service made its demands and it was not until his release by the RAF that Elsworthy established himself in the Ipswich side. His performances led to a number of top clubs, notably Liverpool, expressing a strong interest in him. Ironically, he then began to lose form and his place in the Ipswich line up. On Boxing Day 1953 he scored his only hat-trick for the club in a 4–1 home win over Coventry City, as Town went on to win the Third Division South title. In October 1955 he was a reserve for the Third Division South side against the Third Division North at Accrington and in 1956–57 he represented the South against the North in matches at both Coventry and Stockport. John Elsworthy was actually listed in the Wales 22 for the 1958 World Cup Finals in Sweden, but unfortunately the Welsh FA were short of funds at the time and, at the last moment, reduced their travelling party to 18. Having won the Second Division Championship in 1960–61, Ipswich found themselves in the First Division for the first time in their history. In the year that Town won the League Championship, Elsworthy helped break the deadlock in the final match of the season at home to Aston Villa. It was his diving header that rebounded off the crossbar for Ray Crawford to fling himself forward and head home the opening goal in a 2–0 win. Elsworthy's only goal in the European Cup came in the record-breaking 10–0 victory over Floriana of Malta. He went on to score 52 goals in 435 games, making his last appearance against Bolton Wanderers in September 1964.

FEARON Ronald Thomas

Goalkeeper

Born: Romford, 19 November 1960.
Career: Dover Town; Reading 1980; San Diego Sockets (United States); Sutton United; IPSWICH TOWN 1987; Brighton & Hove Albion (loan) 1988; Leyton Orient 1991; Sutton United; IPSWICH TOWN 1992; Walsall 1993; Sutton United; Southend United 1993; Ashford Town; Leyton Orient 1995.

■ Goalkeeper Ron Fearon was spotted playing for non-League Dover Town and was signed by Reading in February 1980. He spent two seasons at Elm Park, making 61 League appearances, before moving to play in the NASL for San Diego Sockets. Signed by Ipswich from non-League Sutton Town in September 1987, Fearon made his debut at home to Hull City in March 1988 and in his first season with the club helped them finish eighth in Division Two. The following season he appeared on a more regular basis and again the club finished eighth, with Fearon playing his last game against the club he had made his debut against, Hull City. After spells with numerous League and non-League clubs, he ended his career with Leyton Orient, finally calling it a day at the end of the 1995–96 season.

FEENEY James McBurney

Full-back

Born: Belfast, 23 June 1921.
Died: March 1985.
Career: Linfield; Swansea City 1946; IPSWICH TOWN 1950.

■ Classical full-back Jim Feeney joined Swansea from Irish League side

Linfield in December 1946 and, over the next four seasons, made 88 League appearances for the then Vetch Field club. He won a Third Division South Championship medal in 1948–49, but in March 1950 he joined Ipswich Town with fellow Northern Ireland international Sam McCrory for a combined fee of £10,000. Feeney made his Ipswich debut in the East Anglian derby at Carrow Road just a few days after joining the club and was a virtual ever present for the next six seasons. In 1953–54 he missed just two matches as the Portman Road club won the Third Division South title and the following season was outstanding in the Town defence even though the team were relegated from the Second Division. He played the last of his 232 League and Cup games at Brighton in September 1956. In that game he suffered a broken nose in the sixth minute, reducing the side to 10 men.

FILLINGHAM Thomas

Centre-half/Left-half

Born: Bulwell, 6 September 1904.
Died: 2 May 1960.
Career: Bromley United; Birmingham City 1929; IPSWICH TOWN 1938.

■ Tom 'Tosha' Fillingham worked at Hucknall Colliery for a number of years, playing centre-forward for Bromley FC in the Miners' Welfare League. He later worked in a dye factory and in the summer of 1929 was given a trial by Birmingham. He impressed and was signed on professional forms almost immediately. He worked his way up through the ranks before scoring twice on his debut in a 4–1 win at Manchester City in April 1930. On his home debut a few days later, he scored the only goal of the game against Portsmouth. In 1930–31, Fillingham played in a variety of positions before settling at centre-half. He went on to appear in 189 League and Cup games, scoring nine goals, before leaving to join Ipswich Town in June 1938. Fillingham was Ipswich's captain for their first-ever Football League game against Southend United, going on to appear in 34 games. His only goal for the club came in the 4–0 home win over Bristol City. He did not play in any competitive football after World War Two and in 1950 he lost an eye as a result of an injury sustained on the field of play some years earlier.

FISH Mark Anthony

Centre-half

Born: Cape Town, South Africa, 14 March 1974.
Career: Jomo Cosmos (South Africa); Orlando Pirates (South Africa); Lazio (Italy); Bolton Wanderers 1997; Charlton Athletic 2000; IPSWICH TOWN 2005.

■ South African international Mark Fish joined Bolton Wanderers from Lazio in September 1997. It was quite a coup for the Lancashire club as Manchester United had been interested in signing him a season earlier. He became an instant hit with the Bolton fans and played in all three of South Africa's group games in the 1998 World Cup Finals in France. Although his skill and experience marshalled the Trotters' rearguard superbly, the club versus country wrangles did not help his cause and he frequently had to make energy-sapping trips around the globe to play in the African Nations Cup. Though he did not score too many goals, he did net with a spectacular overhead kick at Swindon. At the end of the 1999–2000 season, Fish announced that he was retiring from international football, having won 60 caps for South Africa. He had appeared in 127 games for the Wanderers when in November 2000 he opted for a move back to the Premiership with Charlton Athletic. A regular at the heart of the Addicks' defence, the injury-prone defender's only goal of the 2002–03 campaign came against his former club Bolton. The following season, after a self-imposed three year exile, he returned to the international scene and, though he appeared on a more regular basis for Charlton, his season was ended prematurely when he suffered severe injuries to his chest following a freak accident at home. His 2004–05 season at The Valley was wrecked by a persistent knee injury and, early the following campaign, he joined Ipswich Town on loan. His only appearance for the Portman Road club came in the club's second Championship game of the season at Queen's Park Rangers. He then returned to the Valley.

FLETCHER Charles Alfred

Outside-left/Left-half

Born: Homerton, 28 October 1905.
Died: 1980.
Career: Clapton Orient 1927; Crystal Palace 1928; Merthyr Town 1929; Clapton Orient 1930; Brentford 1933; Burnley 1935; Plymouth Argyle 1937;

IPSWICH TOWN 1938; Clapton Orient 1945.

■ Charlie Fletcher started his career with Clapton Orient, a club with whom he had three spells during the course of his career. Unable to break into the club's League side, he moved on to Crystal Palace and later Merthyr Town before rejoining the London club in 1930. His impressive form – he scored 32 goals in 120 League outings – prompted Brentford to sign him and in 1934–35 he was an important member of the Bees side that won the Second Division Championship. Fletcher, having scored 25 goals in 104 games for the Griffin Park club, then moved to the North West and Burnley, where he averaged a goal every three games, a good return for a winger. After a season with Plymouth Argyle, he joined Ipswich and made his Town debut in a 2–0 defeat of Port Vale. Fletcher played in every remaining game that season, scoring 10 goals in 30 League and Cup games, including two in the 3–3 draw with Bristol Rovers – a game Town had led 3–0 at half-time. Fletcher, who reached double figures in each of the full seasons in which he played, returned to Clapton Orient at the end of World War Two, but failed to make their League side.

FLETCHER Leonard Gerald George

Wing-half

Born: Hammersmith, 28 April 1929.
Career: RAF Didcot; IPSWICH TOWN 1949; Falkirk.

■ Tough-tackling wing-half Len Fletcher was spotted playing football for RAF Didcot and given his chance in League football by Town manager Scott Duncan. He made his debut in a 4–2 defeat at Bristol City towards the end of the 1949–50 season, going on to play in a handful of games before the season's end. He did not appear at all the following season, but was recalled to the side in 1951–52, only to be part of a Town side beaten 5–1 by Swindon. Fletcher remained at Portman Road until the end of the 1954–55 season, but in that time made only 21 League appearances before leaving to continue his career north of the border with Falkirk.

FORREST Craig Lorne

Goalkeeper

Born: Vancouver, Canada, 20 September 1967.
Career: IPSWICH TOWN 1985; Colchester United (loan) 1987; Chelsea (loan) 1996; West Ham United 1997.

■ Vancouver-born goalkeeper Craig Forrest paid his own air fare to England, confident that he could make the grade with Ipswich Town. After signing professional forms in the summer of 1985, he found he was unable to claim a first-team place and was loaned out to Colchester United. He made his Football League debut for the Layer Road club against Wrexham in March 1988. The following season, after making his Ipswich debut in a 1–1 draw at Stoke, he appeared in the opening 22 games until he was deemed at fault for all of the goals in a 3–0 defeat at Chelsea. Ron Fearon displaced him but Forrest worked hard at his game and won his place back. He was an ever present in 1989–90 and continued to impress the following season as he reaped the benefit of the club's specialist goalkeeping coaching provided by Phil Parkes. In 1991–92 he was again ever present as Town won the Second Division Championship and earned automatic promotion to the Premiership. Forrest was also selected for the Canadian national team after the season had ended, but his first season in the top flight was ruined by injury and suspension. His suspension came after he was sent off in the second minute of the home game against Sheffield United for serious foul play. He thus became the first Ipswich goalkeeper ever to be sent off in the Football League. Despite the emergence of Richard Wright, Forrest, who went on to win 56 caps for Canada, appeared in 304 games for the Portman Road club before leaving to join West Ham United. Much of his time at Upton Park was as understudy to Shaka Hislop, until he broke a leg and Forrest was given his chance. Playing for Canada in the 2000 Gold Cup, he was voted the 'Most Valuable Player' of the tournament, but on rejoining the Hammers he was diagnosed with testicular cancer. He had early treatment and has since been keen to do all he can to raise awareness of this particular problem.

FORSTER Nicholas Michael

Forward

Born: Caterham, 8 September 1973.
Career: Horley Town; Gillingham 1992; Brentford 1994; Birmingham City 1997; Reading 1999; IPSWICH TOWN 2005.

■ Signed from non-League Horley Town, Nicky Forster was a regular goalscorer for his first club Gillingham, prompting Brentford to pay £100,000 for his services in the summer of 1994. A striker with electrifying pace, he scored 26 goals in his first season for the Bees, including a hat-trick at Chester. Capped by England at Under-21 level, he was recognised by his fellow professionals when it came to the PFA Division Two team award. With constant press speculation concerning his future, he had a disappointing 1995–96 season, but had taken his tally of goals for the Griffin Park club to 47 in 136 games when Birmingham City paid £700,000 to take him to St Andrew's in January 1997. He scored three goals in his first four games for City before seriously damaging his knee ligaments. Out of action for almost a year, his return to the side certainly helped City's upturn in fortunes. He then found himself left out of the side, went on the transfer list at his own request and, in June 1999, joined Reading for a fee of £650,000. Forming a superb striking partnership with Martin Butler, he contributed to the Royals' best run of the 1999–2000 campaign. Unfortunately he suffered torn knee ligaments prior to the start of the following season and only returned to action in the latter stages of the 2000–01 campaign. Back to his best the following season, he was Reading's leading scorer and netted a hat-trick against Blackpool, both of which helped him win selection for the PFA Division Two team of the season. In 2002–03 he spearheaded Reading's drive for promotion, helping them reach the Play-off semi-finals before being injured in the game against Wolves. During the course of that season, Forster netted hat-tricks in the wins over Ipswich Town and Preston North End, and as well as setting up his own soccer school, was studying part-time for a degree at Roehampton University. Though he continued to score some spectacular goals for the Royals, he was hampered by injuries and he left to join Ipswich. Though he scored on his Town debut against Cardiff, he suffered more injuries before returning to action. He smashed in a sizzler to help Ipswich beat Derby – their first win in nine games – and in doing so, made it a goal in each of his three games back from injury. Town fans will be hoping the experienced striker can steer clear of injuries.

FOX Geoffrey Roy

Wing-half/Full-back

Born: Bristol, 19 January 1925.
Died: 1 January 1994.
Career: IPSWICH TOWN 1945; Bristol Rovers 1947; Swindon Town 1955.

■ An all-round sportsman who played cricket for Gloucestershire 2nd XI, Fox started out as a young half-back with Bristol City and was on the fringes of the first team when he signed for Ipswich Town. He made his debut for the Portman Road club in a 2–0 win over Watford during the early stages of the 1946–47 season, going on to appear in 11 games. He scored his only goal for the club in another 2–0 success, this time against Reading. In June 1947, Bristol Rovers manager Bert Tann signed him and, on his arrival at Eastville, he was converted into a full-back. A great shouter and organiser on the pitch, he offered a marked contrast to his illustrious partner Harry Bamford. Between them they were arguably the finest full-back pairing Rovers have ever had. He had appeared in exactly 300 games for Bristol Rovers when he found himself in dispute with the club over his wish to go part-time. In 1955 he moved to Swindon Town, before later going into business where he was a huge success.

FRIARS Sean Martin

Midfield

Born: Londonderry, 15 May 1979.
Career: Liverpool 1996; IPSWICH TOWN 1998; Portadown (loan); Newry Town; Carlisle United 2001; Newry Town; Cliftonville.

■ Northern Ireland Under-21 international Sean Friars was unable to make the grade with Liverpool and joined Ipswich, where it was thought he was the man to take over from the recently departed Bobby Petta, who had joined Celtic. It did not work out that way and, despite possessing a good left foot and the ability to beat players, his only appearance for the first team was for the last 20 minutes of the home game against Crewe during the 1999–2000 season. He went on loan to Irish League side Portadown before signing for Newry Town. He subsequently had a trial at Carlisle United, but his only appearance was again off the bench. Unfortunately this earned the club a substantial fine for a breach of the registration rules. Later released, Friars rejoined Newry but is now playing his football for Cliftonville.

FULLER Ricardo Dwayne

Forward

Born: Kingston, Jamaica, 31 October 1979.
Career: Tivoli Gardens (Jamaica); Crystal Palace 2001; Heart of Midlothian (loan) 2001; Preston North End 2002; Portsmouth 2004; Southampton 2005; IPSWICH TOWN (loan) 2006.

■ This exciting Jamaican striker originally arrived in England for a trial with Charlton Athletic in December 1999. In fact, he was on the verge of signing for the Addicks when a routine medical revealed a back problem that required corrective surgery. Once he was fully fit again, Fuller was released to join South London neighbours Crystal Palace shortly before the transfer deadline in February 2001. He featured regularly for the Eagles during the closing stages of the 2000–01 season and though he failed to score, he came close on a number of occasions.

Capped by Jamaica, he contributed to their campaign to qualify for the 2002 World Cup Finals in the Far East. Leaving Selhurst Park to rejoin Tivoli Gardens, he joined Preston North End in the summer of 2002 for a fee of £500,000, this after a successful loan spell with Hearts. A natural entertainer, he became an instant hit with the North End fans. Fuller scored on his League debut for Preston on the opening day of the 2002–03 season, but the team lost 2–1 to his former club Crystal Palace. He had scored 11 goals in 20 games for North End, including two against neighbours Burnley and both goals in the 2–0 defeat of promoted Leicester City, when a serious knee injury at Coventry curtailed his season. Despite talk of interest from Everton, Leeds, Spurs and Manchester City, Fuller started the 2003–04 season with a hat-trick against Burnley but, as the season wore on, the goals began to dry up. He had scored 31 goals in 63 games when he moved up to the Premiership with Portsmouth. He went on to become a regular in the Pompey squad, although the majority of his appearances were made from the bench. Unable to force his way into the Portsmouth side, he joined their nearest rivals Southampton, but as a former Pompey player, he received a fair amount of stick from the Saints fans. In February 2006 he joined Joe Royle's Ipswich side on loan and had a most eventful time. He was stopped from playing against Wolves because of a work permit problem, but netted on his debut at home to Leicester City. He received two yellow cards and in the 2–2 draw with his former club Crystal Palace was given his marching orders for making a hand gesture to the linesman, although he insisted he was giving the salute to the Palace fans, who had barracked him throughout the afternoon. However, 11 minutes before his dismissal, the Jamaican had grabbed Ipswich's second equaliser. It was his last game in Ipswich colours before he rejoined Southampton.

GAARDSOE Thomas

Centre-half

Born: Randers, Denmark, 23 November 1979.
Career: AAB Aalborg (Denmark); IPSWICH TOWN 2001; West Bromwich Albion 2003.

■ A Danish Under-21 international when he joined Ipswich from AAB Aalborg in the summer of 2001, Gaardsoe made his debut against West Ham United at Portman Road at the start of the 2001–02 season. His appearances were restricted by minor but niggling injuries and the competition for defensive places, but he certainly impressed Town fans with his attitude, skills and ability to keep calm under pressure. Having scored his first goal for the club against Sunderland, Thomas Gaardsoe blossomed in 2002–03 as a result of an extended run in the first team and the confidence shown in him by Joe Royle. The Ipswich manager seemed to build his defensive tactics around the Dane, who scored four goals including three in successive games. It came as a great surprise when, in August 2003, he was allowed to join West Bromwich Albion for £520,000. He produced some sterling displays at the heart of the Albion defence and was instrumental in helping the Baggies regain their Premiership status. Contributing vital goals against promotion-chasing Wigan and Sheffield United, he was not only named Albion's Player of the Year, but also won full international honours when selected to play for Denmark against England at Old Trafford, a match the Danes won 3–2. Though he was able to help Albion avoid relegation in 2004–05, he was not as successful in 2005–06 as the Baggies lost their place in the top flight.

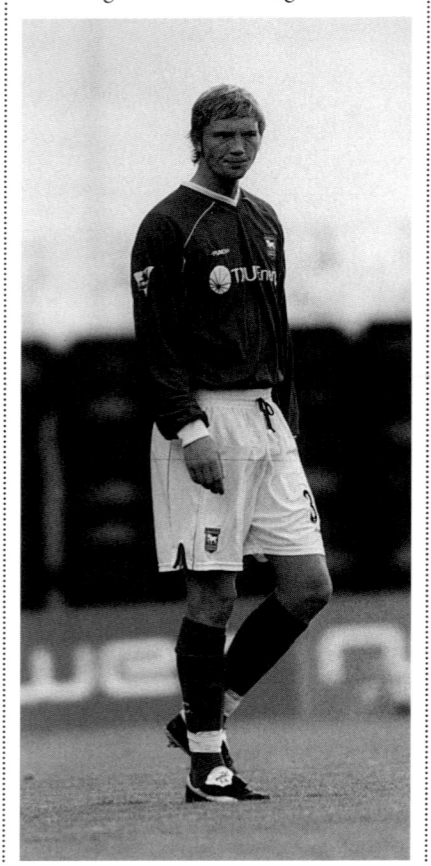

GARNEYS Thomas Thurston

Centre-forward
Born: Leyton, 25 August 1923
Career: Leytonstone; Notts County 1948; Chingford Town; Brentford 1949; IPSWICH TOWN 1951.

■ One of the unlucky footballers whose career was put on hold by the outbreak of World War Two, Garneys was 25 years old by the time he signed for Notts County after playing non-League football for Leytonstone. With Tommy Lawton – who scored four goals in the 9–2 win for County over Ipswich in 1948 – still at the club, there were few opportunities for him and, after a brief spell with Chingford Town, he joined Brentford. His performances for the Bees attracted interest from a number of clubs, but it was Ipswich manager Scott Duncan who won the race for his signature. He made his debut in the opening game of the 1951–52 season, scoring in a 4–1 defeat of Southend United. He ended the season with 20 goals in all competitions to top the club's scoring charts – a feat he achieved in five of his eight seasons at Portman Road. In 1953–54 he scored 19 goals in 44 League games to help the Blues win the Third Division South Championship and the following season, despite missing half the campaign with a bad injury, he netted 20 goals in 24 games including four in a 5–1 win over Doncaster Rovers. Garneys had just returned after a four-match absence and was playing against doctor's orders. It was the first time that an Ipswich player had scored more than three goals in a Football League match. In 1955–56 he scored a hat-trick in a 5–0 win at Northampton Town but, despite scoring 19 goals in 36 League games, it was the first season he had not finished as the club's leading scorer. The following campaign was Tom Garneys's last. In January 1959, having scored 143 goals in 273 games for the Portman Road club, he retired from the game to run the Mulberry Tree Inn in Ipswich.

GARRETT Leonard George

Full-back

Born: Hackney, 14 May 1936.
Career: Eton Manor; Arsenal 1954; IPSWICH TOWN 1958; Haverhill.

■ Before joining Arsenal, Len Garrett had represented London Youth and England Amateur Boys' Club as well as winning three England Youth caps. His career at Highbury was hindered by his call up for National Service in September 1954. Eventually released on a free transfer, he joined Ipswich Town in May 1958, but his only appearance for the Blues came in April 1959 in a 4–1 defeat at Brighton & Hove Albion. On being released, Garrett, who played Minor Counties cricket for Suffolk, left to play local football for Haverhill.

GARVAN Owen

Midfield

Born: Dublin, 29 January 1988.
Career: IPSWICH TOWN 2004.

■ One of the club's Academy graduates, Garvan got his first taste of first-team football when, at the age of just 16, he was named as substitute for the win over Brighton & Hove Albion in November 2004. Garvan, who has been capped by the Republic of Ireland from Under-15 to Under-17 levels, was a regular member of Town's FA Youth Cup-winning side in 2004–05, though he unfortunately missed the decisive second leg of the Final against Southampton after being rushed into hospital with a virus on the eve of the game. He eventually made his League debut for the Tractor Boys against Cardiff City in August 2005 and impressed throughout the remainder of the 2005–06 campaign, scoring three goals in 31 League appearances. One of these put Town ahead against Millwall, 24 hours after he had signed a new contract.

GATES Eric Lazenby

Forward

Born: Ferryhill, 28 June 1955.
Career: IPSWICH TOWN 1972; Sunderland 1985; Carlisle United 1990.

■ Although Eric Gates made his Ipswich Town debut as a substitute for Roger Osborne in a 2–0 home win over Wolverhampton Wanderers in October 1973, it was another two years, almost to the day, before he made his full first-team debut in a 1–0 defeat at Derby County, after having made 13 appearances from the bench. All Eric Gates's football with the Portman Road club was played in the First Division, although it was 1977–78 before he established himself as a first-team regular. Two seasons later, Gates netted his first hat-trick for the club in a 4–0 home win over Manchester City. In his previous game at Portman Road, his strike in Ipswich Town's 3–1 defeat of Southampton had been selected as *Match of the Day*'s Goal of the Month for November 1979. Gates continued to find the net during the next two seasons, in which Town finished runners-up in the First Division on both occasions. His form led to him winning two full caps for England, his first in the World Cup qualifying match against Norway at Wembley in 1981. Injuries hampered his progress in 1982–83, but the following season he was the club's top scorer with 16 goals, including another hat-trick, this time in a 3–0 third-round FA Cup win at Cardiff City. Gates was the club's leading scorer again in 1984–85, but at the end of that season the Ferryhill-born player, who had scored 96 goals in 378 first-team outings, left Portman Road to join Sunderland. At Roker Park, Gates was a first-team regular for five seasons, with his best campaign undoubtedly being the club's Third Division Championship-winning season of 1987–88 when he scored 20 goals including four in a 7–0 defeat of Southend United and a hat-trick in a

Eric Gates

3–0 win over Rotherham United. He went on to score 55 goals in 236 games before leaving the Wearsiders in the summer of 1990 to end his career with Carlisle United. After a spell coaching Hartlepool United, Gates now works in the media in the North East.

GAYLE Brian Wilbert

Centre-half

Born: Kingston, 6 March 1965. Career: Wimbledon 1984; Tooting & Mitcham (loan); Manchester City 1988; IPSWICH TOWN 1990; Sheffield United 1991; Exeter City 1996; Rotherham United 1996; Bristol Rovers 1997; Shrewsbury Town 1997; Telford United.

■ Brian Gayle was discovered as a 16-year-old by Wimbledon and, after having a spell on loan with local Vauxhall League team Tooting & Mitcham, made his League debut for the Dons in a 4–1 home win over Shrewsbury in March 1985. Gayle kept his place for the remainder of the season, but during the club's promotion-winning season of 1985–86 he lost his place to Mick Smith. He did not regain his position in the side until the following season, but in the summer of 1988, after not being selected for the FA Cup Final team, he was sold to Manchester City for £325,000. Gayle, who had appeared in 100 League and Cup games for the Dons, helped City win promotion to the First Division, but when Howard Kendall took over he lost his place and joined Ipswich Town. John Duncan's investment of £330,000 was a masterstroke and Gayle, who played his first game in Town's colours in a 2–1 defeat at Wolves, went on to play for a season under new manager John Lyall before leaving to join his former boss Dave Bassett at Sheffield United. Appointed club captain, his career with the Blades was hampered by injuries and he underwent four operations on his knee. Released in 1996 after making 138 appearances, he joined Exeter City on a monthly basis before signing for Rotherham United. Showing all his experience, he helped shore up the Millers' defence before moving to Bristol Rovers. Freed in the summer of 1997, he joined Shrewsbury Town, where he added some stability to the Gay Meadow club's defence before ending his playing days with non-League Telford United.

GAYNOR James Michael

Outside-right

Born: Dublin, 22 August 1928. Career: Shamrock Rovers; IPSWICH TOWN 1952; Aldershot 1953.

■ During his days with Shamrock Rovers, winger James Gaynor played representative football for the League of Ireland XI. He arrived at Portman Road in March 1952 and made his debut in a 2–1 win at Swindon Town. He kept his place in the side for the remainder of the campaign, scoring his first goal for the club in a 3–1 defeat of Walsall. The following season he appeared in the majority of the club's games and, though he only got on the scoresheet himself in two League games, he did provide Elsworthy and Garneys with plenty of goalscoring opportunities. His last game for Town was against Aldershot and in the close season the Shots were the club that Gaynor joined. He stayed at the Recreation Ground for five seasons, scoring 39 goals in 165 League games before deciding to retire.

GEDDIS David

Forward

Born: Carlisle, 12 March 1958. Career: IPSWICH TOWN 1975; Luton Town (loan) 1977; Aston Villa 1979; Luton Town (loan) 1982; Barnsley 1983; Birmingham City 1984; Brentford (loan) 1986; Shrewsbury Town 1987; Swindon Town 1988; Darlington 1990.

■ After coming through the youth ranks at Portman Road, David Geddis, a strong, determined player with a good shot, made his League debut in a goalless draw at Derby County in May 1977. He scored the only goal of the game against Arsenal on the opening day of the 1977–78 season and two in a 3–2 defeat of Queen's Park Rangers. After Town had reached that season's FA Cup Final, where their opponents were Arsenal, manager Bobby Robson sprang a surprise by naming Geddis on the right wing for the first time in his career. His main task was to keep Arsenal's Northern Ireland international full-back Sammy Nelson with his hands full. It was a Geddis cross that led to the miskicked clearance by Willie Young that gave Roger Osborne his chance for glory with his 78th-minute winner. The following year, the Ipswich striker was fortunate to escape a terrible car

THE WHO'S WHO OF IPSWICH TOWN

David Geddis

GEORGE Finidi
Midfield/Forward
Born: Nigeria, 15 April 1971.
Career: Port Harcourt (Nigeria); Calabar Rovers (Nigeria); Ajax (Holland); Real Mallorca (Spain); IPSWICH TOWN 2001; Real Mallorca.

■ Nigerian international Finidi George, who joined Ipswich Town from Spanish club Real Mallorca for £3.1 million in the summer of 2001, made an immediate impact on his home debut for Ipswich against Derby County. George scored twice and produced an outstanding performance in a 3–1 win. He received a setback at Fulham in October 2001 when he broke his jaw and was out of action for five weeks. He then returned to the

accident that claimed the life of one of Town's young players, Peter Canavan. Though he was not to blame, he needed a change of environment and moved to Aston Villa for a fee of £300,000. He did not really hit it off at Villa and moved on to Barnsley, where he scored 24 goals in 50 games. He then joined Birmingham City, where he continued to find the net with great regularity. After leaving St Andrew's his career went downhill, although he did help Darlington regain their Football League status by scoring three goals in nine games during the run-in of the Quakers' GM Vauxhall Conference campaign of 1989–90. On hanging up his boots he took up a coaching appointment with Middlesbrough under Bryan Robson. Changes at the top at the Riverside meant another move, this time back to his old boss Bobby Robson at Newcastle United.

side with a mini-scoring streak before leaving to play in the African Nations Cup. Before he departed, he scored the goal of the season at Portman Road against Sunderland, when he ran on to Matt Holland's through ball and chipped the ball into the net from the right-hand corner of the Black Cats' penalty area. On his return he found himself in and out of the side, while in 2002–03 he was hampered by a series of niggling injuries that kept him on the sidelines. Obviously not part of the manager's plans, he left the club in the 2003 close season following a settlement of his contract and rejoined Real Mallorca.

GERNON Frederick (Irvin) Anthony John

Defender

Born: Birmingham, 30 December 1962.
Career: IPSWICH TOWN 1980; Northampton Town (loan) 1986; Gillingham 1987; Reading 1988; Northampton Town 1989.

■ England Under-21 international defender Irvin Gernon worked his way up through the ranks at Portman Road before making his Football League debut in a 1–1 draw at Nottingham Forest in March 1982. He appeared in three other games that season – all victories – as Town finished runners-up to Liverpool in the First Division. He appeared on a more regular basis in 1982–83 following Mick Mills's departure to Southampton. Though never an automatic choice, in spite of starting the following campaign in the number-three shirt, Gernon made 76 League appearances for the club before joining Gillingham. It was while with the Kent club that he scored his first League goal, but after a little over a season he left the Priestfield Stadium to join Reading. He spent a season with the Royals before ending his first-class career with Northampton Town, a club where he had earlier spent a period on loan while with Ipswich.

GERRARD Paul William

Goalkeeper

Born: Heywood, 22 January 1973.
Career: Oldham Athletic 1991; Everton 1996; Oxford United (loan) 1998; IPSWICH TOWN (loan) 2002; Sheffield United (loan) 2003; Nottingham Forest 2004.

■ England Under-21 international goalkeeper Paul Gerrard, who kept 13 clean sheets in 18 appearances at that level, started out with Oldham Athletic, where after two operations on a horrifically injured knee he was ready to quit the game. He was sent out on loan to Crewe Alexandra, in order to gain experience, only to dislocate the same knee the day before his debut! Returning to Boundary Park, he decided to give it one more go and, following injuries to both Jon Hallworth and John Keeley, he made his Premier League debut at Queen's Park Rangers in December 1992. After that he never looked back, becoming the Latics' first-choice 'keeper. His only time out of the side was towards the end of the 1995–96 season when he suffered a broken jaw. Gerrard had played in 136 games for Oldham when, in the summer of 1996, Everton paid £1 million to take him to Goodison Park. He had to wait patiently for his first taste of Premiership football for the Merseyside club. It came, surprisingly, at the instigation of Neville Southall, who with the Blues beating Southampton 5–1 at half-time, volunteered to make way for him. Everton went on to win 7–1. When the Welsh international left Goodison, Gerrard seemed the perfect choice to replace him, but the club signed Thomas Myhre and Gerrard remained in the reserves. He then had a loan spell with Oxford United before, following an injury to Myhre, he returned to Everton and impressed Walter Smith so much that he was offered a new long-term contract. Though he showed occasional lapses of concentration, he proved himself a great shot-stopper and was instrumental in 2000–01 in the Blues maintaining their top-flight status. Following the appointment of David Moyes as manager, he had a frustrating time at Everton and in November 2002 he joined his former Oldham boss Joe Royle at Ipswich. He went straight into the Town team at Watford and kept a clean sheet in a 2–0 win. He played in five consecutive games, but a dislocated knee ended his loan spell early. Though he was linked with a permanent move back to Ipswich in the close season, he had loan spells with Sheffield United and Nottingham Forest. After being released by Everton, having made 99 League and Cup appearances, he returned to the City Ground to sign permanently for Forest. An ever present, he was unable to prevent their relegation at the end of the 2004–05 season.

GIBBONS John Ronald

Centre-forward

Born: Charlton, 8 April 1925.
Career: Dartford; Queen's Park Rangers 1947; IPSWICH TOWN 1949; Tottenham Hotspur 1950.

■ Centre-forward John Gibbons was a prolific scorer in non-League football for Dartford when he was signed by Queen's Park Rangers in December 1947. After impressing in the club's reserves, he appeared in eight games during the 1948–49 season, but at the end of that campaign he was allowed to leave and signed for Ipswich Town. He made his debut in a 2–0 defeat at

Crystal Palace, but on his next appearance he scored twice in a 4–4 draw with Leyton Orient. Town led 3–2 at half-time but then fell behind and it was Gibbons who rescued a point with a late equaliser. Even then he could not win a regular place and though he scored the only goal of the game against Exeter City, he left to join Spurs before the end of the season. Unable to break into the North London club's side, he returned to non-League football.

GIBSON Joseph
Forward
Born: Banknock, 20 March 1926.
Career: Polkemmet Juniors; IPSWICH TOWN 1947; West Ham United 1949.

■ Signed from Scottish junior football, versatile forward Joe Gibson made just one League appearance for Ipswich Town and that was in a 3–0 defeat at Newport County on New Year's Day 1949. He remained at Portman Road playing in the reserves until the end of the campaign when he left to try and further his career with West Ham United. However, he could not force his way into the Hammers' side and returned north of the border.

GILLESPIE Ian Colin
Forward
Born: Plymouth, 6 May 1913.
Died: 1988.
Career: Harwich & Parkeston; Crystal Palace 1937; IPSWICH TOWN 1946; Colchester United 1947; Leiston.

■ Discovered playing non-League football for Harwich & Parkeston, Ian Gillespie joined Crystal Palace in February 1937 and, in the seasons leading up to World War Two, scored a number of vital and spectacular goals for the club. He remained with Palace through the war years but, prior to the resumption of League football, he signed for Ipswich Town. He did not have the best of debuts as Town crashed 4–1 at Aldershot and he only appeared in six games that season, scoring his only goal for the club in a 3–1 win at Queen's Park Rangers. Unable to hold down a regular place in the Ipswich side, Gillespie left to play for Colchester United, later becoming player-manager of Leiston.

GLEGHORN Nigel William
Midfield
Born: Seaham, 12 August 1962.
Career: Seaham RS; IPSWICH TOWN 1985; Manchester City 1988; Birmingham City 1989; Stoke City 1992; Burnley 1996; Brentford (loan) 1997; Northampton Town (loan) 1998; Altrincham.

■ Nigel Gleghorn was a Newcastle-on-Tyne fireman playing non-League football for Seaham Red Star when Ipswich manager Bobby Ferguson signed him for just £3,000 in the summer of 1985. Making his debut in a 1–0 defeat at Arsenal, the left-sided midfielder fitted into Ferguson's pattern of play and the following season netted a hat-trick in a 4–3 win at Bradford City. When Ipswich and Ferguson parted company, Gleghorn found he could not adapt to new manager John Duncan's long-ball game and, with his contract expiring, he asked to leave the club. An independent tribunal decided that Manchester City should pay only £47,500 for his services – 13 goals in 82 League and Cup games – a fee that seemed a travesty! After just one season at Maine Road, Birmingham City splashed out £175,000 to take him to St Andrew's. He missed very few games in his time with the Midlands club and appeared in the defeat of Tranmere Rovers in the Leyland DAF Final at Wembley. In 1991–92 he was in outstanding form, top scoring with 22 League and Cup goals as Birmingham won promotion from the Third Division. In the early part of the following season Gleghorn, who had scored 43 goals in 176 games, left to join Stoke City for £100,000. In his first season at the Victoria Ground he helped the Potters win the Third Division Championship and in four seasons with the club was a virtual ever present. After switching from the left-wing to the centre of midfield at the start of the 1995–96 season, Gleghorn played in all 56 games as the club reached the First Division Play-offs, only to lose to Leicester City. Having scored 31 goals in 208 games, he was allowed to join Burnley. Unable to settle at Turf Moor, he had loan spells with Brentford and Northampton Town before moving into non-League football with Altrincham.

GODDARD Paul
Forward
Born: Harlington, 12 October 1959.
Career: Queen's Park Rangers 1977; West Ham United 1980; Newcastle United 1986; Derby County 1988; Millwall 1989; IPSWICH TOWN 1991.

■ At his most dangerous when balls were played into him on the edge of the penalty area, Paul Goddard began his career with Queen's Park Rangers where, after making his debut as a substitute against Arsenal in April 1978, he scored in his first full game against Coventry City. Although he claimed a regular place shortly afterwards, it was not until 1979–80 that he really came to the fore, scoring 16 League goals in a great partnership with Clive Allen. On the basis of that form, West Ham United parted with a fee of £800,000 for him to act as the foil for David Cross. In his first season at Upton Park he won a Second Division Championship medal and reached the League Cup Final but, although he scored in the replay, the Hammers were beaten 2–1 by Liverpool. He was honoured by England when he came off the bench against Iceland in June 1982, but later during his time with West Ham he suffered a serious injury and on his return could not dislodge Tony Cottee and Frank McAvennie. Transferred to Newcastle United, he and his family became homesick and after topping the Magpies' goalscoring charts he was allowed to move to Derby County. Despite forming a great strike partnership with Dean Saunders and with the Rams going well, the County board received an offer from Millwall for the 30-year-old striker that they could not refuse. Sadly, it was a disastrous move for both player and club and a year later Millwall wrote off their hasty £800,000 investment and granted him a free transfer. Goddard's former manager at Upton Park, John Lyall, then signed him for Ipswich Town and after making his debut against his former club, Millwall, he showed a brief glimpse of his previous form with six goals in 10 games before injury ended his season. In 1991–92 he played only a minor role in Ipswich's Second Division Championship campaign after losing his place in September and when drafted back into the side in late season it was in midfield. He had a disappointing season in 1992–93 when it was felt that his experience would be invaluable to the younger members of the side as the club tried to cement its place in the Premier League. Although playing fairly regularly, earlier on Bontcho Guentchev had established himself in the side as Goddard's form fell away. He went on to score 15 goals in 109 first-team outings before he and John Wark took charge of first-team affairs at the start of the 1994–95 season with coach Mick McGiven handed another role within the club. Following the appointment of George Burley as manager, Goddard worked with the youth academy before becoming Glenn Roeder's assistant at West Ham United.

GRANT Wilfred

Winger/Centre-forward

Born: Ashington, 31 August 1920.
Died: 1990.
Career: Morpeth Town; Manchester City 1943; Southampton 1946; Cardiff City 1950; IPSWICH TOWN 1954; Llanelli.

■ A Geordie who had been on the books of Manchester City, Wilf Grant moved to Southampton, scoring 11 goals in 61 games for the Saints before Cardiff manager Cyril Spiers brought him to Ninian Park in exchange for Ernie Stevenson. Eight months after his arrival, both Grant's career and Cardiff's future were to be changed forever when Mike Tiddy was signed and Grant moved from the wing to centre-forward. Using his speed through the middle, Grant netted 14 goals in just 25 League games, including a hat-trick in a 5–2 home win over Grimsby Town. When the Welsh club were promoted to the First Division the following season, Grant was the club's only ever present and top scored with 26 League goals. He continued to score on a regular basis in the top flight and his form won him an England B cap. Following the signing of Trevor Ford, Grant reverted to his wing position, but after scoring 67 goals in 159 League and Cup games, he left Cardiff in October 1954 to join Ipswich Town. After making his debut at Fulham, he scored on his home debut against Port Vale, but in his first season at Portman Road he struggled to make much impact. It was a different story in 1955–56 as Town finished third in the Third Division South with Grant scoring 16 goals in 35 games, including hat-tricks in two successive games: Millwall (home 6–2) and Reading (away 5–1). He netted another treble against Millwall in the return games. On hanging up his boots, he became player-coach at Llanelli and then accepted an invitation from Cardiff manager Bill Jones to become a member of the Ninian Park club's coaching staff. He spent five years with City during their rise and fall from the First Division in the early 1960s.

GREEN Donald

Centre-half

Born: Needham Market, 30 November 1924.
Died: 1996.
Career: Bramford; IPSWICH TOWN 1947; Stowmarket.

■ A strong-tackling centre-half and good in the air, Don Green was spotted playing non-League football for his home-town club Bramford and was signed by Ipswich in March 1947. In a season in which Town finished sixth in the Third Division South, Green, who made his debut in a 1–0 win over Southend United, played in four games. He was outstanding at the heart of the Ipswich defence in 1947–48 as the club finished fourth, playing in 33 games. A bad injury kept him out of contention for the entire 1948–49 campaign and after that he appeared only occasionally before leaving Portman Road to play non-League football for Stowmarket. Don Green later worked as a driver for a local petrol company.

GREGORY David Spencer

Midfield/Right-back

Born: Sudbury, 23 January 1970.

Career: IPSWICH TOWN 1987; Hereford United (loan) 1995; Peterborough United 1995; Colchester United 1995; Canvey Island.

■ Brother of teammate Neil Gregory, David worked his way up through the junior ranks to make his Town debut at Chelsea in December 1988, nearly two years after signing professional. Prior to 1990–91 he had made only one full League appearance, but temporarily claimed a place in midfield when David Lowe had a spell out of the side early on in the season. However, he made only fleeting appearances in Ipswich's Second Division Championship-winning season of 1991–92 and automatic promotion to the new Premier League. He rarely appeared the following season after breaking a finger in training and then picking up a groin strain during a reserve match against Portsmouth. However, he stood in for Eddie Youds in the penultimate game of the campaign and scored Town's only goal in a 3–1 defeat at Crystal Palace. Following a loan spell with Hereford United he joined Peterborough United, but never quite fitted in at Posh and moved on to Colchester United. Inspired management saw him switched from midfield to right-back, where he soon looked a natural. In 1997–98 he played in a variety of positions and was Colchester's leading scorer, including three goals in the Play-offs – one of which was an all-important penalty at Wembley to take United up. He continued to find the net in the higher grade of football, netting 14 goals, a total which included nine spot-kicks. Gregory always gave wholehearted and hard-working displays for Colchester but was then laid low by a series of knee injuries, culminating in an operation. He had scored 26 goals in 259 games before leaving to continue his career alongside his brother at non-League Canvey Island.

GREGORY Neil Richard

Forward

Born: Ndola, Zambia, 7 October 1972. Career: IPSWICH TOWN 1992; Chesterfield (loan) 1994; Scunthorpe United (loan) 1995; Torquay United (loan) 1996; Peterborough United (loan) 1997; Colchester United 1998; Canvey Island.

■ Neil is the younger brother of David Gregory, despite the vast geographical disparity of their birthplaces. He was selected as a substitute for the Premier League game at home to Wimbledon in 1992–93 and, although he did not play, was part of the most inexperienced bench ever, as not one of the three men had played first-team football. He finished the season as the reserves' leading scorer and made a couple of appearances off the bench before making his full debut against the Dons in 1994–95 – a match in which he crashed a shot against the bar. Having had a brief spell on loan with Chesterfield, he joined Scunthorpe, also on loan, towards the end of the season and netted seven goals in 10 games for the Glanford Park club. Back at Portman Road he found himself still on the bench but injuries to Alex Mathie and Ian Marshall gave him his chance and he responded by scoring a double at the expense of Watford. He also had the experience of taking over from Craig Forrest after the 'keeper was injured against Charlton, having four goals knocked past him for his pains! He went in goal again the following season after an injury to Richard Wright. Another loan spell, this time with Torquay United, was followed by a recall to the Ipswich side and his first-ever hat-trick for the senior side in the defeat of Sheffield United. His loan spell at Peterborough saw him score after five minutes of his debut. After a three-month loan spell with Colchester United, he returned to Portman Road while protracted transfer negotiations took place. Colchester eventually broke the club's transfer record by paying £50,000 for his services in January 1998. He scored in each of the last two League games to cement the club's place in the Play-offs and when he played alongside David at Wembley, they became the first brothers to appear in a Play-off Final. Finding goals harder to come by in the Third Division, he eventually parted company with the U's and left to join non-League Canvey Island.

GREW Mark Stuart

Goalkeeper

Born: Bilston, 15 February 1958.
Career: West Bromwich Albion 1976; Wigan Athletic (loan) 1978; Leicester City 1983; Oldham Athletic (loan) 1983; IPSWICH TOWN 1984; Fulham (loan) 1985; West Bromwich Albion (loan) 1986; Port Vale 1986; Blackburn Rovers (loan) 1990; Cardiff City 1992; Stafford Rangers; Hednesford Town.

■ Goalkeeper Mark Grew began his career with West Bromwich Albion, where his debut was a real oddity for the time: coming on as a substitute goalkeeper in a 1978–79 UEFA Cup tie against Galatasaray. Grew joined Wigan Athletic on loan during the club's first season in the Football League, where he replaced the injured John Brown. On leaving the Hawthorns he joined Leicester City, but had an unhappy time at Filbert Street and in March 1984 he moved to Ipswich Town. He made his debut in a 1–1 draw with Manchester United, going on to play in the next five games, only one of which was lost. However, he was in the shadow of Paul Cooper and there followed loan spells with Fulham and West Bromwich Albion before he joined Port Vale. He suffered a serious knee injury early in his Vale career, but returned to perform heroically in both their 1988 Cup run and their 1989 promotion campaign. Twice voted the club's Player of the Year, he ended his League career with Cardiff City before playing non-League football for Stafford Rangers and Hednesford Town. Grew later returned to Vale Park as the club's Youth Development Officer before being appointed assistant manager.

GUDMUNDSSON Niklas

Forward

Born: Sweden, 29 February 1972.
Career: Halmstads (Sweden); Blackburn Rovers 1995; IPSWICH TOWN (loan) 1997.

■ Swedish international Niklas Gudmundsson joined Blackburn Rovers, initially on loan, from Halmstads – for whom he scored 46 goals in 141 games – in December 1995. Although he was not rushed into first-team action – playing mainly for the reserves and making the odd first-team appearance as a substitute – he did enough to persuade the club to take him on a permanent basis. Unable to win a regular place in 1996–97, he spent the last two months of the season on loan with Ipswich Town. During his time at Portman Road he scored three goals – a tap-in at Swindon Town, a long-range effort in the game against Birmingham City and a header in the second leg of the Play-off semi-final against Sheffield United. Although not an out-and-out centre-forward, he had the ability to hold the ball up well and possessed some neat touches. After returning to Ewood Park, he left these shores without a further appearance for the Lancashire club to continue his career in his native Sweden.

GUENTCHEV Bontcho Lubomisov

Midfield/Forward

Born: Tchoshevo, Bulgaria, 7 July 1964.
Career: Lokomotiv (Bulgaria); Etar (Bulgaria); Sporting Lisbon (Portugal); IPSWICH TOWN 1992; Luton Town 1995; CSKA Sofia (Bulgaria); Hendon Town.

■ Bulgarian international Bontcho Guentchev was signed by Ipswich Town from Sporting Lisbon midway through the 1992–93 season, along with Vlado Bozinowski, who would act as his interpreter. Both men were recommended by the former Ipswich and England manager Bobby Robson, then managing the Portuguese club. Guentchev had earlier joined Lisbon from the unlikely Bulgarian League champions of 1990–91, provincial team Etar Veliko Tarnova, for whom he was leading scorer with 15 goals from 27 games. Of all the Scandinavian and Eastern European players signed in droves by Premier League managers during 1992–93, which provoked an understandable protest by the PFA, Guentchev's credentials appeared the least impressive. On arriving at Portman Road, however, a dispute arose over his international appearances. Ipswich had a letter from the Bulgarian FA stating that he had played 12 times for Bulgaria. Although the FA launched an enquiry, they eventually decided to leave things as they were. It was ironic therefore that his early performances for Ipswich showed far more promise than any of the more qualified imports. After making his Premier League debut against Manchester City in December 1992, he scored in his third game against front-runners Blackburn Rovers and held his place with five goals in three FA Cup matches, which included a splendid hat-trick against Grimsby Town. He quickly built up a rapport with Town fans because of his ball skills, but there were some who thought him a bit lightweight for English football, especially on the heavy grounds. Continuing to demonstrate his good passing ability with either foot, Guentchev returned to Ipswich full of enthusiasm following his participation in the 1994 World Cup, where he helped Bulgaria reach the semi-finals (he scored the vital goal in a penalty shoot-out with Mexico). Unable to play for the club the following season because he did not make the required number of appearances to earn an extension to his work permit, he joined Luton Town and, though he was unable to prevent their relegation, was the Hatters' leading scorer in the League. Included in Bulgaria's Euro '96 squad, he figured in most of Luton's games the following season but seemed to lack the appetite for the hurlyburly of life in the lower reaches. He later played for CSKA Sofia before returning to see out his career with non-League Hendon Town.

HALL Wilfred

Goalkeeper

Born: St Helens, 14 October 1934. Career: Earlstown; Stoke City 1953; IPSWICH TOWN 1960; Macclesfield; Stafford Rangers; Altrincham; Stafford Rangers.

■ At 5ft 8in, Wilf Hall was on the short side for a goalkeeper, but his impressive displays between the posts for non-League Earlstown prompted Stoke City to give him a chance at League level. It took him 18 months to break into the Potters' side and even after making his debut he had to vie with Bill Robertson for the number-one jersey. He was Stoke's goalkeeper in all four FA Cup replays against Bury in 1954–55. After over six years with the club, in which he made 57 appearances, he moved to Ipswich Town, making his debut in August 1960 in a 4–1 defeat of Derby County. He had a run of four games – three wins and a draw – but was primarily understudy to Roy Bailey as Town won the Second Division Championship. It was a slightly different story in the First Division – Hall made five appearances and, though the club won the League Championship, his appearances saw him play in defeats by Everton (away 2–5) Fulham (home 2–4) and Birmingham City (away 1–3). He played in seven games in 1962–63 but was never on the winning side. His final appearance coincided with Town being beaten 6–1 by West Bromwich Albion. After leaving Ipswich he played football for a number of top non-League clubs: Macclesfield, Stafford Rangers and Altrincham.

HALLWORTH Jonathan Geoffrey

Goalkeeper

Born: Stockport, 26 October 1965. Career: IPSWICH TOWN 1983; Bristol Rovers (loan) 1985; Oldham Athletic 1989; Cardiff City 1997.

■ Though he started his Football League career with Ipswich Town, goalkeeper Jon Hallworth made his debut while on loan to Bristol Rovers at Reading in January 1985, conceding three goals in a 3–2 defeat before his first game for Ipswich the following November. Prior to the 1987–88 season, Hallworth spent most of his time at Portman Road deputising for Paul Cooper, but started that campaign as the club's first choice and played in 31 consecutive games before making way for Ron Fearon and Craig Forrest. Hallworth never played again for Town's first team and one year later was transferred to Oldham Athletic. He appeared in every game of Oldham's 1990–91 Second Division Championship-winning season and in the top flight, the following season, was consistent to a fault, missing only the final game. In 1992–93 he damaged his wrist diving at the feet of Mark Hughes and carried on playing, not realising his wrist was broken in three places! On regaining full fitness, he found he had to share the goalkeeping duties with Paul Gerrard and then Gary Kelly. Having appeared in 217 games for the Latics, he was given a free transfer and joined Cardiff City. He had an outstanding first season at Ninian Park and won every Player of the Year award that was available. His displays in 1998–99 led to the Bluebirds winning promotion to Division Two and he was included in the PFA award-winning Third Division side. Unfortunately the following season he suffered a knee problem and gradually lost confidence. Though he had come to the end of his three-year contract, he was offered new terms and stayed at the club as cover for Mark Walton before deciding to retire.

HAMILTON Bryan

Midfield

Born: Belfast, 21 December 1946. Career: Distillery; Linfield; IPSWICH TOWN 1971; Everton 1975; Millwall 1977; Swindon Town 1978; Tranmere Rovers 1980.

■ Bryan Hamilton started his playing career with Distillery and earned the first of his 50 Northern Ireland caps while starring for Linfield before Ipswich Town won the race for his signature in August 1971. It was at Portman Road that Hamilton enjoyed his best moments as a player, under Bobby Robson in a talented Ipswich side. He made his debut in a goalless draw at home to Everton on the opening day of the 1971–72 season and, although he only played in a handful of matches during that campaign, he was ever present and joint top scorer with 11 League goals in 1972–73. The following season he was the club's leading scorer with 16 goals in 41 games as Town finished fourth in Division One. He netted his only hat-trick for the club in March 1975 as Newcastle United were beaten 5–4 at Portman Road. Hamilton had scored 56 goals in 199 first-team games when he left Ipswich to join Everton for £40,000. Though Hamilton was not a prolific scorer at international level, he had the happy knack of scoring vital goals – three of his four goals for Northern Ireland came in 1–0 wins over Wales (twice) and Yugoslavia. He played for the Goodison club in the League Cup Final of 1977, although he will always be remembered on Merseyside for scoring the 'goal that never was'. In the FA Cup semi-final against Liverpool, the game stood at 2–2 when, with just seconds remaining, Bryan Hamilton's thigh deflected a Duncan McKenzie flick into the Liverpool net. Everyone in Maine Road thought Hamilton had put Everton into the 1977 FA Cup Final. It was to become an infamous slice of Everton folklore that referee Clive Thomas disallowed the effort for alleged handball; the score remained at 2–2 and the Reds marched on to win the replay. Though his goalscoring tally on Merseyside slumped, Hamilton compensated with precise passing and mature reading of the game, as well as formidable eagerness and lung power. He lost his place in the Everton side and moved to Millwall in the summer of 1977. He later played for Swindon Town before joining Tranmere Rovers as player-manager. Later he took the reins at Wigan Athletic and led the Latics to Freight Rover Trophy success at Wembley in 1985. Appointed manager of Leicester City, he was unable to prevent the Foxes from being relegated and was sacked. Returning to Wigan as chief executive, he later assumed control of team matters. On leaving Wigan a second time, he was a surprise appointment as manager of Northern Ireland. Since leaving his post with the national side, he has twice been called in to add his experience to the Ipswich backroom staff and had a spell in charge of Norwich City.

HAMMOND Geoffrey

Full-back

Born: Sudbury, 24 March 1950. Career: IPSWICH TOWN 1968; Manchester City 1974; Charlton Athletic 1976.

■ After working his way up through the junior and reserve teams, full-back Geoff Hammond made his League debut for Ipswich in a 2–1 defeat at Ipswich in September 1970. In a season in which Town struggled to retain their First Division status, the tough-tackling full-back appeared in 29 games and scored the first of two goals for the club in a 2–1 win over Blackpool. The following season he shared the number-two shirt with Mick Mills, but in 1972–73 he made just one start and appeared twice from the bench. He had a run of six consecutive games the following season but was then transferred to Manchester City, appearing against Town in two 1–1 draws in the 1974–75 season. Hammond later left Maine Road to see out his first-class career with Charlton Athletic.

HANCOCK Kenneth Paul

Goalkeeper

Born: Hanley, 25 November 1937.
Career: Stoke City; Port Vale 1958; IPSWICH TOWN 1964; Tottenham Hotspur 1969; Bury 1971; Stafford Rangers; Northwich Victoria; Leek Town.

■ Goalkeeper Ken Hancock had five years as an amateur with local club Stoke City, but when they failed to offer him professional terms he joined the Potters' nearest rivals, Port Vale. After making his League debut in a 4–2 defeat at Millwall in December 1958, he was ever present during the rest of Vale's 1958–59 Fourth Division Championship-winning season. He spent six years with Vale and made 269 League and Cup appearances before signing for Ipswich Town for a fee of £10,000 in December 1964. He conceded four goals on his Ipswich debut as the Blues lost 4–1 at Preston North End, but went on to prove himself a reliable, clean-handling and competent 'keeper. He was ever present in seasons 1966–67 and 1967–68, playing in 108 consecutive League and Cup games. In the 1967–68 campaign, Hancock kept 12 clean sheets and made a number of memorable saves as the club won the Second Division Championship. After David Best signed for the Tractor Boys, Hancock joined Tottenham Hotspur as cover for the legendary Pat Jennings and appeared in four League and Cup games before leaving for Bury. At Gigg Lane he proved himself to be one of the best 'keepers in the Fourth Division, but later left to play non-League football for Stafford Rangers and then Northwich Victoria. He then returned to Port Vale as part-time coach and standby goalkeeper. However, it was discovered that because he had received a pay out from the provident fund, he could not play for the club and he moved to become player-coach and later manager of Leek Town.

HARBEY Graham Keith

Left-back/Midfield

Born: Chesterfield, 29 August 1964.
Career: Derby County 1982; IPSWICH TOWN 1987; West Bromwich Albion 1989; Stoke City 1992; Gresley Rovers; Burton Albion.

■ Graham Harbey began his career with Derby County where, following an outstanding debut against Charlton Athletic at The Valley in September 1983, he was offered a full contract by Rams' boss Peter Taylor. Though his opportunities at left-back at the Baseball Ground were few while Steve Buckley remained, he did make a number of appearances from the bench during the club's Third Division promotion-winning season of 1985–86. As the Rams were on the way to winning the Second Division title the following season, he had an important spell in midfield but, at the end of the campaign, he was allowed to leave and join Ipswich Town for a fee of £65,000. Over the next two seasons, Harbey missed very few games for the Portman Road club and in October 1987 he netted his only League goal for the club with a spectacular long-range drive in a 3–0 win over Manchester City. Harbey's strong tackling and good distribution of the ball were the major features of his play and it came as a shock when he was allowed to join West Bromwich Albion in November 1989. Harbey was a virtual ever present for the Baggies during his time at the Hawthorns, appearing in over 100 League and Cup games. His fourth and last first-class club was Stoke City and in his only season at the Victoria Ground he helped the Potters win the Third Division Championship. He later played non-League football for Gresley Rovers and Burton Albion.

HAREWOOD Marlon Anderson

Forward

Born: Hampstead, 25 August 1979.
Career: Nottingham Forest 1996; FC Haka (Finland) (loan); IPSWICH TOWN (loan) 1999; West Ham United 2003.

■ A product of Nottingham Forest's youth scheme, this striker made his League debut against West Bromwich Albion on the final day of the 1997–98 season with the club already promoted to the Premiership. A player out of the Emile Heskey mould, he was loaned out to Finnish side FC Haka before being given a place in Forest's Worthington Cup side. Unable to hold down a regular place in Forest's League side, he was loaned out to Ipswich Town in January 1999. With Jamie Scowcroft out injured he certainly added to Town's attack, scoring the only goal of his stay at Bury. Happy to be a team member rather than to promote himself, Harewood later returned to the City Ground, where he eventually won a regular spot in the side. A great favourite with the Forest fans, he showed that he had pace to burn and could give defenders a yard or two start and still overtake them. A player with all the key attributes for a goalscorer, in 2002–03 he formed a deadly strike partnership with David Johnson and his personal tally of 21 goals included four goals against Stoke City and a hat-trick in the defeat of Gillingham. The following season he was the most improved striker in the First Division, netting 11 goals in the opening 19 games. However, after announcing he was not going to sign a new contract at the end of the season, he was allowed to join West Ham United in November 2003 for a bargain fee of £500,000. He was an instant hit for the Hammers, scoring two goals on his debut against Wigan Athletic and finishing the campaign as the club's leading scorer with 14 goals. In 2004–05 he had a fine season, netting 17 Championship goals as the Hammers gained promotion to the Premiership via the Play-offs. Unfortunately he was awesome in the Play-off semi-final against Ipswich, scoring once and setting up another for Bobby Zamora. In 2005–06 he had another outstanding campaign, helping the Upton Park club to a respectable mid-table position in the Premiership and a place in the FA Cup Final, where they lost on penalties in a memorable game against Liverpool.

HARPER Colin George

Left-back

Born: Ipswich, 25 July 1946.
Career: IPSWICH TOWN 1964; Grimsby Town (loan) 1976; Cambridge United (loan) 1977; Port Vale 1977; Chelmsford City; Sudbury Town.

■ Local-born Colin Harper joined the Tractor Boys during the reign of Bill McGarry, making his debut in a 3–0 defeat at Plymouth Argyle in February 1966. He then appeared in the next five games before making four appearances the following season, including one at left-half. It was not until the appointment of Bobby Robson as manager that Harper established himself fully in the Ipswich side. Harper was ever present at left-back in the 1971–72 season and scored his first goal for the club the following term in a 4–1 home win over Manchester United. He was a regular in the side for the next few seasons, prior to having loan spells with Grimsby Town and Cambridge United. He suffered a serious knee injury in the Olympic Stadium in Rome in the UEFA Cup tie against Lazio in November 1973 and was never the same afterwards. He left Portman Road in the summer of 1977, joining Port Vale as their player-coach. He appeared in a handful of games before, in October of that year, being appointed the club's acting manager. A few weeks later he left the club after new manager Bobby Smith brought in his own backroom staff to Vale Park. He then had a spell with Chelmsford City before becoming player-manager at Sudbury Town. He later returned to Ipswich to work as a builder.

HARPER David

Wing-half

Born: Peckham, 29 September 1938.
Career: Millwall 1957; IPSWICH TOWN 1965; Swindon Town 1967; Leyton Orient 1967.

■ England Youth international wing-half Dave Harper began his career with his local club Millwall, helping them win the Fourth Division Championship in 1961–62. He had appeared in 165 League games for the Lions when, in March 1965, Ipswich manager Bill McGarry brought him to Portman Road. Harper, who made his Town debut in a 2–0 win at Portsmouth, was also the club's first-ever substitute when he came off the bench to replace Frank Brogan in the match at Charlton Athletic on 28 August 1965. Dave Harper appeared in 72 League games for the club before leaving to join Swindon Town in the summer of 1967. He failed to settle at the County Ground and, a couple of months after putting pen to paper, he moved on to Leyton Orient. After two seasons of struggling in the lower reaches of the Third Division, Harper played his part in helping the Brisbane Road club win the Third Division Championship in 1969–70, shortly afterwards parting company with the club.

HAVENGA William Stephanus

Inside-forward

Born: Bloemfontein, South Africa, 6 November 18924.
Career: Bremner OB (South Africa); Birmingham City 1948; Luton Town 1950; IPSWICH TOWN 1952; Kettering Town; Worcester City; Hinckley Athletic; Halesowen Town.

■ During the late 1940s and early 1950s, a string of triallists arrived at Birmingham City from South Africa. Willie Havenga was one of the earliest and one of the few to make a Football League appearance. He then moved on to Luton Town and scored six goals in 18 games for the Hatters during one-and-a-half seasons at Kenilworth Road. Joining Ipswich in January

1952, he became the club's first overseas player, making his debut in a 2–0 win over Torquay United, when he laid on the first of Tom Garneys' two goals in a 2–0 win. Havenga went on to play in 19 League games for Ipswich over the next couple of seasons, scoring three goals. On leaving Town he remained in this country for several years, playing non-League football for a number of clubs.

HAYES Hugh

Wing-half

Born: Bangor, 23 June 1925.
Career: Bangor City; IPSWICH TOWN 1946; Bangor City.

■ Tough-tackling wing-half Hugh Hayes had impressed the Ipswich scouts while playing non-League football for his home-town club Bangor. Signed in the summer of 1946, he had to wait until October 1948 before playing his first game for the club in a 2–1 home defeat of Port Vale. Town had been 1–0 down at half-time, but an inspired second-half showing prompted by the hardworking Hayes led to goals from Jackie Brown and Tommy Parker. Hayes appeared in three successive games, the last a disastrous 4–0 beating by Swindon, before returning to the reserves. He appeared in both wing-half positions the following season, his last game being a 1–0 win over Newport County. Not retained at the end of the season, he returned to his former club where he gave a good number of years of sterling service.

HAYNES Daniel

Forward

Born: London, 19 January 1988.
Career: Charlton Athletic; IPSWICH TOWN 2005.

■ Danny Haynes was a product of the Charlton Athletic youth academy before signing a deal to play for Ipswich Town. The pacy striker, who can play down the middle or out wide, was a member of the East Anglian club's FA Youth Cup-winning squad before making his debut against Leeds United in September 2005. Scoring his first goal for the club after leaving the bench in the match against Queen's Park Rangers, his popularity was dramatically increased in February 2006 when he scored the winner in the last minute for Ipswich against arch-rivals Norwich City. This goal meant that he had achieved the unusual feat of scoring against the Canaries for the youth, reserves and first team in 2005–06. There are many similarities between the young Haynes and former Town striker Darren Bent. Both have electric pace and both are more than able finishers when goalscoring opportunities arise. Ipswich fans will hope that the club are able to hang on to Haynes, something they could not manage with Darren Bent.

HEGAN Daniel

Midfield

Born: Coatbridge, 14 June 1943.
Career: Albion Rovers; Sunderland 1961; IPSWICH TOWN 1963; West Bromwich Albion 1969; Wolverhampton Wanderers 1970; Sunderland 1973.

■ Danny Hegan was a player with lots of skill, but he allowed his social activities to rule his life and, though the Coatbridge-born midfielder won seven full caps for Northern Ireland through parentage, he was never the outstanding player he should have been. He began his career with Albion Rovers before moving into the Football League with Sunderland. Unable to break into the first team at Roker Park, he joined Ipswich Town in September 1963. He did not have the best of debuts, as Town were thrashed 6–0 by Bolton Wanderers at Burnden Park. Over the next six seasons, Hegan was a virtual ever present in the Ipswich side and in 1967–68 missed just one game as the club won the Second Division Championship. It was during the 1968–69 season, when the club were back in the top flight, that midfield general Hegan began to feel that he was getting into a rut, but the Town player, who had an Irish father, gave a series of displays that brought him very close to full international honours for Northern Ireland. Hegan was on the transfer list for a number of months before, in the 1969 close season, having scored 38 goals in 230 games, he was allowed to join West Bromwich Albion in exchange for Ian Collard. While at the Hawthorns, Hegan won the first of his seven international caps when he played against the USSR in October 1969. He later joined Albion's rivals Wolverhampton Wanderers, collecting a runners'-up medal in the 1972 UEFA Cup Final. After ending his Football League career with Sunderland, he played in South Africa before hanging up his boots to become a soccer coach at Butlin's holiday camp in Clacton. In January 1982 Danny Hegan was sued for libel by Billy Bremner and the former Leeds United skipper was duly awarded £100,000 in damages.

HIGGINS Augustine (Ossie) Robert

Centre-forward

Born: Dublin, 19 January 1931.
Career: Shamrock Rovers; Aston Villa 1949; IPSWICH TOWN 1952.

■ Ossie Higgins shot to fame while playing League of Ireland football for Shamrock Rovers and was the Hoops' leading scorer in his only season in the first team. Aston Villa gave him the chance to make a career for himself in the First Division of the Football League but, despite some impressive displays for the club's reserve side and scoring a number of spectacular goals, especially with his head, he could not force his way into the Villa side. Higgins was transferred to Ipswich Town in the summer of 1952 and made a couple of appearances in the Ipswich side in 1952–53 against Millwall – a match Town lost 6–1 – and Leyton Orient. Unable to displace Tom Garneys or John Elsworthy, he returned to his native Ireland to continue his career.

HILL David Michael

Midfield

Born: Nottingham, 6 June 1966.
Career: Scunthorpe United 1985; IPSWICH TOWN 1988; Scunthorpe United 1991; Lincoln City 1993; Chesterfield (loan) 1994.

■ A hardworking, left-footed midfield player, Dave Hill began his career with Scunthorpe United and was a regular member of the Irons' side for four seasons before signing for Ipswich in July 1988. In his first season at Portman Road he appeared in 36 League games as Town flirted with a promotion place but ended up just missing out on a Play-off spot in eighth place. Hill remained at Portman Road for three seasons, also demonstrating his skill as a free-kick specialist. Sadly, he then broke a leg in a Combination match against Norwich City. On recovering he had a spell on loan at his former club Scunthorpe and then returned to Glanford Park on a permanent basis in September 1991. He went on to make 245 first-team appearances before signing for Lincoln City. His early days at Sincil Bank saw him play some of his best football, but a series of niggling injuries and a loss of form saw him loaned out to Chesterfield before he rejoined the Imps and won back his first-team spot, prior to being released in the summer of 1995 and going to play in Ireland.

HILL Michael Richard

Centre-forward

Born: Hereford, 3 December 1947.
Career: Bethesda Athletic; Sheffield United 1965; IPSWICH TOWN 1969; Crystal Palace 1973; Cape Town City (South Africa).

■ Qualifying for Wales on the basis of his father's birthplace, Mick Hill was called up for his full international debut against Czechoslovakia in October 1971 after scoring six goals in six games for Ipswich Town. He had begun his career with Cardiff City, but was released in 1965 without having made a first-team appearance. He decided to give up soccer and took a clerical job in Hereford. His father persuaded him to have another try and he joined Welsh League North club Bethesda Athletic. Sheffield United were very impressed with his goalscoring exploits and the 17-year-old was signed on. In his very first League appearance for the Bramall Lane club, he scored his side's first goal against Chelsea and was voted Man of the Match. Strong in the air and skilful on the ground, Ipswich boss Bobby Robson paid £33,000 for his services in October 1969. Having made his debut in a goalless draw against Arsenal at Highbury, he proceeded to hit some spectacular goals. During the 1970–71 season, in front of the BBC *Match of the Day* cameras, he notched a fine goal against Liverpool following a solo run from the halfway line. He was Town's leading scorer in 1971–72 and continued to score on a regular basis until Crystal Palace manager Malcolm Allison took him to Selhurst Park in December 1973. Hampered by injuries during his time with the Eagles, he later emigrated to South Africa and scored for Cape Town City in their 1976–77 South African Cup Final.

HODGES Lee Leslie
Midfield

Born: Plaistow, 2 March 1978.
Career: West Ham United 1995; Exeter City (loan) 1996; Leyton Orient (loan) 1997; Plymouth Argyle (loan) 1997; IPSWICH TOWN (loan) 1998; Southend United (loan) 1999; Scunthorpe United 1999; Rochdale 2002; Bristol Rovers 2003; Thurrock.

■ A creative, attacking left-sided midfield player, Lee Hodges failed to win a place in the West Ham United side and during the course of the 1996–97 season had spells on loan at Exeter City and Leyton Orient. There followed another loan spell, this time with Plymouth Argyle in November 1997, but on his return to Upton Park he managed five first-team appearances from the bench for the Hammers. Although on the small side, Hodges was a bundle of energy and unlucky not to appear on a more regular basis for Harry Redknapp's side. In November 1998 he was loaned out to Ipswich Town, where he came off the bench on four occasions without ever really making his mark. There followed another loan spell at Southend, where he produced a number of Man of the Match performances as the club battled to save its League status. A fee of £130,000 took him to Scunthorpe United in the summer of 1999 and, though he took some time to settle in the North, he had an outstanding first season and was named the Irons' Player of the Season. Though he had to undergo a cartilage operation the following season, his displays led to him winning selection for the PFA award-winning Third Division team. A couple of knee operations in 2001–02 reduced his appearances, but he was still selected for the PFA Select XI before he was surprisingly released. He then joined Rochdale, but suffered with niggling injuries during his time at Spotland and moved on to Bristol Rovers, where he again had to undergo surgery on his knee. On parting company with the Pirates, he moved into non-League football with Thurrock.

HOLLAND Matthew Rhys
Midfield

Born: Bury, 11 April 1974.
Career: West Ham United 1992; Bournemouth 1995; IPSWICH TOWN 1997; Charlton Athletic 2003.

■ Unable to make the grade at West Ham United, midfielder Matt Holland joined Bournemouth in January 1995. In his first full season at Dean Court, he swept the board in the Player of the Year awards. Playing mainly in a central midfield position, though he also had a number of games as a sweeper, he scored 10 goals, the majority from outside the area.

Matt Holland

Appointed the Cherries' captain, he demonstrated his defensive qualities in 1996–97 when, because of injuries, he played in the centre of defence. In the summer of 1997 he joined Ipswich Town for a fee of £800,000 and soon became a firm favourite. Influential in Town's second-half surge up the table, he played in a variety of positions, displaying his wholehearted endeavour in every game. His most eventful experience was probably the game against Oxford United, where he took over from Richard Wright in goal while the 'keeper had stitches in a facial injury. Though he was powerless to prevent Kevin Francis from scoring, he scored the fourth goal himself in a 5–2 win, all before conceding a penalty! Not surprisingly he was voted Player of the Year by the supporters. Instrumental in the club reaching the Premiership via the Play-offs, Holland was appointed club captain. He made his full international debut for the Republic of Ireland against Macedonia in October 1999 and also appeared in the end-of-season Nike Cup games in the United States. The following season he netted his first international goals against Andorra and Portugal, while at club level he continued to epitomise all that is good about the Suffolk club – playing in the right spirit, hard but fair. Unable to prevent the Tractor Boys from being relegated from the Premiership, he remained a regular member of the Republic of Ireland squad and was picked to go to the 2002 World Cup. Ipswich Town's Player of the Year for 2002–03, he was surprisingly allowed to leave Portman Road in the close season, having scored 46 goals in 314 games. He joined Charlton Athletic, who paid £750,000 for his signature. Made club captain on his debut, he was ever present in his first season for the Addicks, soon becoming a huge crowd favourite. A regular in the Republic of Ireland side, having won 46 caps, he built up a good understanding with his fellow midfielders at The Valley and chipped in with some valuable goals during his time with the London club.

HOLSTER Marco

Midfield

Born: Weesp, Holland, 4 December 1971. Career: AZ67 Alkmaar (Holland); SC Heracles (Holland); IPSWICH TOWN 1998

■ Signed in the 1998 close season from the Dutch club SC Heracles, having previously played for AZ67 Alkmaar, the left-footed central midfielder took some time to adjust to English football at Ipswich. He made his debut in the opening game of the 1998–99 season at Grimsby Town – his only full appearance of the campaign – and was on the bench intermittently from then on, being unable to dislodge Matt Holland or Keiron Dyer from the club's first team. Though he looked a useful man to have around, after one more season at Portman Road in which he failed to add to his total of first-team appearances, the Dutchman parted company with the club.

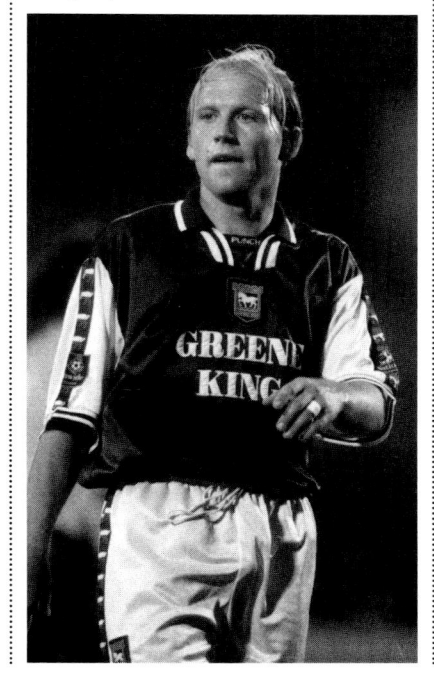

HORLOCK Kevin

Midfield

Born: Erith, 1 November 1972. Career: West Ham United 1991; Swindon Town 1992; Manchester City 1997; West Ham United 2003; IPSWICH Town 2004; Doncaster Rovers 2006.

■ With opportunities scarce and with no first-team games under his belt, Kevin Horlock was transferred from West Ham United to Swindon Town at the start of the 1992–93 season. Not expected to feature quickly in first-team action, an injury crisis pitched him into service and in only his third appearance he helped the Robins beat his former team at Upton Park. Equally at home in midfield or at left-back, Horlock soon became a regular member of the Swindon side. His consistency following the arrival of player-manager Steve McMahon culminated in his selection for a full Northern Ireland cap against Latvia in April 1995. The following season was a remarkable one for Horlock. Having missed the opening game after undergoing a knee operation, he appeared in each of Swindon's subsequent 58 games en route to a Second Division Championship medal. Also that season, Horlock scored a hat-trick at Bristol Rovers. He had scored 26 goals in 192 League and Cup games when Manchester City paid £1.25 million for his services. By now a regular in the Northern Ireland side, he was rewarded with the club captaincy at Maine Road. Although not an aggressive player, he began to pick up more than his fair share of yellow and red cards. In 1999–2000 he scored a number of vital goals and passed his personal goal tally from the previous season. He demonstrated his willingness to follow his own forward passes and get into goalscoring positions to receive a lay-off from the strikers. Horlock had just begun to get to grips with life in the Premiership when, in the game against Charlton Athletic, he fractured an ankle. The 2001–02 season, probably Horlock's best in a City shirt, he played in a midfield 'holding' role and helped his side equal their record for goals in one season as they won the First Division Championship. After losing his place to Joey Barton, he joined West Ham United to make his long-awaited first-team debut. After one season with the Hammers, he joined Ipswich during the summer of 2004 and quickly established himself as a regular in the Town side, playing in a defensive midfield role just in front of the back line. Following the arrival of Darren Currie from Brighton, Horlock's place came under threat and in the second half of the 2004–05 season he found himself on the bench as much as he was in the starting line up. In 2005–06 he was in and out of the side and after joining Doncaster Rovers on loan he signed for the Yorkshire club on a permanent basis.

HOUGHTON Scott Aaron

Midfield

Born: Hitchin, 22 October 1971. Career: Tottenham Hotspur 1990; IPSWICH TOWN (loan) 1991; Gillingham (loan) 1992; Charlton Athletic (loan) 1993; Luton Town 1993; Walsall 1994; Peterborough United 1996; Southend United 1998; Leyton Orient 2000; Halifax Town 2002; Stevenage Borough.

■ One of a crop of talented young midfielders on the books of Tottenham Hotspur at the start of the 1990s, Scott Houghton joined the North London club after graduating from the FA School of Excellence. An England Youth cap, he helped Spurs win the 1990 FA Youth Cup. To gain experience, he was loaned out to Ipswich in March 1991, making his debut off the bench in a 2–2 home draw against Portsmouth. He was then involved in all the remaining games of that 1990–91 season, scoring his only goal for the club in a 3–2 defeat of Leicester City. He returned to White Hart Lane and began to make his mark as a regular member of the first-team squad, but, although he came off the bench 14 times in all competitions, he never actually started a game. He had further loan spells at Gillingham and Charlton before signing for Luton Town. The midfielder-cum-winger spent just one season at Kenilworth Road before joining Walsall. He proved his willingness to take on defenders and scored a number of vital goals during his time with the Saddlers, but in the summer of 1996 he joined Peterborough United for a fee of £60,000. At the end of his first season at London Road, he was Posh's leading scorer, while in 1997–98 he was selected for the PFA award-winning Third Division team. Following a loan spell at Southend, he joined the Roots Hall club on a permanent basis, featuring regularly under manager Brian Little. When David Webb took over the reins, Houghton was sold to Leyton Orient, proving himself to be one of the finest crossers of a ball in the lower divisions. He lost his place following a change of manager and, after a spell with struggling Halifax Town, he moved into non-League football with Stevenage Borough prior to becoming a policeman.

HOUGHTON William Gascoigne

Defender

Born: Hemsworth, 20 February 1939. Career: Barnsley 1957; Watford 1964; IPSWICH TOWN 1966; Leicester City 1969; Rotherham United 1970.

■ Billy Houghton was a schoolboy prodigy and an England Youth international during his early days with Barnsley, where he made his League debut after just four appearances in the Oakwell club's reserve side. He went on to appear in 206 League games for the Yorkshire club before moving to Watford, where Bill McGarry was manager. A physically strong defender, Houghton spent a couple of seasons at Vicarage Road before McGarry, who by now had taken over as boss of Ipswich, signed him for Town. Houghton made his Ipswich debut in a 2–0 win over Cardiff City on the opening day of the 1966–67 season. He went on to make 38 appearances, scoring his only goal of the campaign in a 3–2 win over Rotherham as Ipswich finished fifth in Division Two. He missed just one game the following season as Ipswich won the Second Division Championship, one of his two goals coming in the 4–3 win over Norwich City – this after Town had been 2–1 down at half-time. Allowed to join Leicester City, he had the shortest spell of his League career at Filbert Street and moved on to Rotherham United. Billy Houghton played in over 500 League games for his various clubs before hanging up his boots and returning to the joinery trade.

HOWE Stephen Robert

Forward

Born: Cramlington, 6 November 1973. Career: Nottingham Forest 1990; Kettering (loan); IPSWICH TOWN (loan) 1997; Swindon Town 1998; Havant and Waterlooville.

■ Unable to break into the Nottingham Forest side, Howe went on loan to non-League Kettering Town before returning to the City Ground to make his bow as a substitute in the first leg of the UEFA Cup against French club Lyon and his full Premiership debut a week later against Manchester United. Thereafter he made occasional appearances both as a first choice and substitute before being loaned out to Ipswich Town following the Portman Road club's exit from the FA Cup at the City

Ground. He made his debut in a 2–1 win over Barnsley, but was on the bench for the following game as West Bromwich Albion were thrashed 5–0. He appeared in the club's fifth-round League Cup defeat at home to Leicester City before making his final appearance in the number-10 shirt against Queen's Park Rangers. During his time at Portman Road, Howe was played further up front than he would have liked. Finding himself back in Forest's reserves, he joined Swindon Town for a fee of £30,000, soon rediscovering his form following an extended run in the side. He then suffered an Achilles injury during the 2000–01 season before returning to action the following term. It proved to be his last at the County Ground and, having made 135 appearances for the Robins, he moved into non-League football with Havant and Waterlooville.

HREIDARSSON Hermann

Defender

Born: Iceland, 11 July 1974.
Career: IBV Iceland; Crystal Palace 1997; Brentford 1998; Wimbledon 1999; IPSWICH TOWN 2000; Charlton Athletic 2003.

■ Icelandic international defender Hermann Hreidarsson signed for Crystal Palace immediately prior to the start of the 1997–98 season having had a trial the previous term. Following his containment of Arsenal's Dutch international Dennis Bergkamp, he became a great crowd favourite at Selhurst Park. Despite his outstanding displays for Palace, where he was not merely content to defend and often brought the ball out of defence to set up an attack, he could not prevent them losing their Premiership status. In September 1998 he joined Brentford for a club record fee of £850,000 and soon showed an ability clearly well above that of Division Three. Selected by his fellow professionals for the PFA divisional side, he helped the Bees win promotion as champions of the Third Division. He began the 1999–2000 season in majestic form and his performances attracted the attention of Wimbledon, who paid £2.5 million for his services – a new record for the club. After a little over a season with the Dons, Hreidarsson moved back into the Premiership with Ipswich Town, who paid a club record £4 million to take him to Portman Road. After going straight into the team to face Tottenham Hotspur, he went on to miss just two games through injury and scored his first goal for the club against Manchester City. Earlier in the season he thought he had netted against Bradford at Portman Road and made a celebratory dive into the crowd but, unbeknown to the Icelandic defender, Mark Burchill had got a touch to his goalbound header and claimed the goal. Runner-up in the supporters' Player of the Year competition, the following season he was the only Ipswich Town player, apart from Matt Holland, to play in every Premiership game. He was appointed captain for the FA Cup match that the Republic of Ireland international missed. Hreidarsson, who can play at centre-back or as a wing-back, was hugely popular with Ipswich fans, who adored him charging down the left wing. Sadly, he damaged knee ligaments in the game against Stoke during the 2002–03 season and while still recovering he agreed to join Charlton Athletic for a bargain fee. The following season he was outstanding in the Addicks defence and ended the campaign as runner-up to Dean Kiely in the club's Player of the Year competition. One of Alan Curbishley's best signings, he suffered a cruciate ligament injury the following season and this hampered the 61-cap Icelandic international's progress during the early stages of the 2005–06 season.

HUMES Anthony

Centre-half

Born: Blyth, 19 March 1966.
Career: IPSWICH TOWN 1983; Wrexham 1992.

■ Though he was regarded as a resolute defender, Tony Humes appeared in five different positions for Ipswich Town, including centre-forward. He made his debut for the Tractor Boys in a goalless draw at Blackburn Rovers in November 1986, after a couple of seasons of impressive displays in the reserves. Though not a prolific scorer from any position, Humes scored both Ipswich goals in a 3–2 defeat at Leeds and his goal in the FA Cup tie against Manchester United in January 1988 was a spectacular header. Sadly, during his time at Portman Road, Tony Humes suffered more than his fair share of injuries. These included two broken arms, a broken foot, a broken jaw, a cartilage operation and a hernia operation – all of which kept him out of the Ipswich side for lengthy periods. Humes left Ipswich to join Wrexham for a fee of £40,000 in March 1992. The following season he was the Welsh club's Player of the Year as they won promotion and impressed in the FA Cup tie with

Ipswich, which the Robins won 2–1. Appointed the club's captain, he continued to receive more than his fair share of injuries and suspensions, but formed a very solid central defensive partnership with Brian Carey. A player who always gave 100 percent, Humes was one of Brian Flynn's finest investments, appearing in 239 games before injuries forced his retirement.

HUNT Jonathan Richard
Midfield

Born: Camden, 2 November 1971.
Career: Barnet 1990; Southend United 1993; Birmingham City 1994; Derby County 1997; Sheffield United (loan) 1998; IPSWICH TOWN (loan) 1998; Sheffield United 1999; Cambridge United (loan) 2000; Wimbledon 2000.

■ After starting out with Barnet, Jon Hunt moved to Southend United in July 1993. His displays for the Shrimpers alerted a host of clubs and Birmingham City paid £50,000 for his services a little over a year later. He had the honour of scoring Birmingham's first hat-trick for nine years against Peterborough United in the Auto Windscreens Shield. Damaged knee ligaments put him out of the game for four months, but he returned in time to win a Second Division Championship medal, having already participated in the club's AWS win at Wembley. He netted another hat-trick against Norwich early the following season, finishing the campaign as the club's leading scorer with 15 goals from midfield. Voted the club's Player of the Season, he badly damaged his knee against Ipswich and on recovery was condemned to reserve-team football. He joined Derby County for £500,000 during the summer of 1997 but disappointed Rams fans with a lack of consistency. After a loan spell with Sheffield United, he joined Ipswich Town on a similar basis. He impressed during his stay at Portman Road, but not enough to be asked to stay, and after six appearances – only two in the starting line up – he joined Sheffield United on a permanent basis. Finding himself in and out of the Blades side, he went on loan to Cambridge United before joining Wimbledon. However, when established players returned from injury, he was released by the Dons.

HUNT Robert Rex
Forward

Born: Colchester, 1 October 1942.
Career: Colchester United 1959; Northampton Town 1964; Millwall 1966; IPSWICH TOWN 1967; Charlton Athletic 1970; Northampton Town (loan) 1972; Reading 1973.

■ Robert Hunt is the brother of Ron and William Hunt, and all three of them started out with their hometown team Colchester United. During his time at Layer Road, Bobby Hunt was a prolific scorer, finding the net 81 times in 149 League games and helping the team win promotion to the Third Division in 1961–62. His next club was Northampton Town, where in 1964–65 he helped the side win promotion to the First Division for the first time in the club's history. Relegated after just one season of top-flight football, Hunt left the County Ground to play for Millwall before signing for Ipswich just over a year later. He made his Town debut in a 2–1 win over Aston Villa. His only goal that season, as Town went on to win the Second Division Championship, earned his side a point against his former club, Millwall. Never able to hold down a regular place in the Ipswich side, he spent two more seasons with the Suffolk club before joining Charlton Athletic. Following their relegation to the Third Division he rejoined Northampton on loan before signing for his last League club, Reading.

HUNTER Allan
Centre-half

Born: Sion Mills, Northern Ireland, 30 June 1946.
Career: Coleraine; Oldham Athletic 1967; Blackburn Rovers 1969; IPSWICH TOWN 1971; Colchester United 1982.

■ The winner of 53 full caps for Northern Ireland, centre-half Allan Hunter began his career with Coleraine, for whom he played in the European Cup-winners' Cup competition before entering the Football League with Oldham Athletic in January 1967. A virtual ever present in the Latics defence, he had made 83 appearances for the Boundary Park club when, in the summer of 1960, he joined their Lancashire neighbours Blackburn Rovers for a fee of £30,000. He had a similar playing record with the Rovers and, after appearing in 84 League games, left Ewood Park to join Ipswich Town for £60,000 in a deal that saw Bobby Bell move in the opposite direction. It proved to be an inspired signing, as Hunter formed formidable central defensive

Allan Hunter

partnerships, first with Derek Jefferson and then with Kevin Beattie. The low point of Hunter's 11-year stint at Portman Road came in March 1974 when he missed a penalty in the shoot-out in Leipzig that ended the club's UEFA Cup hopes. It was a cruel blow because Hunter had been a rock at the heart of the Ipswich defence that night after Mick Mills had been sent off. One of the Irishman's greatest games came the following season, in the fourth of those FA Cup quarter-final battles with the then mighty Leeds United at Filbert Street. Beattie had dropped out through injury and 17-year-old John Wark was introduced for his first taste of senior football – Ipswich won 3–2. During his time at Portman Road Hunter, who was voted the club's Player of the Year in 1975–76, was hailed as the best centre-half in the Football League. A knee injury had made him doubtful for the FA Cup Final against Arsenal but he passed a late fitness test and was outstanding in the club's 1–0 success. Hunter, who won 47 of his international caps while with the Suffolk club, left Ipswich in April 1982 after amassing 355 first-team appearances to become player-manager at Colchester United. The genial Irishman did not relish the managerial side of the game and after only eight months in charge he resigned. Four years later he returned to Layer Road as coach, but nowadays he lives and works as a woodwork teacher at Belstead Special School in Ipswich.

JACKSON John Keith

Goalkeeper

Born: Hammersmith, 5 September 1942.

Career: Crystal Palace 1962; Leyton Orient 1973; Millwall 1979; IPSWICH TOWN 1981; Hereford United 1982.

■ John Jackson worked his way up through the ranks at Crystal Palace before making his League debut as Bill Glazier's deputy at Swindon Town in the second game of the 1964–65 season. But then, when Glazier was sold to Coventry City for a record fee of £35,000 for a goalkeeper, Palace boss Dick Graham signed Welsh international Tony Millington as a replacement. By the turn of the year, Jackson had become the club's first-choice 'keeper. Over the next four years, Jackson was a model of consistency, with the highlight of his career coming in 1968–69 when he was ever present in the side that won promotion to the First Division. In the top flight, Jackson really came into his own, playing in 138 consecutive League games, and it was his performances in those games that salvaged precious points and made all the difference between relegation and survival. In the end though, not even John Jackson's heroics could keep Palace in the First Division. Few goalkeepers had earned more respect and admiration than Jackson did during his time in the top flight. He had the misfortune to be an outstanding goalkeeper in an age of great 'keepers: Banks, Shilton and Clemence. Even so, he surely deserved more honours than his single appearance for the Football League XI. Jackson left Selhurst Park for Leyton Orient. He spent six seasons at Brisbane Road without missing a game, which is a remarkable record. He then went to Millwall and was still playing at 40 years of age. It was at this stage of his career that he collected an unexpected bonus. Bobby Robson's Ipswich Town team were chasing the UEFA Cup in 1980–81 when they were suddenly hit by a series of injuries to their goalkeepers. Robson asked Jackson if he would like to travel to Widzew Lodz in Poland as goalkeeping cover. He went but was not needed, although it was his first and only taste of European football. Jackson's only League appearance for Ipswich was against Manchester United in April 1982, a match Town won 2–1. After being goalkeeping coach and youth development officer at Brighton, Jackson remained in the south coast town where he now installs blinds.

JEAN Earl Jude

Forward

Born: St Lucia, 9 October 1971.
Career: Felgueires (Portugal); IPSWICH TOWN 1996; Rotherham United 1997; Plymouth Argyle 1997; West Connection (Trinidad).

■ This St Lucian international spent six years playing in Portugal for Uniao de Coimbra Felgueires before joining Ipswich Town on a free transfer in December 1996. Signed on a monthly basis, his only League appearance for the Tractor Boys was as a substitute in a 1–1 draw against Stoke City. Early in the New Year he moved to Rotherham United and scored on his debut, again coming off the bench. For a small player, his ability to win the ball in the air was quite remarkable and he soon won over the Millers fans. Surprisingly allowed to join Plymouth Argyle, he missed some of the 1997–98 season due to international commitments. The following season he found goals harder to come by and before the campaign had finished he had left Home Park to return to the Caribbean to play for West Connection of Trinidad.

JEFFERSON Derek

Centre-half

Born: Morpeth, 5 September 1948.
Career: IPSWICH TOWN 1966; Wolverhampton Wanderers 1972; Sheffield Wednesday (loan) 1976; Hereford United 1976.

■ Derek Jefferson made his first-team debut for Ipswich Town in an FA Cup third-round tie against Shrewsbury Town in January 1967 as a replacement for the injured Bill Baxter. Although it was his only appearance that season, he established himself in the heart of the Ipswich defence in 1967–68 and gave the club good service over the next six seasons. In 1968–69, Jefferson made more first-team appearances than any other player and scored his only goal for the club in a 2–2 draw at Tottenham Hotspur. That season also saw Jefferson become the first player to be sent off at Portman Road and only the second in a Football League match when he received his marching orders in a 3–1 home defeat by Chelsea on Boxing Day 1968. Jefferson went on to play in 175 League and Cup games for the Blues before Bobby Robson agreed to transfer him to Bill McGarry's Wolverhampton Wanderers for a fee of £880,000 in October 1972. He spent a little over four years at Molineux, during which time he appeared in 52 games, mainly deputising for John McAlle or Frank Munro in the Wolves defence. He also spent a couple of close seasons in the United States when he played against the legendary Pelé. A stern tackler, he had a brief loan spell with Sheffield Wednesday and then rounded off his senior career with Hereford United, where he was player-coach. After a few years as coach to Jim Smith at Birmingham City, Jefferson decided to quit the professional game to devote himself full-time to the Church.

JENNINGS Henry William

Centre-forward

Born: Norwich, 7 January 1920.
Died: September 1969.
Career: Northampton Town 1938; IPSWICH TOWN 1947; Rochdale 1951; Crystal Palace 1951.

■ The son of a Norwich City player, Bill Jennings's career with Northampton Town was interrupted by the outbreak of World War Two and at the end of the first season of peacetime football he left the County Ground to join Ipswich. He made his debut on the opening day of the 1947–48 season in a 2–0 win over Notts County, but then missed the next five games before scoring in the 5–1 derby win over the Canaries. Jennings went on to top the club's goalscoring charts that season with 14 goals in 36 games, as Town finished fourth in the Third Division South. He made a superb start to the 1948–49 campaign, scoring two goals in the opening game as Bristol Rovers were beaten 6–1 and then another brace in the next game, a 5–1 defeat of Torquay United. He went on to net 23 goals in 37 League outings. After that, Jennings surprisingly found himself in and out of the Ipswich side and two seasons later he was allowed to join Rochdale. Unable to settle at Spotland, he left for Crystal Palace, but was forced to hang up his boots without actually appearing in the Selhurst Park club's first team.

JOHNSON David Anthony

Forward

Born: Kingston, Jamaica, 15 August 1976.
Career: Manchester United 1994; Bury

David Johnson

1995; IPSWICH TOWN 1997; Nottingham Forest 2001; Sheffield Wednesday (loan) 2002; Burnley (loan) 2002; Sheffield United (loan) 2005.

■ Powerfully built, despite his lack of height, David Johnson impressed everyone with his enthusiastic, all-action style in his first season of League football after joining Bury from Manchester United, where he was a member of the club's FA Youth Cup-winning side. After helping the club win promotion in his first season at Gigg Lane, Johnson scored a number of vital goals in 1996–97 to help the Shakers win a second successive promotion as champions of Division Two. Bury's financial position meant that they were unable to hold on to their main asset, and, in November 1997, Johnson became Ipswich Town's record signing when the Portman Road club paid £800,000 for his services. He made a sensational start to his Ipswich career, scoring in seven of his first nine games, including a double against Huddersfield Town and his first-ever hat-trick against Oxford United. His striking partnership with Alex Mathie was an exciting aspect of the second half of the 1997–98 campaign and, not surprisingly, his form attracted international recognition with call-ups to the England Under-21 and B squads, while he also represented the Nationwide League side against a team from Italy's Serie B. Johnson was also reportedly wanted internationally by both Jamaica and Northern Ireland as well as England. After ending that season as leading scorer for both Ipswich and his former club Bury, Johnson started the 1998–99 season where he left off – scoring goals. His new partner up front was Jamie Scowcroft and their form kept Mathie on the bench. Unfortunately he suffered a problem with his knee and tried to come back too soon. The 1999–2000 season was, without doubt, David Johnson's best with the club, certainly in terms of goals scored. He started the season with a bang, scoring in six of the first seven games and notching doubles against Swindon and Barnsley. His prowess in front of goal kept his name in the minds of Premiership managers, while on the international scene Johnson, who scored for Jamaica in a friendly against the United States, accepted an invitation to join the Welsh squad. Injury prevented him from pulling on the red shirt and by the time the next international squads were announced he had pledged his future to Scotland, only to find he was ineligible after all! This seemed to put a brake on his goals for a while but he eventually rediscovered his touch and seven goals in the last nine games helped Town secure third place for the second successive season. In the Premiership, despite all his efforts, he was unable to notch that elusive first top-flight goal as Fabian Barthez pulled off a superb save and then, in the next game against Sunderland, he had what looked a perfectly good goal disallowed. George Burley decided to sell him and he joined Nottingham Forest for £3 million. Unable to settle, he had loan spells with Sheffield Wednesday and Burnley before in 2002–03 he netted 25 goals and was named the supporters' Player of the Year and selected for the PFA Division One team of the season. A broken leg early the following season hampered his progress and on returning to fitness he had a spell on loan with Sheffield United. Then he suffered a dislodged spinal disc, but the player, who is a legend with Forest fans, has made a full recovery.

JOHNSON David Edward

Forward

Born: Liverpool, 23 October 1951.
Career: Everton 1969; IPSWICH TOWN 1972; Liverpool 1976; Everton 1982; Barnsley (loan) 1984; Manchester City 1984; Tulsa Roughnecks (United States); Preston North End 1984.

■ David Johnson began his Football League career with Everton, but despite his early successes, which included a hat-trick in an 8–0 romp over Southampton, he was transferred to Ipswich Town in October 1972, with Rod Belfitt moving in the opposite direction. He made his debut the following month in a 2–2 draw with Leeds United and went on to become an instant hit with the Town supporters. Forming a fine understanding up front with Trevor Whymark, he helped Ipswich finish fourth in Division One, with probably his best performance that season coming against Crystal Palace when he scored both goals in a 2–1 win. He found the net more frequently in 1973–74 as Town maintained their position of fourth in the top flight. The following season, Ipswich moved up to third and Johnson netted his only hat-trick for the club in a 4–0 defeat of Coventry City. Having matured into a more than useful centre-forward, he won eight England caps, the first coming against Wales in 1975 when he scored both England's goals in a 2–2 draw. In August 1976, having scored 46 goals in 178 games for Ipswich, Johnson joined Liverpool for a club record £200,000. Johnson's courageous approach and his speed, skill and unselfishness instantly endeared him to the Kop. Despite being hampered by a series of niggling injuries during his early days at Anfield, he managed to collect a League Championship-winners' medal and figured in the Wembley defeat by Manchester United, but he missed out on European glory. Just when it seemed Liverpool were going to discard him, his luck changed and, after striking up a good understanding with Kenny Dalglish, he won a European Cup-winners' medal and four League Championship medals. In August 1982, Johnson's colourful

David Johnson

career came full circle when he rejoined Everton. Unable to reproduce his form of old, he had a loan spell with Barnsley before signing for Manchester City. He then had a brief spell with Tulsa Roughnecks in the NASL before being transferred to Preston North End, where he ended his first-class career. He occupies a unique place in Merseyside folklore, being the only player to have scored a derby winner for both Everton and Liverpool.

JOHNSON Gavin
Midfield

Born: Stowmarket, 10 October 1970.
Career: IPSWICH TOWN 1989; Luton Town 1995; Wigan Athletic 1995; Dunfermline Athletic 1998; Colchester United 1999.

■ Gavin Johnson made his Football League debut for Ipswich Town against Barnsley at Portman Road in February 1989, just a few days after signing professional forms. Though he only played sporadically over the next couple of seasons, he performed well when required. He finally came to the fore in 1991–92, appearing in most of the games during Ipswich's Second Division Championship-winning campaign. Originally a central defender, he was switched to the left side of midfield and it was his goals in the last two games of the season that clinched the title for Ipswich. He missed just two games in 1992–93 but was unfortunate to pick up a knee injury during the final match against Nottingham Forest when his foot got caught in a hole on the Portman Road pitch. Unable to win back his place on a regular basis, he joined Luton Town, but his stay at Kenilworth Road was brief and in December 1995 he signed for Wigan Athletic for a fee of £15,000. The hardworking midfielder made his Latics debut in a 2–1 defeat of Hereford United, going on to play in the last 27 games of the season. Over the next three seasons, Johnson proved that he could play anywhere on the left flank and scored some spectacular goals, especially from dead-ball situations. After helping Wigan win the Third Division Championship in 1996–97, he found his time at Springfield Park dogged by groin problems and in the summer of 1998 he was released. After a short spell with Dunfermline Athletic, he joined Colchester United, helping the Layer Road club maintain their Second Division status. He was a regular until the second half of the 2001–02 season when he suffered a broken leg at Port Vale. On returning to the side he suffered a setback that required a second operation and spent over a year on the sidelines. He continues to defy his advancing years, remaining an important member of the Colchester squad.

JOHNSTONE Robert Gordon

Wing-half

Born: Edinburgh, 19 November 1934.
Career: Ormiston Primrose; West Ham United 1953; IPSWICH TOWN 1957.

■ Spotted playing junior football in Scotland with Ormiston Primrose, wing-half Bobby Johnstone was given his chance at League level by West Ham United. However, although he impressed in the Hammers' youth and reserve sides, he made just a couple of first-team appearances before being allowed to join Ipswich after four years at Upton Park. He made his Town debut in a 1–0 home defeat at the hands of Swansea and, though he kept his place in the side, he made just a handful of appearances in that 1957–58 season, scoring in the 2–0 win over Doncaster Rovers. He appeared on a more regular basis the following season, scoring three goals in 29 games, including two in the 5–3 defeat of Brighton & Hove Albion. At the end of that season, Johnstone left Portman Road and emigrated to Canada.

JONES Frederick

Centre-forward

Born: Pontypool 1914.
Career: Millwall 1934; Folkestone; IPSWICH TOWN 1938.

■ Unable to make much headway with his first club, Millwall, Fred Jones drifted into non-League football with Folkestone before joining Ipswich towards the end of the 1937–38 season of Southern League football. Making his League debut for the club in Ipswich's very first game – a 4–2 win over Southend United – he not only netted twice but also holds the distinction of scoring Town's first goal in the Football League. Injuries hampered his progress in his only full season with the club before the outbreak of hostilities, but nevertheless he scored eight goals in 21 League games including three in successive games before making his final appearance against Norwich City in one of the three games expunged from the records at the start of the 1939–40 season.

JONES William John

Outside-right

Born: Aberbargoed, 5 May 1925.
Career: Bargoed; IPSWICH TOWN 1949; Sudbury Town.

■ Welsh amateur international winger Willie Jones played his early football for Welsh League side Bargoed before signing for Ipswich in April 1949. Jones made his League debut against Crystal Palace during the early part of the following season, playing at right-half. He appeared in eight consecutive games in the number-four shirt that season before playing at outside-right in 1950–51. Over the next three seasons, Jones made just fleeting appearances, scoring his only goal for the club in December 1952 in a 2–2 draw with Colchester United. In the summer of 1955, having played in just 33 League games, he left Ipswich to play non-League football for Sudbury Town.

JUAN Jimmy

Midfield

Born: Valence, 10 June 1983.
Career: AS Monaco (France); IPSWICH TOWN (loan) 2005; AS Monaco.

■ A highly respected French midfielder, Juan began his career with AS Monaco and, after making his debut towards the end of the 2003–04 season, made four appearances from the bench the following term. He also had a run out as a substitute in the

Champions' League defeat by Liverpool at Anfield. After impressing while on loan with Ipswich, he joined the club for the 2005–06 season. Over the course of the campaign he showed himself to be a free-kick expert, scoring in this way against Cardiff City and promoted Sheffield United. Juan had found the net five times in 27 appearances in the Championship before leaving Portman Road to rejoin Monaco.

JURYEFF Ian Martin

Forward

Born: Gosport, 24 November 1962.
Career: Southampton 1980; Mansfield Town (loan) 1984; Reading (loan) 1984; Leyton Orient 1985; IPSWICH TOWN (loan) 1989; Halifax Town 1989; Hereford United 1989; Halifax Town 1990; Darlington 1992; Scunthorpe United 1993; Farnborough Town.

■ Much-travelled forward Ian Juryeff was on the books of Southampton, but after just a couple of appearances from the bench and loan spells with Mansfield and Reading he joined Leyton Orient. Adept at shielding the ball before laying it off, Juryeff always had an eye for goal and in four seasons at Brisbane Road he scored 60 goals in 140 games, helping the club win promotion to the Third Division via the Play-offs in 1988–89. In February 1989 he had a brief spell on loan with Ipswich, making two appearances from the bench before joining Halifax Town in the close season. With the Shaymen struggling near the foot of the Fourth Division, he left but joined Hereford United, who were in a similar position. He then rejoined the Yorkshire club, taking his tally of goals in his two spells to 24 in 107 games before moving on to Darlington. Juryeff's last League club was Scunthorpe United, for whom he scored on a regular basis before losing his place up front and moving into non-League football with Farnborough Town.

KARBASSIYOON Daniel

Defender

Born: Virginia, United States, 10 August 1984.
Career: Roanoke Star (United States); Arsenal 2003; IPSWICH TOWN (loan) 2004; Burnley.

■ Having won Youth international honours for the United States, Danny Karbassiyoon joined Arsenal from amateur club Roanoke Star at the beginning of the 2003–04 season. Having joined the Gunners as a forward, he adapted his role to that of a left-sided full-back. Karbassiyoon's first match for Arsenal was against Manchester City in the Carling Cup in October 2004, as a substitute for Arturo Lupoli. He marked his debut by scoring a goal in the 90th minute as the Gunners won 2–1. However, despite appearing in all of Arsenal's three Carling Cup games, he could not break into their League side and in December 2004 joined Ipswich Town on loan. Capable of delivering some excellent balls into the opposition penalty area, Karbassiyoon made his debut from the bench in a 3–1 defeat at Millwall. He then made three appearances in the number-three shirt – games in which Town won two and drew one – before reverting to the bench for the game against Leicester City, which Town won 2–1. Released by Arsenal in the summer of 2005, he joined Burnley. After struggling to establish himself at Turf Moor, he was placed on the transfer list.

KARIC Amir

Defender

Born: Oramovica Ponja, Yugoslavia, 31 December 1973.
Career: Rudar (Slovenia); NK Maribor (Slovenia); Gamba Osaka (Japan); NK Maribor; IPSWICH TOWN 2000; Crystal Palace (loan) 2001; NK Maribor.

■ Slovenian international defender Amir Karic appeared in the UEFA Champions' League qualifying rounds for the 1999–2000 Slovenian champions NK Maribor before joining Ipswich Town in the summer of 2000. He made his first-team debut in the home leg of the Worthington Cup tie with Millwall and gave glimpses of his potential with some excellent crosses. However, he found it hard to break into the side at Portman Road and later had a short loan spell with Crystal Palace. Particularly effective at delivering free-kicks, he featured in the Slovenian international team in the Euro 2000 Finals before later rejoining NK Maribor, initially on loan.

KEEBLE Christopher Mark

Midfield

Born: Colchester, 17 September 1978.
Career: IPSWICH TOWN 1997; Colchester United 2000; Heybridge Swifts.

■ A regular in the Ipswich reserve side in 1997–98, where he played in central midfield, Keeble was included in the squad for the game at Port Vale and came off the substitutes' bench to make his first-team debut – playing for the last two minutes. The son of the 1950s Colchester United legend Vic Keeble, he was later told he would not be retained by Ipswich and so went to Layer Road on trial. Signed on a permanent basis, he made his debut as a substitute against Cambridge and scored the goal which kept the U's safe from relegation. Injuries, notably a ruptured Achilles tendon, hampered his progress and he was out of action for the entire 2001–02 season. Unable, bar the odd handful of substitute appearances, to force his way back into the side, he left to play non-League football for Heybridge Swifts.

KEELEY Glenn Matthew

Centre-half

Born: Barking, 1 September 1954.
Career: IPSWICH TOWN 1972; Newcastle United 1974; Blackburn Rovers 1976; Everton (loan) 1982; Oldham Athletic 1987; Colchester United (loan) 1988; Bolton Wanderers 1988; Chorley.

■ Glenn Keeley had stood out in Youth internationals for England and in Ipswich Town's FA Youth Cup-winning side prior to making his League debut for the Portman Road club against Manchester United in February 1973 – a match Ipswich won 4–1. It was his only appearance that season, though he did appear in three games the following season before Newcastle United manager Joe Harvey saw him as a replacement for Bobby Moncur and paid £70,000 for his services. Following the appointment of Gordon Lee, he lost his place in the side and was transferred to Blackburn Rovers for a cut-price £30,000. Affectionately nicknamed 'Killer' Keeley because of a number of reckless challenges and brushes with authority, he went on to acquire cult status. With Derek Fazackerley he formed one of the best central defensive partnerships outside the top flight. When former Rovers boss Howard Kendall was in charge of Everton, he offered Keeley a loan spell and the chance to show what he could do in the First Division. Keeley played only 30 minutes for Everton, but was sent off in the Merseyside derby against Liverpool. He returned to Ewood Park and was immediately made club captain. He led Rovers to success in the Full Members' Cup of 1987 before, having scored 24 goals in 413 League and Cup games, he left to play for Oldham Athletic. Unable to give of his best for the Latics on the Boundary Park plastic, he joined Bolton Wanderers, but after just one season his contract was cancelled so he could pursue a commercial pilot's licence in the United States. He later returned to these shores to play non-League football for Chorley.

KELLARD Robert Sydney William

Midfield

Born: Edmonton, 1 March 1943.
Career: Southend United 1960; Crystal Palace 1963; IPSWICH TOWN 1965; Portsmouth 1966; Bristol City 1968; Leicester City 1970; Crystal Palace 1971; Portsmouth 1972; Hereford United (loan) 1975; Torquay United 1975; Chelmsford City; Grays Athletic.

■ A small, stocky, ball-winning midfielder, Kellard served eight League clubs and had two spells with both Crystal Palace and Portsmouth. An England Youth international, he won acclaim for his tireless and industrious performances at his first club Southend United, where at 16 years 208 days he was then the club's youngest debutant. He had made 106 appearances when Dick Graham signed him for Crystal Palace. He was important to the club's successful drive for promotion in the spring of 1964 and he continued as a valued member of the squad until November 1965, when he moved to Ipswich Town for a fee of £16,000. Kellard made his Town debut in a 2–1 defeat at Manchester City. However, after scoring three goals in 13 League games, he left Portman Road after just four months to join Portsmouth. He appeared in over 100 games for Pompey before signing for Bristol City. He then had a spell playing for Leicester City before rejoining Palace, where he replaced Steve Kember, who had moved to Chelsea. Appointed club captain, he later left Selhurst Park a second time, having appeared in 137 games, to rejoin Portsmouth for a fee of £12,000. Following a loan spell with Hereford United, he ended his League career with Torquay United. Moving into non-League football, he played for Chelmsford City and Grays Athletic before running a taxi business prior to managing Harlow Town with Len Glover. He is now an antiques dealer.

KENNEDY John Neil

Left-back

Born: Newmarket, 19 August 1978.
Career: IPSWICH TOWN 1997.

■ An ever present for Ipswich reserves in 1997–98, Kennedy's solid performances earned him a place in the first-team squad for the trip to Port Vale and he made his debut as a substitute, coming on for the final 10 minutes. Following Mauricio Taricco's transfer to Spurs and Micky Stockwell's subsequent injury, he made his first full appearance in the 1–0 win at Barnsley. Playing in seven of the next 10 games, the run gave him confidence to develop his game. Nicknamed 'Spider' by his teammates because of his resemblance to the character of the same name in *Coronation Street*, he was surprisingly given a free transfer.

KERSLAKE David

Full-back

Born: Stepney, 19 June 1966.
Career: Queen's Park Rangers 1983; Swindon Town 1989; Leeds United 1993; Tottenham Hotspur 1993; Swindon Town (loan) 1996; IPSWICH TOWN 1997; Wycombe Wanderers (loan) 1997; Swindon Town 1998.

■ An England Schoolboy international, Kerslake joined his local club, Queen's Park Rangers, where he was thought to be the 'next Duncan Edwards'. Though he turned professional in 1983, he had to wait two years before making his debut for the Loftus Road club. In November 1989 he joined Swindon Town for a fee of £110,000 and immediately slotted into the Robins side at right-back. In his first season at the County Ground he helped the club reach the Play-offs. Sadly, the Football League management committee waited until Swindon had beaten Sunderland in the Final and then announced that the Robins would be demoted to the Third Division. Justice prevailed when, on appeal, the club were restored to the Second Division. Though Kerslake continued to impress, the next couple of seasons were an anti-climax for Swindon supporters, and in 1992–93, with the club again heading for the Play-offs, Kerslake was sold to Leeds United for £500,000. He had been named in the PFA First Division team and his sale to the Yorkshire club sparked an outcry among supporters. Injury curtailed Kerslake's season and he was released after only six months to join Spurs for £450,000. With tremendous competition for places, he rejoined Swindon on loan before signing for Ipswich Town on a free transfer. Although featuring regularly on the substitutes' bench for the Portman Road club, he failed to establish himself in the first team and, after a brief loan spell with Wycombe Wanderers, he joined Swindon for a third time. A nagging abdominal injury reduced his number of appearances and, after taking his total number of appearances to 197, he was released in the summer of 1999.

KINSELLA Antony Steven

Left-winger

Born: Grays, 30 October 1961.
Career: Millwall 1978; Tampa Bay Rowdies (United States); IPSWICH TOWN 1982; Millwall 1984; Enfield; Doncaster Rovers 1987.

■ A Republic of Ireland Under-21 international, left-winger Tony Kinsella started out with Millwall. After three seasons of first-team football, he left to play in the NASL for Tampa Bay Rowdies. On his return to these shores in April 1982, he signed for Ipswich Town and made his debut in the local derby against Norwich City, a game that ended goalless. Kinsella made a handful of appearances that season and played in a similar number the following season before rejoining Millwall. In his second spell at The Den he helped the Lions win promotion to the Second Division as Third Division runners-up. On leaving Millwall a second time, he played non-League football for Enfield before ending his first-class career with a couple of seasons playing for Doncaster Rovers.

KIWOMYA Christopher Mark

Forward

Born: Huddersfield, 2 December 1969.
Career: IPSWICH TOWN 1987; Arsenal 1995; Le Havre (loan) (France); Selangor (loan) (Malaysia); Queen's Park Rangers 1998; Aalborg (Denmark).

■ An athletic striker with great pace, Chris Kiwomya followed his brother Andy into League soccer when he joined Ipswich Town as a trainee in the summer of 1986. On turning professional, he had to wait a further 18 months before making his League debut as a substitute against Bradford City at Portman Road in September 1988. Despite showing some early promise, he did not really become a regular until 1990–91, when he played in 34 matches and topped the club's goalscoring charts. When he arrived at Portman Road he was a winger, but he was converted into a central striker by Town manager John Lyall. Surprisingly overlooked for England Youth and Under-21 honours – although he was an unused substitute against Germany and tore a thigh muscle days before he was due to play against Turkey – he was a regular in the Ipswich side as they won the Second Division Championship in 1991–92, leading the way with 16 League goals and another three in Cup competitions. He made quite an impact in the new Premier League and in the 4–0 League Cup victory over Wigan Athletic he scored his first hat-trick for the club. Although he was the club's leading League goalscorer for three consecutive seasons from 1990–91 to 1992–93, his all-round confidence and ability in front of goal seemed to have disappeared when Arsenal manager George Graham paid £1.25 million, a figure set by a tribunal, to take him to Highbury in January 1995. At the end of that season he had scored three goals in 14 League games, but he was never to appear in the Gunners' first team again. Beset by injuries and a loss of form, he had loan spells with French club Le Havre and Selangor of Malaysia before starting the 1998–99 season with Queen's Park Rangers. He spent three seasons at Loftus Road, scoring 30 goals in 96 games, before joining Danish club Aalborg.

KNIGHTS Darryl James

Forward

Born: Ipswich, 1 May 1988
Career: IPSWICH TOWN 2005.

■ After some excellent performances for Ipswich Town's reserves, striker Darryl Knights was promoted to the club's first-team squad and made his League debut in the match against Sunderland at the Stadium of Light when, aged just 16, he came off the bench for the last 10 minutes of the match. Without doubt the highlight of his 2004–05 season was being a member of the club's FA Youth Cup-winning side. He was inspirational in both legs of the Final, in which he played as a lone striker. A regular for England at Youth level, he played for his country in the Under-17 European Championship qualifiers during the close season but failed to make an appearance for Town's first team in 2005–06.

KUQI Shefki

Forward

Born: Albania, 10 November 1976.
Career: HJK Helsinki (Finland); FC Jokerit (Finland); Stockport County

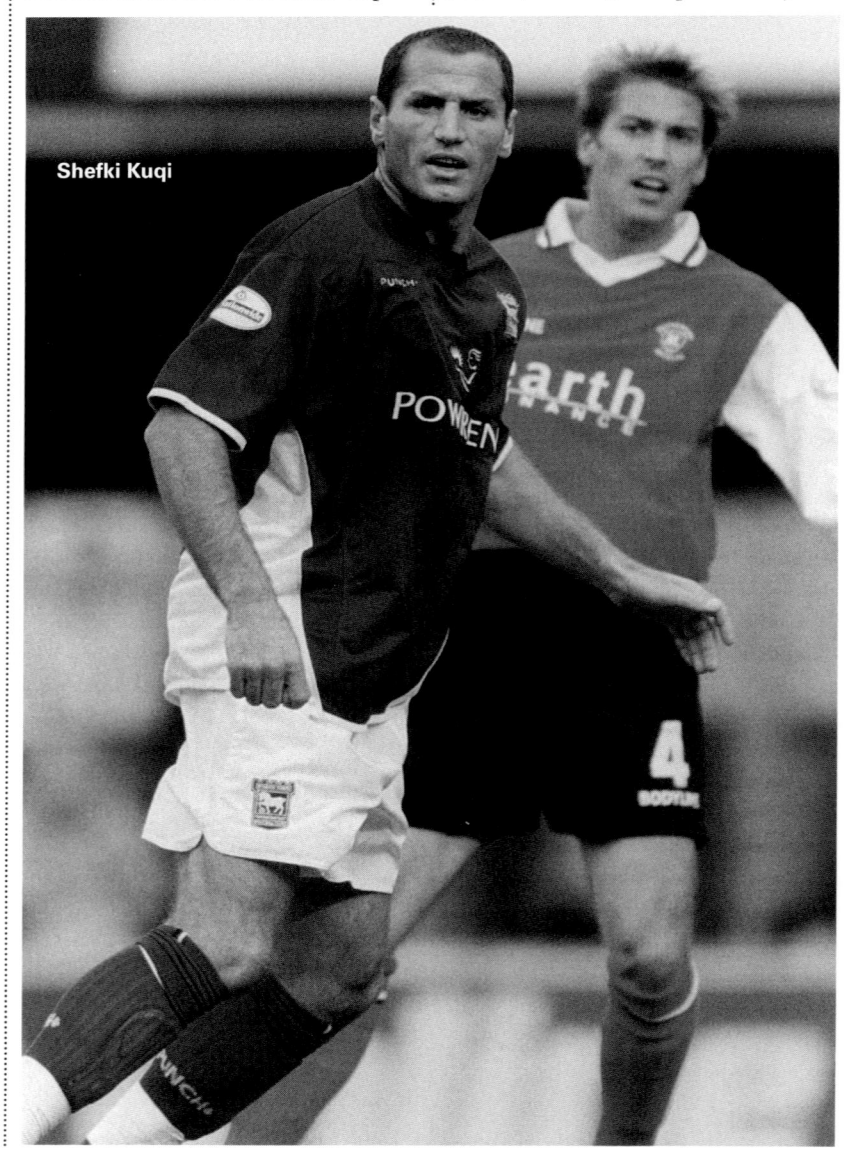

Shefki Kuqi

2001; Sheffield Wednesday 2002; IPSWICH TOWN 2003; Blackburn Rovers 2005.

■ A striker in the old-fashioned English centre-forward mould, Kuqi was a revelation at Edgeley Park following his transfer to Stockport County from Finnish side FC Jokerit in January 2001. His powerful play reaped early dividends with six goals from 17 appearances as he continued representing Finland at international level. He played a prominent role in County's forward line at the beginning of the 2001–02 season, scoring four times in his first 10 appearances. He had found the net 12 times in 38 games when Sheffield Wednesday paid £700,000 for his services 12 months after he joined County. He made an immediate impact for the Owls with his bustling style but, though he ended the 2002–03 season as the club's leading scorer with eight goals, he did not fully realise his potential. Though he began the following season with Wednesday, in September 2003 he joined Ipswich on a three-month loan deal which was later converted into a permanent contract. His non-stop running and commitment immediately endeared him to the Ipswich faithful and the fans did not have long to wait for his first goal as he scored with just his second touch after coming off the bench against Watford. He held his place in the side for most of the season, scoring 11 goals in 36 League games. He was a regular again in 2004–05 and scored goals consistently throughout the campaign, finishing as joint top scorer with 19 Championship goals. Kuqi, who has the knack of being in the box at the right time to pick up rebounds or knock-ons, demonstrated this best in the game against Plymouth Argyle when Town were 2–1 down. He came off the bench and grabbed a brace of goals to complete a most unlikely victory. He was named the club's Player of the Year by the supporters but sadly left the club to play Premiership football for Blackburn Rovers, where his displays throughout the campaign led to the Lancashire club winning a place in the UEFA Cup.

LAMBERT Michael Arnold

Winger

Born: Balsham, 20 May 1950.
Career: IPSWICH TOWN 1967; Peterborough United 1979.

■ Mick Lambert, who was also an excellent cricketer, had the honour of being 12th man for England in the 1969 Lord's Test Match against the West Indies. He worked his way up through the club's ranks at Portman Road before making his first-team debut in a goalless draw at home to Coventry City in March 1969. Over the next few seasons, Lambert found himself in and out of the Ipswich side before replacing Scottish international Jimmy Robertson for the club's 1972–73 First Division campaign. A brave, direct winger who often shot on sight, he was well established in the Ipswich side when he had a clash of heads with Chelsea's Gary Locke in February 1974 and fractured his skull. Lambert played in one of the club's greatest games, a goalless draw with

Mick Lambert

Spanish giants Real Madrid in the Bernabeu Stadium. Ipswich stunned the Spaniards as Bobby Robson's tactics of attacking from the outset paid dividends. Lambert was a constant thorn in the Madrid team's side and his crosses created havoc in the Real defence. He missed very few games over the next four seasons and in 1975–76 scored his only hat-trick for the club in a 3–1 FA Cup third-round win over Halifax Town. He also came off the bench in the 1978 FA Cup Final win over Arsenal after Roger Osborne had gone off in a daze after scoring what turned out to be the winner against the Gunners. Lambert went on to score 45 goals in 263 games for the club before leaving Portman Road in the summer of 1979 to join Peterborough United. He was not at London Road long as an injury forced his retirement from League football.

LANG Thomas

Outside-left

Born: Larkhall, 3 April 1905.
Died: 1988.
Career: Larkhall Thistle; Newcastle United 1926; Huddersfield Town 1934; Manchester United 1935; Swansea City 1937; Queen of the South; IPSWICH TOWN 1946.

■ Tommy Lang was signed by Newcastle United while he was still working on his father's fruit farm in Lanarkshire. Following Stan Seymour in the number-11 shirt, Lang proved to be a splendid replacement. He had a deft touch, was accurate with his crosses and could score with either foot. He was a regular in the Magpies side for over seven seasons and helped the club win the FA Cup in 1931–32: in the semi-final against Chelsea he made one goal and scored another. He had scored 58 goals in 230 games for Newcastle when, in December 1934, he joined Huddersfield Town. After a season at Leeds Road, he moved on to Manchester United and in 1935–36 helped them win the Second Division Championship, although they were relegated after just one season of top-flight football. Following a spell with Swansea, he tried his luck north of the border with Queen of the South before joining Ipswich Town in October 1946. When he made his debut against Brighton & Hove Albion he was, at 41 years 220 days, the club's oldest debutant. He appeared in a handful of games before being appointed the club's trainer.

LAUREL John Albert

Centre-half

Born: Bexleyheath, 11 June 1935.
Career: Tottenham Hotspur 1952; IPSWICH TOWN 1959; King's Lynn.

■ England Youth international centre-half John Laurel was on the books of Tottenham Hotspur for a good number of years without ever making a Football League appearance. He was initially understudy to Harry Clarke and then Maurice Norman, but in the summer of 1959 he left White Hart Lane to join Ipswich Town. He had to bide his time at Portman Road as well, and did not make his Football League debut until October 1960, when he played in a 5–2 win over Leeds United. This was a remarkable game because, with only half an hour left, Town trailed 2–1. Laurel appeared in the next two games but then did not play again until midway through the 1962–63 season in a 3–0 defeat at Leicester. It was his last appearance in an Ipswich shirt and shortly afterwards he left to play non-League football for King's Lynn.

LEA Cyril

Wing-half

Born: Wrexham, 5 August 1934.
Career: Bradley Rovers; Leyton Orient 1957; IPSWICH TOWN 1964.

■ Originally a full-back, Cyril Lea's career blossomed when he was converted to wing-half. He established himself in Leyton Orient's team in 1960–61 and went on to make 205 League appearances for the O's. Though he helped the Brisbane Road club into the First Division in 1962, he lost his place soon afterwards and in November 1964 he joined Ipswich Town. After making his first-team debut in a 1–1 home draw against Charlton Athletic, he played in the remaining 24 games of the season, captaining the side on six occasions. That season his form was such that he was capped twice by Wales at full international level, against Northern Ireland in Belfast and Italy in Florence. Appointed the Portman Road club's captain, he missed very few games over the next two seasons, the latter of which saw Ipswich finish fifth in Division Two. In 1967–68, when Ipswich won the Second Division Championship, Lea made just four appearances, and he made only one, as substitute, the following season when the club were in the top flight. On retiring, he had a brief spell as Town's caretaker manager before being appointed Bobby Robson's first-team coach. The two worked in harmony until the summer of 1979, the year after Town's FA Cup success over Arsenal, when Lea left to take up an appointment as coach at Stoke City. He later coached the Welsh national side and, along with Mike Smith, had a spell in charge of Hull City between 1979 and 1982. Lea was manager of Colchester United between 1983 and 1986, having three good seasons when they just missed promotion in each of those campaigns. Despite this relative success, he was sacked. Having been youth coach at West Bromwich Albion and scouted for George Burley at Ipswich, he later worked with the youth squad at Rushden and Diamonds when former Town favourite Brian Talbot was manager.

LEADBETTER James Hunter

Outside-left

Born: Edinburgh, 15 July 1928.
Career: Edinburgh Thistle; Ammandale; Chelsea 1949; Brighton & Hove Albion 1952; IPSWICH TOWN 1955; Sudbury Town.

■ Jimmy Leadbetter played his early football for Edinburgh Thistle, a nursery club for Hibernian. He won a Scottish Juvenile Cup medal with Thistle before turning professional with Ammandale. Chelsea manager Billy Birrell spotted his potential and, in the summer of 1949, he joined the Stamford Bridge club. Unable to make much of an impression, he made just three appearances in three years with the club. He was the first player to leave when Ted Drake was appointed manager, moving to Brighton & Hove Albion in an exchange deal involving Johnny McNichol. He was a regular for the south coast club, scoring 29 goals in 107 League games. Though he was never officially placed on the transfer list, he joined Ipswich in the summer of 1955 and made his debut for the Blues in a 1–0 home win over Bournemouth in October of that year. After that he was one of the first names to be pencilled in on the club's team sheet and was an ever present in the seasons of 1957–58, 1959–60 and 1960–61. He played in 138 consecutive League matches between 11 October 1958 and 23 December 1961, and was one of only five players to win Championship medals for all three divisions with the same club. Developing a perfect understanding with Ray Crawford and Ted Phillips, for whom he laid on numerous goalscoring chances, he also netted 49 goals himself in his 375 League and Cup games, including a hat-trick in the 3–2 FA Cup win over Mansfield Town in January 1963. His best season in terms of goals scored was 1956–57, when the club won the Third Division South Championship, with Leadbetter netting 13 goals. On leaving Portman Road, he played non-League football for Sudbury Town before later returning to his native Scotland, where he took a job as a driver delivering newspapers.

LEE Alan Desmond

Forward

Born: Galway, 21 August 1978.
Career: Aston Villa 1995; Torquay United (loan) 1998; Port Vale (loan) 1999; Burnley 1999; Rotherham United 2000; Cardiff City 2003; IPSWICH TOWN 2005.

■ Unable to get a game at Aston Villa, this big, strong striker went on loan to Torquay United and Port Vale to gain League experience and scored vital goals for both clubs. Shortly after returning to Villa Park he joined Burnley in a £150,000 deal, but had little chance to make his mark in his first season at Turf Moor due to the consistency of the Clarets' regular front two. Allowed to leave the club for a similar fee, he moved to Rotherham United and soon netted his first Football League hat-trick in a 3–1 home defeat of Cambridge United. Having helped the Millers win promotion to the First Division, he adjusted well to life in the higher division and, though he was not as prolific, he did score some vital goals in the battle against relegation. In 2002–03 he was soon into double figures in terms of goals and thoroughly deserved his call-up into the full Republic of Ireland side. He had scored 41 goals in 122 games for the Yorkshire club when Cardiff City paid out a club record fee of £850,000 for him. Although troubled by injury at Ninian Park, when fit he was a regular in the Welsh club's side, but during the early stages of the 2005–06 season he found himself confined to the bench. It came as no surprise when he was allowed to leave Ninian Park to join Ipswich Town for a fee of £100,000. Giving the club a physical presence, his performances for the Tractor Boys in the latter half of the season were very impressive as he struck twice at Southampton – being denied a hat-trick by the heroics of Paul Smith – and netted a superb equaliser against his former club Burnley. Lee, who will be hoping to score the goals that see Ipswich return to the Premiership, continues to represent the Republic of Ireland on the international stage.

LEGG Andrew

Midfield

Born: Neath, 28 July 1966.
Career: Briton Ferry; Swansea City 1988; Notts County 1993; Birmingham City 1996; IPSWICH TOWN (loan) 1997; Reading 1998; Peterborough United (loan) 1998; Cardiff City 1998; Peterborough United 2003.

■ Fast and skilful, Andy Legg started out with Briton Ferry before joining Swansea in August 1988. He was an important member of the Swans side for five seasons, scoring 38 goals in 207 games before Notts County paid £275,000 to take him to Meadow Lane. Two and a half seasons later he was on the move again, this time to Birmingham City, where he soon settled down on the left side of the St Andrew's club's midfield. His form with Birmingham was such that he won full international honours for Wales, but midway through the 1997–98 season the long throw specialist – whose world record throw of 44.54 metres was beaten by Tranmere's Dave Challinor – had a loan spell with Ipswich before joining Reading. At Ipswich he appeared in half a dozen games, scoring his only goal for the club in a 2–2 home draw against Sheffield United. Failing to impress the manager at Reading, he spent a month on loan at Peterborough before signing for Cardiff. Showing total commitment to the team, he won the 1999–2000 Player of the Year award and the following season, after switching to sweeper, he won the award for a second time. He played an important part in Cardiff's promotion to the First Division in 2002–03 before returning to London Road to become Peterborough's player-coach. Towards the end of the 2004–05 season he was diagnosed as having a cancerous lump on his neck and after surgery he announced he would be hanging up his boots after more than 700 senior appearances.

LE PEN Ulrich

Left-winger

Born: Auray, France, 21 January 1974.
Career: Rennes (France); Lavallois (France); Lorient (France); IPSWICH TOWN 2001; Strasbourg (France).

■ An experienced left-winger, having played in France for Rennes and Lavallois, Le Pen was playing for Lorient when Ipswich paid £1.4 million to bring him to Portman Road in November 2001. He made his Town debut from the substitutes' bench against Bolton soon after putting pen to paper, but had the misfortune to suffer an ankle injury minutes after coming on to the pitch. He returned for the FA Cup defeat by Manchester City, but made no further appearances in that 2001–02 season. He featured as a substitute the following season in the UEFA Cup tie away to Avenir Beggin before returning to France to join Strasbourg on a 12-month loan deal. He featured regularly for them and later signed on a permanent basis.

LINIGHAN David

Centre-half

Born: Hartlepool, 9 January 1965.
Career: Hartlepool United 1982; Derby County 1986; Shrewsbury Town 1986; IPSWICH TOWN 1988; Blackpool 1995; Dunfermline Athletic 1998; Mansfield Town 1999; Southport.

■ The son of Brian, who played for Darlington in 1958 and whose brother, Andy, also joined Hartlepool United from Smiths Dock, David Linighan made his League debut at home to Bradford City in March 1982. For a long while he played mainly in the shadow of Andy and it was not until 1985–86 that he held down a regular place. He impressed Arthur Cox enough for Derby County to pay £30,000 for his services, but after just four months and no first-team appearances, he was sold to Shrewsbury Town. He missed only three matches in 18 months at Gay Meadow and, with Ipswich looking to replace Ian Cranson following his move to Sheffield Wednesday, they signed Linighan for a fee of £300,000. He soon became a fixture in central defence and in 1990–91 he had an outstanding season as the club's captain, which was recognised by the Ipswich faithful when he picked up the fans' Player of the Year award. Linighan also played a sterling role in the Blues' Second Division Championship campaign in 1991–92 until he was injured in the home game against Barnsley, which ruled him out for the rest of the season. He went on to maintain a high level of defensive consistency in the Premiership and had played in 327 first-team games for Ipswich before joining Blackpool for £80,000 in November 1995 after an extended loan spell with the Seasiders. He had begun his last season at Portman Road on a weekly contract and lost the captaincy as a result, though he did recover it after many consistent displays in a beleaguered Town defence. After making 100

League appearances for Blackpool, he had a spell north of the border with Dunfermline Athletic before signing for Mansfield Town. He performed resolutely at the heart of the Stags' back four until breaking a wrist towards the end of the 1999–2000 season. Freed by the Field Mill club, he then played non-League football for Southport.

LITTLE John (Jackie)

Winger

Born: Gateshead, 17 May 1912.
Career: Needham Market; IPSWICH TOWN 1937; Stowmarket.

■ Gateshead-born winger Jackie Little joined Ipswich as an amateur in the summer of 1935 and made his debut in a 3–1 home win over Gorleston in an Eastern Counties League game in September of that year. It was not until the 1937–38 season that he established himself as a first-team regular and, in what was the club's last season in the Southern League, he scored 11 goals in 28 games including a hat-trick in the 3–1 home win over Tunbridge Wells Rangers. He appeared in Town's first match in the Football League, a 4–2 defeat of Southend United, and went on to score six goals in 32 games that season. During the war he guested for Bath City, where he played alongside the Blackpool and England forward Stan Mortensen. When League football resumed in 1946–47, Little was still a member of the Town side and went on to score 20 goals in his 146 Football League games for the club before, at the end of the 1949–50 season, he left Portman Road to become player-manager of Stowmarket.

LOGAN Richard James

Forward

Born: Bury St Edmunds, 4 January 1982.
Career: IPSWICH TOWN 1999; Cambridge United (loan) 2001;
Torquay United (loan) 2001; Boston United 2002; Peterborough United 2003; Shrewsbury Town (loan) 2004.

■ Richard Logan progressed from the YTS scheme through the Ipswich academy and reserve sides, where he scored regularly, to the fringes of the first team. Still a trainee, he made his senior debut at Wolverhampton Wanderers just after Christmas 1998 when he came on as a substitute in the last minute. He then signed professional and three days later got a longer run in the game against Grimsby Town. Though he only made one more appearance from the bench the following season, he was called up by the England Youth side, appearing for the Under-18s against France and the Under-17s against Luxembourg. He continued his development in the club's reserve side in 2000–01, prior to a loan spell at Cambridge United during which he scored against Wycombe Wanderers. The following season he had a three-month loan spell at Torquay United before returning to Portman Road. Still unable to establish a regular place, he moved to Boston United on loan prior to the move being made permanent. He scored six goals in his first five starts before being moved into midfield. A powerful leader of the line, he joined Peterborough United but spent most of his time on the bench, as Posh's playing style did not suit his strengths. Following a loan spell at Shrewsbury, where he scored against his former club Boston, he returned to London Road to fight for his place in the Peterborough side.

LOWE David Anthony

Right-winger

Born: Liverpool, 30 August 1965.
Career: Wigan Athletic 1983; IPSWICH TOWN 1987; Port Vale (loan) 1992; Leicester City 1992; Port Vale (loan) 1994; Wigan Athletic 1996; Wrexham 1999; Rushden and Diamonds (loan) 2000.

■ Despite his early football being restricted to school and local League level, David Lowe's teacher recommended him to Wigan manager Harry McNally and, after a week training with the Latics, he was offered an apprenticeship. After injuries had depleted the first-team squad, Lowe made his Wigan debut against Reading in October 1981 and, though he appeared out of his depth, the club stuck with him. He won a Freight Rover Trophy medal in 1985, scoring one of the goals in a 3–1 win over Brentford. In June 1987 he signed for Ipswich Town for a fee of £80,000 and made his debut in a 1–1 draw at home to Aston Villa on the opening day of the 1987–88 season. He ended the campaign as the club's top scorer with 17 goals in 41 League games. The hardworking midfielder won England Under-21 honours and continued to find the net for the Portman Road club. He was the leading scorer again in 1989–90 but two seasons later found himself on loan at Port Vale. He left Ipswich in the summer of 1992 when Leicester City paid £250,000 for the services of a player who had scored 42 goals in 159 first-team games. He shattered his cheekbone in a pre-season friendly against Borussia Moenchengladbach, but settled well after his delayed debut for the Foxes, though he missed out on the 1993 Play-offs. After another loan spell at Port Vale, Lowe rejoined the Latics for a second spell in March 1996 for a fee of £125,000. In 1996–97 he celebrated his 300th game for the club and his goal in the final match of the season against Mansfield ensured the Latics of the Championship and him of a medal. The following season he was Wigan's top scorer with 18 goals, setting up a new club aggregate scoring record. He ended the season by collecting both the supporters' and the club's Player of the Year trophies. After that he was hampered by injuries, but he declined an offer to combine playing and coaching at the club and joined Wrexham. Later he had a loan spell with Rushden and Diamonds before hanging up his boots to become a regional FA coach.

LUNDSTRUM Colin Francis

Winger

Born: Colchester, 9 October 1938.
Career: West Ham United; IPSWICH TOWN 1956; Colchester United 1961.

■ Winger Colin Lundstrum had been an amateur on the books of West Ham United prior to joining Ipswich Town in November 1956. He spent a couple of seasons in the club's reserve side before being given his League debut against Swansea Town in February 1958, a match that ended goalless. He kept his place in the side for a run of five games, but then did not appear at all the following season. He returned to action in 1959–60 and, in his first game back, scored one of Town's goals in a 3–2 defeat by Cardiff City. However, he managed just 13 League starts in five years at the club and in 1961 joined Colchester United. He made just one appearance for the Layer Road club before drifting into non-League football.

McCALL Stephen Harold

Midfield/Left-back

Born: Carlisle, 15 October 1960.
Career: IPSWICH TOWN 1978; Sheffield Wednesday 1987; Carlisle United (loan) 1990; Plymouth Argyle 1992; Torquay United 1996; Plymouth Argyle 1998.

■ After making his first-team debut against Skeid Oslo in the UEFA Cup first-round first-leg tie in Norway, midfielder Steve McCall played his first League game three days later in a 1–1 draw at home to Everton. Never a prolific scorer in his time at Portman Road, he netted two of Town's goals in the return leg against Skeid Oslo, which the Suffolk club won 7–0. After winning a regular place in the Ipswich side in 1980–81, McCall was capped by England at Under-21 level to add to those he won at Youth level. He went on to play in six internationals at Under-21 level before being chosen for the England B team in 1984–85. In 1981–82 he was one of four ever presents in the Ipswich side as they finished runners-up to Liverpool in the First Division. In fact, McCall played in every League game for the next two seasons, appearing in 166 consecutive games. On 13 April 1985 he broke a bone in his foot in the 2–1 home defeat by Sheffield Wednesday and had to miss the rest of the season. He bounced back in 1985–86 and went on to score 12 goals in 340 first-team games before being transferred to Sheffield Wednesday for £300,000 in the summer of 1987. At Hillsborough he suffered with injuries and a loss of form and, in almost five years with the Yorkshire club, only appeared in 36 League and Cup games. In March 1992 he joined Plymouth Argyle for £25,000 and spent four years at Home Park before becoming player-coach at Torquay United. He later rejoined Plymouth, where he acquired some management experience before leaving the West Country to work with George Burley during his time at Portman Road.

McCRORY Samuel McKee

Inside-forward

Born: Belfast, 11 October 1924.
Career: Linfield; Swansea City 1946; IPSWICH TOWN 1950; Plymouth Argyle 1952; Southend United 1955.

■ Belfast-born forward Sam McCrory began his footballing career with Linfield before Swansea brought him into League football. In three seasons at Vetch Field, he scored 46 goals in 103 League games and helped the Swans win promotion to the Second Division. He arrived at Portman Road in March 1950, along with Irish international full-back Jim Feeney, for a combined fee of £10,500, a record for Ipswich. He made his debut in a 1–1 draw at Norwich City, but before the end of the season he had the dubious distinction, in a 5–0 defeat at Aldershot, of becoming the first Ipswich player to be sent off since the club joined the Football League. In 1950–51 he was the club's top scorer with 21 League goals, including a hat-trick in a 3–1 win at Crystal Palace. He headed the scoring charts again the following season with 16 goals, but in the summer of 1952 he joined newly-promoted Plymouth Argyle. Never an automatic choice at Home Park, his career was revived somewhat after his transfer to Southend United in 1955 and at the age of 33 he received his sole international cap for Northern Ireland, scoring in a rare win over England in 1957.

McDONALD Dean

Forward

Born: London, 19 February 1986.
Career: Arsenal; IPSWICH TOWN 2005; Hartlepool United (loan) 2005.

■ A former Arsenal Academy player, Dean McDonald joined Ipswich Town on trial at the turn of 2005 and impressed in his time playing for the reserves. A player who can operate wide or down the middle, he signed a year's contract in the summer of 2005 and made his League debut for the Tractor Boys against Sheffield Wednesday in September 2005, having an outstanding game. A huge crowd favourite, he loves running at people and was loaned out to Hartlepool United before returning to Portman Road. Definitely one for the future!

McEVELEY James (Jay)

Defender

Born: Liverpool, 11 February 1985.
Career: Blackburn Rovers 2002; Burnley (loan) 2003; Gillingham (loan) 2005; IPSWICH TOWN (loan) 2005.

■ Jay McEveley made his bow in senior football for Blackburn Rovers in the Worthington Cup third-round tie against Walsall in November 2002, and it soon became apparent that he was an outstanding prospect. His progress was recognised when he made his debut for the England Under-21 side against Italy in February 2003. The strapping young defender then went on loan to rivals Burnley and showed great promise before dislocating his knee in an FA Cup game against Mansfield. After recovering from injury he was given a chance in the Rovers side prior to joining Gillingham on loan. He was very impressive for the Kent side as they almost retained their Championship status. In August 2005 he went on a season's loan to Ipswich Town and, after making his debut against Sheffield United the following month, he went on to appear in 19 League games, with his last appearance coming on the final day of the 2005–06 season at Plymouth.

McGINN Francis

Outside-left

Born: Cambuslang, 2 March 1919.
Career: Wrexham 1947; IPSWICH TOWN 1948.

■ Flying winger Francis McGinn started out with Wrexham, but despite his pace down both flanks he was released after a little over a year at the Racecourse Ground and joined Ipswich Town. He scored on his debut in a 1–1 draw against Crystal Palace and appeared in eight games in that 1948–49 season, scoring another goal in a 3–2 defeat of Walsall. A player whose pinpoint crosses in the few games he played laid on a number of goalscoring opportunities for the likes of Bill Jennings and Tommy Parker, he was surprisingly released at the end of the campaign.

McGOURTY John (Jimmy)

Inside-forward

Born: Fauldhouse, 10 July 1912.
Career: Fauldhouse St John's; Partick Thistle; Everton 1932; Hamilton Academicals; Waterford; IPSWICH TOWN 1938.

■ Scottish inside-forward Jimmy McGourty had impressed with Partick Thistle in the Scottish League First Division, prompting Everton to offer him his chance in the Football League just prior to the start of the 1932–33 season. McGourty scored a couple of goals in 14 League appearances that season, but was not a member of the Everton side that contested the FA Cup Final. Unable to make much progress at Goodison Park, he returned north of the border to play for Hamilton Academicals and, following a brief spell in the League of Ireland with Waterford, he signed for Ipswich Town. McGourty's only appearance in an Ipswich shirt came in September 1938 in a 2–1 home defeat at the hands of Cardiff City. He remained at Portman Road until the early part of the following year when his contract was cancelled.

McGREAL John

Defender

Born: Liverpool, 2 June 1972.
Career: Tranmere Rovers 1990; IPSWICH TOWN 1999; Burnley 2004.

■ Cultured central defender John McGreal made his Tranmere debut in a 1–1 draw at Southend United in April 1992, though it was towards the end of the 1993–94 season before he established himself as a first-team regular. Strong in the tackle, he revelled in bringing the ball out of defence and was often compared in his younger days to the Liverpool and Scotland international Alan Hansen. He was appointed Tranmere's club captain for the 1996–97 season and, though there were rumours he was going to pursue a move to France, he stayed at Prenton Park, appearing in 233 games for the club until joining Ipswich in the summer of 1999 for a fee of £650,000. He immediately settled into the side in the middle of the back three between Manu Thetis and Mark Venus. Cool under pressure, he was unlucky to be shown a red card in the game against Portsmouth. Once Tony Mowbray was fully fit, McGreal moved to the right side of the back line, which gave him more space to join the attack. His accurate crosses to the far post created a number of scoring opportunities for his forwards. Following the club's promotion, he showed he was not overawed in the top flight and, being Merseyside-born, thoroughly enjoyed the wins at both Everton and Liverpool. Indeed, it was his goal, his first for the club – a superb header – which paved the way for the 3–0 win at Goodison Park. Adept at the last-minute tackle, more often than not coming away cleanly with the ball, McGreal then suffered a spate of injuries that reduced his number of first-team appearances. Whenever he did play he formed a particularly effective defensive unit with Matt Elliott, but injuries had the last laugh when he picked up a calf strain in the first leg of the 2004 Play-off semi-final against West Ham United. This prevented him from playing in the return leg. Allowed to join Burnley on a free transfer, he was the key man in the transformation of the Clarets' leaky defence of the previous two seasons, helping the club stay clear of relegation worries during his time at Turf Moor.

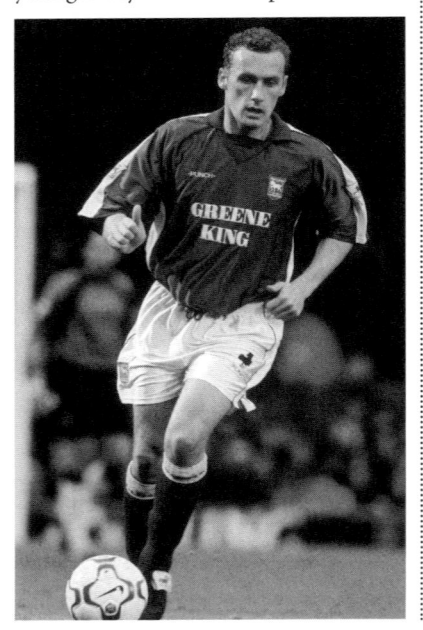

MACKAY Angus MacDougall

Inside-forward

Born: Glasgow, 24 April 1925.
Career: Hamilton Academicals; IPSWICH TOWN 1946; Exeter City 1947; Millwall 1955.

■ Scheming inside-forward Angus Mackay joined Ipswich from Hamilton Academicals prior to the start of the 1946–47 season, making his debut on the opening day of the campaign in a 2–2 draw with Leyton Orient. He made a handful of appearances that season, but the following summer left Portman Road to join Exeter City. He went on to score 78 goals in 257 League games for the Grecians, all of them in the Third Division South, with his best season being 1953–54 when the club finished ninth. Allowed to leave St James's Park in 1955, he signed for Millwall, but after just one season at The Den, he decided to retire.

MacLUCKIE George Robertson

Outside-left

Born: Falkirk, 19 September 1931.
Career: Lochore Welfare; Blackburn Rovers 1952; IPSWICH TOWN 1953; Reading 1958.

■ Winger George MacLuckie began his Football League career with Blackburn Rovers, but could not dislodge England international winger

Bobby Langton. In May 1953 he opted for a move to Ipswich Town, managed by Scott Duncan. He made his Town debut against Walsall on the opening day of the 1953–54 season, scoring one of the goals in a 2–0 win. He was an ever present that season, as Town won the Third Division South Championship, scoring 12 goals and laying on numerous chances for Tom Garneys and John Elsworthy. Liking nothing better than to cut inside from the left-wing and test the opposing goalkeeper, MacLuckie scored 25 goals in 152 League and Cup games before moving to Reading. He made 85 appearances for the then Elm Park club as they challenged for promotion to the Second Division.

McLUCKIE James Sime

Left-half/Inside-right

Born: Stonehouse, Lanarkshire, 2 April 1908.
Died: November 1986.
Career: Tranent Juniors; Hamilton Academicals; Manchester City 1933; Aston Villa 1934; IPSWICH TOWN 1936; Clacton Town.

■ Jimmy McLuckie was a Scottish international, being capped against Wales in 1934 when he was a Manchester City player. When he joined Ipswich from Aston Villa in July 1936, he was the biggest name so far to join the Portman Road club. He was Ipswich Town's first professional captain and made his debut in a 4–1 home win in the club's first Southern League fixture of 1936–37, going on to score five goals in 27 games as Town won the League Championship. McLuckie was also the first player to be sent off in Town's professional history, receiving his marching orders against Guildford City in the Southern League Cup in September 1937. The following season he scored four goals in 32 games as Ipswich finished third in the Southern League and then in 1938–39 he guided the club into their first season in the Football League. Leading by example, he missed just one game as the club finished in a very creditable seventh position. During the war years he was one of a number of Ipswich players who guested for Norwich City, but in 1945–46, when the football authorities decided to operate some organised leagues, he appeared in 17 games, the last against Watford in April 1946. Having played an important part in the development of the professional club at Ipswich, he left to become player-manager of Clacton Town.

McMILLAN George Sorbie

Goalkeeper

Born: Stonehouse, 10 August 1929.
Career: Newarthill Juniors; IPSWICH TOWN 1953; Stirling Albion.

■ Goalkeeper George McMillan played his early football for Newarthill Juniors before arriving at Portman Road in 1953. After some impressive displays for the club's reserve side he made his Football League debut in place of Jack Parry in March 1955 as Town beat Nottingham Forest 2–1. He kept his place in the side for the remaining 12 games of the season, but could not prevent the club's relegation to the Third Division South. After losing out to Charlie Ashcroft at the start of the following season, McMillan won back his place and, apart from two games when Roy Bailey deputised, he made 37 appearances as Town finished third in Division Three South. When Bailey became Town's first-choice 'keeper, McMillan played for the club's reserves until he appeared in four games towards the end of the 1957–58 season. He later left Portman Road to continue his career in his native Scotland with Stirling Albion.

McNEIL Michael

Full-back

Born: Middlesbrough, 7 February 1940.
Career: Middlesbrough 1957; IPSWICH TOWN 1964; Cambridge City.

■ Mick McNeil began his Football League career with his home-town club, making his debut in a remarkable 6–4 win for Middlesbrough at Brighton & Hove Albion in December 1958. His early appearances for the club were at left-half but, after losing his place to Ray Yeoman, he switched to full-back and never regretted the move. In 1959–60, McNeil was ever present as Boro finished fifth in the Second Division. He was selected for an FA XI against the Army at St James' Park and followed this up with a number of appearances for the England Under-21 side. His performances in the Middlesbrough defence led to him winning nine full caps for England, never once appearing on the losing side. In the summer of 1964, after appearing in 193 games for Boro, McNeil was allowed to join Ipswich Town and made his debut in a goalless draw against Cardiff City on the opening day of the 1964–65 season. Although he did not add to his international caps while at Portman Road, he did captain an FA XI to a 10–0 win over Jersey in a match played to commemorate the centenary of the Jersey FA. He played the last of his 173 first-team games for Ipswich in a 1–0 FA Cup fourth-round defeat against Birmingham City in February 1972 before playing non-League football with Cambridge City.

MACROW Geoffrey Cyril

Outside-right

Born: East Harling, Norfolk 26 September 1932.
Died: 1987.
Career: Thetford Town; IPSWICH TOWN 1955; Stowmarket.

■ Winger Geoff Macrow had impressed playing non-League football for Thetford Town before Ipswich manager Alf Ramsey gave him his chance at Football League level. Unfortunately he could not force his way into the side on a permanent basis and made just a single appearance in each of the two seasons after he signed. On his debut it was his cross that led to Tom Garneys scoring the game's only goal and, although he was a regular member of the club's reserve side, he was allowed to leave Portman Road after another season of reserve-team football and join Stowmarket.

MAFFEY Denis

Centre-forward

Born: Sunderland, 22 February 1922. Died: 1995.
Career: Walton United; IPSWICH TOWN 1947; Colchester United.

■ Following his impressive goalscoring exploits for non-League Walton United, bustling centre-forward Denis Maffey joined Ipswich in July 1947 and was given his debut in a 3–2 defeat at Southend United in the second game of the 1947–48 season. Maffey kept his place in the Ipswich side for five consecutive games, his only goal coming in the return game against the Shrimpers at Portman Road when Town won 4–0. He then returned to the club's reserve side and, although he proved quite a consistent goalscorer at that level, he was not given another chance in the League side and in May 1948 he was allowed to join Colchester United, for whom he had a number of seasons of good service.

MAGILTON James

Midfield

Born: Belfast, 6 May 1969.
Career: Liverpool 1986; Oxford United 1990; Southampton 1994; Sheffield Wednesday 1997; IPSWICH TOWN 1999.

■ Recently appointed Ipswich boss Jim Magilton joined Liverpool as an apprentice in May 1986, but as he was unable to break into the Reds' first team, he joined Oxford United for £100,000 in October 1990. Impressive displays for the Manor Ground club, where he scored 39 goals in 167 games, led to a number of top-flight clubs showing an interest in securing his services. In February 1994, Southampton manager Alan Ball paid £600,000 for the Northern Ireland international – who had scored from the penalty spot in a 3–1 defeat of Poland on his debut – and he made his first appearance for the Saints in the 4–2 home win over Liverpool when Matt Le Tissier netted a hat-trick. Jim Magilton was a commanding presence in the centre of the Southampton midfield and a neat and indefatigable 'fetcher and carrier' between penalty areas. However, he did not seem to fit into new manager Dave Jones's plans, and he made a surprise move to Hillsborough soon after the start of the 1997–98 season. The fact that the fee was £1.6 million showed just how highly Owls manager David Pleat rated him. However, when Pleat was replaced by Ron Atkinson, Magilton's days with the Yorkshire club were numbered. On losing his place, he also found that his position in the Northern Ireland side was not assured. After a loan spell with Ipswich Town, the move became permanent and in 1999–2000 he netted his first-ever professional hat-trick in the Play-off semi-final win over Bolton Wanderers. He also had a second penalty attempt brilliantly saved by the Wanderers' 'keeper. To cap a fine season, he won a recall to the Northern Ireland side, now managed by Sammy McIlroy, and on occasions captained the side. One of the main inspirations of Ipswich's successful return to the top flight, Magilton was then hampered by a series of niggling injuries and could not halt the club's slide back into the First Division. Appointed club captain by newly appointed boss Joe Royle, he played in every game in 2003–04 and always led by example. Sorely missed when absent, he led Town to the Play-off semi-finals where they lost to West Ham United in 2004–05 and remained a first-team regular until he replaced Joe Royle as the club's manager in June 2006.

MAHON Alan Joseph

Winger

Born: Dublin, 4 April 1978.
Career: Tranmere Rovers 1995; Sporting Lisbon (Portugal); Blackburn Rovers 2000; Cardiff City (loan) 2003; IPSWICH TOWN (loan) 2003; Wigan Athletic 2004.

■ An attacking midfielder who burst onto the Football League scene with Tranmere Rovers in 1995–96, the Irish Youth international also made his debut for the Republic of Ireland Under-21 side during the course of that campaign. After finding himself in and out of the side, he won a regular place, though towards the end of the 1997–98 season a combination of a recurring stomach injury and the burden of expectancy conspired to give him a frustrating time. However, the following season he found a rich seam of form and caused endless problems for his unfortunate markers. Developing a probing and tricky style of play, rumours began to circulate about a big money move to the Premiership, but in the summer of 2000, after making his full international debut for the Republic against Greece, he chose to move to Sporting Lisbon. He found it difficult to break into the side, although one of his rare appearances came in a European Champions' League game against Real Madrid. In December 2000 he joined Blackburn Rovers, going on to produce some fine performances to assist the club in their bid for promotion. However, during the following season he was used mainly as cover for Damien Duff on the left or even at left-back. With the exception of UEFA Cup ties, he was never in the frame at Ewood Park and joined Cardiff City on loan. After providing the width that had been missing all season, he returned to Blackburn shortly before the end of the term, thus missing out on the Bluebirds' Play-off excitement. In September 2003 he joined Ipswich on a three-month loan deal and was an instant hit with the fans because of his exciting wing play and accurate crosses. He opened his account at Portman Road with the only goal of the win at Bradford City, but was hampered by injuries in the latter stages of the loan. He returned to Ewood before Wigan paid £250,000 for his services. He brought a balance to the Latics midfield, but lost his place following the signing of Graham Kavanagh, although he remained an important squad member during the club's first season in the Premiership.

MAKIN Christopher Gregory

Full-back

Born: Manchester, 8 May 1973.
Career: Oldham Athletic 1991; Wigan Athletic (loan) 1992; Marseilles (France) 1996; Sunderland 1997; IPSWICH TOWN 2001; Leicester City 2004; Derby County 2005.

■ Spotted by Oldham Athletic playing in Manchester Schools football, Chris Makin worked his way up through the ranks prior to turning professional during the 1991 close season. Unable to break into the Boundary Park club's first team, he joined Wigan Athletic on loan at the start of the 1992–93 season and impressed during a 15-match spell. Wigan wanted to sign him but were turned down flat and, on his return to Oldham, he was capped by England at Under-21 level and represented the Football League Under-21 side against the Italian Serie B at Huddersfield. He had appeared in 114 games for Oldham when, with his contract up, he left the English soccer scene to play for Marseilles. After a year playing in France, he returned to these shores to play for Sunderland for a fee of £500,000. In his first season in the North East, he helped the Wearsiders reach the Play-off Final, where they lost to Charlton Athletic. The following season he picked up a deserved First Division Championship medal and had little problem in adapting to life in the Premiership, thanks to his all-action style and commitment. In March 2001 he was rather surprisingly allowed to leave the Stadium of Light and join Ipswich Town for £1.25 million. After a handful of games towards the end of the 2000–01 campaign, he kept his place in the Ipswich side throughout the following season until an ankle ligament injury against Aston Villa ended his season a month early. Following the appointment of his former Oldham boss Joe Royle, he was handed a central defensive role, where his tackling and pace were the main features of his game. He was then injured in the home game against West Ham United in August 2003 and never played again during that 2003–04 season. Eventually diagnosed as having damaged his hip joint, he required corrective surgery. Offered a short-term contract, he opted to join Leicester City, but was allowed to move on to Derby County following a change in management. George Burley was well aware of his capabilities, having recruited him when he was at Portman Road.

MALCOLM Kenneth Campbell

Full-back

Born: Aberdeen, 25 July 1926.
Career: Arbroath; IPSWICH TOWN 1954.

■ Aberdonian Ken Malcolm joined Ipswich from Arbroath in May 1954 and, although he was not in the side for the opening game of the season, he did not have long to wait before making his debut, playing in the 4–2 defeat at Hull City in September of that year. Despite only playing in 21 League games that season due to a niggling groin injury, he showed his versatility by turning out in eight different positions. Playing a couple of games up front, he scored in a 3–3 draw against Port Vale and in the 5–1 home defeat of Doncaster Rovers. At the start of the 1955–56 season, Malcolm established himself at left-back and over the next eight seasons played in 291 League and Cup games for the Portman Road club, winning a Third Division Championship-winners' medal in 1956–57 and a Second Division Championship-winners' medal in 1960–61. In 1961–62, when Ipswich won the First Division title, Malcolm only played in three matches because he strained a knee and was then hospitalised with a bad attack of sciatica. Although he returned to first-team action the following season, it proved to be his last in the Football League. Malcolm did not appear in the Town side again after the 6–1 defeat at West Bromwich Albion in March 1963. During the close season he retired from the playing side of the game and coached the club's juniors for two years.

MARINER Paul

Forward

Born: Bolton, 22 May 1953.
Career: Chorley; Plymouth Argyle 1973; IPSWICH TOWN 1976; Arsenal 1984; Portsmouth 1986; Naxxar Lions (Malta); Albany Capitals (United States).

■ Paul Mariner began his footballing career with non-League Chorley before being transferred to Plymouth Argyle for a small fee in July 1973. Within weeks of the start of the 1973–74 season he had displaced Jimmy Hinch and became recognised as one of the leading forwards in the Third Division. His scoring partnership with Billy Rafferty did much to ensure Argyle's promotion to the Second Division in 1975–76. It also attracted the attention of First Division clubs Ipswich, West Bromwich Albion and West Ham United, but it was Bobby Robson who made the Home Park club an offer they could not refuse in October 1976. With seven goals in 10 League games, Mariner had already demonstrated that he could get goals in the Second Division as well as the Third and Argyle accepted Ipswich's valuation of the player at £220,000, including two Town players: Terry Austin and John Peddlety. Mariner made his Ipswich debut in a 1–0 win at Manchester United and had a hand in the club's goal, scored by Clive Woods. Robson's high opinion of Mariner continued after he had left Ipswich to become manager of the national team and Mariner was awarded the first of his 35 caps some six months after moving to Portman Road. In his first season with the club, he scored 13 goals in 31 League and Cup games, including a hat-trick in a 4–1 home win over West Ham United. In 1977–78 he was the top scorer with 22 goals, including another hat-trick in a 6–1 sixth-round FA Cup win at Millwall. He ended the campaign with an FA Cup-winners' medal after the Blues had beaten Arsenal 1–0 in the Final. He led the scoring charts again in 1978–79 and 1979–80 and in this latter season netted his third hat-trick for the club in a 6–0 win over Manchester United. Although his goalscoring achievements were less over his last three seasons at Portman Road, he had scored 135 goals in 339 League and Cup games when he signed for Arsenal in February 1984 for £150,000. Although hardly a veteran, he had seen his best years and in August 1986, after scoring 17 goals in 70 first-team games for the Gunners, he joined Portsmouth. In his first season at Fratton Park he helped the club gain First Division recognition for the first time in almost 30 years. He later played for Naxxar Lions and Albany Capitals before having a brief spell as commercial manager of Colchester United, but he now spends most of his time coaching in the United States.

MARSHALL Andrew John

Goalkeeper

Born: Bury St Edmunds, 14 April 1975.
Career: Norwich City 1993; Bournemouth (loan) 1996; Gillingham (loan) 1996; IPSWICH TOWN 2001; Wolverhampton Wanderers (loan) 2003; Millwall 2004.

Paul Mariner

■ An England Under-21 international, goalkeeper, Andy Marshall began his career with Norwich City, where initially he was understudy to Bryan Gunn. After loan spells with Bournemouth and Gillingham, where he gained invaluable experience, he replaced the Scottish international as the Canaries' first-choice 'keeper. Selected to represent the Football League Under-21s against the Italian Serie B equivalent, he was gaining in confidence all the time and making some truly outstanding saves. Tremendously athletic, he possesses fantastic reflexes and agility, making him a top-class shot-stopper. He had made 219 appearances for Norwich when he took advantage of the Bosman ruling and joined Ipswich Town on a free transfer, but a back injury in a pre-season friendly meant he was not fully fit for the start of the 2001–02 season. This caused the club to bring in Matteo Sereni and it was not until the turn of the year that he got a look in. However, with Sereni on a 12-month loan, Marshall had the opportunity to confirm his status as Ipswich Town's number-one 'keeper the following season before he was surprisingly made available on a free transfer with one year of his contract still to run. He began the 2003–04 season on loan with Wolves before returning to Portman Road. Unable to dislodge Kelvin Davis, he opted for a move to Millwall, where he replaced the injured Tony Warner before losing out to Graham Stack.

MARSHALL Ian Paul

Centre-half/Forward

Born: Oxford, 20 March 1966.
Career: Everton 1984; Oldham Athletic 1988; IPSWICH TOWN 1993; Leicester City 1996; Bolton Wanderers 2000; Blackpool 2001.

■ Ian Marshall began his career with Everton and made his League debut when deputising for the injured Derek Mountfield against West Bromwich Albion at Goodison Park in August 1985. However, first-team chances were few, with Kevin Ratcliffe and Dave Watson holding down the central defensive positions, and so in March 1988 he moved to Oldham Athletic for a fee of £100,000. On his arrival at Boundary Park, he tried to convince Oldham manager Joe Royle that there was a frustrated centre-forward in him trying to get out. Royle did try him up front during the club's great twin Cup runs of 1989–90, with some success. But after scoring in the first FA Cup semi-final against Manchester United in 1990, he was injured and missed selection for the League Cup Final against Manchester United the same year. In 1990–91 he scored a superb hat-trick in a 3–2 win at Wolverhampton Wanderers and ended the season as the club's top scorer with 17 goals from only 26 League games as Oldham stormed to the Second Division Championship. During the inaugural season of the Premier League, he played in 13 games up front and 13 at the back. With no one seeming to know what his best position was, he joined Ipswich Town for a fee of £750,000 in the summer of 1993. He proved his worth as a striker with three goals in the opening three matches of the 1993–94 campaign and ended the season as the club's top scorer. He was hampered by injuries the following season, but in 1995–96 he notched up 19 goals, the same number as his strike partner, Alex Mathie, even though he helped out in defence on a number of occasions. His classic header against Leicester City

Ian Marshall

earned him the club's Goal of the Season award. He had scored 37 goals in 96 games for Ipswich when, in August 1996, he left Portman Road to join newly promoted Premier League club Leicester City for £800,000. Cup-tied as far as the Coca-Cola Cup was concerned, he missed out on the Foxes' run to Wembley. Sadly he continued to be prone to injury during his time with Leicester, but he still managed to play a crucial role in City's Worthington Cup triumph in 2000 and made an appearance from the bench in the Final. Released, he joined Bolton Wanderers and, although most of his appearances for the Trotters were from the bench, he proved he could still handle the pace of First Division football. Hugely popular with the fans, he left the Reebok Stadium to join Blackpool and made an appearance in the LDV Vans Trophy Final before, following an injury, he announced his retirement from the game.

MASON Paul David

Midfield

Born: Liverpool, 3 September 1963. Career: Everton; Groningen (Holland); Aberdeen 1988; IPSWICH TOWN 1993; Woodbridge Town.

■ Although he was born in Liverpool, Paul Mason started his career in mainland Europe and continued it in Scotland before entering League football in England with Ipswich 10 years later. He was signed as an associate schoolboy by Everton, but left Goodison without being offered an apprenticeship by the club. After playing non-League football on Merseyside, he went to work in Holland, where he was discovered by Groningen FC when playing for a works side. After five seasons of playing in Dutch football, he signed for Aberdeen for a fee of £200,000 in the summer of 1988. He spent another five years at Pittodrie, winning a Skol Cup-winners' medal in 1989 when he scored both goals in a 2–1 extra-time win over Rangers. Helping the Dons finish runners-up in the League on four occasions, he had scored 37 goals for the Dons in 192 first-team outings when, in the summer of 1993, he joined Ipswich Town for £400,000. He made his debut against Oldham Athletic on the opening day of the 1993–94 season, scoring the club's last goal in a 3–0 win. Although he could play up front, Mason preferred a wide role, which allowed him to cut in looking for the shot. He was the club's top scorer in 1996–97, with 15 League and Cup goals, and although a broken hand followed by an Achilles tendon injury kept him out for most of 1997–98 he did, albeit belatedly, forge a reputation in English football. Though he was told he would be offered a new contract if he proved his fitness – which he seemed to do after scoring a cracking goal in the Worthington Cup tie against Exeter City – the club did a U-turn and he was sent on his way. On leaving Ipswich, he appeared briefly for Woodbridge Town in the FA Vase before moving to Southport, where he runs a hotel.

MATHIE Alexander

Forward

Born: Bathgate, 20 December 1968. Career: Glasgow Celtic 1987; Morton 1991; Port Vale (loan) 1993; Newcastle United 1993; IPSWICH TOWN 1995; Dundee United 1998; Preston North End (loan) 1999; York City 2000; Pickering Town.

■ A product of Parkhead, Alex Mathie only appeared rarely for Celtic in senior action and moved to Morton in search of regular football. There he became a prolific scorer and was top goal-getter in his two seasons, netting over 40 times. The Cappielow Park club eventually cashed in when Newcastle United took an interest, selling Mathie to the Magpies for a fee of £285,000. Unable to break into the Newcastle side on a regular basis, he had a spell on loan to Port Vale before Ipswich paid £500,000 for his services in February 1995. He scored on his debut against Southampton and, in his first full season, his partnership with Ian Marshall blossomed. Mathie scored in each of Town's first four games, including a brace against Stoke City and a hat-trick in a 3–0 win over the eventual champions, Sunderland. Following Marshall's departure, Mathie found that the burden of goalscoring fell heavily on his shoulders. He bore it well, scoring nine goals in 17 games, including doubles against Oldham, Fulham and Crystal Palace, until a dislocated shoulder at the Palace game ended his season prematurely in October. Tests proved that he needed operations on both shoulders, but the nature of things meant that they could not be carried out individually. On 21 February 1998, Alex Mathie ensured he had a place in Ipswich folklore when he scored a first-half hat-trick against Norwich City. Despite forming a lethal and exciting partnership with David Johnson, which helped spark Ipswich's revival, he often found himself the odd man out as George Burley juggled his three strikers around. Finding himself permanently on the bench, Mathie opted for a return to Scotland with Dundee United, where he knew he would almost certainly be guaranteed first-team football. He was later loaned to Preston North End, where his performances went a long way towards helping the Lilywhites win the Second Division Championship. On leaving Tannadice he returned to Football League action with York City, but his early progress at Bootham Crescent was hampered by a spate of injuries and after being released he linked up with Northern Counties East outfit Pickering Town.

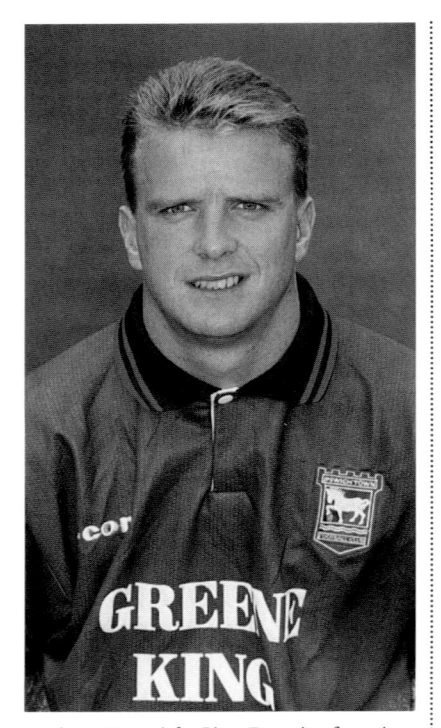

MEADE Raphael Joseph

Forward

Born: Islington, 22 November 1962. Career: Arsenal 1988; Sporting Club Lisbon (Portugal); Dundee United; Luton Town 1989; BK Odense (Denmark); IPSWICH TOWN 1990; BK Odense; Plymouth Argyle 1991; Brighton & Hove Albion 1991; Dover; Singapore; Brighton & Hove Albion 1994.

■ Meade's prolific goalscoring feats for the youth and reserve teams at Arsenal earned him his League debut for the Gunners in October 1981, when he scored the only goal of the game against Manchester City. He went on to play in 16 games that season, but a cartilage operation forced him to miss the entire 1982–83 season. In December 1983 he hit a rich vein of form when scoring a hat-trick against Watford and nine days later two in a 4–2 victory at Tottenham Hotspur. The following season, with Woodcock, Mariner and Nicholas operating in the striking positions, his first-team chances were limited and he moved to Sporting Club Lisbon for £60,000. Over the following eight years, Meade roamed from country to country at will. He played in Scotland for Dundee United, in England for Luton, Ipswich (for whom he made just a single appearance from the bench), he had two spells in Denmark with BK Odense and then came back to England to play for Plymouth, Brighton and Dover as well as playing in Singapore.

MIDGLEY Neil Alan

Forward

Born: Cambridge, 21 October 1978. Career: IPSWICH TOWN 1997; Luton Town (loan) 1999; Kidderminster Harriers (loan) 2000; Barnet 2001.

■ Unable to force his way into the Ipswich side, Neil Midgley joined Luton Town on a two-month loan in September 1999 and made his League debut as a Luton player, scoring three goals in 10 games. A busy worker in attack, he made his Ipswich debut the following December against West Bromwich Albion as a substitute and scored with a fine far-post header. After another couple of outings from the bench, he made his first full start at Port Vale, but found his opportunities limited when Marcus Stewart joined the Tractor Boys. Midgley then went on loan to Kidderminster Harriers, scoring some vital goals that helped them clinch the Conference title. He later signed for Barnet, but a combination of a lack of match fitness and the Bees' relegation problems meant that he received few opportunities. Following the club's relegation to the Conference, he was placed on the open to offers list.

MILLER John Tony

Winger

Born: Ipswich, 21 September 1950. Career: IPSWICH TOWN 1968; Norwich City 1974; Mansfield Town 1976; Port Vale 1980; Oakham United; Selston.

■ An exciting right-winger who could provide pinpoint crosses, Miller worked his way up through the ranks at Portman Road before making his debut in a goalless draw against

Coventry City in March 1969. He was never an automatic choice for Ipswich, playing in 60 League and Cup games in five seasons with the club, and in October 1974 he was allowed to join Norwich City. In his first season at Carrow Road he helped the Canaries win promotion at the first attempt following relegation from the First Division the previous season. Miller later played for Mansfield Town for four seasons, scoring 14 goals in 113 League appearances and helping them win the Third Division Championship in his first season at Field Mill. His last League club was Port Vale where, after making an immediate impact, a knee injury forced his retirement from the first-class game, though he later made a comeback with Oakham United and then Selston.

MILLER Thomas William
Midfield

Born: Easington, 8 January 1979. Career: Hartlepool United 1997; IPSWICH TOWN 2001; Sunderland 2005.

■ Voted Hartlepool United's Young Player of the Year for 1996–97, Miller eventually gained a regular first-team place towards the end of the following season. His performances began to attract the attention of the bigger clubs, particularly Crystal Palace, but Miller indicated his willingness to learn the game at Victoria Park by signing a new contract that would keep him at the club until the end of the 2000–01 season. During the early part of the 1999–2000 season, Miller proved himself a more than useful goalscorer, netting a hat-trick against Barnet and finishing the season as the club's leading scorer with 16 goals. He was recognised by his fellow professionals with a place in the PFA Division Three team. He was ever present for Hartlepool in 2000–01, finished the season as top goalscorer in all competitions and was named in the PFA Division Three team for the second year in a row. After previously being on Ipswich's books as a schoolboy, he returned to Portman Road for a substantial fee. Initially his first-team opportunities were limited as he adjusted to the standards required in the Premiership. He had to wait until Easter Monday 2002 for his full Premiership debut against Chelsea and he took full advantage with a Man of the Match performance. He eventually won a regular place in the starting line up in 2002–03, thriving under Joe Royle's influence. Playing alongside Jim Magilton, he operated from box to box but, keen to support the attack, he notched up 10 goals during the campaign. Injuries hampered his progress the following season, but in 2004–05 he was able to stay injury-free and featured in most games for the club. He finished the season with 13 Championship goals and maintained his record of never having missed a penalty. Released in the close season of 2005 after Ipswich failed in their bid for promotion to the Premiership via the Play-offs, Miller turned down offers from Celtic, Wigan, Leeds and Crystal Palace to join his boyhood heroes, Sunderland. However, he failed to show his true form as the Black Cats were relegated after a disastrous season.

MILLS Michael Denis
Full-back

Born: Godalming, 4 January 1949. Career: Portsmouth; IPSWICH TOWN 1966; Southampton 1982; Stoke City 1985.

■ Mick Mills began his career with Portsmouth but was released when the Fratton Park club abandoned their youth policy. Ipswich Town snapped him up and it was not long before he made his League debut, aged 17 years 123 days, against Wolverhampton Wanderers, a match Town won 5–2. Just over three years later, he became the first player in Ipswich history to make 100 League appearances before his 21st birthday. Following Bill Baxter's departure midway through the 1970–71 season, Mills was appointed the club captain and over the next 12 years led the Blues by example. It was 1973, when his name was extremely well-known around England's big grounds as a full-back or midfield player of non-stop momentum and perception, that he was called up to the national side for the first time when he played against Yugoslavia. It was a personal honour when he captained his country for the first time against Wales at Cardiff in 1978, but his proudest moment was to lead England against the challenge of Switzerland in a World Cup eliminator at Wembley in 1980. An unobtrusive yet invaluable part of the England defensive set-up, Mills won 42 caps, his last coming against Spain in 1982. For Ipswich, he was ever present in four successive seasons from 1972–73, appearing in 198 consecutive League games. Known as 'Captain Fantastic' the highlights of his career were the winning of the FA Cup in 1978 when Arsenal were beaten 1–0 and the defeat of AZ67 Alkmaar in the UEFA

Mick Mills

Cup Final in 1980–81. Mills, who appeared in 741 first-team games – a club record – left Portman Road in November 1982 to join Southampton for a fee of £50,000. He soon fitted into the Saints' style of play and over the next three seasons played in 121 League and Cup games, including being ever present in 1984–85 when the club finished fifth in the First Division. In the summer of 1985 he moved to Stoke City as player-manager, but after a number of mediocre seasons he was replaced by Alan Ball, whom he had recently appointed as his assistant. He also managed Colchester United and had a spell as assistant manager at Coventry City before becoming first-team coach at both Sheffield Wednesday and Birmingham City.

MILLWARD Horace Douglas

Inside-forward

Born: Sheffield, 10 August 1931.
Died: United States, December 2000.
Career: Doncaster Rovers; Southampton 1952; IPSWICH TOWN 1955.

■ Unable to make the grade with Southampton, Doug Millward joined Ipswich Town and made his debut in the East Anglian derby game against Norwich City in April 1956, a match the Canaries won 3–2. The following season, he scored nine goals in 35 games as Town won the Third Division South Championship, but created many of Ted Phillips's 41 strikes. Millward missed very few games and for two years from September 1956 he missed just two matches. Millward's only hat-trick for the club came in January 1960 when Ipswich beat Leyton Orient 6–3, while the following season he netted some vital goals – six in 19 games – as Town won the Second Division title. He did not appear in any of the games when the club won the League Championship in 1961–62, but made three top-flight appearances the following season before parting company with the club. After managing Poole Town, he took over the reins at St Mirren, becoming in those days a rarity – an English manager in the Scottish League. Millward, who was a qualified FA coach, later moved to the United States, where the anticipated football boom never happened. Instead, he turned his attention to coaching tennis. In December 2000, Millward sadly died in the United States and his ashes were brought back to England and scattered over the Solent, where the talented and competitive player had been involved in an air-sea rescue operation while on National Service.

MILTON Simon Charles

Midfield

Born: Fulham, 23 August 1963.
Career: Bury Town; IPSWICH TOWN 1987; Exeter City (loan) 1987; Torquay United (loan) 1988; Braintree Town.

■ Simon Milton was 23 years old when he joined Ipswich Town from local Eastern Counties League club Bury Town in the 1987 close season. He made his League debut while on loan with Exeter City, at home to Stockport County in November 1987, scoring two goals. He was soon back at Portman Road, but another loan spell at Torquay United followed before he returned to Ipswich to play in the club's last six games of the season. In the final match of the campaign he scored the winning goal in a 3–2 win at Bradford City that lifted Town three places in the Second Division to eighth. The following year he had the chance to join rivals Norwich City, but opted for a new deal at Portman Road instead. Over the next few seasons, Milton proved himself capable of scoring explosive goals after bursting through from midfield, even though he was extremely unfortunate with injuries. He also showed his versatility, playing wide on the right, in central midfield and as a ball winner. He was voted the supporters' Player of the Year for 1995–96, but was given a free transfer at the end of 1997–98, which was his testimonial season after scoring 55 goals in 332 first-team games for the Blues. On leaving Portman Road he went to play non-League football for Braintree Town.

MITCHELL Alexander Russell

Full-back

Born: Gourock, 24 May 1918.
Died: 1990.
Career: Bute Athletic; IPSWICH TOWN 1946; Bury Town.

■ Tough-tackling full-back Alex Mitchell was spotted playing in Scottish junior football for Bute Athletic and brought to Portman Road in the summer of 1946. He made his Ipswich debut wearing the number-11 shirt in a 2–1 defeat of Torquay United towards the end of the 1947–48 season. It was his only appearance that season and, after just one more appearance in 1948–49, Mitchell played in 40 of the following season's games, operating in both full-back positions. However, following the signings of Jim Feeney and Len Tyler, Mitchell was released and moved into non-League football with Bury Town.

MITCHELL David John

Centre-forward

Born: Stoke-on-Trent, 24 August 1945.
Career: Port Vale 1964; IPSWICH TOWN 1966.

■ David Mitchell worked his way up through the ranks at Port Vale before making his first-team debut in a League Cup tie against Luton Town in September 1984. He was then selected intermittently the following season. He rarely played in 1965–66 and at the end of that campaign he was given a free transfer and moved to Ipswich Town. He made his debut as a substitute in the East Anglian derby against Norwich City in September 1966, replacing Dave Harper in a 2–1 win for Town. He came off the bench two games later to replace goalscorer Gerry Baker in a 1–1 draw against Bristol City, but they were his only appearances for the club and after a season of reserve-team football he left Portman Road.

MITCHELL Scott Andrew

Full-back

Born: Ely, 2 September 1985.
Career: IPSWICH TOWN 2004.

■ A product of the Ipswich Town Academy, Scott Mitchell is a versatile player who can operate in defence or midfield. He made his first-team bow in 2003–04, making two appearances as a substitute in the games against Derby County (drew 2–2) and Watford (won 4–1). The following season he played his first full game for Ipswich at left-back in the Carling Cup tie with Brentford. Later in the season he played right-back in the FA Cup defeat by Bolton Wanderers. Surprisingly overlooked throughout the entire 2005–06 season, there is talk that he will move north of the border to join Livingston once his contract has expired.

MONCUR John Frederick

Midfield

Born: Stepney, 22 September 1966.
Career: Tottenham Hotspur 1984; Doncaster Rovers (loan) 1986; Cambridge United (loan) 1987; Portsmouth (loan) 1989; Brentford (loan) 1989; IPSWICH TOWN (loan) 1991; Swindon Town 1992; West Ham United 1994.

■ Influenced by his father – one of the backroom staff at Tottenham Hotspur – it came as no surprise when John Moncur junior made his League debut for the White Hart Lane club against Everton in May 1987. He had already acquired League experience during loan spells with Doncaster Rovers and Cambridge United and later had further spells while on loan to Portsmouth, Brentford and Ipswich Town. While with the Portman Road club in October 1991, Moncur made five starts and made an appearance from the bench, but was only on the winning side in his last appearance, as Town beat Wolves 2–1. In March 1992, Glenn Hoddle signed him for Swindon Town for a fee of £80,000. A member of the Robins side that earned promotion to the Premiership, he scored in the crucial Play-off semi-final at Tranmere and was involved in two of the goals in the 4–3 victory over Leicester City in the Play-off Final at Wembley. Despite Swindon finishing bottom of the Premier League in 1993–94, Moncur impressed with his excellent passing skills. He signed for West Ham United in June 1994 for a fee of £900,000, but unfortunately missed the start of the season due to an ankle injury. A player who could not get enough of the ball, he suffered more than his fair share of groin and calf injuries during his time at Upton Park. His tremendous work-rate and combative approach to the game saw him remain an important member of the West Ham squad for a number of seasons, even though he did not feature regularly. He remained a great favourite of the Hammers fans and had appeared in 203 games for the club when he eventually ended his career.

MORAN Douglas Walter
Inside-forward

Born: Musselburgh, 29 July 1934.
Career: Falkirk 1956; IPSWICH TOWN 1961; Dundee United 1964.

■ Doug Moran was a part-timer with Scottish League side Hibernian but, finding himself in competition with Scottish international inside-forward Bobby Johnstone, he opted to join Falkirk on loan. The move was made permanent shortly afterwards and the following year he scored the winning goal in extra-time in the Scottish Cup Final against Kilmarnock. Transferred to Ipswich Town for a fee of £12,000 in the summer of 1961, Moran made his debut for the Portman Road club in a goalless draw against Bolton Wanderers on the opening day of the 1961–62 season. He was an ever present that season as Town went on to win the League Championship, scoring 14 goals including a brace against West Bromwich Albion and creating many more for Ray Crawford and Ted Phillips. In September 1963, Doug Moran netted another brace, this time against Manchester United, but it is not a match he would wish to remember as the Red Devils won 7–2. While with Ipswich, Doug Moran won the Southern Area professional footballers' golf championship and came fifth in the all-England Final. On leaving Portman Road, he returned north of the border to continue his career with Dundee United.

MORGAN Philip Jonathan
Goalkeeper

Born: Stoke-on-Trent, 18 December 1974.
Career: IPSWICH TOWN 1993; Stoke City 1995; Chesterfield (loan) 1996; Halifax Town.

■ England Youth international goalkeeper Philip Morgan was a brave and excellent shot-stopper who waited over two years in the wings before making his Town debut in a 2–0 defeat at Leicester City in 1994–95. Though he had spent a number of occasions on the bench, he was released in the close season and joined Stoke City. Unable to oust Carl Muggleton and Mark Prudhoe, he was loaned out to Chesterfield, where he kept clean sheets in his two appearances. After Billy Mercer's injury cleared up, he returned to the Potteries before later joining Conference side Halifax Town.

MORRIS Peter John
Midfield

Born: Shirebrook, 8 November 1943.
Career: Mansfield Town 1960; IPSWICH TOWN 1968; Norwich City 1974; Mansfield Town 1976; Peterborough United 1979.

■ Peter Morris began his League career with Mansfield Town, where his manager was the legendary Raich Carter. He made his debut for the Stags in February 1961 at Workington when only 17 and a year later he was made captain – the youngest in the club's history. In 1962–63 he helped the Stags win promotion from the Fourth Division and went on to score 50 goals in 287 League games for Mansfield before joining Ipswich Town for a fee of £12,000 in March 1968. He made his debut for the Blues in a 3–2 win over Derby County and played in the last 14 matches of the club's Second Division Championship-winning season. In 1972–73, Ipswich won the Texaco Cup, with Morris scoring both goals in the 2–1 first-leg win over Norwich City at Portman Road. Also that season, his well-judged long passes helped the club finish fourth in the First Division and so qualify for Europe. With young talent such as Beattie and Mills coming through at Portman Road, Morris, who had scored 16 goals in 258 first-team games, left to join rivals Norwich for £60,000. After a couple of seasons at Carrow Road, he turned down manager John Bond's offer of a player-coach position to manage Mansfield Town, where he took his total League appearances for the Field Mill club to 328. He later managed Peterborough United and Southend United. After spells coaching in Saudi Arabia and with Leicester City, he managed Kettering Town, where he gave them four years of FA Cup runs and almost a place in the Football League when they finished runners-up in the Conference in 1988–89.

MORRIS Trevor
Inside-left

Born: Gorslas, 6 September 1920.
Career: West Bromwich Albion 1936; Caerphilly Town; IPSWICH TOWN 1938; Cardiff City 1939.

■ Trevor Morris started out with West Bromwich Albion, but on being unable to break into their League side, left to play Welsh League football for Caerphilly Town. His impressive displays, in which he scored a number of spectacular goals, attracted a number of League clubs, including Ipswich Town, who signed him in the summer of 1938. He spent almost the entire 1938–39 season in the club's reserves, playing in his one and only League game against Bournemouth on the final day of the season – a match that ended goalless. He returned to his native Wales to play for Cardiff City, but his career was interrupted by World War Two. When football resumed after the hostilities, Trevor Morris was appointed secretary to the Welsh FA.

MORROW Samuel

Forward

Born: Derry, 3 March 1985.
Career: IPSWICH TOWN 2002; Boston United (loan) 2003; Hibernian 2004.

■ This young striker made an appearance off the bench for Ipswich in the Carling Cup tie at Notts County, but was unable to establish a regular place in the side. In December 2003, he joined Boston United on loan, but found it difficult to adjust to the pace of Third Division football. He had a couple of appearances as a substitute before returning to Portman Road. Released in the summer of 2004, he went north of the border to play for Hibernian and, although the majority of his 22 appearances were from the bench, he helped the Easter Road club to finish third in the Scottish Premier League.

MOWBRAY Anthony Mark

Centre-half

Born: Saltburn, 22 November 1963.
Career: Middlesbrough 1981; Glasgow Celtic; IPSWICH TOWN 1995.

■ One of Middlesbrough's all-time greatest captains, Tony Mowbray, or 'Mogga', was the linchpin around

Tony Mowbray

which the Boro team was built for more than a decade. A rock at the heart of the Middlesbrough defence, Mowbray stood firm through the liquidation and was a key figure in the club's resurgence under Bruce Rioch. Mowbray had supported Boro as a boy and, after putting pen to paper, he progressed through the ranks to make his debut against Newcastle United in September 1982. Mowbray was a regular throughout the 1980s and an inspirational captain after the liquidation saga of 1986. He was part of the Middlesbrough team that climbed into the First Division in 1987–88 and at the end of the following season he was called up, with Gary Pallister, for an England B tour. Mowbray also had the honour of leading Boro out in the Zenith Data Systems Cup Final at Wembley in March 1990. But Boro's stint in the top flight was short-lived, and after another two years playing Second Division football, Mowbray, who had scored 29 goals in 424 games, decided it was time for a move and made a £1 million switch to Celtic. Injuries then began to play a part as the giant central defender spent periods out of the team at Parkhead and in October 1995 he moved to Ipswich Town for £300,000. He was immediately installed as club captain prior to making his debut at home to Wolves. He took a while to settle in and was not helped by having six different central-defensive partners in as many games. In February 1996 he sustained a nasty groin injury and this kept him out of action for longer than anticipated. When he did return to the side, it coincided with a resurgence in the form of the team, although when the injury flared up again he had to undergo an operation. He had a much better season in 1998–99 when he helped Town equal the club record of 26 clean sheets in a season. Despite his advancing years, he remained a commanding figure at the centre of the Town defence. In the summer of 1999 he was appointed first-team coach at Portman Road, although he retained his registration as a player. He featured strongly in the Play-off Final at Wembley, captaining the club to success over Barnsley and headed home the club's 28th-minute equaliser from a Jim Magilton cross – it was his last appearance in an Ipswich shirt. Then, with Ipswich back in the Premiership, he hung up his boots and turned his attention to coaching Ipswich. He had a brief spell as the club's caretaker manager prior to the appointment of Joe Royle, and went into management himself as boss of Scottish League club Hibernian.

MUHREN Arnold Johannes Hyacinthus

Midfield

Born: Holland, 2 June 1951.
Career: Ajax Amsterdam (Holland); Twente Enschede (Holland); IPSWICH TOWN 1978; Manchester United 1982; Ajax Amsterdam.

■ A classy midfielder, Arnold Muhren began his career with the great Ajax team of the 1970s and was substitute for them in the European Cup Finals of 1972 and 1973, although he never came on in either game. Having learnt his trade at Europe's premier club, he moved to Twente Enschede, where he impressed Ipswich Town's Bobby Robson during a pre-season tour. Robson had to move swiftly, as Ajax were keen to bring him back, but £165,000 was enough to have him move across the Channel and settle in Suffolk. After missing the opening game of the 1978–79 season, he made his first-team debut for the Portman Road club in a 3–0 home defeat by Liverpool, going on to score eight goals in 41 League games. He was a great favourite with the Town fans, but not before the club had altered their style of play. There was now a lot more variety in their approach, with many moves being built up through Muhren in midfield, as well as the club's previous moves which were often based on the long-ball game. Not surprisingly he ended the season as the supporters' choice as Player of the Year. Muhren returned to Holland in 1981 to collect a UEFA Cup-winners' medal with Ipswich, but when his contract at Portman Road expired in the summer of 1982, he moved to Manchester United. The popular Dutchman had scored 29 goals in 214 first-team outings. At the end of his first season at Old Trafford, he helped United to victory in the FA Cup Final replay against Brighton, scoring a second-half penalty. He was hit by injuries towards the end of the 1983–84 season and his demise coincided with the Reds dropping out of the Championship race. Thereafter, he struggled to find a first-team place and in June 1985 he returned to Ajax and appeared in the 1987 European Cup-Winners' Cup Final. He was also in the Dutch side that captured the 1988 European Championship, but announced his retirement from international football after the Final. He then moved into coaching at youth level and with Muhren guiding them, the next generation have a chance of being as good as the last.

MULRANEY Ambrose

Outside-right

Born: Wishaw, 18 May 1916.
Career: Carluke Rovers; Dartford; IPSWICH TOWN 1936; Birmingham City 1945; Shrewsbury Town 1947; Kidderminster Harriers 1948; Aston Villa 1948; Cradley Heath.

■ A fast raiding Scottish winger who could occupy either flank, 'Jock' Mulraney failed to break into the Celtic side and, after a spell with non-League Dartford, he joined Ipswich Town. He made his debut against his former club in a Southern League fixture, going on to help the club win the Championship. He made a

Arnold Muhren

goalscoring Football League debut against Walsall in the club's second game of the 1938–39 season. Mulraney has the distinction of scoring Ipswich Town's first-ever hat-trick in the Football League as Bristol City were beaten 4–0 in April 1939. In March 1940 he went into the RAF and rose to the rank of Flt Sgt PT Instructor. On joining Birmingham, he won a League South Championship medal in 1946 but then played non-League football for Shrewsbury and Kidderminster before returning to League action with Aston Villa. He later ended his involvement with the game following a spell as player-manager of Cradley Heath.

MURCHISON Ronald Angus

Wing-half
Born: Hurlford, 12 February 1927.
Career: Auchterader Primrose; IPSWICH TOWN 1950; Newmarket.

■ Wing-half Ron Murchison spent five seasons at Portman Road in the early 1950s, making 42 League appearances and scoring two goals, both in 1–1 draws against Gillingham – the first in April 1952 and the second in March 1953. The majority of his appearances came in 1951–52, when he played in the last 29 games of the season. With the likes of Harry Baird, Tommy Parker and Neil Myles on the staff, competition for places was tough and in the summer of 1955 Murchison left Ipswich to play non-League football for Newmarket.

MURRAY Antonio

Midfield
Born: Cambridge, 15 September 1984.
Career: IPSWICH TOWN 2002.

■ Another product of the Ipswich Town Academy, Antonio Murray is the son of the former Cambridge United and Brentford left-back Jamie Murray. A promising midfielder, he impressed in the club's reserve side throughout the 2002–03 campaign and was rewarded with his Football League debut as a second-half substitute for Tommy Miller in the last game of the season against Derby County, a match Town won 4–1.

MYLES Neil Thomson

Wing-half
Born: Falkirk, 17 June 1927.
Died: 1993.
Career: Third Lanark; IPSWICH TOWN 1949; Clacton Town.

■ Falkirk-born Neil Myles joined Ipswich Town from Third Lanark in August 1949 but had to wait four months before making his debut. The wait was worthwhile because on his debut on 24 December 1949 he netted two of the Ipswich goals in a 4–4 home draw against Crystal Palace. During his first three seasons with the club, he played in just 20 games, scoring eight goals from a variety of forward positions. He was then converted to wing-half and was ever present over the next two seasons, going on to appear in 110 consecutive League games. When Ipswich won the Third Division South Championship in 1953–54, Myles was a key member of the side, as he was three seasons later when the club won the Championship for a second time. He went on to score 18 goals in 245 League and Cup games for the Blues, making his last appearance at Villa Park in September 1959. At the end of that season, Myles left Portman Road to play non-League football with Clacton Town.

NASH Gerard Thomas

Centre-half/Midfield
Born: Dublin, 11 July 1986.
Career: IPSWICH TOWN 2003; Hartlepool United (loan) 2005; Southend United (loan) 2006.

■ A player who turned down Arsenal and Manchester United to join

Ipswich, Gerard Nash has captained age-groups for the Republic of Ireland from Under-14s to Under-17s. A product of Town's Academy, he made his League bow at the age of 17 as a substitute in the 6–1 win over Burnley in October 2003 and was on the bench a further eight times during the 2003–04 campaign. Nash suffered a knee injury in training a couple of months after his debut which scans revealed as cruciate ligament damage.

He was forced to undergo major surgery on the knee for the second time in three years but recovered to make a number of appearances for the reserves prior to going out on loan, first with Hartlepool United and then, towards the end of the campaign, with Southend United. Popular around the club, Town fans will be hoping he has got over the worst and can help them regain their place in the Premiership.

NAYLOR Richard Alan

Centre-half
Born: Leeds, 28 February 1977.
Career: IPSWICH TOWN 1995; Millwall (loan) 2002; Barnsley (loan) 2002.

■ Originally a central defender when he first joined Ipswich as a youngster, Naylor was later played up front in the youth team when there was a shortage of strikers. He certainly made his presence felt in 1996–97, making his full debut at Birmingham and scoring his first goal in the Coca-Cola Cup tie against Gillingham. Knee problems and the fantastic form of David Johnson, Alex Mathie and Jamie Scowcroft meant that he was restricted to substitute appearances the following season. Even though he was still down the pecking order in 1998–99, when he did get a chance he took it with both hands. He scored a last-minute winner in the televised game with Sheffield United and then notched a double in the next match against Portsmouth. He started the following season as the club's first-choice striker and indeed scored Town's first goal of the campaign against Nottingham Forest. Midway through the season, following George Burley's change of tactics, Naylor found himself back on the bench. However, he saved his best for the Play-off Final at Wembley. Replacing the injured Johnson, he put Ipswich into the lead when he ran on to Stewart's flick and beat the goalkeeper with a right-foot shot. He was also involved in the build-up to Stewart's goal, holding the ball up on the edge of the box then passing to Jamie Clapham, who made the cross, and in injury time he put the ball through for Martyn Reuser to score the goal that sealed the win. Summer operations on both knees meant that he missed much of the 2000–01 season – especially when it was discovered that he had been playing with a broken femur. There followed another campaign of injuries and increased competition for places and with loan spells at Millwall and Barnsley, there was little opportunity to put together a first-team run at Ipswich. However, following the appointment of Joe Royle, it was decided that Naylor had the potential to be a better central defender than a striker and he was given a run in this position towards the end of the 2002–03 season. The following season was one of his best in Town's colours, as he not only contributed some vital goals at set pieces, but also showed his courage by not being afraid to go in where it hurts. 'Bam Bam' won the John Kerridge Award in 2004–05 for the most improved player at the club, after he was the only Ipswich player to appear in all 46 Championship games. Captaining the side in the absence of Jason De Vos and Jim Magilton, he has now taken his total of first-team appearances for Ipswich to over 300.

NEILSON Thomas

Half-back
Born: Armadale, 28 July 1922.
Career: Heart of Midlothian; IPSWICH TOWN 1948.

■ After a couple of seasons playing Scottish League football for Heart of Midlothian, tough-tackling half-back Tommy Neilson joined Ipswich Town in the summer of 1948. He played for a season in the club's reserves before making his Football League debut in a 2–0 defeat at Bristol City in April

1949. It was his only League appearance though he did play in a couple of other games, his last against Norwich City in the Norfolk Jubilee Cup a month later, a match the Canaries won 1–0.

NELSON Andrew Nesbitt

Centre-half

Born: Silvertown, 5 July 1935.
Career: West Ham United 1953; IPSWICH TOWN 1959; Leyton Orient 1964; Plymouth Argyle 1965.

■ Andy Nelson's displays for the London and Essex youth sides persuaded West Ham United to offer him professional terms in 1953. After nearly six years as a part-timer at Upton Park, in which he made just 15 League appearances due to the fine form of Ken Brown, he moved to Ipswich Town for £8,000. He made his first-team debut in a disastrous 4–1 home defeat by Huddersfield Town on the opening day of the 1959–60 season and went on to be one of four ever presents in a side that finished 11th in the Second Division. The following season he was captain of the Town side that scored 100 goals in winning the Second Division Championship and in 1961–62 was again ever present in the Ipswich team that won the League Championship. Although he never scored a goal for the Blues, the popular centre-half made 215 League and Cup appearances before joining Leyton Orient in September 1964. He had one season at Brisbane Road before moving to Plymouth Argyle for a fee of £4,000 in October 1965. He was just one short of 100 appearances for the Devon club when he ended his playing career. On hanging up his boots, he managed both Gillingham and Charlton Athletic before subsequently working for the Addicks' commercial department. On ending his involvement with the game, he emigrated to Spain where he now plays bowls to a very high standard.

NEVILLE Christopher William

Goalkeeper

Born: Downham Market, 22 October 1970.
Career: IPSWICH TOWN 1989.

■ Goalkeeper Chris Neville was a youth trainee with the Portman Road club when an injury to Ipswich's first-choice 'keeper Craig Forrest forced the club to throw the youngster in at the deep end for the game at West Bromwich Albion. He had a very satisfactory debut in a game Town won 3–1. It was his only appearance at League level and he drifted into the local non-League scene.

NEWMAN Eric Ivan Alfred

Goalkeeper

Born: Romford, 24 November 1924.
Died: 1971.
Career: Romford; Arsenal 1946; IPSWICH TOWN 1950; Chelmsford City.

■ Signed by Arsenal from non-League Romford, goalkeeper Eric Newman spent four years at Highbury without playing a League game due to the fine form of Welsh international Jack Kelsey. He joined Ipswich in September 1950 and for a couple of seasons understudied Mick Burns and Jack Parry. Following his debut in a 2–1 defeat at Bournemouth in September 1952, he made 18 appearances. He performed most creditably, with the exception of the home game against Bristol Rovers, when he was deemed responsible for all of the goals in a 5–1 defeat. At the end of that season, he decided there was no future for him at Portman Road and he left to play for Chelmsford City.

NIVEN Stuart Thomas

Midfield

Born: Glasgow, 24 December 1978.
Career: IPSWICH TOWN 1996; Barnet 2000.

■ Stuart Niven made his Ipswich Town debut at Sheffield United in September 1996 and his home debut in front of the BSkyB cameras against Charlton Athletic two games later. After putting in two solid displays, he was called up to the Scotland Under-18 side and played against teammate Keiron Dyer when England played Scotland. An attacking midfielder, he was unable to break into the Ipswich side and spent the next three seasons in the club's reserves until he joined Third Division Barnet in September 2000. He had a memorable start to senior football at Underhill, scoring in the first minute of their trip to Carlisle United – the goal giving the Bees a 1–0 win. Later his form dipped and, following the club's relegation to the Conference, he was placed on the open to offers list but remained with the club.

NORFOLK Lee Richard

Midfield

Born: New Zealand, 17 October 1975.
Career: IPSWICH TOWN 1994; Bishop's Stortford; Sudbury Wanderers.

■ A New Zealand-born midfielder who played with great determination, Norfolk made his Ipswich debut as a substitute against Southampton in 1994–95 and created the second goal in a 2–1 win with a perfect cross for Lee Chapman to head home. He had an unfortunate follow-up season, making just one Anglo-Italian Cup appearance at home to Salernitana due to hectic competition for midfield places at the club. Retained for another season, he could not add to his number of first-team appearances and moved into non-League football with Bishop's Stortford and later Sudbury Wanderers.

O'BRIEN Joseph
Outside-left

Born: Dublin, 9 May 1924.
Career: Dundalk; Luton Town 1946; IPSWICH TOWN 1949.

■ Flying winger Joe O'Brien played his early football in the League of Ireland for Dundalk and it was his impressive performances in the first season after World War Two that alerted Luton Town. He made his debut for the Hatters in a 2–1 home win over Doncaster Rovers in December 1946 and, in a run of eight games, he scored three goals. One of these came in a 6–1 defeat of Leeds United, when the Irish-born winger also had a hand in all of his side's goals. At the end of the following season O'Brien, who could not force his way into the Luton side on a regular basis, left to join Ipswich. He scored on his debut against Bournemouth on the opening day of the 1949–50 season, going on to score 11 goals in 41 games, including a brace against Bristol City in a match Town lost 4–2. He started the following season as the club's first-choice number-11, but later lost his place to Jimmy Roberts and parted company with the Portman Road club.

O'CALLAGHAN Kevin
Left-winger

Born: Dagenham, 19 October 1961.
Career: Millwall 1978; IPSWICH TOWN 1980; Portsmouth 1985; Millwall 1987; Southend United 1991.

■ After joining Millwall as an apprentice in 1977, Kevin O'Callaghan went on to appear for four League clubs. But undoubtedly the most famous side he appeared in was the one which included Pelé, Ossie Ardiles, John Wark, Bobby Moore and Sylvester Stallone – in the box office hit *Escape to Victory*, when he volunteered to have his arm broken so that Sylvester 'Hatch' Stallone could be freed from isolation. At Millwall he was a member of the Lion's FA Youth Cup-winning side and he had played in just 20 League games when, in January 1980, the Republic of Ireland international was transferred to Ipswich Town for a club record £250,000. During his five years at Portman Road, O'Callaghan helped the club to runners'-up spot in Division One, the UEFA Cup Final in 1980–81 and second place in the First Division the following season. He made 115 top-flight appearances, though 43 were started from the dugout. In January 1985 he joined Portsmouth on a month's loan. Two months later the move became permanent when Pompey paid Ipswich £90,000 for the player. In 1986–87, his final season at Fratton Park, he helped the club complete a remarkable decade by winning promotion to Division One, having been in Division Four in 1979–80. He returned to Millwall for a second spell, but his time there was blighted by injury and discord after he had won a Second Division Championship medal in his first season back. After trying to shake off a mystery knee problem, and following a bust-up with manager Bruce Rioch, he left to end his career with Southend United.

O'DONNELL Christopher
Defender

Born: Newcastle-upon-Tyne, 26 May 1968.
Career: IPSWICH TOWN 1985; Northampton Town (loan) 1988; Leeds United 1989; Exeter City 1991; Gateshead.

■ A stocky, red-haired defender, Chris O'Donnell joined Ipswich as a trainee, making his debut in a 1–1 draw against Sunderland in September 1986. He went on to make 10 appearances that season, but then lost his place in the side and after a few more appearances and a loan spell with Northampton Town, he joined Leeds United. His only first-team action at Elland Road was a one-match appearance as a substitute for Jim Beglin against Hull City. He then switched to Exeter City, but made only a couple of appearances before moving into non-League football in his native North East with Gateshead.

O'MAHONEY Matthew Augustine

Centre-half

Born: Kilkenny, 19 January 1913.
Died: 1992.
Career: Hoylake; Southport 1935; Wolverhampton Wanderers 1935; Newport County 1936; Bristol Rovers 1936; IPSWICH TOWN 1939; Yarmouth Town.

■ Capped by both the Republic of Ireland and Northern Ireland, centre-half Matt O'Mahoney started his League career with Southport, where his impressive performances alerted a number of leading clubs. It was Wolverhampton Wanderers who won the race for his signature, but injuries and a loss of form at Molineux saw him switch to Newport County. His stay at Somerton Park was brief and in the summer of 1936 he joined Bristol Rovers. Despite the club struggling in the lower reaches of the Third Division South, O'Mahoney was the club's most consistent player and his displays at the heart of the Rovers defence saw him win full international honours – six caps for the Republic and a single appearance for Northern Ireland. Ipswich signed him in the summer of 1939 and, although his League career was then put on hold, he was the club's first-choice when League football resumed in 1946–47. In that first season of peacetime football, O'Mahoney missed just the last two games of the campaign, scoring four goals, the last in a 4–3 defeat against Mansfield Town. After playing in just a handful of games the following season he was back to his best form in 1948–49, but an injury in the 2–1 home defeat at the hands of Norwich City in October 1948 forced him to quit the first-class game. He later played non-League football for Yarmouth Town.

O'ROURKE John

Centre-forward

Born: Northampton, 1 February 1945.
Career: Arsenal; Chelsea 1962; Luton Town 1963; Middlesbrough 1966; IPSWICH TOWN 1968; Coventry City 1969; Queen's Park Rangers 1971; Bournemouth 1974.

■ After playing as an amateur with both Arsenal and Chelsea, John O'Rourke joined Luton Town. A former England Youth international, he made his Hatters debut against Reading in December 1963, keeping his place in the side for the remainder of that season and scoring a remarkable 22 goals in 23 games. That total included four goals in a 6–2 win at Brentford and a hat-trick in a 4–2 defeat of Bristol Rovers. Injuries hampered his progress the following season, but in 1965–66 O'Rourke netted 32 goals in 40 games, including hat-tricks in the wins over Doncaster Rovers, Crewe Alexandra, Chester and Rochdale. At the end of the season O'Rourke, who had scored 66 goals in 90 first-team outings, joined Middlesbrough. Forming a formidable strike partnership with Arthur Horsfield, O'Rourke scored 30 goals in 43 games to help Boro win promotion to the Second Division. At the end of the season, O'Rourke won international recognition when he was selected for the England Under-23 side against Turkey in Ankara where, not surprisingly, he scored one of the England goals. He went on to score 42 goals in 72 games for Boro when Ipswich Town manager Bobby Robson took him to Portman Road and First Division football. He scored twice on his Town debut in a 4–2 defeat of Cardiff City. O'Rourke scored six goals in his first four games, including another double at Bolton. He ended the season with 12 goals in 15 games, helping Ipswich win the Second Division Championship. The following season of First Division football saw O'Rourke finish the campaign as joint top scorer in the League with Ray Crawford, both players netting 16 times. He lost his goalscoring touch in the first half of the 1969–70 season and was allowed to join Coventry City. He later helped Queen's Park Rangers win promotion to the First Division before seeing out his career with Bournemouth. A prolific scorer wherever he played, John O'Rourke netted 165 goals in 327 games for his six League clubs.

OSBORNE Roger Charles
Midfield
Born: Otley, 9 March 1950.
Career: Grundisburgh; IPSWICH TOWN 1971; Colchester United 1981.

■ One of the game's unsung heroes, Roger Osborne made his debut in a 2–0 home win over Wolverhampton Wanderers in October 1973 but then had to wait until the 1975–76 season before establishing himself as a first-team regular at Portman Road when he appeared in 36 games as Town finished sixth in the First Division. Although never a prolific scorer – finding the net just 10 times in 149 appearances – his goal that gave Ipswich a 1–0 FA Cup Final win over Arsenal in 1978 will always endear him to Town fans. It came in the 77th minute as Geddis's cross was cut out by Arsenal centre-half Willie Young, only for the ball to run loose to Roger Osborne who hit home a left-foot shot out of the reach of the Gunners' Irish international 'keeper Pat Jennings. The excitement of scoring proved too much for Osborne and he was replaced immediately by Mick Lambert. Sadly, Osborne missed the entire 1978–79 season with a knee injury and although he made a handful of appearances over the next couple of seasons, his Portman Road career was over and in February 1981, the club's goalscoring hero left to join Colchester United for a fee of £25,000. During his eight seasons at Ipswich, he showed his versatility and ability to man mark the opposing team's top player. There is no better example than when he completely marked Johann Cruyff out of the game in a 3–0 home win over Barcelona in the 1977–78 UEFA Cup. He went on to play in 206 League matches for the Layer Road club before leaving the first-class game.

OSMAN Russell Charles
Centre-half
Born: Ilkeston, 14 February 1959.
Career: IPSWICH TOWN 1976; Leicester City 1985; Southampton 1988.

■ Russell Osman, the son of Rex who played a couple of League games for Derby County in the 1953–54 season, began his career with Ipswich Town. Under the managership of Bobby Robson, he formed an excellent central defensive partnership with Terry Butcher. In 1975 he won an FA Youth Cup-winners' medal though he had to wait until September 1977 before making his first-team debut in a 1–0 home win over Chelsea. He was unlucky, having played in 28 games and three cup ties in 1977–78, not to make an appearance in the FA Cup Final victory over Arsenal. In May 1980 he won the first of 11 full international caps for England when he played against Australia and made his last appearance for his country against Denmark in a European Championship match in September 1983. He twice went close to a League Championship medal – as the club finished runners-up in the First Division in 1980–81 and 1981–82. He also helped them win the UEFA Cup in 1981 when they beat AZ67 Alkmaar 5–4 on aggregate. Osman was ever present in the seasons of 1979–80 and 1980–81 and had played in 385 first-team games for the club when he left Portman Road in the summer of 1985 to join Leicester City for a fee of £240,000. He made 108 League appearances for the then Filbert Street club before signing for Southampton for £325,000 in June 1988. Osman's first managerial role was with Bristol City where he was initially caretaker manager but in 1994 he lost his job. He became manager of Cardiff City in November 1996 but midway through the following season, he was replaced by Frank Burrows. After a spell back at Ashton Gate as Bristol City's coach, he was joint manager of Bristol Rovers before trying his hand at media work, both radio and television.

OVERTON Paul Henry

Goalkeeper

Born: Ely, 18 April 1961.
Career: IPSWICH TOWN 1978; Peterborough United 1979; Northampton Town 1980.

■ Paul Overton will probably not want to remember his one and only Football League appearance. Replacing the injured Paul Cooper for the game at Aston Villa in April 1978, he conceded six goals as the Midlands club ran out winners 6–1. He remained at Portman Road for another season but due to Cooper's consistency and ability to stay injury-free he was not called upon again. He left to play for Peterborough United and later had a spell with Northampton Town but at both clubs he did not make a single appearance in their League sides.

OWEN Aled Watkin

Winger

Born: Caeysgawen, 7 January 1934.
Career: Bangor City; Tottenham Hotspur 1953; IPSWICH TOWN 1958; Wrexham 1963; Holyhead Town.

■ Having impressed with non-League Bangor City, winger Aled Owen was signed by Tottenham Hotspur in September 1953. Though he impressed in a friendly against Hibernian during the early part of the 1953–54 season, he had to wait until the end of the campaign for is lone League game for the North London club. He spent almost five years at White Hart Lane, playing for the reserve and A teams without seriously challenging for a place in the first team. He was transferred to Ipswich Town in the summer of 1958 and made his debut at Sunderland in the 1958–59 season. The following season was his best at Portman Road, the winger scoring twice in 18 appearances. He made eight appearances in the club's Second Division Championship-winning season whilst his solitary appearance in the League Championship-winning campaign of 1961–62 was against Leicester City when he provided the cross for Ray Crawford to score the game's only goal. He ended his first-class career with a few appearances for Wrexham before playing non-League football for Holyhead Town.

PALMER Stephen Leonard

Midfield

Born: Brighton, 31 March 1968.
Career: Cambridge University; IPSWICH TOWN 1989; Watford 1995; Queen's Park Rangers 2001; MK Dons 2004.

■ One of the very few footballers who have come into professional soccer from Cambridge University, Steve Palmer signed for Ipswich Town in the 1989 close season following an impressive display in the Varsity match and ironically made his Football League debut at Oxford United in September 1989. He only appeared in a couple more matches that season but in 1990–91 after a long period on the bench, he was given an extended run in the side. Still not a regular in 1991–92, though he did play a part in

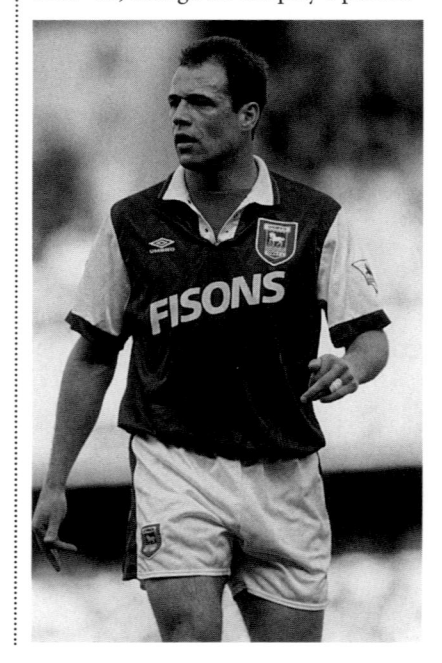

Ipswich's Second Division Championship campaign as deputy for Paul Goddard, he was one of a number of players to suffer from injuries the following season when he needed two operations on a thigh problem. In September 1995, Watford paid £135,000 to take him to Vicarage Road and he soon became one of the mainstays of the side. His versatility showed when in 1997–98 he actually started a League match in every shirt from number-one to 14 during the campaign – a unique feat which required only a little help from the manager. With promotion assured as Second Division champions, he started the home match against Bournemouth in goal, keeping a clean sheet for all of 10 seconds before changing places with regular 'keeper Alex Chamberlain! Voted the club's Player of the Year in 1998–99, he was an ever present the following season and continued to serve Watford well until the end of the 2000–01 season when after appearing in 272 games he joined Queen's Park Rangers. Immediately appointed captain, he was the club's only ever present in seasons 2001–02 and 2002–03, going on to play in 101 consecutive League games. Released in the summer of 2004 he joined the MK Dons where he reverted to mainly bench and coaching duties.

PARKER Stanley Frederick

Inside-forward

Born: Worksop, 31 July 1920.
Died: 14 November 1994.
Career: Worksop LBOB; IPSWICH TOWN 1946; Norwich City 1951.

■ After scoring on his League debut in a 2–1 win over Port Vale in November 1946, inside-forward Stan Parker found the net three times in his first four games and ended the campaign with 10 goals in his 27 appearances. His total of nine goals in 1947–48 included three doubles in the games against Notts County (2–0) Norwich City (5–1) and Watford (3–2), while the following season he did not play in as many games but had his best season to date in terms of goals scored – 11 in 22 matches. In 1949–50, Parker was Town's leading scorer with 13 goals but the following season he fell out of favour and spent most of the campaign in the reserves. In the summer of 1951, he opted to leave Portman Road and try his luck with the club's main rivals, Norwich City, but though he spent a season at Carrow Road, he failed to break into the Canaries' League side.

PARKER Thomas Robertson

Inside-forward

Born: Hartlepool, 13 February 1924.
Died: 18 March 1996.
Career: IPSWICH TOWN 1946.

■ Tommy Parker 'guested' for the club in the 1945–46 season when he was in the Royal Navy at Shotley and in the 12 games he played, scored three goals – including two in his first game in a 3–2 defeat against Watford. He made his Football League debut in the game against Norwich City in September 1946, scoring two goals in a 5–0 win for the Portman Road club and ended the season with 11 goals in 40 games. Having established himself in the Ipswich side, Parker missed just one game in each of seasons 1950–51, 1951–52 and 1952–53 before being an ever present in 1953–54 when the club won the Third Division South Championship. Although he scored his fair share of goals, his most prolific term for the club was 1955–56 when he broke the club's scoring record with 30 goals in the League and another in the FA Cup. His only hat-trick that campaign came in a 6–2 home win over Swindon Town. Remarkably, Parker lost his first-team place to Ted Phillips the following season and the Leiston-born forward smashed Parker's record with 41 League goals and five more in the FA Cup. Parker, who had scored 95 goals in 475 outings – the club appearance record until overhauled by Mick Mills – left Portman Road at the end of that season before returning in 1965 to take charge of the club's Development Association. He finally retired some 20 years later, receiving a watch and a commemorative certificate to mark his loyal service to Ipswich Town.

PARKES Phillip Benjamin Neil Frederick

Goalkeeper

Born: Sedgley, 8 August 1950.
Career: Walsall 1968; Queen's Park Rangers 1970; West Ham United 1979; IPSWICH TOWN 1990.

■ Goalkeeper Phil Parkes began his career with Walsall before moving to Queen's Park Rangers in the summer of 1970. He stayed with the Loftus Road club for eight seasons, his performances helping the club win promotion to the First Division in 1974–75 and then the following season, runners'-up spot in the top flight behind Liverpool. Parkes, who represented England at Under-21 and Under-23 level won his one and only international cap in April 1974 when he kept a clean sheet in a goalless draw against Portugal. In February 1979,

Parkes moved to West Ham United for a fee of £525,000, at the time the highest fee ever paid for a goalkeeper. In May 1980 he won an FA Cup-winners' medal as the Hammers beat Arsenal 1–0 and was back at Wembley in March 1981 for the League Cup Final against Liverpool which the club lost after a replay. In 12 seasons at Upton Park, Parkes made 436 appearances before giving way to Czech international Ludek Miklosko. In the summer of 1990 he followed former West Ham boss John Lyall to Portman Road where he was understudy to Craig Forrest. After all realistic hopes of making the Play-offs disappeared, Parkes played in three games of that 1990–91 season, with Town beating Leicester City 3–2 on his debut. On leaving Ipswich, Parkes returned to Loftus Road as Queen's Park Rangers goalkeeping coach.

PARKIN Samuel

Forward

Born: Roehampton, 14 March 1981.
Career: Chelsea 1998; Millwall (loan) 2000; Wycombe Wanderers (loan) 2000; Oldham Athletic (loan) 2001; Northampton Town (loan) 2001; Swindon Town 2002; IPSWICH TOWN 2005.

■ Sam Parkin started his career with Chelsea, progressing through the youth ranks and was on the fringes of the first team on occasions. He joined Millwall on loan and in what was his Football League debut scored twice against Oxford United. Having scored four goals in five games for the Lions, he went on loan again, this time to Wycombe Wanderers where he played an important role in the Chairboys' FA Cup campaign. Later that season he had another spell on loan, this time at Oldham where he made a great start, scoring in each of his first three games. He spent the whole of the 2001–02 season on loan at Northampton Town and featured regularly for the Cobblers throughout the campaign. In the 2002 close season, Parkin joined Andy King's Swindon Town and in his first season at the County Ground he netted 26 goals, starting with a hat-trick against Barnsley on the opening day of the season. Tall, useful in the air and with two good feet, he quite understandably romped away with the Player of the Year award. He enjoyed another fine season with the Wiltshire club in 2003–04 before weighing in with another 20–plus haul of goals for Swindon the following season. Voted again as the club's Player of the Year, he had scored 73 goals in 142 games for the Robins when Joe Royle swooped to sign him on a four-year deal in the face of competition from Crewe, Norwich and Watford. He made his debut against Cardiff City and though a target for the boo-boys, he netted both Town's goals in a 2–0 win at Leeds United and despite 20 stitches in a head wound he returned to score the winner at Millwall. Sidelined for part of the season with a broken ankle, Town fans will be hoping he can rediscover the goalscoring prowess he displayed whilst with Swindon.

PARKIN Thomas Aichison

Midfield

Born: Gateshead, 1 February 1957.
Career: IPSWICH TOWN 1973; Grimsby Town (loan) 1976; Peterborough United (loan) 1976.

■ Midfielder Tommy Parkin was a member of the Ipswich Town youth team that won the FA Youth Cup in 1973, a side that also contained Robin Turner, George Burley and Eric Gates. He had been spotted by Bobby Ferguson, then the club's youth coach, while playing for St Mary's Boys Club in Newcastle. He made his first-team debut in the FA Cup third-round tie at Cardiff City in January 1978 and over the next nine seasons or so became an important squad member at Portman Road. He can certainly look back on a remarkable full debut for Town, coming into the midfield in the 1978 FA Charity Shield defeat at the hands of Nottingham Forest at Wembley, when he came close to scoring with a great early shot that was brilliantly saved by Peter Shilton. Versatility was always an important part of his contribution to the side and besides right-back and midfield in the first team, he also played at left-back and up front for the reserves. His only time away from Portman Road were spells on loan at Grimsby Town and Peterborough United. A player who showed great loyalty to the club, he is a proud holder of a UEFA Cup-winners' medal – he was on the substitutes' bench in Amsterdam when Town beat AZ67 Alkmaar.

PARRY Brinley John (Jack)

Goalkeeper

Born: Pontardawe, 11 January 1924.
Career: Clydach; Swansea City 1946; IPSWICH TOWN 1951; Chelmsford City.

■ Jack Parry's form for his first League club, Swansea, impressed the Welsh FA selectors. But he had an unhappy debut for Wales against

Scotland – the team lost 3–1. Despite showing great consistency over the following season, he was overlooked thereafter. Parry joined the Swans from local team Clydach in September 1946 and made his League debut in 1946–47, the first season of League football after World War Two. Over the next four seasons, Parry went on to appear in 98 League games. He won a Third Division South Championship medal in 1948–49 when he appeared in 22 games. Jack Parry earned a reputation for being a brave and agile goalkeeper, never afraid to dive at the feet of an onrushing forward. His performances for the Swans not only won him selection at full international level for Wales, but also attracted a number of the game's leading clubs. However, it was Third Division Ipswich Town's manager Scott Duncan who finally persuaded Parry to leave the Vetch Field. Making his Ipswich debut in a 2–0 defeat against Colchester United in October 1951, he was the club's first-choice 'keeper for the next four seasons. He was ever present in 1953–54 when Town won the Third Division South Championship, finishing three points clear of Brighton. At the end of the following season when Town were relegated from Division Two, Parry left Portman Road to play non-League football for Chelmsford City.

PARRY Oswald

Full-back

Born: Merthyr Tydfil, 16 August 1908. Died: 1991.
Career: Wimbledon; Crystal Palace 1931; IPSWICH TOWN 1936.

■ Ossie Parry joined Ipswich from Crystal Palace in the summer of 1936, having made 141 League appearances for the Selhurst Park club. The Town's first professional player, he made his debut for the club in a 4–1 home win over Tunbridge Wells Rangers on the opening day of the 1936–37 Southern League season. He went on to appear in all but two of the club's games in that campaign as they won the Southern League Championship. In 1937–38, the strong-tackling full-back was the club's only ever present as they finished third in their last season of Southern League football. The following season, which was Town's first in the Football League, Ossie Parry and goalkeeper Mick Burns were the only ever presents as the club ended the campaign seventh in the Third Division South. Parry's career, like so many others, was hampered by World War Two, although he did play in 31 of the matches played in 1945–46 when the Third Division South was split into two halves to prevent clubs from having to travel to far. When football resumed after the hostilities, Parry continued to be an integral member of the Ipswich side, playing the last of his 104 League games in a 6–1 defeat at Brighton on 7 May 1949 at the age of 40 years 264 days.

PAZ Charquero Adrian

Forward

Born: Uruguay, 9 September 1968.
Career: Penarol (Uruguay); IPSWICH TOWN 1994; Columbus Crew (United States).

■ Uruguayan international Adrian Paz joined Town from Penarol for a fee of £900,000 in September 1994. A right-sided player, more suited to a wide role rather than that of a central striker, he took time to settle to the English game and had the additional burden of being expected to score the goals that would carry Ipswich up the table. He made his debut against Manchester United where he learnt the harsh realities of close marking, before being substituted because of an injury. Possessing great ability on the ball and often able to beat opponents with ease, he had his best game for the club against Liverpool at Portman Road, scoring his side's only goal and running Phil Babb ragged. As Town's season drew to a close, he was back home in his native country, negotiating terms with a new club but he eventually joined American club Columbus Crew.

PEDDELTY John

Centre-half

Born: Bishop Auckland, 2 April 1955.
Career: IPSWICH TOWN 1973; Plymouth Argyle 1976.

■ Central defender John Peddelty made his Ipswich debut in the number-six shirt for the FA Cup tie against non-League Chelmsford City in January 1973, a match Town won 3–1. His League debut followed a couple of months later against Liverpool. With Allan Hunter and Kevin Beattie occupying the two central defensive positions, Peddelty found it difficult to establish himself in the Ipswich side and in October 1976, having made 44 League appearances, the former England Youth international became part of the deal that brought Paul Mariner to Portman Road, when he moved in the opposite direction to play for Plymouth Argyle. After two seasons of struggle near the foot of the Second Division, the second culminating in the Pilgrims' relegation to Division Three, Peddelty parted company with the Devon club.

PENNYFATHER Glenn Julian

Midfield

Born: Billericay, 11 February 1963.
Career: Southend United 1981; Crystal Palace 1987; IPSWICH TOWN 1989; Bristol City 1993; Colchester United; Stevenage Borough; Canvey Island.

■ A former Southend United apprentice, he made his first-team debut for the Shrimpers before signing professional in February 1981. Pennyfather was a key figure in the club's 1986–87 promotion success and had appeared in 238 League games for the Roots Hall side when in November 1987 he was sold to Crystal Palace for a record £150,000. While at Selhurst Park, he helped the Eagles win promotion via the Play-offs in 1988–89 before joining Ipswich Town early the following season. His Portman Road career was short-lived and though he featured in the club's 1991–92 Second Division title campaign, he made just 15 League appearances and scored one goal, that against Oxford United in March 1990. Bristol City manager Russell Osman paid £80,000 for his services in March 1993, this after a loan spell with the club. He spent just over a season at Ashton Gate before in the summer of 1994 being released. He then played for Colchester United, Stevenage Borough and Canvey Island before returning to Southend as coach.

PERALTA Sixto Raimundo

Midfield

Born: Comodoro Riv, Argentina, 16 April 1979.
Career: Huracan (Argentina); Racing Club de Avellaneda (Argentina); Inter Milan (Italy); Torino (Italy) (loan); IPSWICH TOWN 2001; Racing Club de Avellaneda; Tigres (Mexico).

■ Peralta started his playing career with Argentina League sides Huracan and Racing Club de Avellaneda before moving to Italy in August 2000. Inter Milan's purchase of Peralta appears to have been on a 'one for the future' basis with the player training for the club for just two weeks before they looked to loan him to another club side in Italy. Indeed that happened prior to the start of the 2000–01 season when he joined Torino. In the summer of 2001, he joined Ipswich on a year's loan from Inter Milan and became an instant hit with the fans once he had established himself in the first team with his battling qualities and never-say-die attitude. After scoring his first goal for the club on Boxing Day 2001 as Town beat Leicester City 2–0, Peralta showed his ability to change a game with a flash of inspiration. Indeed, it was his skill that set up the goal for Alun Armstrong in the UEFA Cup tie against Inter, thus rather ironically making the Argentinian responsible for the exit from the competition of his own club! Following a loan spell with one of his former clubs, Racing Club de Avellaneda, he joined Mexican side Tigres.

PERRETT George Richard
Wing-half

Born: Kennington, 2 May 1915.
Died: 1952.
Career: Fulham; IPSWICH TOWN 1936.

■ George Perrett had played as an amateur for Fulham before signing for Ipswich in the summer of 1936. He made his Town debut in the opening game of the following season in a 4–1 home win over Tunbridge Wells Rangers in the club's first Southern League game. The wing-half went on to score four goals in 25 outings as the Blues won the Championship at the first attempt. Perrett was an important member of the Ipswich side at this time and after the club had been elected to the Football League, he made his Third Division South debut in the opening game of the 1938–39 season, a 4–2 win over Southend United. Unfortunately, his career was interrupted by World War Two but he returned to the side for the 1945–46 regional League game against Southend United after his demob. It was a game he would probably want to forget as he missed the chance to equalise from the penalty spot in a 2–1 defeat. When League football resumed in 1946–47, Perrett was a regular in the Ipswich line up and in 1948–49 was an ever present as the Blues finished seventh in the Third Division South. He played the last of his 115 League games for the club in a 4–0 home defeat by Notts County in December 1949. Sadly, the popular Londoner died in August 1952, aged only 37.

PETERS Jaime
Midfield

Born: Pickering, Ontario, Canada, 4 May 1987.
Career: Moor Green; IPSWICH TOWN 2005.

■ Capped by Canada at full international level, midfielder Jaime Peters was just 17 when he made his debut against Guatemala. He also represented Canada in the Under-20s World Youth Cup. Peters turned down the offer of joining Chelsea, Manchester United and several other leading clubs after impressing on trial to join Ipswich Town in the summer of 2005. Recommended to the Portman Road club by former town favourite Frank Yallop, he made his Football League debut against Cardiff City in August 2005, going on to appear in 13 games. He netted a hat-trick for the reserves in a 7–0 win and is definitely one for the future.

PETTA Robert Alfred Manuel
Midfield

Born: Rotterdam, Holland, 6 August 1974.
Career: Feyenoord (Holland); IPSWICH TOWN 1996; Glasgow Celtic 1999; Fulham (loan) 2004; Darlington 2005.

■ Bobby Petta joined Ipswich from Feyenoord during the summer of 1996 and his impressive form against Arsenal in John Wark's testimonial, earned him a place in the starting line up for the opening game of the 1996–97 season against Manchester City. Although able to operate as a winger or as an out-and-out striker, with the ability to get past players, he found it difficult to adjust to the English games and together with illness and some niggling injuries he soon became the forgotten man of Portman Road. However, the following season, he began to show the form which persuaded George Burley to bring him across the North Sea to Ipswich. Having scored his first goal for the club against Swindon Town, he notched a notable double in the local derby against Norwich City. Also his pin-point crosses created several goals for the team's strikers. Unable to reproduce this consistency in 1998–99, he also refused to sign a new contract and this did not endear him to the club's supporters. In July 1999 he left Ipswich to sign for Celtic and in 2000–01 he helped the Glasgow giants win the League and League Cup, retaining the Championship title the following season. Eventually finding himself out of the first team picture at Parkhead, he joined Fulham on loan in January 2004. Used mainly as a squad player, the Cottagers did not pursue a permanent signing. Released from his contract at Parkhead by mutual consent, he had trials with a number of clubs before signing for Darlington in January

2005. He scored on his debut at Bury but this proved to be his only goal and he was more of a provider than a scorer in his subsequent appearances.

PETTERSON Andrew Keith

Goalkeeper

Born: Freemantle, Australia, 29 September 1969.
Career: East Freemantle (Australia); Luton Town 1988; IPSWICH TOWN (loan) 1993; Charlton Athletic 1994; Bradford City (loan) 1994; IPSWICH TOWN (loan) 1995; Plymouth Argyle (loan) 1996; Colchester United (loan) 1996; Portsmouth (loan) 1998; Portsmouth 1999; Torquay United (loan) 2001; West Bromwich Albion 2002; Brighton & Hove Albion 2002; Bournemouth 2002; Derry City; Rushden and Diamonds 2003; Southend United 2003; Walsall 2004; Notts County 2004; Farnborough Town 2005.

■ Australian-born 'keeper Andy Petterson's first League club were Luton Town but in over five seasons at Kenilworth Road he made just 23 League and Cup appearances. In March 1993 he joined Ipswich on loan and made his debut in the Premier League game against Nottingham Forest, a match Town won 2–1. He later signed for Charlton Athletic but after failing to establish himself in the side he went on loan to Bradford City and then Ipswich for a second spell. This time he figured in the game against Derby County which ended all-square at 1–1 before following this with loan spells at Plymouth and Colchester United. A good shot stopper, on his return to The Valley he appeared on a more regular basis and in 1996–97 was voted Player of the Year. Losing his place to Mike Salmon and then Sasa Ilic, Petterson joined Portsmouth, having made 83 appearances for the Addicks. He found it difficult to keep a clean sheet playing behind a constantly changing defence and eventually lost his place. Loaned to Torquay, he also had spells with south coast clubs Brighton and Bournemouth before playing for League of Ireland outfit Derry City. Not featuring for Rushden and Diamonds, he had brief spells with Southend and Walsall before joining non-League Farnborough Town.

PHILLIPS Edward (Ted) John

Inside-forward

Born: Leiston, 21 August 1933.
Career: Leiston; IPSWICH TOWN 1953; Leyton Orient 1964; Luton Town 1965; Colchester United 1965.

■ When Ipswich Town won the Third Division South Championship in 1953–54, Ted Phillips played in four of the last few games, scoring two goals, one of which came in the 2–1 home win over Northampton Town on the final day of the season as 22,136 welcomed home the champions. The following season he scored both goals on his first appearance in a 4–2 defeat at Hull City and went on to score four goals in 12 games, but in 1955–56 he went to play for Stowmarket in the Eastern Counties League. However, the club held his registration and in 1956–57 he returned to Portman Road. That season, Town won the Third Division South title and Ted Phillips broke the goalscoring record with a phenomenal 41 goals in 41 League games. He also scored five goals in three FA Cup appearances to become the leading goalscorer in the Football League. Included in his total were five hat-tricks: Colchester United (home 3–1), Queen's Park Rangers (home 4–0), Watford (home 4–1), Shrewsbury Town (home 5–1) and Reading (away 3–1). In 1957–58 Phillips suffered badly from illness and injuries but still managed to score a goal a game in his 11 appearances including a hat-trick in a 4–2 home win over Bristol City. The following season was not much better, for after having undergone a cartilage operation and then straining his knee ligaments, he only managed to play in half of the club's games. He was back to full fitness in 1959–60 and was an ever present and top scorer with 24 goals including hat-tricks against Swansea (home 4–1) and Sunderland (home 6–1). The following season, the Blues won the Second Division Championship and Phillips, who was again ever present, scored 30 goals as he and Ray Crawford terrorised the opposing defences. During this period, he played in 128 consecutive League games. Phillips and Crawford continued to find the net in 1961–62 as the club won the League Championship at the first time of asking. The Leiston-born forward scored 28 goals in 40 League games and ended the season with 36 goals in 50 first-team appearances. He went on to score 181 goals in 295 games before leaving Portman Road for Leyton Orient. He scored 17 goals in 36 games for the Brisbane Road club before later playing for Luton Town and finally Colchester United where he took his tally of League goals to 199 in 349 appearances for his four clubs.

PICKETT Reginald Arthur

Wing-half

Born: Bareilly, India, 6 January 1927.
Career: Weymouth; Portsmouth 1949; IPSWICH TOWN 1957; Stevenage Town.

■ Born in India where his father was in the Army, he returned to England after attending school in Reading, joined the Royal Navy and was involved in the final year of World War Two. After the hostilities, he joined Weymouth of the Western League but a little over a year later, he was on the staff of Portsmouth, alongside such illustrious names as Jimmy Dickinson, Peter Harris and Jack Froggatt. He enjoyed almost nine years at Fratton Park and was a member of Pompey's First Division Championship-winning side in 1948–49. He had appeared in 123 League games for the south coast club when in July 1957 Alf Ramsey decided that Pickett was just the kind of experienced player they needed as they attempted to consolidate their position in Division Two. Pickett made his Ipswich debut in a goalless draw against Blackburn Rovers on the opening day of the 1957–58 season. He scored on his home debut a week later as Barnsley were beaten 3–0 and missed very few games as Town finished the season in mid-table. He replaced Doug Rees as Ipswich captain and was a regular member of the side for the next couple of seasons, playing in the opening 24 games of the 1960–61 Second Division Championship-winning season, before Bill Baxter took over from him. Ramsey still held Pickett in high regard and he used his vast experience in the European Cup second-round tie against AC Milan in the San Siro stadium, this in spite of him having played in only a handful of matches in the last couple of seasons. On leaving Ipswich he had a couple of seasons playing non-League football for Stevenage Town before returning to Portsmouth to work in the taxi business.

POLE Harold Edward (Ted)

Forward

Born: Kessingland, 25 March 1922.
Career: IPSWICH TOWN 1946; Leyton Orient 1951.

■ Versatile forward Ted Pole had played football in the forces prior to joining Ipswich in October 1946. He had to wait until New Year's Day before making his Football League debut in a 1–1 draw with Bournemouth. He went on to score five goals in consecutive games to help Town finish sixth in the Third Division South. He scored a number of spectacular goals the following season as Town moved up to fourth but then lost his place in the side. He remained at Portman Road until the summer of 1951, mainly playing reserve team football, before joining Leyton Orient where he later ended his playing days.

PRICE Lewis Peter

Goalkeeper

Born: Bournemouth, 19 July 1984.
Career: IPSWICH TOWN 2002; Cambridge United (loan) 2004.

■ Lewis Price joined Town's successful Academy in October 2001 and after being an unused substitute for much of the 2003–04 season, finally made his debut at Gillingham in April 2004 when Kelvin Davis had a stomach upset. The promising young 'keeper acquitted himself well before featuring for the club in their Carling Cup ties against Brentford and Doncaster early the following season. Then, following an injury to Davis, he had a brief run in the club's Championship side and marked that spell with a brilliant penalty save in the televised game against Coventry City. Later in the season he went on loan to Cambridge United where he covered for the injured John Ruddy and made another penalty save, this time against Notts County. He also established himself as first choice for Wales' Under-21 side, having qualified to play through his father, and was named in John Toshack's senior squad for the World Cup clash against Austria. Last season he appeared in 25 League games before losing out to Shane Supple towards the end of the campaign.

PROUDLOCK Adam David

Forward

Born: Telford, 9 May 1981.
Career: Wolverhampton Wanderers 1999; Clyde (loan) 2000; Nottingham Forest (loan) 2002; Tranmere Rovers (loan) 2002; Sheffield Wednesday (loan) 2002; Sheffield Wednesday 2003; IPSWICH TOWN (loan) 2005.

■ A tall, hard-working striker, Adam Proudlock began his career with Wolverhampton Wanderers but was loaned out to Scottish First Division club Clyde at the beginning of the

2000–01 season. He responded in style with a hat-trick on his debut against Falkirk and a tally of five goals in six appearances. On his return to Molineux, he found himself in and out of the side but still ended the season as the club's leading scorer with nine goals in all competitions. The following season he netted a fine hat-trick against Bradford City but was then loaned out to Nottingham Forest, Tranmere Rovers and Sheffield Wednesday. He eventually joined the Owls for a fee of £150,000 in September 2003 and although he suffered from a lack of service, he did net a hat-trick in the FA Cup first-round victory over Salisbury Town. Injuries then began to hamper his progress at Hillsborough and in October 2005 he joined Ipswich Town on loan. After making his debut away to Championship leaders Reading, Proudlock struggled to find any form during his stay at Portman Road and made the last of his nine appearances – six of which came from the bench – at his former club Wolves in February 2006.

PULLEN James Daniel

Goalkeeper

Born: Chelmsford, 18 March 1982.
Career: Heybridge Swifts; IPSWICH TOWN 1999; Blackpool (loan) 2001; Dagenham & Redbridge (loan) 2003; Peterborough United 2003; Heybridge Swifts (loan); Gravesend & Northfleet.

■ Signed from Heybridge Swifts, the young goalkeeper went on loan to Blackpool at the start of the 2001–02 campaign and eventually stayed all season. He made his League debut for the Seasiders at Oldham and retained his place in the side until the Bloomfield Road club's FA Cup game against Newport County. On his return to Portman Road, the promising 'keeper made his Town debut in the Worthington Cup tie with Middlesbrough and then made his League debut against Grimsby Town. Surprisingly given a free transfer at the end of the season, he had a brief spell on loan with Dagenham & Redbridge before being transferred to Peterborough United. Although he only started three games, he never let the side down and after rejoining his first club Heybridge Swifts on loan, he signed for Gravesend & Northfleet.

PUTNEY Trevor Anthony

Midfield

Born: Harold Hill, 9 April 1960.
Career: Brentwood Town; IPSWICH TOWN 1980; Norwich City 1986; Middlesbrough 1989; Watford 1991; Leyton Orient 1993; Colchester United 1994.

■ When Putney joined Ipswich from Brentwood Town in September 1980 the Portman Road club were one of the best teams in the country, and towards the end of that season they were in line for a unique treble of FA Cup, Football League Cup and UEFA Cup. Putney made his Ipswich debut as a substitute for Irvin Gernon in a 1–0 home defeat by Arsenal in October 1982. During his six years with the Blues, he showed his versatility by wearing nine different numbered outfield shirts and scored nine goals in 127 League and Cup games. In June 1986 he joined Norwich City in exchange for John Deehan and went on to appear in exactly 100 first-team games for the Canaries before a £300,000 move took him to Middlesbrough. Sadly, a Gordon Cowans tackle in a Zenith Data Systems Cup match broke his leg, and although he eventually made a full recovery he could not win a place in the Middlesbrough first team. After a spell at Vicarage Road playing for Watford, the quick-witted midfielder joined Leyton Orient before ending his League career with Colchester United. After a spell coaching Ryman League side Romford, he now visits Portman Road from time to time as a statistician for the Press Association, who tend to use former professional footballers for this job.

REDFORD Ian Petrie

Winger

Born: Perth, 5 April 1960.
Career: Dundee 1976; Glasgow Rangers 1980; Dundee United 1985; IPSWICH TOWN 1988; Raith Rovers 1994.

■ Winger Ian Redford began his career in his native Scotland for Dundee where he won Scottish Youth and Under-21 honours and in 1978–79 helped them win a place in the Scottish Premier League after finishing as First Division champions.

Redford had scored 34 goals in 85 League games for Dundee when he left to play for Rangers. He spent five seasons at Ibrox, scoring 23 goals in 162 League games before switching to Dundee United. His form for the Tannadice club alerted a number of sides south of the border but it was Ipswich boss John Duncan who brought him to Portman Road. He made his Town debut against Brighton & Hove Albion in November 1988 and over the next three seasons was an important member of the Portman Road club's squad. After leaving the game for a spell, he returned to action with Raith Rovers but nowadays Ian Redford, who was a founder of Fair Game, Scotland, plays golf with a handicap of two.

REED William George

Outside-right

Born: Rhondda, 25 January 1928.
Career: Rhondda Town; Cardiff City 1947; Brighton & Hove Albion 1948; IPSWICH TOWN 1953; Swansea City 1958.

■ Billy Reed became the first player to receive full international honours while on the books of Ipswich Town when in 1955 he played for Wales against Yugoslavia and Scotland. The Rhondda-born winger played his early football with his home town before joining Cardiff City. Unable to make the grade at Ninian Park, the former Welsh amateur moved to Brighton & Hove Albion in the summer of 1948. Reed found himself in and out of the Seagulls' side over the next couple of seasons but in 1951–52 he was not only ever present but the club's top scorer with 19 goals – a total which included a hat-trick in a 5–1 win over Ipswich Town. Reed was leading the south coast club's scoring charts again the following season when he was transferred to Ipswich, having scored 37 goals in 132 games for Brighton. At Portman Road, Reed was considered the best right-winger in the lower divisions. Possessing exceptional dribbling skill, he was dubbed the 'Stanley Matthews' of the Third Division. In 1953–54 he helped Ipswich win the Third Division South pipping his former club by three points. In fact, Reed scored in both matches against Brighton, including the winner in a 2–1 victory at the Goldstone Ground. Although the club were relegated in 1954–55, Reed was one of Ipswich Town's best players, scoring 12 goals including a hat-trick in a 5–2 home win over Walsall. During the Third Division South Championship-winning season of 1956–57, Reed was involved in one of the most controversial incidents in the club's history. An FA Cup third-round tie with Second Division Fulham was nearing its end with the Cottagers leading 3–2. With the seconds ticking away, Tom Garneys crossed from the left and Reed knocked the ball into the net. The referee blew his whistle at the same time and no one knew if the goal stood or not. It transpired that referee Ken Stokes had blown his whistle a split second before the ball crossed the line and so Town had been beaten. A crowd massed outside the changing rooms and the club were subsequently reprimanded by the FA for the misbehaviour of their supporters. In 1958 Reed returned to his native Wales to play for Swansea where he ended his career prior to working as a laboratory technician and later commissionaire at the Swansea Guildhall.

REES Douglas (Dai) Charles

Centre-half

Born: Neath, 12 February 1923.
Died: February 2000.
Career: Troedyrhiw; IPSWICH TOWN 1949; Sudbury Town; Halstead Town.

■ Doug 'Dai' Rees was already a Welsh amateur international centre-half when he joined Ipswich Town from Troedyrhiw in February 1949 with the Blues making a £350 donation to the Welsh club. He took over from George Rumbold on his debut in a 1–1 draw at Leyton Orient in April that year and went on to play in 387 games over the next 10 years, including being ever present in the seasons of 1950–51 and 1955–56. He played in 41 games in 1953–54 and helped the club win the Third Division South Championship. When he was appointed club captain the popular defender only scored one goal for Ipswich and that came in the 2–2 draw at Shrewsbury Town towards the end of the 1952–53 season when he was pressed into emergency service at centre-forward. Rees was selected in the preliminary list of 40 Welsh players for the 1958 World Cup but unfortunately did not make the final 22. He played his last game for the club at Grimsby Town in April 1959 before falling out with Town boss Alf Ramsey. He later played for Sudbury Town and was player-coach at Halstead Town before working for William Brown's Timber Merchants for a good number of years.

REES William Derek

Outside-left

Born: Swansea, 18 February 1934.
Died: April 1998.
Career: Portsmouth 1954; IPSWICH TOWN 1957; Welling Town.

■ Able to play in any of the forward positions, Derek Rees started out with Portsmouth, having signed for the Fratton Park club in May 1954. He found it quite difficult to secure a regular spot in a Pompey side that was going through a transitional period after so much success in the late 1940s and early 1950s. During his three-year stay on the south coast, Rees scored 15 goals in 47 games before in May 1957 being transferred to Ipswich Town. He made his debut for the Portman Road club in the goalless draw against Blackburn Rovers on the opening day of the 1957–58 season before scoring in his first game at home the following week against Barnsley. He scored 13 goals in 31 games including doubles in the wins over Rotherham United and Cardiff City. The following season he struggled in front of goal, though he did net both goals in the 2–0 defeat of Sunderland and strike an upright when a hat-trick was on the cards. Derek Rees remained at Portman Road until the early 1960s, helping the club win the Second Division title in 1960–61 when he scored twice on the opening day in a 3–1 defeat of Leyton Orient. On finding himself surplus to requirements at Ipswich, he left to play non-League football for Welling Town.

REUSER Martijn Franciscus

Midfield

Born: Amsterdam, Holland, 1 February 1975.
Career: Ajax Amsterdam (Holland); Vitesse Arnhem (Holland); IPSWICH TOWN 2000; Willem II Tilbury (Holland).

■ Dutch international Martijn Reuser joined Ipswich initially on loan from Vitesse Arnhem before transfer deadline day in March 2000. He made his debut from the substitutes' bench against Fulham with just 15 minutes remaining and immediately became a hero with the fans, when in the last minute, with the game goalless, he ran on to Jim Magilton's through-ball and fired under the 'keeper to secure the three points. He featured in most games thereafter, albeit from the bench and adjusted well to the English game. A scorer of vital goals he got the clinching goal against Bolton in that season's Play-off semi-final and then, in the Final at Wembley, showed tremendous composure to run onto Richard Naylor's ball, shrug off a defender and power a shot past the 'keeper. Signing for Town on a permanent basis for a fee of £1 million, he found the first half of the 2000–01 season a little harder than his opening campaign with the club but then proved his worth by scoring six goals in 11 games including one against Manchester City that sealed his opponents' relegation to Division One. He suffered from injuries and a lack of confidence the following season and this affected the whole team. He was made available on a free transfer before the January 2003 transfer window but continued to play for Ipswich until the end of the season when one of his goals was enough to beat leaders Portsmouth. His appearances in 2003–04 were again restricted by injury but even when fit he found himself on the bench and it was no surprise when he returned to the Netherlands to continue his career with Willem II Tilbury.

RICHARDS Matthew Lee

Left-back

Born: Harlow, 26 December 1984.
Career: IPSWICH TOWN 2002.

■ Another product of the Ipswich Town Academy, having progressed to the club's first team via the reserve and youth teams, he benefited greatly by the departure of Jamie Clapham midway through the 2002–03 season. Richards became the youngest player to represent the club when aged 17 he made his debut in the UEFA Cup tie against Avenir Began in August 2002. Primarily a left wing-back or full-back, he has an excellent tackle and pace to match even the most fleet-footed of attackers. The following season he established himself as the club's regular left-back. He joined the attack on frequent occasions, scoring his first goal against Stoke City when he hooked home a loose ball following a corner. The 2004–05 season was something of a disappointment for Matt Richards as Joe Royle preferred to introduce loan signings into the left-back berth. It was a different story last season with Richards, an England Under-21 international, appearing in 38 League games, his attacking runs proving a nuisance to the majority of the club's opponents.

RIMMER Ellis James
Outside-left
Born: Birkenhead, 2 January 1907.
Died: 1965.
Career: Whitchurch; Tranmere Rovers 1924; Sheffield Wednesday 1927; IPSWICH TOWN 1938.

■ Ellis Rimmer joined Sheffield Wednesday from Tranmere Rovers in February 1928 as the Owls battled against the threat of relegation, contributing a number of vital goals as safety was secured. The 1928–29 campaign saw him play a major role as Wednesday won the League Championship, netting a hat-trick in the 4–2 derby win over Leeds United. The following season he scored 17 times as the Owls successfully defended their title and reached the FA Cup semi-final. However, it is not with that FA Cup run which Rimmer is most associated with but the victorious FA Cup campaign of 1935. He scored in every round and added two goals in the last four minutes against West Bromwich Albion in the Final to ensure the cup went back to Hillsborough. His second hat-trick for the Yorkshire club came in 1935–36 when he scored all three goals in a 3–3 draw with Everton, the club that had overlooked him in his younger days. Rimmer's form earned him four England caps, scoring twice on his debut in a 5–2 defeat of Scotland and he was a member of the Sheffield Wednesday teams which contested two FA Charity Shield matches against Arsenal in 1930 and 1935. He had scored 140 goals in 418 games for the Owls when in the summer of 1938 he joined Ipswich. After playing in the Football League Jubilee Cup match against Norwich, which ended all-square at 1–1, he made his League debut against Cardiff City the following month. Rimmer appeared in three successive games for the Portman Road club but on each occasion was on the losing side, after which he decided to hang up his boots.

RIMMER Neill
Midfield
Born: Liverpool, 13 November 1967.
Career: Everton 1984; IPSWICH TOWN 1985; Wigan Athletic 1988; Altrincham.

■ A former England Schoolboy and Youth international, Neill Rimmer began his Football League career with Everton, making his debut as a substitute for Paul Wilkinson in a 2–0 defeat at Luton on the final day of the 1984–85 season. However, it was his only appearance for the Goodison club's first team and in the close season he joined Ipswich Town. He made his debut against Leicester City in September 1985 but it was his only appearance and it was not until 1987–88 that he established himself in the side, scoring three goals in 19 games. However, the competition for places at Portman Road was stiff and in the summer of 1988 he joined Wigan Athletic on a free transfer. Neill Rimmer was an important member of the Latics' side for the next eight seasons. A great midfield competitor, strong in the tackle and a good ball-winner, he unfortunately suffered more than his fair share of injuries in his time at Springfield Park. A willing worker who was also the club's captain, in his last campaign with the club in 1995–96, he was the Latics' longest-serving player.

ROBERTS James Dale
Centre-half
Born: Newcastle-upon-Tyne, 8 October 1956.
Died: 5 February 2003.

Career: IPSWICH TOWN 1974; Hull City 1980; North Ferriby United; Bridlington Town.

■ Dale Roberts won international Youth honours and was a member of the Ipswich Town team that won the FA Youth Cup in 1973 and 1975. He made his first-team debut against Birmingham City in December 1974, a match Town won 3–0. Though he spent six seasons at Portman Road, he was a regular reserve-team player due to the embarrassment of riches at Bobby Robson's disposal. Unable to shine in the League side on a regular basis, he had a spell playing in the NASL for Atlanta Chiefs before in February 1980, joining Hull City for a fee of £60,000. He helped the Tigers win promotion from the Fourth Division in 1982–83 and again into the Second Division two years later. He went on to play in 153 League games for Hull before a pelvic injury brought his League career to an end. He then had brief spells playing non-League football at North Ferriby United and Bridlington Town before being invited back to Hull as the youth-team coach. He later teamed up with George Burley in a managerial capacity, first at Ayr United, then Colchester before returning to Portman Road in early 1995. He went on to lead the reserves to the FA Premier League South title in 2001–02 and played a highly influential role in the club's promotion to the Premiership in 2000 and qualification for the UEFA Cup the following season.

ROBERTS James Nicoll

Outside-left

Born: Larbert, 12 June 1923.
Career: Dundee; IPSWICH TOWN 1949; Barrow 1952.

■ Jimmy Roberts, who represented Scotland at Under-23 level, started out with Dundee, whom he helped win promotion to the top flight in 1946–47 as champions of the B Section. He joined Ipswich in September 1949 and after spending the majority of his first season in the reserves he was called up for his League debut against Millwall. It was not the happiest of debuts for though the game was goalless going into the last quarter, the Lions won 3–0. The following season he appeared on a more regular basis, scoring nine goals in 35 games from his position on the left-wing, including four in his first five games. He scored twice in the 4–1 defeat of Southend United on the opening day of the 1951–52 season and netted another brace against Northampton Town in a 3–2 win over the Cobblers. Allowed to leave Portman Road in the summer of 1952, he joined Barrow for one season of Third Division North football.

ROBERTSON James Gillen

Winger

Born: Glasgow, 17 December 1944.
Career: Cowdenbeath; St Mirren; Tottenham Hotspur 1964; Arsenal 1968; IPSWICH TOWN 1970; Stoke City 1972; Walsall 1977; Crewe Alexandra 1978.

■ Jimmy Robertson played in the Cowdenbeath side as a 16-year-old amateur, represented Scotland at Youth level and won an amateur cap against Northern Ireland before joining St Mirren. Three months after winning his first Under-23 cap for Scotland against Wales, he was transferred to Tottenham Hotspur for £25,000. A fast, well-balanced winger who loved to cut inside and try a shot on goal, Jimmy Robertson was able to play on either flank but is best remembered at White Hart Lane as the player who supplied the ammunition for the likes of Jimmy Greaves and Alan Gilzean. After his move to White Hart Lane, Robertson won more caps at Under-23 level before winning his one and only full international cap against Wales in October 1964. He was a popular player with the Spurs faithful and his finest performance for the North London club came in the 1967 FA Cup Final against Chelsea when he scored the opening goal to launch Spurs on their way to their fifth FA Cup victory. Robertson was surprisingly allowed to leave Spurs and moved to rivals Arsenal in October 1968 in a £55,000 deal which saw David Jenkins travel in the opposite direction. He never really settled at Highbury and after less than two years, he joined Ipswich Town. Robertson made his Town debut in a 2–0 home win over Sunderland in March 1970. With him in the side, Town collected nine points out of a possible 14 and rose to safety from their previous position at the foot of the table. He went on to score 12 goals in 98 League and Cup games before being allowed to move to Stoke City for £80,000. He later wound down his career with Walsall and Crewe Alexandra. After becoming a director of the Task Force Group, a computer insurance company, he is now more often than not to be found working and playing at Newcastle-under-Lyme Golf Club.

RODGER Robert

Centre-half

Born: Dumbarton, 1917.
Career: Rhyl; Belfast Distillery; Hibernian; IPSWICH TOWN 1937; Hull City 1939.

■ Bob Rodger started out with Rhyl before having brief spells with Belfast Distillery and Hibernian. When he joined Ipswich in the summer of 1937, it meant that he had played for clubs from each of the four home countries. He played in the 2–1 defeat of Folkestone in the opening game of the 1937–38 Southern League Championship, missing just one game as the club finished third behind Guildford City and Plymouth Argyle. His Football League debut came in the second game of the club's inaugural season as Town overcame Walsall 1–0. Though he went on to appear in nine games that season, he was only on the winning side once more and on being unable to oust Tom Fillingham, left to play for Hull City. Unfortunately for Bob Rodger, the war interrupted his progress and was responsible for the end of his involvement with the game.

ROY John Robin

Outside-right

Born: Southampton, 23 March 1914.
Died: 1980.
Career: Sholing; Norwich City 1933; Mansfield Town 1936; Sheffield Wednesday 1937; Notts County 1938; Tranmere Rovers 1938; Aberaman; IPSWICH TOWN 1946; Yeovil Town.

■ Having joined Norwich City from local amateurs Sholing, he proved himself a lively winger and a great crowd pleaser. He worked his way up through the club's ranks and scored 56 goals in A and reserve-team fixtures including three hat-tricks. However, he failed to score in any of his six League appearances for the Canaries and moved on to Mansfield Town. Roy, who was to appear for six League clubs, appeared in 25 games for the Stags, his most at any one club before switching to Sheffield Wednesday. There followed spells with Notts County and Tranmere Rovers until World War Two intervened. Signed from Welsh side Aberaman, Roy made his Ipswich debut on the opening day of the 1946–47 season as Town fought back from being two goals down at half-time to share the spoils in a 2–2 draw. In 15 League games that season, Roy scored two goals including one on his last appearance as Swindon Town were beaten 3–1. At the end of the season, Roy left Portman Road to play non-League football for Yeovil Town.

RUMBOLD George

Full-back

Born: Alton, 10 July 1911.
Died: 1995.
Career: Faringdon; Crystal Palace 1934; Leyton Orient 1937; IPSWICH TOWN 1946.

■ Strong-tackling full-back George Rumbold began his career with Crystal Palace but was unable to force his way into the side on a regular basis and in July 1937 opted for a move to Leyton Orient. He spent the last two seasons prior to World War Two at Brisbane Road but though he was one of the club's most consistent players, he could not lift them away from the lower reaches of the Third Division South. When League football resumed in 1946–47, Rumbold joined Ipswich and made his debut against his former club on the opening day of the campaign. He was the club's only ever present that season. In 1947–48, playing in both full-back positions, he scored a number of spectacular goals that lifted the club up to fourth place in the Third Division South. The following season, his tally of six League goals from 35 games was a club record for someone playing at full-back, but after one more season he decided to retire.

SANTOS Georges

Midfield/Defender

Born: Marseilles, France, 15 August 1970.
Career: Olympique Marseille (France); Toulon (France); Tranmere Rovers 1998; West Bromwich Albion 2000; Sheffield United 2000; Grimsby Town 2002; IPSWICH TOWN 2003; Queen's Park Rangers 2004.

■ A tall, seemingly awkward Frenchman, he became a cult figure at Tranmere Rovers after joining them from Toulon, thanks to his enthusiasm and commitment. More ungainly and uncompromising than vicious, he picked up 14 bookings during his first season at Prenton Park. Rumoured to be the target for several top French clubs, he was sent off during the early part of the 1999–2000 season and thereafter did not figure in manager John Aldridge's plans. Allowed to join

West Bromwich Albion on transfer deadline day in March 2000 for a fee of £25,000 he was a key performer at the Hawthorns in the last few weeks of the season when relegation threatened. Even so, he moved on to Neil Warnock's Sheffield United where he impressed with his ball-winning abilities and all-round commitment. Unfortunately his season was brought to a premature end when he sustained a broken nose and a shattered eye socket in the game against Nottingham Forest. On his return to action, he was dismissed for a challenge in the notorious match against his former club and his two-minute substitute appearance in that game marked the end of his career with the Blades. He joined Grimsby and in his only season at Blundell Park was voted the Mariners' Player of the Year. In the summer of 2003 he joined Ipswich and started the following season as a defensive midfield player, struggling to produce his best form. His confidence and form improved once he was moved to central defence and his partnership with Richard Naylor blossomed. However, he then found himself a casualty after a poor team performance against Crystal Palace and was unable to re-establish himself in the side. His only goal for the club was scored in a 3–2 win at Cardiff City. Moving on to Queen's Park Rangers he soon won over the fans with his determined displays.

SCALES John Robert

Centre-half

Born: Harrogate, 4 July 1966.
Career: Leeds United; Bristol Rovers 1985; Wimbledon 1987; Liverpool 1994; Tottenham Hotspur 1996; IPSWICH TOWN 2000.

■ After signing for Leeds United on a YTS scheme in the summer of 1984, John Scales was released the following year and joined Bristol Rovers. He spent two years with the Pirates but when Bobby Gould was made the manager of Wimbledon, Scales was among his former manager's first signings. At the end of his first season with the Dons, Scales won an FA Cup-winners' medal after coming on as a substitute for Terry Gibson during the 1–0 victory over Liverpool. He later switched from full-back to a more central role, replacing Eric Young, and was the rock upon which Joe Kinnear built his defence. His consistent displays at the heart of the Wimbledon back four led to him being voted the club's Player of the Year in seasons 1992–93 and 1993–94. Scales had appeared in 288 games for Wimbledon when in September 1994 he was transferred to Liverpool for £3.5 million. Full international honours came his way soon after, the first of his three caps coming against Japan. Despite being Liverpool's best player in the 1996 FA Cup Final defeat by Manchester United, he was allowed in December of that year to join Tottenham Hotspur for £2.6 million. He soon demonstrated his great aerial ability with Spurs but during his three-and-a-half seasons with the club, he was ravaged by injuries and only made 37 appearances. Given a free transfer, he joined Ipswich Town. He began brightly, making his debut in the 2–1 defeat by Leicester City, but he was constantly dogged by injuries and made only three more first-team appearances at Portman Road. He finally left the club by mutual consent in April 2001, announcing that he intended to gain coaching qualifications and also concentrate on his business interests.

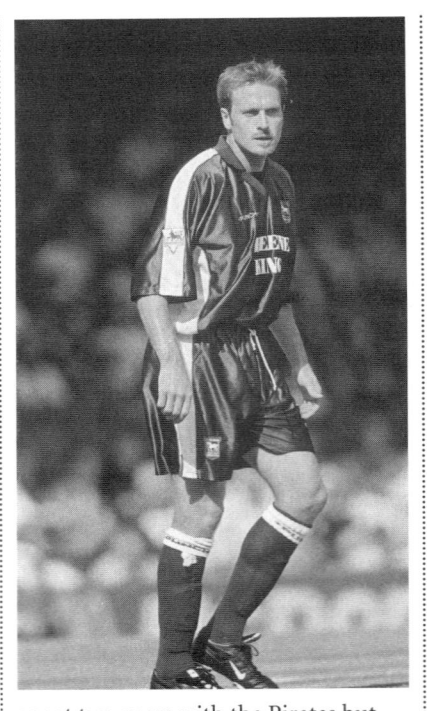

SCOWCROFT James (Jamie) Benjamin

Forward

Born: Bury St Edmunds, 15 November 1975.
Career: IPSWICH TOWN 1994; Leicester City 2001; IPSWICH TOWN (loan) 2005; Coventry City 2005.

■ First called up to deputise for the injured Ian Marshall at home to Wolves in October 1995, he made good use of his height to win more than his fair share of high balls. In 1996–97 he won a regular place in the Ipswich side, scoring 11 goals including doubles at Sheffield United and Bolton and one in the second-leg Play-off at home to the former. The goals at Bolton were a bit of a milestone as they enabled Town to become the first team to win at Burnden Park in 1996–97. His talent was recognised by regular call-ups to the England Under-21 side but the following season in the local derby against Norwich City he was badly injured and was carried from the field in a neck brace after being paralysed down one side. Although recovering completely within a few days, he then tore a cartilage in his knee which required surgery. After being suspended for a sending-off, he found on his return that the Johnson-Mathie partnership had blossomed and he could not get back in the side. Even so,

James Scowcroft

he was asked to join the England B squad for the game against Chile and played for the Nationwide League team. In 1998–99 he developed as a target man and though he was unfortunate to break his collarbone in an accidental collision with the Barnsley 'keeper, he did net his first hat-trick for the club against Crewe Alexandra. He had his best season to date in 1999–2000, finally matching his undoubted skills with a consistency of performance. Playing both in midfield and up front he was deservedly voted the club's Player of the Year. He found it hard to match his achievements the following season and after scoring 55 goals in 248 games he joined Leicester City for a fee of £3 million. Injuries hampered his progress at the Walker's Stadium but new manager Mickey Adams seemed to get the best out of him. He was a regular choice under all the club's managers both in midfield and attack before returning to Portman Road on loan in February 2005. He led the line as a replacement for the injured Shefki Kuqi before dropping back to a place on the bench. He later signed for Coventry City and was a regular in the Sky Blues side throughout the 2005–06 season.

SEDGLEY Stephen Philip

Midfield/Centre-half

Born: Enfield, 26 May 1968.
Career: Coventry City 1986; Tottenham Hotspur 1989; IPSWICH TOWN 1994; Wolverhampton Wanderers 1997.

■ A Spurs fan as a boy, he trained at the club in his schoolboy days and even appeared in the junior team. However, he was not offered a chance with the North London club and joined Coventry City. He made his League debut against Arsenal in August 1986 and although he appeared in 25 games that season, he was considered too inexperienced to be included in the club's 1987 FA Cup Final team which defeated Spurs 3–2. After three years of steady progress at Highfield Road he found himself the subject of a substantial offer by Spurs, who splashed out £750,000 for his services. Signed to provide defensive stability, he went on to win an FA Cup-winners' medal in 1991 following the 2–1 victory over Nottingham Forest. He went on to appear in 222 League and Cup games for the White Hart Lane club before becoming Ipswich Town's first £1 million player in June 1994. He proved to be most versatile, in midfield or defence and in his first season scored more than his fair share of goals. However, the campaign started badly for him when a shin injury forced him to delay his debut, which finally came in the local derby against Norwich, which the Canaries won 2–1. Following the appointment of George Burley as manager, Sedgley was made captain prior to heavy defeats by Manchester United and Spurs after which he was left on the sidelines. In 1995–96, he played equally well whether it was in central defence, midfield or even as a sweeper. A true competitor who was aggressive and made decisive tackles, he was Town's dead-ball specialist, taking most corners, free-kicks and penalties. Despite being troubled by a foot injury, he attempted to play through the pain barrier prior to joining Wolves in the summer of 1997 in exchange for Mark Venus and a cash adjustment. During his early days at Molineux he had to have an operation to remove a small piece of bone in his knee and this, coupled with a recurring foot injury, restricted his appearances. On leaving League football he became coach to non-League Kingstonian.

SERENI Matteo

Goalkeeper

Born: Parma, Italy, 11 February 1975.
Career: Sampdoria (Italy) 1999; Crevalcore (Italy) (loan); Piacenza (Italy) (loan); Empoli (Italy) (loan); IPSWICH TOWN 2001; Brescia (Italy) (loan) 2002; Lazio (Italy) 2003.

■ Ipswich Town had to see off the challenge of Serie A side Fiorentina and break the club record transfer fee for the signing of Sampdoria's goalkeeper Matteo Sereni. The Italian Under-21 international, who cost the Blues £4.5 million, had made his first-team debut for Sampdoria in a goalless draw against Cremonese at the age of 20 but there followed loan spells with Crevalcore, Piacenza and Empoli before he rejoined Sampdoria to become their first-choice 'keeper at the start of the 1999–2000 season. An agile 'keeper and excellent shot-stopper, he made his Ipswich debut at Sunderland and in the first half of the campaign was called upon many times to keep his side in the game. He received a red card in the game at Leicester, which was later rescinded and asked to be rested from the FA Cup game at Dagenham – not an unusual request in Italy. But then he did not get his place back in the side for the next Premiership game and had to sit and watch from the substitutes' bench. He spent the 2002–03 campaign on a season's long loan with Brescia before later signing on a permanent basis for Lazio.

SHANAHAN Terence Christopher

Forward

Born: Paddington, 5 December 1951.
Career: Tottenham Hotspur; IPSWICH TOWN 1969; Blackburn Rovers 1971; Halifax Town 1971; Chesterfield 1974; Millwall 1976; Bournemouth 1977; Aldershot 1978.

■ Unable to make the grade with Spurs, Terry Shanahan joined Ipswich in the summer of 1969 and played two seasons of reserve-team football before being given his Football League debut in a 3–1 defeat at Southampton. He was on the bench for the game against his former club Spurs before playing in the final two games of the 1970–71 season against Wolves and Chelsea, both goalless draws. Having had a spell on loan with Blackburn, he joined Halifax Town and in three seasons at The Shay he scored 23 goals in 96 League games. He continued to find the net for his next club, Chesterfield – 28 goals in 60 games – but the Spireites were no more than a mid-table Third Division team. He played Second Division football for Millwall before finishing his career with spells at Bournemouth and Aldershot.

SHARKEY Patrick Gerald Sharp

Midfield

Born: Omagh, Northern Ireland, 26 August 1953.
Career: Portadown; IPSWICH TOWN 1973; Millwall (loan) 1976; Mansfield Town 1977; Colchester United 1978; Peterborough United 1979; Po Chai Pills (Hong Kong).

■ Signed from Irish League side Portadown, Pat Sharkey made his Town debut against Manchester City in October 1975, coming off the bench to replace Kevin Beattie in a 1–1 draw. Towards the end of the season, he got an extended run of 12 games in the Ipswich side and scored his only goal for the club in a 2–1 defeat of Arsenal. His form led to him winning his one and only full international cap for Northern Ireland against Scotland but then he suffered from a spate of injuries and, following a spell on loan with Millwall, he left to play for Mansfield Town, who had just won the Third Division Championship. After a brief spell with Colchester United, he wound down his first-class career with Peterborough United and later spent some time in Hong Kong.

SHUFFLEBOTTOM Frank

Full-back

Born: Chesterfield, 9 October 1917.
Career: Margate; IPSWICH TOWN 1938; Nottingham Forest 1942; Bradford City 1946.

■ Signed from non-League side Margate, full-back Frank Shufflebottom was a regular throughout the two seasons of Southern League football prior to the club being admitted into the Football League for the 1938–39 season. However, he only made two League appearances for the club, the first in a 2–0 defeat against Bournemouth and the other a goalless draw against Bristol Rovers when he made a goal-line clearance to deny the Pirates. He later made a couple of appearances for Nottingham Forest before signing for his last League club, Bradford City. He appeared in 56 League games for the Bantams before hanging up his boots and becoming their first-team trainer.

SIDDALL Alfred Brian

Inside-forward

Born: Northwich, 2 May 1930.
Career: Wolverhampton Wanderers; Witton Albion; Northwich Victoria; Stoke City 1951; Bournemouth 1954; IPSWICH TOWN 1957; Haverhill Rovers.

■ Brian Siddall originally joined the groundstaff at Wolves and was a professional there, but persistent knee trouble led to the Molineux club releasing him. He returned to Cheshire and had a few games for Witton Albion and then Northwich Victoria before being given a second chance at League level by Stoke, who snapped him up ahead of Arsenal who were also tracking his progress. He spent four seasons at the Victoria Ground, scoring 10 goals in 59 games but with his first-team opportunities limited, Frank Taylor let him join Bournemouth. He spent another four seasons on the south coast, scoring 14 goals in 86 League games, before leaving Dean Court to sign for Ipswich in May 1957. He scored on his Town debut but it was only a consolation goal as the Blues were beaten 5–1 by Barnsley. He was one of the club's most consistent players that season and had scored both goals in the 2–1 defeat of West Ham United when towards the end of the game he suffered a knee injury that kept him out of action until towards the end of the campaign. Over the next two seasons, he found himself in and out of the side and in the 1960 close season, he left to join Haverhill Rovers.

SITO Luis Castro

Defender

Born: Coruna, Spain, 21 May 1980.
Career: Deportivo La Coruna (Spain); Lugo (Spain); Racing Club de Ferrol (Spain); IPSWICH TOWN 2005.

■ Able to play in either full-back position, he spent a couple of seasons at Deportivo La Coruna until at the age of 19 he moved to Spanish Second Division side, Lugo. He spent four years there before signing for Racing Club de Ferrol. He arrived at Portman Road on trial in the summer of 2005 and played in two pre-season friendlies before making his League debut against Queen's Park Rangers in August. The following month he was sent off in the matches against eventual promotion winners Sheffield United and in the East Anglian derby against Norwich City which Town lost 1–0. He remained a regular in the Ipswich side for most of the season, appearing in 38 League games.

SIVELL Laurence

Goalkeeper

Born: Lowestoft, 8 February 1951.
Career: IPSWICH TOWN 1969; Lincoln City (loan) 1979.

■ Goalkeeper Laurie Sivell played his first game for the club against Liverpool at Anfield in March 1970, when he had to face a penalty at the Kop End from which Tommy Smith scored the Reds' second goal in a 2–0 win. The following season, Sivell replaced David Best following an injury to the club's first-choice 'keeper and impressed so much that Best was unable to regain his place until the Lowestoft-born 'keeper broke a finger in the home match against Everton. One of Sivell's best performances in this extended run came in the goalless draw at Elland Road against the League leaders, Leeds United – only the second home point the Yorkshire club had dropped all season. Sivell's best season was 1974–75 when, despite the signing of Paul Cooper from Birmingham City at the end of his loan spell, he made 40 League appearances as Ipswich finished third in Division One. After letting in three goals at Newcastle United on the opening day of the following season, he lost his place to Cooper before winning a recall for the match against Aston Villa. As the game, which was goalless, entered its last minute Sivell made a brilliant save from Chris Nicholl. However, the ball ran loose to Andy Gray and Sivell, who dived at the Scottish international's feet to prevent a certain goal, received horrific injuries. He was taken off on a stretcher with blood pouring from a face wound which required 11 stitches in and around his mouth. The brave goalkeeper also lost a number of teeth and suffered a black eye. He went on to make a full recovery and appeared in 175 games before at the end of the 1983–84 season, he gave the game up after suffering for a while with knee injuries.

SLATER Stuart Ian

Left-winger

Born: Sudbury, 27 March 1969.
Career: West Ham United 1987; Glasgow Celtic 1992; IPSWICH TOWN 1993; Leicester City 1996; Watford 1996; Carlton 1999; Forest Green 2000; Weston-super-Mare 2003.

■ Stuart Slater turned down the chance to join his local club – Ipswich Town – and signed as an apprentice for West Ham United in the summer of 1985. He turned professional two years later and six months after that made his League debut as a last-minute substitute against Derby County at Upton Park. After establishing himself as a first-team regular, Slater developed into one of England's most exciting young prospects. He won England Under-21 honours before coming off the bench in a B international against Switzerland in May 1991. Not a prolific scorer, he went through the entire 1991–92 season, playing in 53 League and Cup games without finding the net. He had scored 16 goals in 174 games for the Hammers when in the summer of 1992 he joined Celtic for £1.5 million. Unable to settle at Parkhead, he had played in just 55 games before signing for Ipswich Town for £750,000 where he linked up with former Hammers boss John Lyall. He made his Town debut in a 3–0 reversal at Queen's Park Rangers and though he was never an automatic selection, he was at his best when given a free role, having the ability to take on defenders and leave them in his wake. In 1995–96 he scored two goals in an outstanding display against Stoke City and came close to netting a hat-trick, but later in the campaign he broke down with an Achilles tendon injury. After turning down a move to Stoke, he had a trial with Leicester City before settling down at Watford. He proved an excellent free-signing for the Hornets before an operation was necessary on his Achilles tendon. Even so, he had played in enough games to win himself a Second Division Championship medal before leaving Vicarage Road to play non-League football.

SMITH George Casper

Centre-half

Born: Bromley, 23 April 1915.
Died: 1983.
Career: Bexleyheath; Charlton Athletic 1938; Brentford 1945; Queen's Park Rangers 1947; IPSWICH TOWN 1949.

■ George Smith played for Charlton Athletic in the war and appeared in an FA Cup Final against Chelsea at Wembley in 1944, which the Addicks won 3–1. He also gained a wartime cap for England against Wales in May 1945 and gained a Third Division Championship-winners' medal during his time with Queen's Park Rangers in

1947–48. He arrived at Portman Road in September 1949 as the club's assistant manager but also registered as a player and made his debut in a 2–1 defeat by Nottingham Forest. He played in eight consecutive games from his debut, one of which was a 5–1 home defeat at the hands of Walsall. He remained as assistant manager until January 1950 before managing a number of non-League clubs. After taking over the reins at Crystal Palace he managed Portsmouth and in 1961–62 led them to the Third Division Championship, later becoming the south coast club's general manager. He lost his job in 1973 when Pompey's new chairman John Deacon restructured the management.

SMITH John

Inside-forward

Born: Liverpool.
Career: IPSWICH TOWN 1945.

■ Little is known about this inside-forward who joined the Portman Road club from the army towards the end of 1945 and played in some wartime games for the Blues before making the first of his two League appearances in a goalless draw against Exeter City in November 1946. A week later he laid on the winning goal for Stan Parker in a 2–1 defeat of Port Vale but then drifted into the club's reserve team before later parting company with the club.

SMITH Trevor Richard

Full-back

Born: Lowestoft, 12 August 1946.
Career: IPSWICH TOWN 1964; Crewe Alexandra 1968.

■ Attacking full-back Trevor Smith worked his way up through the ranks at Portman Road before making his Football League debut in the East Anglian derby game against Norwich City in September 1964. He had a good first half and Town were leading 1–0 but he was deemed at fault for the Canaries' equalising goal, which spurred them on to go for the winner which they did, to claim a 2–1 victory. Though he was never a first-team regular he was an important member of the squad that contested the next couple of seasons before staying with the club to play reserve-team football. When he did leave Portman Road, he joined Crewe Alexandra but despite his efforts, he never made the Railwaymen's League side.

SMYTHE Herbert Robert

Wing-half

Born: Manchester, 28 February 1921.
Career: HMS Ganges; IPSWICH TOWN 1945; Halifax Town 1950; Rochdale 1950; Accrington Stanley 1951.

■ One of the club's earliest utility players in the Football League, Bob Smythe played his early football for HMS Ganges while serving in the Royal Navy and joined Ipswich in December 1945. He appeared for the club throughout the 1945–46 season before playing the first of just a couple of League games against Cardiff City in December 1946. His second appearance in Town's League side came the following season when he wore the number-nine shirt in a 2–1 win over Reading. On leaving Ipswich, Bob Smythe played for a number of clubs in the north – Halifax Town, Rochdale and Accrington Stanley – but never really established himself at any of them.

SNELL Victor Derek Robert

Full-back

Born: Samford, 29 October 1927.
Career: IPSWICH TOWN 1945.

■ Vic Snell was a loyal servant to Ipswich Town Football Club for 18 years even though he only appeared in 64 League games during nine seasons as a player. His first League game for Town came in October 1949 when he played in a 2–1 defeat by Nottingham Forest, this after Town led 1–0 until the closing moments. Midway through that season he appeared in four consecutive games – games that included a 4–4 draw against Crystal Palace, a 4–0 home defeat by Notts County and a 6–0 thrashing at Watford. In 1951–52 he played in just two games, both against Port Vale, one at left-half and one in the number-11 shirt. He continued to appear in a few games each season – with the exception of 1953–54 when the club won the Third Division South title and 1954–55. He played in 11 games when Town won the Third Division South Championship for a second time in four seasons, but made his most League appearances (36) in what turned out to be his last playing season with the club in 1958–59. In his last few seasons with the club, he ran the A team before later emigrating to South Africa where he coached a number of teams.

SONNER Daniel James

Midfield

Born: Wigan, 9 January 1972.
Career: Wigan Athletic; Burnley 1990; Bury (loan) 1992; Preussen Koln (Germany) 1993; FC Erzgebirge Aue (Germany); IPSWICH TOWN 1996; Sheffield Wednesday 1998; Birmingham City 2000; Walsall 2002; Nottingham Forest 2003; Peterborough United 2004; Port Vale 2005.

■ After struggling to break through to senior level at his home-town club Wigan Athletic, the story was much the same for Danny Sonner after he joined Burnley. He contributed goals to Bury's promotion bid during a loan spell at Gigg Lane but in May 1993 he left Turf Moor to try and make his way in German football. In February 1995 he was called up to the Northern Ireland squad for a B international against Scotland. In the summer of 1996 he joined Ipswich Town and quickly settled into the side, scoring a number of spectacular goals including a overhead kick in the Coca-Cola Cup tie against Fulham. The 1997–98 season proved to be a frustrating one for Sonner as he was unable to command a regular place in the Ipswich side and the majority of his appearances were as a substitute. Even so, he won his first full international cap for Northern Ireland when coming off the bench against Albania. He joined Sheffield Wednesday for a cut-price fee of £75,000 in October 1998 and as the term wore on he looked like the Premiership's bargain buy of the season. A loss of form saw him slip out of the first-team picture at Hillsborough in 1999–2000 yet the new Northern Ireland manager Sammy McIlroy kept selecting him for the national team. He moved on to Birmingham City in August 2000 and after a good first season appeared in the Worthington Cup Final defeat by Liverpool before an Achilles tendon injury restricted his appearances. The nagging heel injury required surgery but when he had recovered, Steve Bruce did not select him for the League side and he joined Walsall on a one-year deal. He slipped out of the first-team picture midway through the 2002–03 season and was released early. The right-sided midfielder joined Nottingham Forest but again he faded from the scene after making a promising start to life at the City Ground. He then signed for Peterborough United but could not settle and following a loan spell with Port Vale, he joined the Valiants on a permanent basis in 2005.

SPEARITT Edward Alfred

Full-back/Winger

Born: Lowestoft, 31 January 1947.
Career: IPSWICH TOWN 1965; Brighton & Hove Albion 1969; Carlisle United 1974; Gillingham 1976.

■ Eddie Spearitt worked his way up through the ranks at Portman Road before making his Ipswich debut in a 1–0 home win over Preston North End on the opening day of the 1965–66 season. After a handful of appearances he returned to the reserves prior to having a run of 11 games towards the end of the campaign. He played on a more regular basis the following season, while in 1967–68 he played his part in helping the club win the Second Division Championship. After struggling to hold down a regular place in the top flight, he left the Suffolk club to join Brighton early in 1969. Over the next four seasons or so, Spearitt proved himself to be a versatile performer, appearing in seven different outfield shirts. By the start of the 1971–72 campaign, he had become the club's first-choice left-back and was ever present as the Seagulls won promotion to Division Two. The following season, Spearitt was a model of consistency in a Brighton side that was relegated to the Third Division after finishing bottom of Division Two and not surprisingly was named the club's Player of the Season. Towards the end of the 1973–74 season, Spearitt, who had scored 25 goals in 232 games, was transferred to Carlisle United. Injuries hampered his progress at Brunton Park and he only played in 31 games in two seasons before switching to Gillingham where he ended his career.

STACEY Stephen Darrow

Full-back

Born: Bristol, 27 August 1944.
Career: Bristol City 1961; Wrexham 1966; IPSWICH TOWN 1968; Chester City (loan) 1969; Charlton Athletic (loan) 1970; Bristol City 1970; Exeter City 1971.

■ Though he signed professional forms with his home-town club

Bristol City in November 1961, he had still not broken into the first team at Ashton Gate by February 1966 and was happy to move to Wrexham. In his first season at the Racecourse, he saw Wrexham finish 92nd in the Football League but became a regular over the next couple of seasons as the club began to rebuild. He gained a Welsh Cup runners'-up medal in 1967 when Wrexham lost in the Final to Cardiff City. He had appeared in 119 games for the Robins when in September 1968 Ipswich paid £25,000 to take him to Portman Road. He made his Town debut in a 2–0 defeat at the hands of Liverpool but appeared in only three games, the last a 4–0 defeat by the Reds in the return fixture before having spells on loan with both Chester and Charlton Athletic. He then returned to his first club, Bristol City, before joining Fourth Division Exeter City. On leaving the Grecians he had a season playing non-League football for Bath City.

STEGGLES Kevin Peter

Defender

Born: Ditchingham, 19 March 1961.
Career: IPSWICH TOWN 1978; Southend United (loan) 1984; Fulham (loan) 1986; West Bromwich Albion 1987; Port Vale 1987; Bury Town; Brantham Athletic; Great Yarmouth; Woodbridge Town.

■ Versatile defender Kevin Steggles started out with Ipswich, making his debut against St Etienne in a UEFA Cup quarter-final second leg in March 1981. He was never an automatic choice for the Portman Road club, but had his most successful season in 1981–82 when he appeared in 18 League games as the club finished runners-up in the First Division and scored his only goal for the club in a 1–1 draw at Sunderland. He had appeared in 50 League games when, following loan spells with Southend United and Fulham, he joined West Bromwich Albion. His stay at the Hawthorns was brief and in November 1987 he moved to Port Vale. On losing his place he left to play non-League for a number of clubs including Bury Town, Brantham Athletic, Great Yarmouth and Woodbridge Town.

STEIN Earl Mark Sean

Forward

Born: Cape Town, South Africa, 29 January 1966.
Career: Luton Town 1984; Aldershot (loan) 1986; Queen's Park Rangers 1988; Oxford United 1989; Stoke City 1991; Chelsea 1993; Stoke City (loan) 1996; IPSWICH TOWN (loan) 1997; Bournemouth 1998; Luton Town 2000; Dagenham & Redbridge.

■ Mark Stein was a lively striker with a knack of being in the right spot at the right time. He began his career with Luton Town where his brother Brian, an England international, was a prolific scorer but following a loan spell with Aldershot, he joined Queen's Park Rangers. He won the League Cup with the Loftus Road club in 1988. Continuing to find the net on a regular basis, Stein then played for Oxford United before joining Stoke City in September 1991. While with the Potters he won the Freight Rover Trophy and the Second Division Championship in 1992 and 1993 respectively. In October 1993 he moved to Chelsea for a fee of £1.45 million but after a fine first season at Stamford Bridge niggling injuries began to interrupt his game. He returned to the Victoria Ground on loan before joining Ipswich in a similar capacity for two months at the start of the 1997–98 season, as cover for Alex Mathie. Linking up with Jamie Scowcroft, he led the line well while being able to feed off the tall striker's flick-ons. Although he scored three times in his 11 appearances during his time at Portman Road, there was never any question of him joining the Tractor Boys on a permanent basis and he went back to Chelsea before being loaned out to Bournemouth. Signed by the Cherries in the close season, he ended the 1998–99 season with 23 League and Cup goals and won selection to the PFA award-winning Second Division side. Top scorer for a second successive season at Dean Court he then could not agree terms and rejoined his first club Luton to help them through a transitional period prior to leaving to play non-League football for Dagenham & Redbridge.

STEPHENSON Roy

Outside-right

Born: Crook, 27 May 1932.
Died: January 2000.
Career: Burnley 1949; Rotherham United 1956; Blackburn Rovers 1957; Leicester City 1959; IPSWICH TOWN 1960; Lowestoft Town.

■ Roy Stephenson was a flying winger who started his career with Burnley, laying on the Clarets' winning goal on his First Division debut at Anfield over Easter 1950. Although he scored regularly when called upon, he was never quite able to hold down a regular place in Burnley's League side. His best season was 1954–55 when he scored 10 goals in 22 games and was invited to an FA trial match at Highbury for the England Under-23 side to play Italy but unfortunately was not selected. In September 1956, Stephenson moved to Rotherham United and a little more than a year later joined Blackburn Rovers in the Second Division. He helped Rovers to promotion to the top flight in 1958 and also played in every game in Blackburn's run to the FA Cup semi-final where they were beaten by Bolton. On leaving Ewood Park, he had a season with Leicester City before his career suddenly took off following his transfer to Second Division Ipswich Town in the summer of 1960. Making his debut in a 4–0 win over Brighton & Hove Albion, he had a hand in all of the goals as Ted Phillips and Ray Crawford scored two apiece. His fast, direct wing play and pin-point crosses contributed in no small measure to the century of goals Town scored that season as the club swept to the Second Division Championship. The story was the same the following season as Ipswich carried all before them to win the League Championship. Stephenson missed only one game during that momentous campaign, his delivery from out wide on the right once more serving the prolific Phillips and Crawford. He also figured on the scoresheet himself, netting seven times. He scored in Ipswich's Charity Shield clash with Tottenham Hotspur in August 1962 but sadly it was only a consolation goal in a 5–1 defeat. It was a sign that the bubble was about to burst and sure enough, after a season of struggle in 1962–63, Town were relegated the following season. Stephenson, who had scored 26 goals in 163 games, left Portman Road in June 1965 to join nearby Lowestoft Town.

STEVENSON Walter Harry Horace

Outside-right

Born: Derby, 26 June 1923.
Career: Nottingham Forest 1944; IPSWICH TOWN 1948.

■ Winger Horace Stevenson was on the books of Nottingham Forest when League football resumed in 1946–47 but despite having impressed in a number of wartime games and in a few outings for the reserve side, he could not force his way into the Forest side. In February 1948 he opted for a move to Ipswich Town and the following month made his long-awaited League debut against Watford, a match Town lost 3–1. He kept his place in the side for the next two games – a defeat by Queen's Park Rangers and a 2–1 win over Port Vale when his crosses provided the goalscoring opportunities for Jennings and Parker – but after that he returned to the reserves and left the club at the end of the season.

STEWART William Marcus

Forward

Born: Bristol, 7 November 1972.
Career: Bristol Rovers 1991; Huddersfield Town 1996; IPSWICH TOWN 2000; Sunderland 2002; Bristol City 2005; Preston North End (loan) 2006.

■ Starting out with his home-town team Bristol Rovers, Marcus Stewart added a good goalscoring rate to his fine performances for the club and in 1994–95 broke a 39-year club record of scoring in nine consecutive matches. Also that season an excellent performance at Wembley in the Play-off Final against Huddersfield Town culminated in a superb goal, taking his season's tally to 23. The following season he topped Rovers' goalscoring charts with 30 goals including the Pirates' quickest League goal in their history – just 28 seconds against Hull City – and not surprisingly was selected for the PFA award-winning Division Two team. In the summer of 1996, having scored 79 goals in 207 games, he signed for Huddersfield as the replacement for Andy Booth, with a sum of £1.2 million changing hands. He netted a hat-trick in only his second outing for the Yorkshire club in the Coca-Cola Cup against Wrexham. Following the signing of Wayne Allison, he blossomed in his new surroundings and was the club's leading scorer in 1998–99. The following season he again topped Huddersfield's scoring list, passing the previous season's total by Boxing Day! He also scored his first League hat-trick in the defeat of Crystal Palace. He had scored 68 goals in 160 games when in February 2000 he became Ipswich's record signing when they paid £2.5 million for his services. He made an immediate impact with a goal in his first two games but was then dogged by injuries. He only regained fitness towards the end of the campaign and led the fightback in the

Marcus Stewart

Play-off semi-final at Bolton, scoring both Ipswich goals in a 2–2 draw. He had a fine match in the Play-off Final at Wembley scoring the crucial third goal when he headed Jamie Clapham's cross into the corner of the net. Selected for that season's PFA Division One side, he had an even better season in 2000–01. Between Boxing Day and 20 January he scored in seven successive games, which took him to the top of the Premiership scoring charts. One of the highlights was his hat-trick at The Dell against Southampton in a 3–0 win. He was in contention for the Golden Boot for being the Premiership's leading scorer right up to the last game of the season, made the short list of six for the PFA Player of the Season and was voted Player of the Year by the Ipswich supporters. The following season was a complete contrast. After starting well and enjoying his European experience, he broke his jaw in training and on his return appeared to have lost some of his confidence and with it his place in the starting line up. In August 2002 he moved to Sunderland for a fee of £3.25 million. After a disappointing first season in the North East, he topped the club's scoring charts in 2003–04 and 2004–05 when he netted two hat-tricks as the Black Cats won the Championship. Released by the Wearsiders, he joined Bristol City before joining Preston North End on loan as they made a push for promotion to the Premiership via the Play-offs.

STIRK John

Right-back

Born: Consett, 5 September 1955. Career: IPSWICH TOWN 1973; Watford 1978; Chesterfield 1980; North Shields.

■ An England Youth international, he worked his way up through the ranks at Portman Road to eventually make his League debut in a 1–0 defeat of

Manchester City in November 1977. He then played in five of the next six games and was on the winning side a further three times but at the end of the season, in which Town struggled to hold on to their top-flight status, he left to play for Watford. After helping the Hornets into the Second Division as their ever present right-back, he was discarded without playing League football again for the club. All of his 60 appearances for the Vicarage Road club were consecutive before he ended his first-class career with Chesterfield. On leaving Saltergate, Stirk returned to his native North East to play non-League football for North Shields.

STOCKWELL Michael Thomas

Midfield/Right-back

Born: Chelmsford, 14 February 1965. Career: IPSWICH TOWN 1982; Colchester United 2000.

■ Micky Stockwell graduated to the professional ranks in 1982–83 but waited three years before making his Football League debut in a 1–0 win at Coventry City in December 1985. He played a few more times that season as the club slid into the Second Division but mainly as a substitute. On winning a regular place on the left side of midfield in 1987–88 he was injured during a match at Walsall in January 1989 and did not win his place back until the following October, this time at right-back. In 1990–91 he slotted into Town's midfield and played in all but two League games in the number-four shirt. However, the number on his back was not a reliable guide to the position he would take up in any particular game. He was ever present in 1991–92 as Ipswich swept to the Second Division Championship and then rose to the challenge presented by the Premiership magnificently and ended 1992–93 as the club's Player of the Year. Early in the season he played a few games up front when Chris Kiwomya dropped out and in the game against Wimbledon he netted twice. What made it an even better day for many Town supporters was the fact that Ladbrokes set odds of 14–1 for Stockwell to score the first goal of the game, totally unaware that he was playing as an emergency striker and many fans profited by the bookmaker's generosity. Injuries then hampered his progress and he was laid low by damaged knee ligaments that required surgery. However, he recovered well and had his testimonial at the start of the 1995–96 season when former Town boss Bobby Robson brought his FC Porto side to Portman Road. He was later honoured to be handed the club captaincy but, with his game suffering, it was eventually passed on to new signing Tony Mowbray. He continued to amaze all at Portman Road with his stamina and energy, still running up and down the pitch like a youngster. A fine example for the youngsters in the team to follow, he was always available when required and always ready to give his all for the cause. Given a free transfer in the summer of 2000, he joined Colchester United and was the only player in 2000–01 to start every League and Cup game for the U's. He finished up as the club's leading scorer with 11 goals and was voted Colchester's Player of the Season by the Layer Road faithful. He defied the years again the following season, with a similar total of goals and again named as the club's Player of the Season. After more than 20 years as a professional footballer, he announced his retirement, looking to go into coaching.

STUART Mark Richard

Left-winger

Born: Chiswick, 15 December 1966. Career: Charlton Athletic 1984; Plymouth Argyle 1988; IPSWICH TOWN (loan) 1990; Bradford City 1990; Huddersfield Town 1992; Rochdale 1993; Southport 1999; Stalybridge Celtic 2001; Guisely 2002.

■ Winger Mark Stuart began his career with Charlton Athletic, whom he helped win promotion to the top flight in 1985–86 but after scoring 31 goals in 128 games he joined Plymouth Argyle in November 1988 for a fee of £150,000. He continued to score spectacular goals for the Pilgrims before being loaned out to Ipswich in March 1990. He made his debut at Watford the following month, going on to score twice in his five appearances, playing his last game in Ipswich colours at home to Hull City. After returning to Home Park, Stuart left Plymouth to join Bradford City, later playing for another Yorkshire club – Huddersfield Town. He crossed the Pennines in the summer of 1993 to join Rochdale where he soon impressed as the club's dead-ball specialist. Playing in a variety of positions, he scored some vital and spectacular goals for the Spotland club, this in spite of being troubled by injuries. The longest-serving player at the club, he had a spell on loan with Southport and after scoring 45 goals in 232 games for Rochdale he joined the Sandgrounders on a permanent basis.

SUNDERLAND Alan

Forward/Midfield

Born: Mexborough, 1 July 1953.
Career: Wolverhampton Wanderers 1971; Arsenal 1977; IPSWICH TOWN 1984; Derry City.

■ During his seven seasons with Wolverhampton Wanderers, Alan Sunderland appeared in a number of different positions. By the end of 1971–72, his first season with the club, he had helped them reach the UEFA Cup Final, where they lost to Tottenham Hotspur. A member of the Wolves side that won the 1974 League Cup Final, he top scored for the Molineux club during their 1976–77 Second Division Championship-winning season with 16 goals in 41 games. Then, having scored 35 goals in 198 games for Wolves, he joined Arsenal for £220,000 in November 1977. At the end of his first season with the Gunners, Sunderland played in the FA Cup Final against Ipswich and in 1978–79 he scored six goals in the club's victorious FA Cup campaign, including the winner in the Final against Manchester United. Also collecting a UEFA Cup-winners' medal that season, he was later capped by England and had scored 92 goals in 281 first-team outings for the North London club before signing for Ipswich Town in February 1984. He made his debut in a 3–0 home defeat by Southampton and though he only scored three goals in the last 15 games of that season, they brought victories over former club Wolves, local rivals Norwich City and the mighty Manchester United, helping the club retain their First Division status. The following season, Town again struggled near the foot of the top flight but Sunderland still managed to score some vital goals before leaving to have a brief spell in Ireland with Derry City.

SUPPLE Shane

Goalkeeper

Born: Dublin, 4 May 1987.
Career: IPSWICH TOWN 2005.

■ One of a number of Republic of Ireland youngsters at Ipswich's Academy, Shane Supple was in goal when Town beat Southampton to lift the FA Youth Cup in 2004. Capped by his country at various Youth levels, he was on the bench for Town 12 times during the 2004–05 season. A keen Gaelic football fan, he eventually made his first-team debut as a replacement for Lewis Price in the game against Leicester City in August 2005, having an outstanding game and keeping a clean sheet in a goalless draw. Supple shared the goalkeeping duties with Price throughout the campaign, ending the season as the current holder of the first-team jersey.

SWAILES Christopher William

Defender

Born: Gateshead, 19 October 1970.
Career: IPSWICH TOWN 1989; Peterborough United 1991; Boston United 1991; Bridlington Town; Doncaster Rovers 1993; IPSWICH TOWN 1995; Bury 1997; Rotherham United 2001; Oldham Athletic 2005.

■ A right-sided defender who is quicker than he looks, he started out with Ipswich but was unable to make much headway and joined Peterborough United without having made a first-team appearance. It was a similar story at London Road and he drifted into non-League football, playing for Boston United and Bridlington Town before signing for Doncaster Rovers in October 1993. He eventually made his League debut for the Belle Vue club and had played in 54 games when he returned to Portman Road for a second spell in March 1995, Town paying £225,000 for his services. He made his debut in the Premiership game against Aston Villa and conceded an unfortunate own-goal in the last minute. The tall Ipswich defender found his first-team opportunities limited by the number of quality players in the squad and his cause was further undermined when undergoing a hernia operation in December 1995. The following season was without doubt his best and just shows what an extended run in the side can do for confidence. Playing in the last 20 games of the 1996–97 season, when Town lost just three times, he was part of the defence which set a club record five successive clean sheets, thus guaranteeing Town a place in the Play-offs. The central defender also found time to notch his first goal for the club at Swindon when he headed home Jamie Scowcroft's driven cross. However, following the arrival of Mark Venus, he found himself part of the David

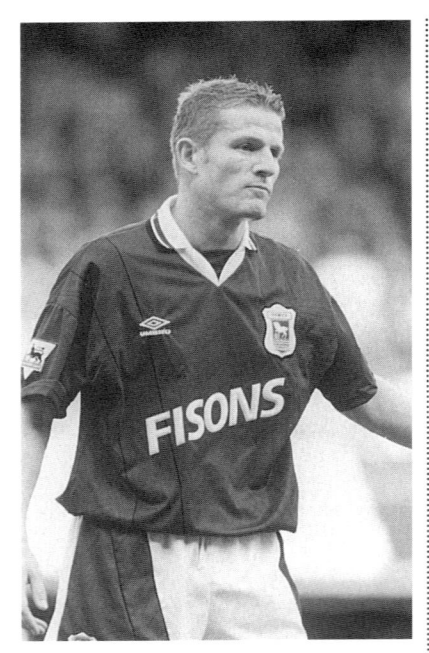

Johnson deal in November 1997. Initially frozen out of the first-team picture, he was given a regular place in the Shakers' defence following Paul Butler's transfer to Sunderland and was voted the club's Player of the Year. Injuries and suspensions then hampered his progress the following season, but he was back to his best in 2000–01 but having played in 146 games he was transferred to Rotherham United. Always giving maximum effort, he was made the Millers' captain and his never-say-die attitude led to him appearing in 184 games before he moved on to Oldham Athletic in 2005.

TALBOT Brian Ernest

Midfield

Born: Ipswich, 21 July 1953.
Career: IPSWICH TOWN 1970; Arsenal 1979; Watford 1985; Stoke City 1986; West Bromwich Albion 1988; Fulham 1991; Aldershot 1991.

■ Brain Talbot began his career as an apprentice with Ipswich Town in July 1968 and before turning professional in the summer of 1972, he had a two-year loan spell with Toronto Metros. He made his first-team debut for the Portman Road club in a 1–0 win at Burnley in February 1974 and played in the remaining 15 games of the season, scoring three goals. He spent seven seasons in the Ipswich first team, playing in 227 first-team matches and won five England caps, the first against Northern Ireland in 1977. He was also in the Ipswich team of 1978 that beat Arsenal to lift the FA Cup. In January 1979, the all-action midfielder joined the Gunners for £450,000 and at the end of that season was a member of Arsenal's FA Cup-winning team against Manchester United. Talbot scored the first and Alan Sunderland grabbed the winner. In doing so he became, and still is, the only player ever to play for different Cup-winning teams in successive seasons. Talbot created an Arsenal club record in 1979–80 when he appeared in all of the club's 70 first-team games and also that season he played in both losing major finals, in the FA Cup against West Ham United and in the European Cup-winners' Cup against Valencia. The driving force behind both Ipswich and Arsenal's midfield, his play was built around his great stamina. In just over six seasons at Highbury, he played in a staggering 327 first-team games. Following the signing of Southampton's Steve Williams, he realised his Arsenal days were over and he joined Watford for £150,000 in June 1985. He later played for Stoke City, West Bromwich Albion and Fulham and after serving as chairman of the PFA, he went into football management with the Baggies and later Aldershot. After a spell in charge of Hibernians of Malta, he returned to these shores and took Rushden and Diamonds into the Football League. He later managed Oldham Athletic and Oxford United.

TANNER Adam David

Defender

Born: Maldon, 25 October 1973.
Career: IPSWICH TOWN 1992; Peterborough United 2000; Colchester United 2000; Canvey Island 2001.

■ Starting out as a central midfield player, showing good vision and good passing ability, he made his belated debut against Leicester in January 1995 and scored with a low volley – a goal that won him the Goal of the Season award from the supporters. He also scored the goal that secured the club's first-ever victory at Anfield. Over the next couple of seasons, his first-team opportunities were limited because of the competition for places and, when he did get in, it was as a central defender as a result of an injury crisis. His season fell apart when he tested positive for cocaine and was suspended for three months by the FA. However, the club stood by him and he received a great reception from the fans when he came on as a substitute in the final League game of the 1996–97 season against Birmingham. Putting all his troubles behind him, he still could not establish a regular first-team place and his versatility made him an ideal person to have on the substitutes'

Brian Talbot

bench. The arrival of Jean-Manuel Thetis and the emergence of Titus Bramble saw the competition for places in defence become even keener and he left to join Peterborough United. Unable to break into their first team, he moved on to Colchester United where he made just a handful of appearances before signing for Ryman League club Canvey Island. He appeared as a substitute in their FA Trophy Final victory over Forest Green in May 2001.

TARICCO Mauricio Ricardo

Defender

Born: Buenos Aires, Argentina 10 March 1973.
Career: Argentinos Juniors 1993; IPSWICH TOWN 1994; Tottenham Hotspur 1998; West Ham United 2004.

■ Able to play at full-back or in midfield, with a preference for the right side, Taricco has an Italian father and therefore can play without a work permit under EEC rules. Able to speak English well, he joined Ipswich from Argentinos in September 1994 and made his debut in the home leg of the Coca-Cola Cup tie against Bolton Wanderers who fielded two wingers. It was a tough baptism and he appeared to be uncomfortable defensively. He was only brought into the side the following season at left-back, following an injury to Neil Thompson, but seemed far more comfortable in the number-three spot. He became more influential as the campaign wore on, combining well with Stuart Slater. He had a tremendous season in 1996–97, culminating in him being voted the supporters' Player of the Year. After scoring his first goal for the club against Reading, he then got the winner at Stoke before opening the scoring in the local derby against Norwich. In 1997–98, following the arrival of Jamie Clapham, he was switched to right-back and it was this formation that produced the wonderful unbeaten run which took Town to the Play-offs. His contribution was recognised when he was named in the PFA Nationwide Division One select team. He continued to excite the locals in the opening weeks of the following campaign but in the game against Wolves in November 1998 he was stretchered off in the last minute with an ankle injury. It proved to be his last appearance in an Ipswich shirt as the next day the club announced that they had accepted a £1.8 million offer from Tottenham Hotspur. Quickly settling in at White Hart Lane, he was one of the North London club's most consistent players before needing a hernia operation. On his return, he suffered an uncharacteristic disciplinary record at Tottenham in 2001–02 but put all that behind him the following season when he scored his first Premiership goal. The pacy defender continued to demonstrate his great distribution skills until November 2004 when after making 156 appearances he joined West Ham United. Yet within days he had left Upton Park to return to Argentina.

After just 21 minutes of his debut against Millwall he was injured. The recovery period was deemed to be long term and his contract was mutually terminated.

TENNENT David

Winger

Born: Ayr, 22 January 1930.
Career: Annbank United; IPSWICH TOWN 1952; Albion Rovers.

■ Signed from Scottish junior club Annbank United, winger David Tennent made his Ipswich debut at Colchester United on the opening day of the season in what turned out to be a goalless draw. After impressing on his next appearance in the East Anglian derby defeat of Norwich City 2–1, he played in two successive defeats but was not called upon again. Midway through the campaign he returned north of the border to continue his career with Albion Rovers in the Scottish B Section.

THETIS Jean-Manuel (Manu)

Defender

Born: Dijon, France, 5 November 1971.
Career: Seville (Spain) 1997; IPSWICH TOWN 1998; Wolverhampton Wanderers (loan) 2000; Sheffield United 2001.

■ A giant of a defender, he joined Ipswich from Spanish club Seville in September 1998, making his debut against Oxford United. He did not take long to endear himself to the fans although he fell foul of the referees who seemed to book him by reputation. Able to play in central defence or as a right-wing back, he showed that he liked to get forward as often as possible and ended his first season with three goals to his credit – the best of which was the overhead kick which earned three points at West Bromwich Albion. Starting the 1999–2000 season on the right of a

Frans Thijssen

three-man central defensive unit at Portman Road he was a key figure in the club's successful start to the campaign. Thetis appeared to carry the can for the club's poor display in the home game against Queen's Park Rangers and that as well as a bad Achilles injury meant that he only played in a further four games. At the beginning of the following season, he joined Wolves on loan but after just three appearances he returned to Portman Road prior to signing for Sheffield United on transfer deadline day in March 2001. He made just one appearance from the bench for the Blades before in the close season returning to play in France.

THIJSSEN Franciscus Johannes

Midfield

Born: Holland, 23 January 1952. Career: NEC Breda (Holland) 1973; FC Twente (Holland) 1973; IPSWICH TOWN 1979; Vancouver Whitecaps (Canada) 1983; Nottingham Forest 1983; Fortuna Sittard (Holland) 1984.

■ The £200,000 paid to Dutch club FC Twente by Bobby Robson in February 1979 for Frans Thijssen was shrewd business by the Ipswich manager. A former teammate of the club's other Dutchman, Arnold Muhren, he 'guested' for Ipswich in Trevor Whymark's testimonial match when Norwich City provided the opposition. He made his League debut in a 1–0 win at Derby County and over the next four seasons was a virtual ever present, although he missed a few games during the 1981–82 campaign because of groin trouble. There was talk during his stay at Portman Road that because his contract was soon to expire he may return to his native Holland. But manager Bobby Robson must have persuaded him that there were better times ahead and that he should stay and enjoy them. The first of his 16 goals for the club was the winner against Norwich City at Carrow Road and so he was a huge favourite with the Ipswich faithful. He also scored one goal in each leg of the 1981 UEFA Cup Final against AZ67 Alkmaar. Thijssen's time with the club was marked by a high standard of application and skill and his crowning achievement was in 1980–81 when the Football Writers' Association named him as their Footballer of the Year. Thijssen's name joined the distinguished roll of many of the British game's finest since Stanley Matthews became its first recipient. Thijssen was only the second foreigner to carry off the accolade, the other being German-born Bert Trautmann, the Manchester City goalkeeper, in 1956. Thijssen proved beyond doubt that skill in whatever circumstances will always come out on top and turned in a superb performance in his final match at Norwich in April 1983. Promised a free transfer, he joined Vancouver Whitecaps before returning to play League football for Brian Clough's Nottingham Forest. He later completed his playing career in his native Holland, playing for Fortuna Sittard. After coaching the youth team at Vitesse Arnhem, he managed Swedish club Malmo.

THOMPSON Kenneth John

Wing-half
Born: Ipswich, 1 March 1945.
Career: IPSWICH TOWN 1962; Exeter City 1966.

■ Having impressed in the club's youth and reserve teams, tough-tackling wing-half Ken Thompson made his League debut for Ipswich against Portsmouth in November 1964, a game Town won 7–0 with Frank Brogan netting a hat-trick. Thompson had helped set up a couple of the Ipswich goals and kept his place in the side for the following game – a 4–0 defeat at Manchester City. His last appearance that season saw Ipswich concede another four goals at Preston. He made a handful of appearances in 1965–66 but again played in two games where the defence let in four goals including his last appearance in the final game of the season when he came off the bench in a 4–1 defeat at Bristol City. On leaving Portman Road, he joined Exeter City where he played just one season of Fourth Division football.

THOMPSON Neil

Left-back
Born: Beverley, 2 October 1963.
Career: Nottingham Forest; Hull City 1981; Scarborough 1983; IPSWICH TOWN 1989; Barnsley 1996; Oldham Athletic (loan) 1997; York City 1998; Scarborough 2000; Boston United 2001.

■ Neil Thompson began his career with Nottingham Forest but when he was not offered professional terms, he joined Fourth Division Hull City. He made his Football League debut at Tranmere Rovers in February 1982. Plagued by injury in Hull's promotion-winning season of 1982–83 he was released and joined Scarborough of the Alliance Premier League. At this point his Football League career seemed to be over and so it proved, at least for four years. However, in 1986–87, Scarborough won the Championship of the re-titled Vauxhall Conference and became the first team to be promoted to the Football League. Missing very few games, he helped his side reach the Play-offs but any disappointment at losing to Leyton Orient was short lived, as he moved up the League to join Ipswich Town. He made his debut against Barnsley in August 1989 and went on to play in all but one game in his first season at Portman Road. He missed a few games through injury in 1990–91 but was back to his best the following season as Ipswich won the Second Division Championship and with it automatic promotion to the new Premier League. An Achilles tendon injury forced him to miss the last few matches of that 1992–93 season. He continued to be an important member of the Ipswich side over the next few seasons, though there were times when his appearances were restricted by injuries. Given a free transfer in the summer of 1996, Neil Thompson had appeared in 246 games before signing for Barnsley. He quickly settled in at Oakwell and by the end of his first season, he had helped the Reds win promotion to the top flight. Surprisingly he found himself in and out of the side in 1997–98 and had loan spells with Oldham and York City before joining the Minstermen as the club's player-coach. When Alan Little was dismissed he became York's caretaker manager but he too was sacked and moved to one of his former clubs, Scarborough, on a non-contract basis. He later joined Boston United as manager but injuries at the club saw him playing League football once more.

THOMSEN Claus

Defender/Midfield
Born: Aarhus, Denmark, 31 May 1970.
Career: Aarhus GF (Denmark);

IPSWICH TOWN 1994; Everton 1997; AB Copenhagen (Denmark); VFL Wolfsburg (Germany).

■ Danish international Claus Thomsen was bought from his home-town club Aarhus for £200,000 in the summer of 1994 but was one of a number of players who had to postpone his Ipswich debut in 1994–95, this time because of a hernia. The tall midfielder who generated much excitement with his penetrating runs, played his first game for the club against Bolton Wanderers in the League Cup second-round first-leg tie at Portman Road. His first League game against Manchester United saw him provide the cross from which Paul Mason scrambled home one of the goals in a 3–2 win for Town. He ended that disastrous relegation season as the club's top scorer with just five goals. At first though he found it quite hard to adjust to the English game and after returning for the 1995–96 with an injury picked up while playing in a pre-season friendly for Denmark, he started the new campaign on the sidelines. On his return to the side he played in central defence, benefiting playing alongside Tony Mowbray and, when these two played together, Town produced their best defensive displays of the campaign. Having played for Denmark in Euro '96, he appeared for Ipswich until midway through the 1996–97 season when Joe Royle, the manager of Everton, took him to Goodison Park for a fee of £900,000. Despite being a virtual ever present, the Dane suffered the misfortune of scoring an own-goal in the Goodison derby against Liverpool. Following Royle's departure, Thomsen did not seem to figure in new manager Howard Kendall's plans and was sold to AB Copenhagen for £500,000, later moving into German football with VFL Wolfsburg.

THORBURN James Hope Forrest

Goalkeeper

Born: Lanark, 10 March 1938.
Career: Raith Rovers; IPSWICH TOWN 1963; St Mirren 1965.

■ Goalkeeper Jim Thorburn began his career playing First Division football in Scotland for Raith Rovers. His displays for the Stark's Park club led to him being signed by Ipswich in the summer of 1963. He made his debut for the Blues in a 2–1 defeat at home to Arsenal towards the end of that season after Roy Bailey and Dave Bevis had occupied the number-one jersey in the earlier games. He appeared in 10 games that season but there were some disastrous results among those games as Town were relegated to Division Two. Thorburn was between the posts for the 9–1 demolition by Stoke, the 6–0 beating by Liverpool and the 6–3 reversal at Spurs. All told, he conceded 36 goals in those 10 games. In 1965–66, he appeared in 14 consecutive games midway through the campaign and though he conceded four goals in the games against Rotherham United and Manchester City, he did keep a clean sheet as Town beat Portsmouth 7–0. On leaving Portman Road he returned to Scotland to play for St Mirren and though they lost their top-flight status in 1966–67, Thorburn was in goal the following season when they won the Second Division Championship.

THROWER Dennis Alan

Wing-half

Born: Ipswich, 1 August 1938.
Career: Landseer Old Boys; IPSWICH TOWN 1955; Bury Town.

■ Wing-half Dennis Thrower played his first game in Ipswich colours in a 1–0 win over Bournemouth in August 1956 and though he made one more appearance that season, he did not appear in the Town side again until the 1962–63 season. A great servant of the Portman Road club, Thrower was used primarily as an understudy to the likes of Reg Pickett, Bill Baxter and John Elsworthy but did play in 17 games in 1964–65 when the club finished fifth in Division Two. Not a great goalscorer, Thrower's two goals for the club were both scored against Bolton Wanderers but in two different seasons. On leaving Portman Road in June 1965, he signed for local non-League club Bury Town.

TIBBOTT Leslie

Full-back

Born: Oswestry, 25 August 1955.
Career: IPSWICH TOWN 1973; Sheffield United 1979.

■ A Welsh Under-21 international, full-back Les Tibbott worked his way up through the ranks at Portman Road to make his debut in a 1–1 draw at home to Coventry City in January 1976. He appeared on a more regular basis in 1976–77 but it was the following season before he established himself as a first-team regular. In March 1979, having appeared in 54 League games, he left Ipswich to play for Sheffield United. He missed very few games in three seasons at Bramall Lane and, following the club's relegation to the League's basement in 1980–81, he was a member of the side that won immediate promotion as Fourth Division champions in 1981–82.

TREACY Francis

Inside-forward

Born: Glasgow, 14 July 1939.
Career: Johnstone Burgh; IPSWICH TOWN 1961; St Mirren.

■ Signed from Scottish junior football with Johnstone Burgh Frank Treacy had to bide his time in the club's reserves before making his Ipswich debut at Nottingham Forest in November 1963 – a match Town lost 3–1. The following season of 1964–65 saw Treacy score five goals in 12 games including two in the 5–2 defeat of Middlesbrough and a last-minute winner against Bury. He played in a handful of games the following season but was then allowed to return north of the border to continue his career with St Mirren. In his second season at Love Street, St Mirren scored 100 League goals in winning the Second Division Championship and Treacy was the Buddies' leading scorer.

TRENTER Ronald Herbert

Outside-right

Born: Ipswich, 13 December 1928.
Career: Whitton; IPSWICH TOWN 1945; Clacton Town 1951; IPSWICH TOWN 1951; Clacton Town 1951.

■ Winger Ron Trenter joined Ipswich from local side Whitton in December 1945 but on being unable to break into the club's first team he left to play non-League football for Clacton Town. His impressive displays for the non-League side led to him being given a second chance by the Blues and at the start of the 1951–52 season he made his two League appearances for the Portman Road club. Trenter's debut on the opening day of the season saw Town beat Southend United 4–1 but then he was part of the side that lost 4–0 at Millwall and did not play for the club again. He rejoined Clacton and gave them a good number of years service before later emigrating to Australia.

TROTTER Liam

Midfield

Born: Ipswich, 24 August 1988.
Career: IPSWICH TOWN 2005.

■ Central midfielder Liam Trotter is another product of the Ipswich Town Academy. He had trials with both Ipswich and Colchester but was never taken on as a schoolboy and ended up playing for Ransomes Youth. He later went to West Suffolk College where he ended up playing under Danny Laws and after finally being given a trial by Ipswich was offered a two-year contract. He made his only appearance for the club off the bench in the last game of the 2005–06 Championship season at Plymouth Argyle.

TURNER Robin David

Forward

Born: Carlisle, 10 September 1955.
Career: IPSWICH TOWN 1973; Swansea City 1985; Colchester United 1985; Bury Town.

■ Though he never set the world alight with his footballing prowess,

Robin Turner demanded the utmost respect from the Ipswich fans, for his undying loyalty to the Portman Road club. He made his first-team debut at Derby County in October 1975 in a match the Rams won 1–0 and between then and his final appearance in a Town shirt against Nottingham Forest in April 1984, when the game ended in a 2–2 draw, he made just 22 League starts and appeared off the bench on 28 occasions. On leaving Ipswich, he signed for Swansea City but could not settle in South Wales and returned to play for Colchester United before entering the world of non-League football with Bury Town.

TWAMLEY Bruce Richardson

Full-back

Born: Canada, 23 May 1952.
Career: IPSWICH TOWN 1969; Vancouver Whitecaps (Canada) 1975; New York Cosmos (United States); Minnesota Kicks (United States); Edmonton Drillers (United States).

■ A Canadian international, full-back Bruce Twamley worked his way up through the ranks at Portman Road to make his League debut in the number-three shirt in a 2–1 defeat at Wolverhampton Wanderers in March 1974. He made just one other appearance for the club, this time in the number-two shirt, a year later as the club came from behind to beat Leicester City 2–1. After that, he returned to his native Canada to play for Vancouver Whitecaps before joining New York Cosmos. He spent three seasons with the Cosmos, playing with the likes of Pele before switching to Minnesota Kicks for a couple of seasons. He ended his playing days with three seasons in the NASL for Edmonton Drillers. Twamley, who won seven of his nine full international caps for Canada whilst with Ipswich, is still involved with the national team, being appointed as an assistant-coach.

TYLER Leonard Victor

Left-back

Born: Rotherhithe, 7 January 1919.
Died: 1988.
Career: Redhill; Millwall 1943; IPSWICH TOWN 1950; Sittingbourne.

■ Able to play in either of the full-back berths, Len Tyler started out with Millwall but in his second season with the club, they finished bottom of the Second Division and dropped down into the Third Division South. Tyler was one of the Lions' mainstays following their relegation but in the summer of 1950 he left the London club and signed for Ipswich Town. He made his debut for the Portman Road club in a 1–1 draw against Northampton Town on the opening day of the 1950–51 season and went on to miss just one game. Injuries disrupted his progress in 1951–52 especially during the second half of the campaign and in the close season, it was decided to release him. A player who had the lost best years of his career to World War Two, he opted for a move into non-League football with Sittingbourne.

UHLENBEEK Gustav Reiner

Defender

Born: Paramaribo, Surinam, 20 August 1970.
Career: Ajax (Holland); Cambuur (Holland); SV Tops (Holland); IPSWICH TOWN 1995; Fulham 1998; Sheffield United 2000; Walsall (loan) 2002; Bradford City 2002; Chesterfield 2003; Wycombe Wanderers 2004; Mansfield Town 2005.

■ Gus Uhlenbeek joined Ipswich on a permanent basis from Dutch side SV Tops prior to the start of the 1995–96 season, having impressed during summer trials as a fast and direct winger with a powerful shot. In an astute tactical gamble by manager George Burley, Uhlenbeek was switched to right-back for the Anglo Italian Cup game against Brescia and looked like he had played there for years. Having started the following season with a cream rinse in his hair, presumably to match the club's new colours of cream and black, he suffered a spate of injuries and was not really match fit until midway through the campaign. A regular for the rest of the season, Uhlenbeek broke his foot during the Play-off game against Sheffield United and as it did not heal properly, he was forced to have surgery during the close season. Again he missed half of a season but showed on his return that he had lost none of his tremendous pace. Setting up Alex Mathie's second goal in the derby game against Norwich, he sadly left Ipswich for Fulham on a free transfer under the Bosman ruling in the summer of 1998. In his first season with the Cottagers, he helped them win the Second Division Championship. Even so, he was never an automatic choice at Fulham and joined Sheffield United. He was a fixture in the Blades' side until losing his place to Rob Kozluk. Following a loan spell with Walsall, when his side beat the Blades 1–0 to secure their First Division status, he signed for Bradford City where he was a virtual ever present. After parting company with the Bantams, he joined Chesterfield but his stay at Saltergate was brief because of disciplinary problems and he moved on to Wycombe Wanderers. He had a fine season with the club but left to play his football for Mansfield Town in 2005.

UNSWORTH David Gerald

Defender

Born: Chorley, 16 October 1973.
Career: Everton 1992; West Ham United 1997; Aston Villa 1998; Everton 1998; Portsmouth 2004; IPSWICH TOWN (loan) 2005; Sheffield United 2005.

■ David Unsworth made his Football League debut for Everton against Tottenham Hotspur in April 1992 while still a trainee. Although he was substituting at left-back for the injured Andy Hinchcliffe, he scored a stunning equalising goal for the Toffees with a first-touch volley from a corner in a 3–3 thriller. In his early days with the club, Everton fans thought he would prove the natural long-term successor to Welsh international Kevin Ratcliffe for, like the former skipper, Unsworth proved to be a quick, powerful and efficient left-sided central defender. During the 1994–95 season he developed a fine central defensive partnership alongside Dave Watson, helping Everton lift the FA Cup at the end of that campaign. England manager Terry Venables called him up to the full international squad and he played against Japan. Much to the consternation of many Everton supporters, Unsworth left Goodison in the summer of 1997, joining West Ham United for a fee of £1 million, with the Hammers' Danny Williamson moving in the opposite direction. Despite having an excellent first season at Upton Park, a year later he was involved in one of the most bizarre transfers in Premiership history. After joining Aston Villa, he realised that his former club Everton also coveted his signature. Following his pleas to the Villa board and without kicking a ball for his new club, he was allowed to rejoin Everton for the £3 million Villa had paid the Hammers. Back at Everton, he was appointed club captain and he developed into one of the Premiership's most solid and reliable defenders, going on to appear in 350 games for the club and equalling the club record of 23 successful spot-kicks while playing against Liverpool. In the summer of 2004 he joined Portsmouth but after a good start when he appeared in a variety of defensive roles he fell out of favour and joined Town on loan. He made an immediate impact in his debut against Sheffield United at Bramall Lane when he cut in from the left-wing to smash the ball home and open the scoring. He kept his place until the end of the season and although he strengthened the club's back four, he never really reached the heights that he had on his debut. The loan agreement with Pompey did not cover the Play-off matches and he returned to Fratton Park before joining Sheffield United for the 2005–06 season and helping them win promotion to the Premiership.

VAUGHAN Anthony John

Midfield

Born: Manchester, 11 October 1975.
Career: IPSWICH TOWN 1994; Manchester City 1997; Cardiff City (loan) 1999; Nottingham Forest 2000; Scunthorpe United (loan) 2002; Mansfield Town (loan) 2002; Motherwell (loan) 2003; Mansfield Town 2003; Barnsley 2004; Stockport County 2005 (loan).

■ Originally a defender who could play at full-back or in central defence, he made his Ipswich debut at Chelsea in October 1994 and had started to stake a regular claim when he injured a knee badly at Manchester City. Though he returned to action in 1995–96 he served three suspensions, mainly due to arriving late for challenges which he put down to a lack of timing and pace following injuries. The following season he scored a number of goals for Town from set pieces and was part of the defence which kept five successive clean sheets in the run-in to the Play-offs. Although he was offered a new contract, he declined to sign it, preferring to keep his options open.

In June 1997, he joined Manchester City for a fee of £1 million. Though the then Maine Road club were relegated from Division One at the end of his first season with the club, Tony Vaughan, who had been switched to midfield, showed commitment and flair from a position he appeared to be more than comfortable in. With the team pushing for promotion, Vaughan missed almost half the games through injury and suspension. Finding himself a fringe player, he had a spell on loan with Cardiff City. The Welsh club were keen to sign him but terms could not be agreed and he signed for Nottingham Forest for a fee of £350,000. Disciplinary problems reared their head the following season and manager David Platt immediately put him on the transfer list. A forgotten figure at the City Ground he had loan spells with Scunthorpe and Mansfield before going north of the border to join Motherwell in a similar capacity. He then spent a season with the Stags before captaining Barnsley throughout 2004–05. He left Oakwell to spend three months on loan with Stockport prior to rejoining the Yorkshire club.

VENUS Mark

Defender

Born: Hartlepool, 6 April 1967. Career: Hartlepool United 1985; Leicester City 1985; Wolverhampton Wanderers 1988; IPSWICH TOWN 1997; Cambridge United 2003; Dagenham & Redbridge 2004; Hibernian 2004.

■ After a handful of appearances as a non-contract player with his hometown club Hartlepool United, Mark Venus joined Leicester City. He struggled in the Foxes' side that languished near the foot of the First Division and in March 1988 he was allowed to move on to Fourth Division leaders Wolverhampton Wanderers for their run-in for a fee of £40,000. A year later he won a Third Division Championship medal with the Molineux club before graduating to the captaincy of the club. Over the next few seasons, Mark Venus proved himself a versatile defender, going on to play in 338 games before in the summer of 1997 joining Ipswich as part of the deal that saw Steve Sedgley move in the opposite direction. He went straight into the Ipswich team for the game at Queen's Park Rangers, partnering Jason Cundy in central defence, and scored his first goal in only his second game, at Charlton in the Coca-Cola Cup. His season then took a turn for the worse in the derby game against Norwich. In what was thought a minor thigh injury, it proved more serious and he was out of action until the end of December. On his return he broke a toe. This too proved difficult to heal and he was out until towards the end of the campaign. His contribution to the club's success in 1998–99 was immense, being a key figure on the left side of the three-man central defence which helped equal a club record 26 clean sheets during the campaign and weighing in with nine goals. His abilities were recognised by his inclusion in the PFA First Division select side. After relinquishing his post as the club's penalty taker, it was inevitable that his seasonal goals tally would drop. However, he scored the first goal of the 2000–01 season at Tottenham and though he started to lose a little of his pace, he more than compensated for this with some great anticipation that enabled him to snuff out any danger at an early stage. In 2001–02 he scooped all the club's Player of the Year awards this in spite of the club having the worst defensive record in the Premiership. Injuries then hampered his progress and he left to play for Cambridge United. He later went on loan to Dagenham & Redbridge and had a game for Hibernian before joining Hornchurch as assistant manager.

VERNAZZI Paolo Andrea

Midfield

Born: Islington, 1 November 1979. Career: Arsenal 1997; IPSWICH TOWN (loan) 1998; Portsmouth (loan) 2000; Watford 2000; Rotherham United 2004; Barnet (loan) 2005.

■ Despite his Italian name, which he owed to his parenthood, Paulo Vernazzi was born in Islington and came through the junior ranks at Arsenal to turn professional in November 1997. He made his first-team debut at Highbury alongside Chris Wreh in the Coca-Cola Cup tie against Birmingham City and later, with nine first teamers out of action, made his League debut at Crystal Palace. The following season, he had a three-month loan spell at Portman Road, making his Ipswich debut in a 1–0 win against Swindon Town and three days later playing his second and final game in the East Anglian derby against Norwich City, a match Town lost by the same scoreline. The following season he had another spell on loan, this time at Portsmouth where he added class and strength to the Pompey midfield. Capped by England at Under-18 and Under-20 levels, he returned to Highbury early after Tony Pulis decided he needed to cut the wage bills. Back with Arsenal, he played against Ipswich in the Worthington Cup before in December 2000 he joined Watford for a fee of £350,000. His early displays for the Hornets led to him winning selection for the England Under-21 side against Germany. In 2001–02 he suffered a number of injuries and one of these, a cartilage injury, required an operation and brought his season to a premature end. He returned to action the following season but his failure to score goals led to him being given a free transfer by the Vicarage Road club. He joined Rotherham United where he always gave of his best in the difficult circumstances of a relegation season. In 2005–06 he had a spell on loan with Barnet before returning to Millmoor.

VILJOEN Colin

Midfield

Born: Johannesburg, South Africa, 20 June 1948.
Career: IPSWICH TOWN 1967; Manchester City 1978; Chelsea 1980.

■ South African-born midfielder Colin Viljoen made a remarkable debut for the Portman Road club when he played against Portsmouth in March 1967. After finding themselves two goals down in the opening quarter of an hour, Town fought back to win 4–2 with Viljoen scoring a hat-trick. He played in the last 10 games of that season, scoring six goals and over the next eight seasons missed very few matches. In 1967–68 he endeared himself to Ipswich fans when in the local derby against Norwich City, he netted another hat-trick after Town had once again been behind to two early goals – this time Ipswich beat the Canaries 4–3. In 1974–75, when Town finished third in Division One, Viljoen was voted Player of the Year, his form winning him the first of two England caps, when he played in a goalless draw against Northern Ireland at Wembley. Sadly, the following season he suffered from Achilles tendon trouble and was forced to miss most of the campaign. In fact, he missed the entire 1976–77 campaign after three operations on the tendon. The following season, with Viljoen still out of action for most of the campaign, Ipswich overcame hurdle after hurdle to reach the FA Cup Final. As the big day approached, Bobby Robson, much to the disgust of the team, opted to give Viljoen a run out instead of Roger Osborne who had played his part in the club getting there. The team obviously did not agree with Robson's decision and Town lost 6–1. The Ipswich boss was obviously upset, but he got the message – Osborne played at Wembley and became the unlikely hero. Later that summer Viljoen, who had scored 54 goals in 372 League and Cup games, left Portman Road to join Manchester City where he was again hampered by injuries. He appeared in just 38 games for the then Maine Road club before ending his League career with Chelsea whom he joined in March 1980. He later ran a public house called Nine Stiles near New Denham for a while before returning to live in his native South Africa.

WALLS James Parker

Centre-half

Born: Crossgates, 11 March 1928.
Died: 1995.
Career: Crossgates; Charlton Athletic 1945; IPSWICH TOWN 1954; Stowmarket 1955.

■ Having played his early football north of the border for Scottish junior side Crossgates near Dunfermline, centre-half Jimmy Walls was given his chance in the Football League by Charlton Athletic. He was at The Valley for eight seasons of League football, but in that time he made just 10 League appearances. Transferred to Ipswich Town in readiness for the 1954–55 season, his one and only appearance in the blue of the Portman Road club came in September 1954, a match the Potters won 1–0 with a late goal. At the end of that season, he realised his chances of regular first-team football at Ipswich were slim and he decided to leave and play non-League football for Stowmarket.

WALSH Roy

Inside-forward

Born: Dedham, 15 January 1947.
Career: IPSWICH TOWN 1965; Southend United 1967.

■ A versatile forward who excelled for the club's reserve side, he made his first-team debut for Ipswich Town against Cardiff City at Ninian Park in a League Cup fifth-round game in November 1965. That season, he appeared in seven League games but could not force his way into the side on a regular basis because of the form of players like Gerry Baker and Danny Hegan. He decided in the summer of 1967 to leave and try his luck with Southend United but following his arrival at Roots Hall he found that competition for places was stiff and he left to play in local non-League football.

WARK John

Midfield

Born: Glasgow, 4 August 1957.
Career: IPSWICH TOWN 1974; Liverpool 1984; IPSWICH TOWN 1988; Middlesbrough 1990; IPSWICH TOWN 1991.

■ After turning professional with Ipswich Town during the 1974 close season, John Wark made his League debut at Portman Road against Leicester City in March 1975 but it was not until 1976–77 that he became a regular in Town's midfield. It was then that he gave early warning of his goalscoring prowess with 10 goals in 33 League appearances. He missed the first half of the following season with injury but returned to help the club to the FA Cup Final where they beat Arsenal 1–0. Ipswich totally outplayed the Gunners and Wark crashed two tremendous shots against the post. He made his international debut for Scotland against Wales in May 1979 and remained a regular selection until 1984. In total he scored seven goals in his 29 international appearances. In three consecutive seasons from 1979 to 1982, the Blues came close to winning the League Championship without actually clinching it and Wark's goals were instrumental in keeping the club at or near the top. Consolation for these near misses was found in the club's UEFA Cup victory of 1980–81 in which the Scotsman's contribution was outstanding. He scored four goals against Aris Salonika in the first round, a hat-trick against Widzew Lodz in the third round, goals in both legs of the fourth round against St Etienne, a goal in the semi-final against Cologne and goals in each leg of the Final against AZ67 Alkmaar which Ipswich won 5–4 on aggregate. In total he scored 14 goals from midfield in 12 games. It brought him the accolade of his fellow professionals – the PFA senior award as Player of the Year. The added honour he received, and one which must have been totally unexpected, was that of European Young Footballer of the Year, an award he travelled specially to Italy to collect. He even made an appearance in a film. He had a small part in *Escape to Victory* alongside Pele and Bobby Moore. In 1982–83 he was top scorer with 20 League goals but had become disaffected and in March 1984 he joined Liverpool for a fee of £450,000, just in time to share in their League Championship triumph. In 1984–85 he was Liverpool's top scorer with 18 League goals including a hat-trick at West Bromwich Albion. Plagued by injury in 1985–86 he again missed out on a League Championship medal and

John Wark

never won his place back at Anfield. In January 1988 he moved back to Ipswich and proved he had not lost his goalscoring touch with 13 League goals in 1988–89 and 10 in 1989–90. Surprisingly he joined Middlesbrough for the following season but never really settled and in September 1991 returned to Ipswich for a third time as a non-contract player, apparently to help on the coaching side rather than as a first-team player. Remarkably he returned to the team a month after rejoining the club as a central defender and held his place to the end of the season as Town won the Second Division Championship. In 1992–93 he proved he was still good enough to play at the highest level as the Blues embarked on the first season of Premier League football. In November 1995, in the game at Norwich, he broke the derby appearance record held jointly by Mick Mills and Kevin Keelan and when he scored from the penalty spot he broke the goalscoring record as well. Always an inspiration to those around him, John Wark scored 190 goals in 678 first-team games in his three spells at Portman Road.

WARNE Raymond

Centre-forward

Born: Ipswich, 16 February 1929.
Career: Leiston; IPSWICH TOWN 1950; Sudbury Town.

■ Signed from non-League Leiston, centre-forward Ray Warne scored on his debut against Plymouth Argyle in December 1950, going on to net 11 goals in 22 games including doubles against Gillingham and Watford. He could not maintain this impressive goals per game ratio and did not add to his total the following season although he was played on the right-wing. At the end of that season, he was released by the Portman Road club and left to play non-League football for Sudbury Town.

WESTLAKE Ian John

Midfield

Born: Clacton, 10 July 1983.
Career: IPSWICH TOWN 2002.

■ Ian Westlake was one of a number of young talents to be offered a first-team chance during the course of the 2002–03 season, when in October 2002, he came off the bench in the home defeat by Gillingham when Tony Mowbray was looking after the team. He made a handful more appearances as a substitute later in the season. He made his first full start against West ham United at the start of the following season, going on to enjoy a remarkable campaign. He quickly established himself in the Town line up and his industrious style of play made it very difficult for Joe Royle to leave him out. Used mainly on the left side of midfield, Westlake also proved that he could man-mark effectively. He ended that season as the club's Player of the Year and won the John Kerridge trophy for the most improved player as determined by the coaching staff. At the start of the 2004–05 season, he was named in the England Under-21 squad but has yet to make his debut at that level. Unable to find that level of consistency throughout the following campaign, he did chip in with a number of goals from midfield. Last season he found himself in and out of the team but the highlight was probably in the home game against Luton Town when he came off the bench to score the only goal of the game – a brilliant piece of individual skill, chesting down Darren Currie's free-kick and shooting home.

WHELAN Philip James

Centre-half

Born: Reddish, 7 March 1972.
Career: IPSWICH TOWN 1990; Middlesbrough 1995; Oxford United 1997; Rotherham United 1999; Southend United 2000.

■ Following a successful trial, central defender Phil Whelan signed professional forms for Ipswich Town. Following an early season Zenith Data Cup outing in 1991–92, he made his Football League debut away to Southend United in April 1992, standing in for the injured Dave Linighan and scoring in a 2–1 win. He also scored in his second League game and showed much composure in his eight end-of-season games as Town swept to the Second Division Championship and promotion to the Premier League. Often played out of position the following season, he still impressed enough to be called up by the England Under-21 side before being released to concentrate on preparing for his final accountancy exams. He made a promising start to Ipswich's Second Division Championship-winning season but suffered a horrendous ankle injury in the last home match of 1993–94 and expected to be out of action for a long time. However, he made good progress

WHITTON Stephen Paul
Midfield/Forward

Born: East Ham, 4 December 1960.
Career: Coventry City 1978; West Ham United 1983; Birmingham City 1986; Sheffield Wednesday 1989; IPSWICH TOWN 1991; Colchester United 1994.

■ One of a number of east-London youngsters discovered by Coventry City, he rose through the ranks at Highfield Road to make his Football League debut in midfield against Spurs in September 1979. However, he did not make the breakthrough until 1981–82 and the following term, having been switched to the forward line, was the club's top scorer with 12 League goals. At the end of that season, he returned to his native east-end to join West Ham United but in three seasons at Upton Park he was never really able to establish a regular place. He returned to the Midlands in the summer of 1986 to join Birmingham City after spending two months on loan at St Andrew's the previous season. At Birmingham he was converted to a central striker, top scoring with 14 goals in his second season. In 1988–89 the club were relegated to the Third Division, but before the end of the campaign he had been sold to Sheffield Wednesday. For most of his time at Hillsborough, Whitton floundered in the club's reserve side until he was rescued from obscurity by his former manager at West Ham, John Lyall, who signed him for Ipswich Town. He scored on his debut against West Bromwich Albion and in his next League outing but then lost form and his place. After several disappointing seasons, he enjoyed probably the best time of his career in 1991–92 while operating in midfield, missing only two League games and guiding Ipswich to the Second Division Championship. He had a disjointed first season in the Premiership mainly due to a variety of niggling injuries. In March 1994 he left Portman Road to become player-coach at Colchester United, later being appointed the Layer Road club's assistant manager.

WHYMARK Trevor John
Forward

Born: Diss, 4 May 1950.
Career: Diss Town; IPSWICH TOWN 1969; Sparta Rotterdam (Holland) 1979; Derby County 1979; Vancouver Whitecaps (Canada) 1980; Grimsby Town 1980; Southend United 1984; Peterborough United 1985; Colchester United 1985; Diss Town.

■ After scoring 65 goals for the club's youth and reserve teams in 1968–69, Diss-born Trevor Whymark was given his first-team debut the following season in a 1–0 defeat at Manchester City. He appeared in eight games at the end of that 1969–70 campaign, scoring his first goal for the club in a 2–0 home win over Sunderland. Over the next three seasons, Whymark scored six goals in 32 League games before establishing himself as a first-team regular in 1972–73 when he was joint-top scorer with 11 goals. Also that season he netted five goals in the Texaco Cup including one in the

with his recovery and was back in the first team in November 1994, but four months later he was transferred to Middlesbrough for £300,000. Following a registration mix-up he did not make his debut until the following season but even then injuries and a suspension limited his first-team opportunities. It was a similar story in 1996–97, before, in the close season, he was transferred to Oxford United. His first season at the Manor Ground was a nightmare: after a back injury in the opening game following a clash with a teammate, he had the misfortune to suffer a bad leg break. On recovery he fell out with the manager and was loaned to Rotherham United but stayed with Oxford to try and win a first-team place. Eventually transferred to Southend, he was appointed the Shrimpers captain, going on to play in 119 games before a serious knee ligament injury forced his retirement.

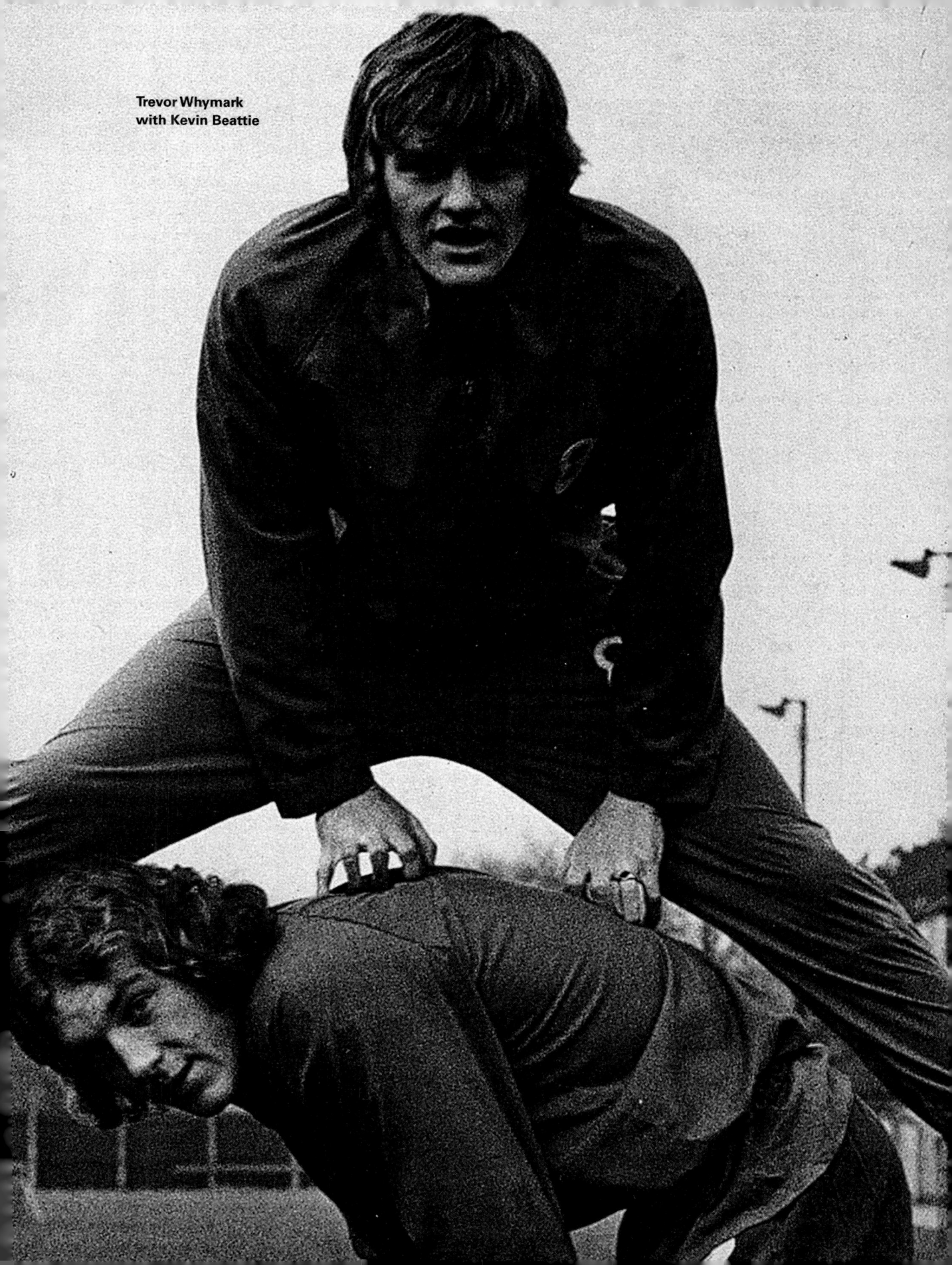

**Trevor Whymark
with Kevin Beattie**

second leg of the Final against Norwich City. In 1973–74 he again scored 11 League goals but in the UEFA Cup second-round first-leg match against Lazio, he scored all the club's goals in a 4–0 win. He was joint-top scorer in 1974–75 as Town finished third in the First Division before becoming the club's leading scorer for the first time the following season. Whymark was the club's top scorer again in 1976–77 with more than half his total of 13 League goals coming in two games! He scored four in the 7–0 demolition of West Bromwich Albion – the first time an Ipswich player had scored four goals in a First Division match – and then a hat-trick in a 5–0 win over Norwich City. In 1977–78, Whymark scored four goals in a match for the third time as Swedish side Landskrona were beaten 5–0. That performance led to him winning his first full cap for England when he came on as a substitute for Terry McDermott in a 2–0 away win in Luxembourg. Sadly, Whymark damaged knee ligaments in a Boxing Day match at Norwich and this kept him out of the club's FA Cup Final line up. Though he played a few games the following season, he was allowed to leave the club and join Vancouver Whitecaps after scoring 104 goals in 335 games. He later played two games for Derby County before Grimsby Town broke their transfer record to sign him. After scoring 16 goals in 93 League games for the Mariners, he ended his League career with spells at Southend United, Peterborough United and Colchester United.

WHYTE David Antony

Forward

Born: Greenwich, 20 April 1971.
Career: Greenwich Borough; Crystal Palace 1989; Charlton Athletic (loan) 1992; Charlton Athletic 1994; Reading 1997; IPSWICH TOWN 1997; Bristol Rovers 1998; Southend United 1998.

■ Unable to hold down a regular place in the Crystal Palace side, he joined Charlton Athletic for a fee of £450,000 in the summer of 1994, this after he had spent a spell on loan there a couple of years earlier. After joining the Addicks on a permanent basis, Whyte became a huge success, for after scoring in is first game he continued to score throughout the campaign on a regular basis. He claimed several spectacular goals among his haul and became the first Charlton player for 14 years to record over 20 in a season. Having failed to recapture his devastating form the following season, he returned to something like his best in 1996–97 before suffering a ruptured Achilles tendon which put him out of the game for six months. After an unsuccessful trial at Reading, he joined Ipswich on loan, making his debut against his former club Charlton Athletic in November 1997. He made just one more appearance, against Stockport County, but having failed to find the net in either game he moved on to play for Bristol Rovers. He showed glimpses of his talent with Rovers but still finished the 1997–98 season playing for Southend United on non-contract forms. The following season he struggled to shine in a poor Southend team and ultimately lost his place before an injury curtailed his playing career.

WIGG Ronald George

Forward

Born: Dunmow, 18 May 1949.
Died: July 1997.
Career: Leyton Orient; IPSWICH TOWN 1967; Watford 1970; Rotherham United 1973; Grimsby Town 1975; Barnsley 1977; Scunthorpe United 1977; Columbus Magic (United States); Cleveland Force (United States).

■ Ron Wigg was an apprentice at Leyton Orient in the mid-1960s, but was snapped up by Ipswich Town in April 1967. He scored twice on his debut in a 3–1 defeat of Carlisle United and though he only played in five games in that 1967–68 season, he netted another double in the 2–1 win over Birmingham City. He did not appear again until towards the end of the following season when he scored six goals in 10 games including netting in his first four consecutive games. He appeared on a more regular basis in 1969–70 but then moved to Watford for what was then a club record £18,000. With the Vicarage Road club, he hit 20 goals in 97 games before in early 1973 he was off to Rotherham United where 22 goals in 65 League outings followed. Less than two years later, Grimsby secured his services but his tally of goals for the Mariners – 11 in 63 games – was a little disappointing. Barnsley became Ron Wigg's fifth port of call before later that year he completed his career by

WILLIAMS Gavin John
Midfield

Born: Pontypridd, 20 June 1980.
Career: Hereford United; Yeovil Town 2002; West Ham United 2004; IPSWICH TOWN (loan) 2005; IPSWICH TOWN 2006.

■ Having started his career with Hereford United, for whom he scored 31 goals in 133 games, midfielder Gavin Williams joined Yeovil Town for a fee of £20,000 in the summer of 2002. In his first season with the Glovers, he helped them win the Nationwide Conference and promotion to the Football League. He was a near ever present in 2003–04 and the club's top scorer with 13 goals in all competitions as Yeovil narrowly missed out on the Play-offs. Voted the club's Player of the Year, his probing and defence-splitting passes attracted the attention of the leading clubs and it was no surprise when in December 2004, West Ham paid £250,000 for his services. He was the Hammers' star man on New Year's Day at Ipswich and only injury prevented him from winning his first full cap for Wales. With stiff competition for places at Upton Park, Williams, who has since gone on to represent Wales, joined Ipswich on loan and netted on his debut in a 1–1 draw at Coventry City. The move was made permanent and he looks like being an important member of the Town squad for years to come.

WILLIAMS David Geraint
Midfield

Born: Treorchy, 5 January 1962.
Career: Bristol Rovers 1980; Derby County 1985; IPSWICH TOWN 1992; Colchester United 1998.

■ Midfielder Geraint Williams, popularly known as 'George', was one of many youngsters from South Wales who joined Bristol Rovers during the 1970s. He made his League debut in a 3–3 home draw with Sheffield Wednesday in October 1980 and held his place for the rest of the season despite Rovers' eventual relegation to the Third Division. He was a regular performer during his five seasons with the Pirates before leaving Eastville in March 1985 to sign for Derby County for a fee of £40,000. He quickly established himself in a defensive midfield anchor role at the Baseball Ground, assisting the Rams to two consecutive promotion-winning seasons. Whilst with Derby he played for Wales against West Germany in the first international to be played at Cardiff Arms Park. Williams, who won 13 caps for Wales, went on to appear in 321 League and Cup games for Derby. After the Rams missed out on the First Division Play-offs, Williams joined Ipswich Town for a fee of £650,000 in the summer of 1992. He scored on his Town debut on the opening day of the 1992–93 season in a 1–1 draw with Aston Villa. Although he was not a prolific scorer, he did net a couple of memorable goals, perhaps none better than his goal at Reading midway through the 1995–96 season when he ran half the length of the Elm Park pitch to score in a 4–1 win for Ipswich. He remained an important member of the Ipswich side until the summer of 1998, when after appearing in 264 games for the Portman Road club, he joined Colchester United. He ended his playing career after just one season but remained at Layer Road as the club's coach.

WILLIAMS John James (Jackie)
Winger

Born: Aberdare, 29 March 1911.
Died: 1979.
Career: Aberaman; Llanelli; Huddersfield Town 1932; Aston Villa 1935; IPSWICH TOWN 1938; Wrexham 1938; Colwyn Bay; Runcorn.

■ Winger Jackie Williams played his early football in his native Wales for Aberaman and Llanelli before being signed by First Division Huddersfield Town in 1932. In his second season at Leeds Road, he helped the Yorkshire club finish runners-up in the First Division, going on to score 15 goals in 50 games before being transferred to Aston Villa. In his only season at Villa Park, the Midlands club were relegated to Division Two and so Williams left to continue his career with Ipswich Town. He played in most of the club's Southern League games over the next couple of seasons before making his Football League debut in the club's first-ever game in the competition, a 4–2 defeat of Southend United. He went on to play in nine League games in that 1938–39 season before leaving to play for Wrexham. On ending his first-class career at the Racecourse Ground, he later stayed in North Wales to play for Colwyn Bay prior to finishing his playing days with Runcorn.

WILNIS Fabian

Defender

Born: Surinam, 23 August 1970. Career: NAC Breda (Holland) 1990; De Graafschap (Holland) 1996; IPSWICH TOWN 1999.

■ This skilful defender came to Ipswich from Dutch club De Graafschap in January 1999 having previously played for NAC Breda, as the replacement for Mauricio Taricco. Although the wing-back role was new to him, having played a more traditional full-back role in Holland, he seemed ideally suited to it. Having made his debut against Grimsby Town, he scored his first goal for the club in a 6–0 win at Swindon Town and the following season once again demonstrated his ability to support his attack with sorties up the wing and pin-point crosses into the box. After being left out of the Ipswich line up for the club's opening game following their return to the Premiership, he made his top-flight debut against Manchester United, scoring in a 1–1 draw. He maintained his position at right-back or wing-back for most of the season, his other goal being an injury-time header that secured the points at Coventry City. In 2001–02 he found himself behind Chris Makin and Hermann Hreidarrson for the full-back berths and struggled to get an opportunity but following the appointment of Joe Royle he bounced back to become a vital member of the team. He became a hero of the fans when he netted the opening goal of the Carrow Road derby, firing home from the penalty spot to set Ipswich on the road to victory. After that, he has produced some excellent performances – a good indication being that he was certainly missed when he was unable to play. Though he was out of contract at the end of the 2004–05 season, he stayed at Portman Road and was a revelation in 2005–06, being voted the supporters' Player of the Year and taking his total of League and Cup appearances to 287.

WILSON Kevin James

Forward

Born: Banbury, 18 April 1961. Career: Banbury United; Derby County 1979; IPSWICH TOWN 1985; Chelsea 1987; Notts County 1992; Bradford City (loan) 1994; Walsall 1994; Northampton Town 1997.

■ A sprightly striker, Kevin Wilson had trials with Sheffield United and Stoke City before Derby County gave him his chance in League football when they signed him from non-League Banbury United in December 1979. Although he was Derby's leading scorer in 1981–82, his most prolific period was the start of Arthur Cox's first season in charge when he scored four goals against Hartlepool United in a League Cup tie and a hat-trick against Bolton Wanderers before breaking an arm against Plymouth Argyle. When he recovered, he joined Ipswich Town for £150,000 and made his debut in an FA Cup tie against Gillingham. Towards the end of that 1984–85 season, he netted a hat-trick in a 5–1 home win over Stoke City. Wilson, who was a bargain buy at a time when funds were short because of the ill-advised decision to develop the Pioneer Stand without first arranging the funding, won the first of 42 Northern Ireland caps. This only came after Town manager Bobby Ferguson informed the Irish FA that Wilson had an Irish mother. Wilson was ever present in the 1986–87 season, netting 20 goals including hat-tricks against Crystal Palace and Blackburn Rovers and another in a League Cup tie against Darlington. Wilson had scored 49 goals in 125 games when Chelsea paid £335,000 for his services in the summer of 1987. He continued to score on a regular basis for the Stamford Bridge club and in almost five seasons of football he netted 47 goals in 172 first-team outings before joining Notts County for £225,000 in March 1992. There followed a loan spell at Bradford City before he left Meadow Lane to join

Walsall on a free transfer. He helped the Saddlers gain promotion from Division Three before joining Northampton Town. Appointed the Cobblers' player-manager, he had three seasons in charge at the Sixfields Stadium before later managing a number of non-League clubs including Bedford Town, Aylesbury United and Kettering Town.

WILSON Ulrich Johan

Defender

Born: Holland, 5 May 1964.
Career: Twente Enschede (Holland); IPSWICH TOWN (loan) 1987.

■ After impressing in the Dutch League with Twente Enschede, versatile defender Ulrich Wilson joined Ipswich on loan, making his debut at Swindon Town in December 1987. Though he was always fully committed during his stay at Portman Road, he could not hold down a regular spot in the side and had appeared in just six games – his last appearance being at Oldham in April 1988 – before he returned to his native Holland to continue his career with Twente Enschede.

WOODS Charles Morgan Parkinson

Forward

Born: Whitehaven, 18 March 1941.
Career: Cleator Moor; Newcastle United 1959; Bournemouth 1962; Crystal Palace 1964; IPSWICH TOWN 1966; Watford 1970; Colchester United (loan) 1971.

■ At his first club, Newcastle United, Charlie Woods had the daunting task of filling George Eastham's boots when the future England player fell into dispute with the Magpies board. He was plunged into United's side for a relegation fight during season 1960–61. Small and compact and a fixture at inside-right he could not prevent the club dropping into the Second Division. Following a change of manager, Woods moved south to Bournemouth where his outstanding form for the Cherries led to Crystal Palace signing him in November 1964. He continued to impress playing for the Eagles before in the summer of 1966 he signed for Ipswich Town. Woods made his debut at Brentford in a League Cup second-round tie, scoring one of the goals in a 4–2 win. Having helped Ipswich into the top flight as champions of the Second Division in 1967–68, he continued to be an important member of the side until the end of the 1969–70 season when he joined Watford. His time at Vicarage Road, where he had a spell on loan at Colchester, was undistinguished and on hanging up his boots he went into coaching first with Blackburn Rovers and then Ipswich Town. At Portman Road after coaching the reserves and the first team, he was appointed assistant manager and later chief scout. He was later Bobby Robson's chief scout when he was manager of Newcastle United.

WOODS Clive Richard

Winger

Born: Norwich, 18 December 1947.
Career: Norwich Gothic; IPSWICH TOWN 1969; Norwich City 1980; Newton Flotman.

■ Norwich-born winger Clive Woods had always been a great fan of the Canaries but after they showed no interest in signing him he joined Ipswich Town, though he continued to live near Norwich. He made his Town debut as a substitute for Ian Collard in a 2–0 home win over Newcastle United in September 1969 and over the next 10 years with the club he baffled the best of defences with his tantalising close skills. Though he was not the most prolific of scorers, he did net some spectacular goals, perhaps the best being the curling left-foot shot that gave Ipswich victory over mighty Leeds United in an FA Cup third-round replay at Filbert Street in March 1975. He will always be remembered though for his marvellous display against Arsenal in the FA Cup Final at Wembley in 1978 when he was voted Man of the Match. He went on to score 31 goals in 338 games for the Portman Road club before moving to Norwich City in March 1980 for a fee of £70,000 with another £50,000 to be paid when he had made 25 appearances for the Canaries. Playing for his home-town club was an ambition realised for Woods but after playing in just 37 games he was given a free transfer by Ken Brown. He had an invitation to play for Twente Enschede of Holland but the terms were not right and he went to play Eastern Counties League football for Newton Flotman.

WOODS Neil Stephen

Forward

Born: York, 30 July 1966.
Career: Doncaster Rovers 1983; Glasgow Rangers 1986; IPSWICH

TOWN 1987; Bradford City 1990; Grimsby Town 1990; Wigan Athletic (loan) 1997; Scunthorpe United (loan) 1998; Mansfield Town (loan) 1998; York City 1998; Southport 1999.

■ A right-footed playmaker adept at holding, shielding and laying off the ball, Neil Woods began his career with Doncaster Rovers where his impressive displays led to a £120,000 move to Glasgow Rangers in December 1986. Unable to make much impression at Ibrox, he joined Ipswich Town for a similar fee in the summer of 1987. Woods made his Town debut at home to Aston Villa and went on to score five goals in 19 games that season. Injuries then prevented him from holding down a regular first-team spot and in March 1990 he left to play for Bradford City. His stay at Valley Parade was brief and in August 1990 he joined Grimsby Town for £82,000. Very fast in the box, with quick reactions in front of goal, Woods scored a number of spectacular goals in his time at Blundell Park. In November 1997 he was loaned out to Wigan Athletic, followed by similar spells with Scunthorpe and Mansfield before the tried and trusted target man, who had scored 48 goals in 258 League and Cup games for the Mariners, was released. He then joined his home-town club York City, but after just one season at Bootham Crescent, he left to play non-League football for Southport.

WOOKEY Kenneth William

Outside-right

Born: Newport, 23 February 1922. Career: Newport County 1939; Bristol Rovers 1946; Swansea City 1948; Hereford United 1949; IPSWICH TOWN 1950.

■ Winger Ken Wookey started out with his home-town club Newport County and was a member of the side that were thrashed 13–0 by Newcastle United in a Second Division game in October 1946. The game saw the debut of future England international Len Shackleton and he scored six of the goals, though, in fact, the sixth should really have been credited to Wookey who put the ball into his own net while under pressure from the Magpies' rampaging forward. Wookey later played for Bristol Rovers and Swansea City before drifting into non-League football with Hereford United. Ipswich Town resurrected his League career in October 1950 and he made his debut in a goalless draw at Nottingham Forest. He went on to appear in 15 games that season, scoring his only goal for the club in a 3–2 defeat of Colchester United.

WOSAHLO Roger Frank

Winger

Born: Cambridge, 11 September 1947. Career: Chelsea 1964; IPSWICH TOWN 1967; Peterborough United 1968; IPSWICH TOWN 1969.

■ An England Schoolboy international, Roger Wosahlo was the leading scorer for Chelsea's junior side but was never given a chance to show off his skills in the first team, his only game coming as a substitute against Stoke City in April 1967 when players were being rested prior to the FA Cup Final with Spurs. On joining Ipswich, he made his Town debut in a 4–1 win at Huddersfield Town when his crosses provided the opportunities for Hegan and Baker to score. Even so, he was allowed to move to Peterborough where he made 15 appearances in 1968–69 as they struggled near the foot of the Fourth Division. On his return to Portman Road in the summer of 1969, he made just one further appearance as a substitute against Liverpool before later emigrating to South Africa.

WRIGHT Jermaine Malaki

Midfield

Born: Greenwich, 21 October 1975. Career: Millwall 1992; Wolverhampton Wanderers 1994; Doncaster Rovers (loan) 1996; Crewe Alexandra 1998; IPSWICH TOWN 1999; Leeds United 2004; Millwall (loan) 2005; Southampton (loan) 2006.

■ Jermaine Wright began his career as a trainee with Millwall but failed to make a first-team appearance at The Den and made a £60,000 move to Wolves in 1994. However, in four years at Molineux, Wright failed to break into the first team on a consistent basis. He had a loan spell at Doncaster Rovers but the experience gained at Belle Vue did not help him break into the Wolves side with any regularity. In February 1998 he was allowed to leave Wolves for just £25,000 and was snapped up by Crewe manager Dario Gradi. It was while he was at Gresty Road that Gradi converted Wright from a winger into a central midfield playmaker. He was improving all the time during his stay with the Railwaymen before his sudden departure to Ipswich in the summer of 1999 for a fee of £500,000. After making a good start against the club who also wanted his services, Nottingham Forest, his early form was a disappointment. He bounced back and after scoring his first goal for

WRIGHT Richard Ian

Goalkeeper

Born: Ipswich, 5 November 1977.
Career: IPSWICH TOWN 1995;
Arsenal 2001; Everton 2002.

■ Goalkeeper Richard Wright made his Ipswich debut at home to Coventry City in May 1995 and kept a clean sheet – only the third Town had achieved all season. After making two wonderful saves from Dion Dublin he kept his place for the remaining two fixtures when he did enough to convince Ipswich fans that the long-term goalkeeping position was in safe hands. Described by his manager as the best young goalkeeper in the country, he started the 1995–96 season as understudy to Craig Forrest but with the Canadian international injured, he played in 26 of the final 27 games. His excellent form was rewarded when he was asked to join the full England squad in training for the Croatia game. The following season he was the club's first-choice 'keeper and won selection for the England Under-21 side. Indeed, he kept five successive sheets in the final games of the campaign and also had a clean sheet on his Under-21 debut during the same period. In 1997–98 he represented England at B level and continued to train with the full national squad. An ever present that season he proved himself extremely agile for a big man, getting down to low shots very quickly. A club record-equalling 26 clean sheets in 1998–99 tells its own story – another tremendous season for Town's ever-present 'keeper. He also won five more caps for England at Under-21 level, keeping four clean sheets and captaining the side against Bulgaria. Not surprisingly he was recognised by his fellow professionals with selection to the PFA award-winning First Division side. In 1999–2000 he began to be talked about as the natural successor to David Seaman and Nigel Martyn in the full England side. His double save against Stockport County when he parried Tony Dinning's spot-kick and managed to knock the rebound to safety was voted 'Save of the Century' by the fans. After helping Ipswich to the Play-off Final against Barnsley at Wembley, he got off to an unfortunate start when he was credited with an own-goal before being adjudged to have fouled Hignett in the penalty area but redeemed himself by saving Barnard's penalty-kick. He won selection to the PFA award-winning side for a second successive season and stepped up to the full international side, making his debut against Malta when he saved a late penalty to save England's blushes. He continued to enhance his credentials with a string of outstanding performances before Arsenal paid £6 million to take him to Highbury. Finding himself unable to dislodge David Seaman, he opted for a move to Everton, the Merseyside outfit paying £3.5 million for his services. After an uneasy start to his Everton career, he found his feet and improved until a knee injury forced him out of the side. On his return he was unable

Town against his former club Crewe in the last minute he never looked back as Town reached the Play-offs. His first season in the Premiership proved to be even better for Wright. In an exciting season for Ipswich fans, he was a key player in George Burley's midfield as the Tractor Boys finished in fifth position and secured a place in the UEFA Cp. Wright also claimed the club's Most Improved Player Award following some superb midfield displays in the top flight. After earning rave reviews there was even talk of a call-up to the full England squad at one stage. Though Town were relegated at the end of their second season back in the Premiership, he enjoyed success in the UEFA Cup and remained loyal following relegation. A hernia operation hampered his progress in 2001–02 but he continued to give of his best until the summer of 2004 when after playing his last game in the Play-off semi-final defeat by West Ham, he joined Leeds United. He was a consistent performer for the Yorkshire club in 2004–05 but had loan spells with Millwall and Southampton in Southampton.

to displace Nigel Martyn but in 2005–06 he appeared on a much more regular basis.

YALLOP Frank Walter

Full-back

Born: Watford, 4 April 1964.
Career: IPSWICH TOWN 1982; Blackpool (loan) 1995; Tampa Bay Mutiny (United States).

■ Having been spotted by Ipswich Town playing in schools football, he made steady progress into the club's professional ranks and eventually, after a wait of over two years, he made his League debut at Everton in March 1984, replacing the injured George Burley. However, it was not until the 1985–86 season that he won a regular place in the Town team at full-back. Unfortunately, it coincided with the club's relegation to the Second Division. He was the club's first-choice right-back for the next six seasons and occasionally filled in on the left-side or in central defence. In 1990–91, Yallop was selected for the Canadian national team and went on to win 34 caps. In 1991–92, when the Blues won the Second Division Championship, he lost his place early in the season and played no further part in the successful campaign. In the first season of Premier League football, he scored two super goals in successive matches – against Spurs at White Hart Lane and then the decider at home to Manchester United later in the same week but it was a season disrupted by World Cup calls. He continued to be an important member of the first-team squad before in November 1995 he went on loan to Blackpool. In February 1996, in a bid to cut the Portman Road club's wage bill, the experienced defender was released on a free transfer to join Tampa Bay Mutiny of the new American League after having appeared in 386 first-team games in 14 years with the Town. He was later voted top coach in America after transforming the fortunes of San Jose Earthquakes.

YOUDS Edward Paul

Centre-half/Midfield

Born: Liverpool, 3 May 1970.
Career: Everton 1988; Cardiff City (loan) 1989; Wrexham (loan) 1990; IPSWICH TOWN 1991; Bradford City 1995; Charlton Athletic 1998; Huddersfield Town 2002; Grays Athletic.

■ Unable to hold down a first-team spot at Everton, Eddie Youds had loan spells with Welsh clubs Cardiff City and Wrexham before in November 1991 joining Ipswich Town. He made his debut for the Portman Road club in a 1–0 reversal at Derby County shortly after his arrival at Portman Road but it was his only appearance that season. Youds remained at Portman Road for four seasons but never really established himself as an automatic member of the Ipswich side. He went on to appear in 59 games during that time, with his only goal for the club coming in a 1–0 win over Blackburn Rovers midway through the 1993–94 season. After a loan spell with Bradford City, he joined the Valley Parade club on a permanent basis and was soon made the club captain. He led the Bantams to promotion to the First Division in 1995–96 and then missed the whole of the following season with serious knee injuries before Charlton Athletic paid £550,000 for his services. A no-nonsense central defender, he continued to make his presence felt in the opposition penalty area and in 1999–2000 helped the Addicks win the First Division Championship. Injuries then hampered his progress at The Valley and in the summer of 2002 he joined Huddersfield Town, later becoming the Terriers' captain before entering non-League football with Grays Athletic.

ZONDERVAN Romeo

Midfield/Full-back

Born: Surinam, 4 March 1959.
Career: Postalia (Holland); Den Haag (Holland); Twente Enschede (Holland); West Bromwich Albion 1982; IPSWICH TOWN 1984; NAC Breda (Holland) 1992.

■ Surinam-born Dutch international Romeo Zondervan played his early football with Dutch sides Den Haag and Twente Enschede before joining West Bromwich Albion in March 1982. Although a skilful, mobile midfielder, Zondervan made his Albion debut at Middlesbrough at left-back. He never really got to grips with the club's relegation battle and was left out of the side as the club eventually survived the drop. The Dutchman's form, along with that of fellow countryman Martin Jol improved under new manager Ron Wylie, but after clocking up almost 100 appearances both Zondervan and Jol were discarded by new manager Johnny Giles. Zondervan signed for Ipswich and made his Town debut in a goalless draw against Watford in March 1984. He went on to become a virtual ever present in the Ipswich side for the next eight seasons. Voted Player of the Year in 1987, he played a key role in the club's 1991–92 Second Division Championship-winning season. Appointed club captain during John Duncan's managerial reign, he went on to score 20 goals in 325 League and Cup games before returning to Holland to continue his career with NAC Breda. On hanging up his boots, he became a players' agent and is now a part-time European scout for Ipswich. Zondervan is also a fully qualified pilot.

Football League Managers

Scott Duncan

November 1937 – August 1955

Third Division South Championship 1953–54.

Dumbarton-born Adam Scott Duncan began his playing career with his home-town club before joining Newcastle United in March 1908. A fast, ball-playing winger, he was part of the Magpies side that won the League Championship in 1908–09 and the FA Cup the following season. In 1911 he played for the Anglo-Scots in an international trial game but after scoring 12 goals in 81 games, he left St James' Park to join Glasgow Rangers for a fee of £600. Later he again played for Dumbarton and then joined Cowdenbeath before hanging up his boots. After serving his managerial apprenticeship with Hamilton Academicals and Cowdenbeath, he took charge at Manchester United on a salary reported to be £800 per annum. In his first couple of seasons with the club he spent a great deal of money but failed to produce good results despite his financial outlay. In 1933–34, United just escaped relegation but two years later he led them to the Second Division Championship. Unfortunately United were relegated after just one season in the top flight. After Ipswich Town became a professional club in 1936, Chairman Captain JM Cobbold asked the secretary of the FA, Stanley Rous, to recommend a possible manager. Rous reported that Scott Duncan was considered the best. Cobbold drove to Manchester and invited Duncan to return with him to Ipswich. Within a year, the club had been elected to the Football League and Duncan, who was to stay at Portman Road for 18 years, transformed the non-League side into one capable of reaching the Second Division when they won the Third Division South Championship in 1953–54. Sadly the club were relegated the following season and Duncan stepped down to be replaced by Alf Ramsey, though he stayed on at the club as secretary for a further three years.

Town record under Scott Duncan

	P	W	D	L	F	A
League	436	175	95	166	656	673
Cup	43	17	13	13	77	68
Total	479	192	108	179	733	741

Alf Ramsey

August 1955 – April 1963

Third Division South Championship 1956–57.
Second Division Championship 1960–61.
First Division Championship 1961–62.

As a player, Alf Ramsey was a strong, polished and distinguished defender who joined Portsmouth as an amateur in 1942 and a year later moved to The Dell to play for Southampton. He made his England debut in a 6–0 victory over Switzerland at Highbury in December 1948 before going on to make 28 consecutive appearances for his country. In all he won 32 caps for England and represented the Football League on five occasions. In May 1949 he moved to Tottenham Hotspur for £21,000, a record fee for a full-back. Virtually an ever present in the teams that won the Second Division and Football League titles in 1950 and 1951, he was very accurate with penalties and free-kicks and developed into a great reader of the game. In May 1955 he retired after appearing in 250 League and Cup games for the White Hart Lane club. He was appointed manager of Ipswich Town in August 1955 and immediately began to refashion the Portman Road side in a manner which was to herald the dawn of a new era. He led the club to the Third Division South title in 1956–57, the Second Division Championship in 1960–61 and the First Division Championship in 1961–62. This was arguably the most remarkable League Championship win in its history, as Ipswich were all but condemned to relegation by virtually all football pundits and journalists at that time. But Alf Ramsey's tactical astuteness, working with a squad of solid but not outstanding players, baffled and astonished the leading clubs of the day, to produce the seemingly impossible task of actually winning the title in Town's first-ever season in the top flight. In January 1963 he was appointed full-time manager of England. His greatest triumph came in 1966 when England, playing on home territory, won the World Cup for the first and only time. In May 1974 after England had failed to qualify for the finals of that year's World Cup competition, he was sacked. Under Ramsey England lost only 17 of 113 games and won 69 of these. In September 1977, at the age of 57, Sir Alf was appointed manager of Birmingham City. He held office for only six months before being forced to relinquish the position due to ill health.

Town record under Alf Ramsey

	P	W	D	L	F	A
League	340	163	71	106	661	524
Cup	29	13	4	12	62	60
Total	369	176	75	118	723	584

Jackie Milburn

May 1963 – September 1964

'Wor Jackie' was an idol of the Geordies for over a decade and was without doubt one of the best centre-forwards in the Football League after World War Two. Fast and with a lethal shot, he scored a number of spectacular goals including two in Newcastle's 1951 FA Cup Final success over Blackpool. In 1955 he scored one of the quickest-ever Wembley goals after just 45 seconds of the Magpies' 3–1 win over Manchester City. He scored 199 goals in 395 games for Newcastle before moving to Linfield where he led the side to two Irish Cup Finals. He returned to England as player-coach at Southern League Yiewsley under Bill Dodgin before succeeding Alf Ramsey as manager of Ipswich Town. He inherited quite an old squad at Portman Road and in a season in which they conceded 121 goals, including a 10–1 defeat against Fulham, the club finished bottom of the First Division with only 22 points and nine wins. He continued to have a difficult time at the start of the 1964–65 season and his health began to suffer. On 4 September 1964 he tendered his resignation and entered the newspaper world. He remained for more than 20 years covering north-eastern football from the press box. When he died of cancer in 1988, the whole of Newcastle city centre ground to a halt for his funeral.

Town record under Jackie Milburn

	P	W	D	L	F	A
League	51	10	10	31	68	140
Cup	5	1	2	2	7	6
Total	56	11	12	33	75	146

Jimmy Forsyth (caretaker)

September 1964 – October 1964

Jimmy Forsyth was Ipswich Town's first-team coach when he was appointed caretaker manager in September 1964. Assisted by Charlie Cowie and Ken Malcolm, Forsyth was responsible for team selection following Jackie Milburn's departure and the appointment of new manager Bill McGarry a month later.

Town record under Jimmy Forsyth

	P	W	D	L	F	A
League	6	2	2	2	11	11
Cup	1	0	0	1	1	4
Total	7	2	2	3	12	15

Bill McGarry

October 1964 – November 1968

Second Division Championship 1967–68.

Discovered by Port Vale in 1945, he moved to Huddersfield Town for a fee of £12,000 in March 1951. He soon established himself in the First Division and in 1954 won the first of four England caps when he played in the World Cup Finals in Switzerland. He was also capped for England B, played for the Football League and went on the FA's 1956 South African tour. He scored 26 goals in 381 League and Cup games for the Yorkshire club before becoming Bournemouth's first player-manager. From July 1963 he was the manager of Watford and in October 1964 he moved to Portman Road as Town manager. Remembered for his competitiveness as a player, he carried that approach into his managerial career and at Ipswich he concentrated on building up the players' strength and stamina. In only his sixth game in charge, the club recorded their highest victory in a League match when they beat Portsmouth 7–0. In 1967–68 he took the club to the Second Division Championship but in November 1968 he moved to Wolverhampton Wanderers and led them into Europe where they reached the Final of the UEFA Cup. He also led them to success in the 1974 League Cup Final before being sacked in May 1986 after the club had been relegated. He later coached in Saudi Arabia and managed Newcastle United. There followed spells as Brighton scout, Power Dynamo (Zambia) coach, Zambian national team manager and periodic coaching in South Africa before he spent 61 days in a second spell managing Wolves.

Town record under Bill McGarry

	P	W	D	L	F	A
League	177	72	59	46	290	238
Cup	19	8	3	8	33	34
Total	196	80	62	54	323	272

Cyril Lea (caretaker)

November 1968 – January 1969

First-team coach and former Welsh international Cyril Lea took over as caretaker manager of Ipswich Town following the departure of Bill McGarry to Molineux. Lea, who later gave way for Bobby Robson, coached the Welsh national side and managed Colchester United.

Town record under Cyril Lea

	P	W	D	L	F	A
League	6	3	0	3	12	9
Cup	1	0	0	1	1	2
Total	7	3	0	4	13	11

Bobby Robson

January 1969 – August 1982

FA Cup winners 1978.
UEFA Cup winners 1981.
Texaco Cup winners 1973.
Division One runners-up 1980–81 and 1981–82.
FA Youth Cup winners 1973 and 1975.

One of the game's most successful managers, Bobby Robson began his career as an amateur with Middlesbrough but was playing for another local side, Langley Park, when Fulham manager Bill Dodgin pipped Newcastle United for his signature. In May 1950, Robson left his coal mining job to join Fulham and soon established himself at inside-right alongside Jezzard and Haynes. However, in March 1956, Vic Buckingham signed him for West Bromwich Albion for £25,000 and in seven years at the Hawthorns he scored 61 goals in 240 League games. Also during this time, he was converted to wing-half and renewed his partnership with Johnny Haynes when he won the first of 20 full caps for England against France in 1958.

Bobby Robson

Like Haynes, he lost his international place after the 1962 World Cup but then linked up again with the Fulham maestro when he returned to Craven Cottage for a second spell in August 1962. He played five more First Division seasons, taking his Fulham record to 80 goals in 370 League and Cup games before retiring. After leaving Fulham he moved to North America to manage Vancouver Royals but in January 1968 he returned to Craven Cottage for a third spell, this time as manager. Sadly, he lasted less than 10 months before being sacked for failing to arrest the club's decline. After a short spell scouting for Chelsea, he was appointed manager of Ipswich Town in January 1969. The first few years in charge proved tough, but he began to put together a useful side. The club finished fourth in the First Division in both the 1972–73 and 1973–74 seasons. They also finished third in seasons 1974–75, 1976–77 and 1979–80 and were runners-up in 1980–81 and 1981–82. The club won the UEFA Cup in 1980–81 but Robson's greatest triumph came in the 1978 FA Cup Final when Town beat Arsenal 1–0. In July 1982, Robson, who had managed the England B side since 1978, replaced Ron Greenwood as the England manager. Although England failed to qualify for the European Championships in 1984, they qualified for the World Cup finals two years later but lost 2–1 to Argentina in the quarter-finals. After qualifying with ease for the 1988 European Championships, England lost all of their games in the finals. In 1990 he took England to the World Cup semi-finals where they were unfortunate to lose to West Germany on penalties after a 1–1 draw. In August 1990, Robson had had enough of the limelight as England's manager and took over at PSV Eindhoven. They won the Dutch title in both 1990–91 and 1991–92 but failed to find success in Europe. Robson later managed Sporting Lisbon, FC Porto and Barcelona before succeeding Ruud Gullit as manager of Newcastle United. He is currently assistant manager to Republic of Ireland boss Steve Staunton.

Town record under Bobby Robson

P	W	D	L	F	A
League					
562	238	141	183	780	661
Cup					
147	78	32	37	251	153
Total					
709	316	173	220	1031	814

Bobby Ferguson

August 1982 – May 1987

Bobby Ferguson came from a footballing family, his father having played for West Bromwich Albion and his uncle for Chelsea. A tough-tackling defender, he began his career with Newcastle United but after making only 11 appearances in seven years with the Magpies, he left to join Derby County in 1962. He became a first-team regular at the Baseball Ground, making 121 League appearances in a little over three years. On New Year's Eve 1965 he joined Cardiff City and soon settled in to give the Bluebirds three years of good service. When he was released he joined Barry Town as player-manager before coming back into League football with Newport County. He had a fairly torrid time at Somerton Park, and, when he was dismissed in 1971, he linked up with Bobby Robson at Ipswich, eventually graduating to the manager's post at Portman Road when Robson became England supremo. In 1984–85 Ipswich reached the sixth round of the FA Cup and the semi-finals of the League Cup but the following season they were relegated. In 1986–87 Ferguson took the club to fifth place in the Second Division but after the club lost to Charlton Athletic in the Play-offs,

Ferguson had the sad distinction of becoming the first manager to be sacked by Ipswich Town.

Town record under Bobby Ferguson

P	W	D	L	F	A
League					
210	71	53	86	256	262
Cup					
48	26	8	14	79	61
Total					
258	97	61	100	335	323

John Duncan

June 1987 – May 1990

John Duncan was a Scotland Schoolboy triallist who turned professional with his home club, Dundee, before being farmed out to Broughty Athletic. However, he was soon in the Dundee side, showing an eye for the goals that led to him being selected as non-playing substitute for the full Scotland side before appearing for the Scottish League against the Football League in 1973. In 1974 he won a Scottish League Cup-winners' medal when Dundee beat Celtic 1–0 in the Final but in October of that year he joined Spurs for £150,000. Lethal inside the penalty area, he ended his first season at White Hart Lane as the club's top scorer. Although a back injury forced him to miss most of the 1976–77 season he went on to score 75 goals in 145 games before leaving to play for Derby County in September 1978. Recurring back problems restricted Duncan to only 37 appearances for the Rams and he moved to Scunthorpe, quickly taking over as manager. He was badly treated by Scunthorpe who sacked him to make way for Allan Clarke. He joined Hartlepool United but after only two months in charge moved to Chesterfield and led them to the Fourth Division Championship in 1984–85. In the summer of 1987 he accepted an offer to manage Ipswich Town but after three seasons when they gained themselves a reputation as a competent Second Division side – always finishing in mid-table – he was dismissed when they failed to make the 1990 promotion Play-offs. After a spell in radio journalism and teaching, he was once again appointed manager of Chesterfield and in 1996–97 led them to the FA Cup semi-finals.

Town record under John Duncan

	P	W	D	L	F	A
League	136	60	28	48	199	179
Cup	25	13	1	11	38	35
Total	161	73	29	59	237	214

John Lyall

May 1990 – December 1994

Second Division Championship 1991–92.

As a player, John Lyall represented England Youth against Luxembourg at Upton Park in 1957 and was a member of the West Ham side beaten by Manchester United in the FA Youth Cup Final later that year. Sadly, Lyall was hampered by injuries and was only able to make 31 League appearances before eventually conceding defeat in the summer of 1963. He worked in the offices at Upton Park for a while before taking up coaching at the club. In 1971 he became assistant manager to Ron Greenwood and then team manager with Greenwood as general manager in August 1974. Lyall was given full managerial responsibilities when Greenwood became England's manager in 1977. During Lyall's management, the Hammers won the FA Cup twice. In 1975 they beat Fulham 2–0 and in 1980 beat Arsenal 1–0. West Ham also reached the European Cup-winners' Cup Final where they lost 4–2 to Anderlecht in the Heysel Stadium. The club were relegated in 1978 but in 1980–81 they won the Second Division Championship and reached the League Cup Final but lost to Liverpool in a replay. After the Hammers were relegated again in 1988–89, Lyall, who was the longest-serving manager in the Football League, was sacked. After working as a technical co-ordinator with Tottenham Hotspur, he was appointed manager of Ipswich Town. He quickly rebuilt the team and the Portman Road club won the Second Division title in 1991–92 to gain promotion to the new Premier League. After enjoying the longest unbeaten start of any Premier League side, Ipswich were fourth in the Premier League come January 1993 with a UEFA Cup place looking possible but a dip in form in the final few weeks of the season saw Town finish a disappointing 16th. It was a similar story the following season and in December 1994, with the club firmly rooted to the foot of the Premier table, Lyall was sacked. He then moved upstairs to become the club's general manager.

Town record under John Lyall

	P	W	D	L	F	A
League	193	61	64	68	231	264
Cup	38	16	11	11	60	44
Total	231	77	75	79	291	308

Paul Goddard (caretaker)

December 1994

Paul Goddard, along with the help of Town legend John Wark, acted as caretaker manager at Portman Road following the dismissal of John Lyall and the appointment of new manager, former Town favourite, George Burley.

Town record under Paul Goddard

	P	W	D	L	F	A
League	3	0	2	1	4	7
Cup	0	0	0	0	0	0
Total	3	0	2	1	4	7

George Burley

December 1994 – October 2002

Division One Play-off winners 1999–2000.

Scottish international full-back George Burley appeared in exactly 500 first-team games for Ipswich before leaving Portman Road in September 1985 to join Sunderland and later ending his career with Gillingham. After spells as manager of Ayr United and coach of Motherwell he took over the reins at Colchester United but in December 1994 his career turned full circle when he returned to Ipswich as manager. At the time of his appointment, the club were firmly rooted to the foot of the Premier League and though they beat Leicester City 4–1 and then gained their first victory at Anfield, the Blues were relegated. After leading the club to seventh place in Division One in 1995–96, Burley's next three seasons in charge brought semi-final Play-off defeats. Ipswich finally returned to the Premiership in 1999–2000 after beating Barnsley 4–2 in the last Division One Play-off Final at Wembley before the old stadium was to be redeveloped. Most observers expected the club to suffer immediate relegation but George Burley's hard-working side defied the odds and finished in fifth place, gaining themselves a UEFA Cup place and George Burley the Manager of the Year award. Though Town beat Inter Milan at home they lost the tie over two legs, but it was their League form that was a cause for concern. Midway through the 2001–02 season, Ipswich were bottom of the Premiership, but George Burley's side then won seven of the next eight games and climbed to 12th place. They appeared safe from relegation but another decline set in and the club's fate was confirmed on the final day of the season with a 5–0 defeat at Liverpool. The loss of income due to relegation led to the club going into administration. They had the minor consolation of again qualifying for the UEFA Cup, this time via UEFA's Fair Play route. Burley was sacked in October 2002 after nearly eight years as Ipswich boss. He later managed Derby County and then Hearts whom he took to the top of the Scottish Premier Division before falling out of favour with the

Tynecastle club's owner. Burley is now manager of Southampton.

Town record under George Burley

P	W	D	L	F	A
League					
338	149	80	109	491	406
Cup					
75	39	16	20	129	91
Total					
413	188	96	129	620	497

Tony Mowbray (caretaker)
October 2002

Tony Mowbray joined Ipswich during the reign of George Burley and took over as the club's caretaker manager following the popular Scot's dismissal in October 2002. Though there were a number of Town supporters who would have liked to have seen him appointed on a permanent basis, he lost out to Joe Royle. He is now manager of Hibernian where his assistant his former teammate Mark Venus.

Town record under Tony Mowbray

P	W	D	L	F	A
League					
4	1	1	2	5	7
Cup					
0	0	0	0	0	0
Total					
4	1	1	2	5	7

Joe Royle
October 2002 – May 2006

Joe Royle began his playing career with Everton, making his debut at the tender age of 16 years and 282 days – the youngest player ever to represent the Merseyside outfit until his record was beaten by Wayne Rooney. Within four years of his debut, Royle had packed a wealth of experience into his sizeable frame and earned himself the reputation as one of Everton's finest post-war strikers and a fitting successor to the traditions of Dixie Dean and Tommy Lawton. Royle was Everton's leading marksman in 1968–69 with 22 goals and again the following season with 23 goals as the Goodison club won the League Championship. His career began to be dogged by injury and he moved to Manchester City, having scored 119 goals in 272 games for Everton. He also won six full caps for England. Royle later played for Bristol City and Norwich before entering management with Oldham Athletic. At Boundary Park he combined integrity, humour and sound judgement as the Latics won promotion from the Second Division and reached the League Cup Final and FA Cup semi-final. In November 1994 he returned to Goodison as manager and though he kept the club in the Premiership there were clashes with the chairman over transfer deals. These led to him leaving the club by mutual consent and he joined Manchester City. He took the then Maine Road club into the Premiership after two successive promotions but lost his job following the club's relegation at the end of the 2001–02 season. When Royle became Ipswich manager, the club was struggling near the First Division relegation zone but following a revival under the new boss they just missed the Play-offs. The 2003–04 season saw the club come out of administration and continue to challenge for promotion back to the top flight. They finished in fifth place but lost in the Play-off semi-final to West Ham United. Despite missing automatic promotion in 2004–05, Joe Royle tried to achieve his fifth promotion success as manager through the Play-offs. However, they suffered another semi-final defeat at the hands of the Hammers. Royle left Ipswich by mutual consent in May 2006 following a 15th place finish in the Coca-Cola Championship – the club's worst League finish to a campaign in over 40 years.

Town record under Joe Royle

P	W	D	L	F	A
League					
170	74	46	50	284	241
Cup					
19	7	2	10	24	25
Total					
189	81	48	60	308	266

Jim Magilton
June 2006 –

Highly regarded by Blues supporters, the Northern Ireland international midfielder won 52 caps for his country and is best remembered for the hat-trick he scored in the Play-off semi-final defeat of Bolton Wanderers in May 2000 that earned Town a place at Wembley and ultimately promotion to the Premiership. Following the departure of Joe Royle at the end of the 2005–06 season, Magilton became his surprise successor in a management change that also saw Academy Director and former Town youth and reserve player Brian Klug appointed as first-team coach.

Ipswich Town Internationals

Until 1972, when Bruce Twamley appeared for Canada, the players winning representative honours were restricted to the countries making up the British Isles although George Burley, the club's first Scottish international did not win his first cap until 1979. Please find below the players who have won full international honours whilst being registered with Ipswich Town.

England
Kevin Beattie 1975 v Cyprus (2), Portugal, Scotland, Switzerland; 1976 v Finland, Italy; 1977 v Holland, Luxembourg – 9.
Terry Butcher 1980 v Australia; 1981 v Spain; 1982 v Czechoslovakia, Denmark, France, Luxembourg, Scotland, Spain, Wales, West Germany (2); 1983 v Australia (3), Denmark, Greece, Hungary (2), Luxembourg, Northern Ireland, Scotland, Wales; 1984 v East Germany, Finland, France, Northern Ireland, Turkey; 1985 v Eire, Finland, Italy, Northern Ireland, Romania, Scotland, United States, West Germany; 1986 v Argentina, Canada, Israel, Mexico, Morocco, Paraguay, Poland, Portugal, Scotland, USSR – 45.
Ray Crawford 1961 v Northern Ireland; 1962 v Austria – 2.
Eric Gates 1980 v Norway, Romania – 2.
David Johnson 1975 v Scotland, Switzerland, Wales – 3.
Paul Mariner 1977 v Luxembourg (2), Northern Ireland; 1978 v Scotland, Wales; 1980 v Australia, Italy, Northern Ireland, Norway, Scotland, Spain, Switzerland, Wales; 1981 v Hungary (2), Norway, Spain, Switzerland; 1982 v Czechoslovakia, Denmark, Finland, France, Greece, Holland, Kuwait, Scotland, Spain, Germany (2); 1983 v Denmark, Hungary, Luxembourg, Wales – 33.
Mick Mills 1972 v Yugoslavia; 1976 v Brazil, Finland (2), Italy (2), Northern Ireland, Scotland, Wales (2); 1977 v Northern Ireland, Scotland, Wales; 1978 v Brazil, Denmark, Hungary, Northern Ireland, Eire, Scotland, Wales, West Germany; 1979 v Austria, Bulgaria, Denmark, Northern Ireland (3), Scotland; 1980 v Spain (2), Switzerland; 1981 v Hungary (2), Norway, Switzerland; 1982 v Czechoslovakia, Finland, France, Kuwait, Scotland, Spain, West Germany – 42.
Russell Osman 1980 v Australia; 1981 v Norway, Romania, Spain, Switzerland; 1982 v Denmark, Iceland; 1983 v Australia (3), Denmark – 11.
Brian Talbot 1977 v Argentina, Brazil, Northern Ireland, Scotland, Uruguay – 5.
Colin Viljoen 1975 v Northern Ireland, Wales – 2.
Trevor Whymark 1977 v Luxembourg – 1.
Richard Wright 2000 v Malta – 1.

Scotland
Alan Brazil 1980 v Hungary, Poland; 1982 v East Germany, England, Holland, New Zealand, Northern Ireland, Spain, Switzerland, USSR, Wales – 11.
George Burley 1979 v Argentina, England, Northern Ireland, Norway, Wales; 1980 v England, Northern Ireland, Poland, Portugal, England, Wales – 11.
John Wark 1979 v Argentina, Austria, Belgium (2), England, Northern Ireland, Norway, Peru, Wales; 1981 v Israel, Northern Ireland, Sweden; 1982 v Brazil, East Germany, Holland, New Zealand, Northern Ireland, Spain, Switzerland, USSR; 1983 v Belgium, East Germany, England, Northern Ireland, Switzerland, Uruguay – 26.

Wales
Mick Hill 1971 v Czechoslovakia, Romania – 2.
Cyril Lea 1965 v Italy, Northern Ireland – 2.
Lewis Price 2005 v Cyprus; 2006 v Paraguay – 2.
Billy Reed 1954 v Scotland, Yugoslavia – 2.
Gavin Williams 2005 v Cyprus – 1.
Geraint Williams 1993 v Northern Ireland; 1995 v Germany – 2.

Northern Ireland
Bryan Hamilton 1971 v USSR (2); 1972 v Bulgaria, Spain; 1973 v Bulgaria, Cyprus (2), England, Portugal, Scotland, Wales; 1974 v England, Norway, Scotland, Sweden, Wales; 1975 v England, Norway, Sweden, Yugoslavia (2) – 21.
Allan Hunter 1971 v USSR (2); 1972 v Bulgaria, England, Scotland, Spain, Wales; 1973 v Bulgaria, Cyprus (2), England, Portugal, Scotland, Wales; 1974 v England, Norway, Scotland, Sweden, Wales; 1975 v England, Norway, Scotland, Sweden, Wales, Yugoslavia (2); 1976 v Belgium, England, Holland, Israel, Scotland, Wales; 1977 v Belgium, Denmark, England, Holland, Iceland (2), Scotland, Wales, West Germany; 1978 v Eire; 1979 v Denmark, England, Eire, Scotland, Wales – 47.
Jim Magilton 2000 v Denmark, Iceland, Luxembourg, Malta, Yugoslavia; 2001 v Bulgaria, Czech Republic, Denmark, Iceland, Malta, Norway; 2002 v Liechtenstein, Poland – 13.
Pat Sharkey 1976 v Scotland – 1.
Danny Sonner 1997 v Albania – 1.
Kevin Wilson 1987 v England, Israel, Yugoslavia – 3.

Republic of Ireland
Tommy Carroll 1968 v Austria, Denmark, Poland (2); 1969 v Czechoslovakia; 1970 v Poland, Sweden, West Germany (8).
Dermot Curtis 1958 v Poland; 1959 v Sweden; 1960 v Chile, Norway, Sweden, West Germany; 1961 v Scotland; 1962 v Austria, Iceland – 9.
Matt Holland 1999 v Macedonia; 2000 v Finland, Mexico, Portugal, South Africa, United States; 2001 v Andorra (2), Cyprus (2), Estonia, Holland, Iran (2), Portugal; 2002 v Cameroon, Denmark, Finland, Germany, Greece, Nigeria, Russia (2), Saudi Arabia, Spain, Switzerland, United States; 2003 v Albania (2), Georgia (2), Norway, Scotland – 33.
Kevin O'Callaghan 1981 v Czechoslovakia, Poland,

West Germany B; 1982 v Algeria, Brazil, Chile, Iceland, Spain, Trinidad and Tobago; 1983 v Holland, Iceland, Malta (2), Spain; 1984 v Denmark, Mexico, Norway – 17.

Bulgaria
Bontcho Guentchev 1994 v Germany, Italy, Mexico (2), Oman, Ukraine; 1995 v Argentina – 7.

Canada
Jason De Vos 2004 v Belize (2), Costa Rica, Honduras (2), Wales – 6.
Craig Forrest 1988 v Chile, Costa Rica, Greece, Poland; 1989 v Belgium, Denmark; 1990 v Mexico, United States; 1991 v Honduras; 1992 v Jamaica, Scotland, United States; 1993 v Australia (2), Costa Rica (2), El Salvador (2), Honduras (2), Mexico (3); 1994 v Brazil, Germany, Holland, Morocco; 1995 v Denmark, Jamaica, Trinidad and Tobago; 1996 v Brazil, Costa Rica, Cuba (2), El Salvador, Honduras, Panama (2); 1997 v Costa Rica, El Salvador, Mexico, United States – 42.
Jaime Peters 2005 v Luxembourg – 1.
Bruce Twamley 1972 v Guatemala, Mexico (2), United States (2); 1973 v Poland, United States – 7.
Frank Yallop 1990 v Mexico, United States; 1991 v Honduras, Jamaica, Mexico; 1992 v Bermuda (2), El Salvador (2), Jamaica (2), Scotland, United States (2); 1993 v Australia (2), Costa Rica, El Salvador (2), Honduras (2), Martinique, Mexico (3); 1994 v Brazil, Germany, Holland, Morocco, Spain; 1995 v Chile, Denmark, Jamaica, Northern Ireland, Trinidad and Tobago, Turkey; 1996 v Brazil, Honduras – 38.

Denmark
Claus Thomsen 1995 v Armenia, Belgium, Macedonia; 1996 v Croatia, Germany, Ghana, Greece, Portugal, Scotland, Slovenia, Sweden, Turkey – 12.

Finland
Shefk Kuqi 2004 v Armenia, Holland, Italy, Malta; 2005 v Czech Republic, Denmark, Holland – 7.

Holland
Arnold Muhren 1981 v Belgium, Cyprus, France (2), Eire; 1982 v England, Scotland – 7.
Frans Thijssen 1979 v East Germany; 1980 v Czechoslovakia, France, Eire, Spain, West Germany; 1981 v Belgium, Cyprus, France, Eire – 10.

Iceland
Hermann Hreidarsson 2000 v Czech Republic, Denmark, Northern Ireland, Poland; 2001 v Bulgaria (2), Czech Republic, Denmark, Malta, Northern Ireland, Poland; 2002 v Andorra, Estonia, Hungary, Lithuania, Scotland – 16.

Jamaica
David A Johnson 1999 v Paraguay, Sweden, Trinidad and Tobago, United States – 4.

Nigeria
Finidi George 2001 v Japan; 2002 v Algeria, Ghana, Liberia, Mali (2), Senegal – 7.

Slovenia
Amir Karic 2000 v Luxembourg, Switzerland; 2001 v Luxembourg, Romania (2), Russia, Switzerland, Yugoslavia; 2002 v China, Croatia, France, Ghana, Honduras, Italy, Malta, Paraguay, South Africa, Spain, Tunisia – 19.

Individual Scoring Feats

Five Goals in a Game
R. Crawford	v Floriana	European Cup	25 September 1962
A. Brazil	v Southampton	Division One	16 February 1982

Four Goals in a Game
F. Chadwick	v Street	FA Cup Round One	26 November 1938
T. Garneys	v Doncaster Rovers	Division Two	21 January 1956
D. Curtis	v Stoke City	Division Two	19 September 1959
R. Crawford	v Southampton	League Cup Round Two	12 September 1967
T. Whymark	v Lazio	UEFA Cup	24 October 1973
T. Whymark	v West Bromwich Albion	Division One	6 November 1976
T. Whymark	v Landskrona Bois	UEFA Cup	28 September 1977
J. Wark	v Aris Salonika	UEFA Cup	17 September 1980
J. Wark	v West Bromwich Albion	Division One	30 October 1982

Three Goals in a Game
A. Mulraney	v Bristol City	Division Three South	8 April 1939
A. Day	v Norwich City	Division Three South	7 September 1946
J. Brown	v Port Vale	Division Three South	19 March 1949
J. Brown	v Norwich City	Division Three South	15 October 1949
S. McCrory	v Crystal Palace	Division Three South	18 November 1950
J. Elsworthy	v Coventry City	Division Three South	26 December 1953
T. Parker	v Swindon Town	Division Three South	3 September 1955
B. Reed	v Walsall	Division Three South	7 September 1955
W. Grant	v Millwall	Division Three South	22 October 1955
W. Grant	v Reading	Division Three South	29 October 1955
W. Grant	v Millwall	Division Three South	3 March 1956
T. Phillips	v Colchester United	Division Three South	6 October 1956
T. Phillips	v Queen's Park Rangers	Division Three South	3 November 1956
T. Phillips	v Watford	Division Three South	26 December 1956
T. Phillips	v Shrewsbury Town	Division Three South	26 January 1957
T. Phillips	v Reading	Division Three South	2 March 1957
T. Phillips	v Bristol City	Division Two	2 November 1957
R. Crawford	v Brighton & Hove Albion	Division Two	15 November 1958
R. Crawford	v Swansea Town	Division Two	21 February 1959
T. Phillips	v Swansea Town	Division Two	26 August 1959
D. Curtis	v Sunderland	Division Two	19 September 1959
T. Phillips	v Sunderland	Division Two	19 September 1959
D. Millward	v Leyton Orient	Division Two	2 January 1960
R. Crawford	v Brighton & Hove Albion	Division Two	7 September 1960
R. Crawford	v Leeds United	Division Two	1 October 1960
R. Crawford	v Leyton Orient	Division Two	17 December 1960
R. Crawford	v Chelsea	Division One	2 December 1961
J. Leadbetter	v Mansfield Town	FA Cup Round Three	9 January 1963
R. Crawford	v Sheffield Wednesday	Division One	20 April 1963
G. Baker	v Oldham Athletic	FA Cup Round Three	4 January 1964
G. Baker	v Tottenham Hotspur	Division One	4 April 1964
F. Brogan	v Portsmouth	Division Two	7 November 1964
R. Crawford	v Hull City	Division Two	22 October 1966
F. Brogan	v Northampton Town	Division Two	5 November 1966
C. Viljoen	v Portsmouth	Division Two	25 March 1967

F. Brogan	v Bristol City	Division Two	26 August 1967
C. Viljoen	v Norwich City	Division Two	3 February 1968
D.E. Johnson	v Coventry City	Division One	16 November 1974
B. Hamilton	v Newcastle United	Division One	15 March 1975
M. Lambert	v Halifax Town	FA Cup Round Three	3 January 1976
T. Whymark	v Norwich City	Division One	15 February 1977
P. Mariner	v West Ham United	Division One	22 March 1977
P. Mariner	v Millwall	FA Cup Round Six	11 March 1978
E. Gates	v Manchester City	Division One	8 December 1979
P. Mariner	v Manchester United	Division One	1 March 1980
J. Wark	v Widzew Lodz	UEFA Cup	5 April 1980
J. Wark	v Norwich City	Division One	15 April 1980
J. Wark	v Blackburn Rovers	League Cup Round Two	5 October 1983
E. Gates	v Cardiff City	FA Cup Round Three	7 January 1984
K. Wilson	v Stoke City	Division One	6 May 1985
K. Wilson	v Darlington	League Cup Round Two	8 October 1985
J. Deehan	v West Bromwich Albion	Division Two	13 September 1986
N. Gleghorn	v Bradford City	Division Two	18 October 1986
K. Wilson	v Crystal Palace	Division Two	15 November 1986
K. Wilson	v Blackburn Rovers	Division Two	2 May 1987
D. Atkinson	v Middlesbrough	Division Two	23 April 1988
S. Milton	v Shrewsbury Town	Division Two	20 September 1988
C. Kiwomya	v Wigan Athletic	League Cup Round Two	6 October 1992
B. Guentchev	v Grimsby Town	FA Cup Round Five	13 February 1993
A. Mathie	v Sunderland	Division One	2 September 1995
N. Gregory	v Sheffield United	Division One	18 March 1997
A. Mathie	v Norwich City	Division One	21 February 1998
D.A. Johnson	v Oxford United	Division One	24 February 1998
J. Scowcroft	v Crewe Alexandra	Division One	28 November 1998
J. Magilton	v Bolton Wanderers	Division One Play-offs	17 May 2000
M. Stewart	v Southampton	Premiership	2 April 2001
P. Counago	v Avenir Beggen	UEFA Cup	29 August 2002
D. Bent	v Walsall	Division One	16 March 2004
D. Bowditch	v Watford	Division One	20 March 2004

Progressive Scoring Records

Fred Chadwick set the first target in Ipswich Town's opening season of League football, scoring 17 League goals and adding another six in the FA Cup. This chart shows how individual scoring records have been equalled and beaten since then.

	League		All Matches	
1938–39	Fred Chadwick	17	Fred Chadwick	23
1948–49	Bill Jennings	23	Bill Jennings	23
1952–53			Tom Garneys	24
1953–54			Tom Garneys	24
1955–56	Tom Parker	30	Tom Parker	31
1956–57	Ted Phillips	41	Ted Phillips	46

Leading scorers for each season from 1938–39 to 2005–06

	League		All Matches	
1938–39	Fred Chadwick	17	Fred Chadwick	23
1946–47	Albert Day	14	Albert Day	14
1947–48	Bill Jennings	14	Bill Jennings	14
1948–49	Bill Jennings	23	Bill Jennings	23
1949–50	Stan Parker	12	Stan Parker	15
1950–51	Sam McCrory	21	Sam McCrory	21
1951–52	Sam McCrory	16	Tom Garneys	20
1952–53	Tom Garneys	18	Tom Garneys	24
1953–54	Tom Garneys	19	Tom Garneys	24
1954–55	Tom Garneys	20	Tom Garneys	21
1955–56	Tommy Parker	30	Tommy Parker	31
1956–57	Ted Phillips	41	Ted Phillips	46
1957–58	Tom Garneys	18	Tom Garneys	19
1958–59	Ray Crawford	25	Ray Crawford	26
1959–60	Ted Phillips	24	Ted Phillips	25
1960–61	Ray Crawford	40	Ray Crawford	40
1961–62	Ray Crawford	33	Ray Crawford	37
1962–63	Ray Crawford	25	Ray Crawford	33
1963–64	Gerry Baker	15	Gerry Baker	18
1964–65	Gerry Baker	16	Gerry Baker	16
1965–66	Gerry Baker	11	Gerry Baker	15
1966–67	Ray Crawford	21	Ray Crawford	25
1967–68	Frank Brogan	17	Ray Crawford	21
1968–69	Ray Crawford	16	Ray Crawford	17
	John O'Rourke	16	John O'Rourke	17
1969–70	Colin Viljoen	6	Colin Viljoen	6
1970–71	Colin Viljoen	10	Colin Viljoen	12
1971–72	Rod Belfitt	7	Mick Hill	8
	Mick Hill	7		
1972–73	Bryan Hamilton	11	Trevor Whymark	16
	Trevor Whymark	11		
1973–74	Bryan Hamilton	16	Bryan Hamilton	19
1974–75	Bryan Hamilton	10	Bryan Hamilton	17
	Trevor Whymark	10		
1975–76	Trevor Whymark	13	Trevor Whymark	15
1976–77	Trevor Whymark	14	Trevor Whymark	15
1977–78	Paul Mariner	11	Paul Mariner	22
1978–79	Paul Mariner	13	Paul Mariner	17
1979–80	Paul Mariner	17	Paul Mariner	22

THE WHO'S WHO OF IPSWICH TOWN

1980–81	John Wark	18	John Wark	36
1981–82	Alan Brazil	22	Alan Brazil	28
1982–83	John Wark	20	John Wark	23
1983–84	Eric Gates	13	Eric Gates	16
1984–85	Eric Gates	13	Eric Gates	16
1985–86	Kevin Wilson	7	Kevin Wilson	15
1986–87	Kevin Wilson	20	Kevin Wilson	25
1987–88	David Lowe	16	David Lowe	18
1988–89	John Wark	13	Dalian Atkinson	13
			Jason Dozzell	13
			John Wark	13
1989–90	David Lowe	13	David Lowe	13
1990–91	Chris Kiwomya	10	Chris Kiwomya	11
1991–92	Chris Kiwomya	16	Chris Kiwomya	19
1992–93	Chris Kiwomya	10	Chris Kiwomya	17
1993–94	Ian Marshall	10	Ian Marshall	15
1994–95	Claus Thomsen	5	Claus Thomsen	5
1995–96	Ian Marshall	19	Ian Marshall	19
1996–97	Paul Mason	11	Paul Mason	14
1997–98	David A. Johnson	26	David A. Johnson	31
1998–99	David A. Johnson	13	David A. Johnson	14
	Jamie Scowcroft	13	Jamie Scowcroft	14
1999–00	David A. Johnson	22	David A. Johnson	23
2000–01	Marcus Stewart	19	Marcus Stewart	21
2001–02	Marcus Bent	9	Marcus Bent	10
			Marcus Stewart	10
2002–03	Pablo Counago	16	Pablo Counago	20
2003–04	Darren Bent	15	Darren Bent	16
2004–05	Darren Bent	19	Shefki Kuqi	20
	Shefki Kuqi	19		
2005–06	Nicky Forster	7	Nicky Forster	7

Player of the Year

The supporters' Player of the Year award is decided towards the end of every season by voting from Town's fans. The winner is presented with a Rosebowl in the final home League game of the season as a token of appreciation from the Town fanbase for their efforts in the season just ended.

The winners have been as follows:

1972–73	Kevin Beattie
1973–74	Kevin Beattie
1974–75	Colin Viljoen
1975–76	Allan Hunter
1976–77	George Burley
1977–78	Mick Mills
1978–79	Arnold Muhren
1979–80	Frans Thijssen
1980–81	Paul Cooper
1981–82	Alan Brazil
1982–83	Paul Mariner
1983–84	Trevor Putney
1984–85	Terry Butcher
1985–86	Terry Butcher
1986–87	Romeo Zondervan
1987–88	Frank Yallop
1988–89	John Wark
1989–90	John Wark
1990–91	David Linighan
1991–92	John Wark
1992–93	Mick Stockwell
1993–94	John Wark
1994–95	Craig Forrest
1995–96	Simon Milton
1996–97	Mauricio Tauricco
1997–98	Matt Holland
1998–99	Jamie Clapham
1999–2000	Jamie Scowcroft
2000–01	Marcus Stewart
2001–02	Mark Venus
2002–04	Matt Holland
2003–04	Ian Westlake
2004–05	Shefki Kuqi
2005–06	Fabian Wilnis

Terry Butcher

Top 20 Scorers

	All Matches			League Matches	
1	Ray Crawford	218	1	Ray Crawford	204
2	John Wark	190	2	Ted Phillips	161
3	Ted Phillips	181	3	John Wark	135
4	Tom Garneys	143	4	Tom Garneys	123
5	Paul Mariner	135	5	Paul Mariner	96
6	Trevor Whymark	104	6	Tommy Parker	86
7	Eric Gates	96	7	Trevor Whymark	75
8	Tommy Parker	95	8	Eric Gates	73
9	Alan Brazil	80	9	Alan Brazil	70
10	Jason Dozzell	72	10=	Gerry Baker	58
11	Frank Brogan	69		David A. Johnson	58
12	Gerry Baker	66		Frank Brogan	58
13=	David A. Johnson	62	13	Jason Dozzell	53
	Chris Kiwomya	62	14	Chris Kiwomya	51
15	Darren Bent	57	15	Darren Bent	49
16	Bryan Hamilton	56	16	Simon Milton	48
17=	Simon Milton	55	17	Jamie Scowcroft	47
	Jamie Scowcroft	55	18	Colin Viljoen	45
19	Colin Viljoen	54	19	John Elsworthy	44
20	John Elsworthy	52	20=	Bryan Hamilton	43
				Jimmy Leadbetter	43
				Stan Parker	43
				Billy Reed	43

Top 20 Appearances

	All Matches			League Matches	
1	Mick Mills	737(4)	1	Mick Mills	588(3)
2	John Wark	670(8)	2	John Wark	533(6)
3	Mick Stockwell	555(53)	3	Mick Stockwell	464(42)
4	Paul Cooper	575	4	Paul Cooper	447
5	George Burley	500	5	Tommy Parker	428
6	Tommy Parker	475	6	Bill Baxter	409
7	Bill Baxter	459	7	John Elsworthy	398
8	John Elsworthy	435	8	George Burley	394
9	Jason Dozzell	393(21)	9	Doug Rees	356
10	Doug Rees	387	10	Jimmy Leadbetter	344
11	Russell Osman	382(3)	11	Jason Dozzell	320(20)
12	Eric Gates	345(39)	12	Ray Crawford	320
13	Jimmy Leadbetter	375	13	Frank Yallop	289(27)
14	Colin Viljoen	367(5)	14	Roy Bailey	315
15	Allan Hunter	354(1)	15	Colin Viljoen	303(2)
16	Ray Crawford	354	16	Eric Gates	267(29)
17	Terry Butcher	350	17	Russell Osman	294
18	Roy Bailey	346	18	Simon Milton	217(64)
19	Steve McCall	321(19)	19	Allan Hunter	280
20	Paul Mariner	339	20	Dave Linighan	275(2)

Ipswich Town Career Records

Below are the career records (League, FA Cup and League Cup) of every Town first-team player since the club's first Football League game on 27 August 1938. The years given are the first years of seasons, thus 1946 means 1946–47. In the 'Others' list are all the competitions not accounted for in the rest of the table. This list contains figures for the FA Charity Shield, the European Cup, the European Cup-winners' Cup, the UEFA Cup, the Anglo Italian Cup, the Texaco Cup, Simod Cup and Zenith Data Systems Cup.

		LEAGUE		FA CUP		FL CUP		OTHERS		TOTAL	
Player	Played	A	G	A	G	A	G	A	G	A	G
Abidallah N.	2000–2003	0/2	0	0/1	0	0	0	0	0	0/3	0
Abou S.	1998	5	1	0	0	0	0	0	0	5	1
Acres B.D.J.	1953–1959	217	6	15	0	0	0	0	0	232	6
Alsop G.A.	1938	9	2	2	1	0	0	0	0	11	3
Ambrose D.P.	2001–2003	20/10	8	1/1	1	2	1	3/1	1	26/12	11
Appleby R.D.	1995	0/3	0	0	0	0	0	1	0	1/3	0
Armstrong A.	2000–2004	50/29	14	2/1	1	2/2	1	5/3	3	59/35	19
Ashcroft C.T.	1955	7	0	0	0	0	0	0	0	7	0
Atkins I.L.	1985–1987	73/4	4	4	0	8	0	9	0	94/4	4
Atkinson D.R.	1985–1988	49/11	18	0	0	5/1	3	2	1	56/12	22
Austin T.W.	1974–1975	10/9	1	1/1	1	0	0	0/2	1	11/12	3
Axeldahl J.M.	1999	1/15	0	0/1	0	0/3	0	0	0	1/19	0
Bailey R.N.	1955–1964	315	0	19	0	7	0	5	0	346	0
Baird H.	1946–1951	216	6	11	1	0	0	0	0	227	7
Baker C.E.	1992–1994	47/1	0	10	0	8	0	0	0	65/1	0
Baker G.A.	1963–1967	135	58	9	4	7	4	0	0	151	66
Baker W.G.	1955	20	0	0	0	0	0	0	0	20	0
Ball J.H.	1951–1952	32	2	6	0	0	0	0	0	38	2
Baltacha S.	1988–1989	22/6	1	0	0	1	0	1	0	24/6	1
Barber F.	1995	1	0	0	0	0	0	0	0	1	0
Barnard C.L.	1966–1970	18/3	0	1	0	1	0	0	0	20/3	0
Barnes D.	1982–1983	16/1	0	0	0	0	0	0	0	16/1	0
Barron S.	2004–2005	14/1	0	1	0	1	0	0	0	16/1	0
Bart-Williams C.G.	2003–2004	23/3	2	1	0	0	0	0/1	0	24/4	2
Baxter W.A.	1960–1970	409	21	23	1	22	0	5	0	459	22
Beattie T.K.	1972–1980	225/3	24	24/2	5	16	0	31/6	3	296/11	32
Belcher J.A.	1958–1959	27	0	2	0	0	0	0	0	29	0
Belfitt R.M.	1971–1972	40	13	2	0	1	0	3	3	46	16
Bell D.	1938–1949	171	3	16	0	0	0	0	0	187	3
Bell R.C.	1968–1971	32	1	4	0	1	0	0	0	37	1
Bent D.A.	2001–2004	103/19	49	2/2	3	6/1	3	5/4	2	116/26	57
Bent M.N.	2001–2003	51/10	21	4	1	0/2	0	2/1	1	57/13	23
Bernal A.	1987	4/5	0	0	0	0	0	0/2	0	4/7	0
Berry P.	1958–1959	38	6	3	0	0	0	0	0	41	6
Bertschin K.E.	1975–1976	19/13	8	0	0	1	0	0	0	20/13	8
Best D.	1968–1973	168	0	7	0	12	0	12	0	199	0
Bevis D.R.	1963–1965	6	0	2	0	0	0	0	0	8	0
Blackman R.H.	1955–1957	27	12	1	0	0	0	0	0	28	12
Blackwood R.R.	1962–1964	62	12	5	1	2	0	4	1	73	14
Bolton J.M.	1963–1965	69	2	4	0	4	0	0	0	77	2
Bolton R.	1965–1967	21/1	0	0/1	0	0	0	0	0	21/2	0
Bowditch D.P.	2002–2005	13/31	7	0/1	0	3/1	1	0	0	16/33	8
Bozinoski V.	1992	3/6	0	0/1	0	1/1	0	0	0	4/8	0
Bramble T.M.	1998–2001	41/7	1	4/1	0	4/1	2	4	1	53/9	4

185

THE WHO'S WHO OF IPSWICH TOWN

Player	Played	LEAGUE A	LEAGUE G	FA CUP A	FA CUP G	FL CUP A	FL CUP G	OTHERS A	OTHERS G	TOTAL A	TOTAL G
Branagan K.G.	2000–2001	2/1	0	0	0	1	0	0	0	3/1	0
Brazil A.B.	1977–1982	143/11	70	18/2	6	14/1	3	20/1	1	195/15	80
Brekke-Skard V.	2005	2/1	0	0	0	0	0	0	0	2/1	0
Brennan M.R.	1983–1987	165/3	19	12	3	21/1	2	10	1	208/4	25
Broadfoot J.J.	1963–1965	100/1	19	8	1	5/1	1	0	0	113/2	21
Brogan F.A.	1964–1969	201/2	58	10/1	5	9	6	0	0	220/3	69
Brown J.	1948–1950	98	25	5	2	0	0	0	0	103	27
Brown T.	1946–1950	111	0	5	0	0	0	0	0	116	0
Brown T.	1952–1955	84	17	11	4	0	0	0	0	95	21
Brown W.L.	1996–2001	28/12	0	2	0	3	0	4/1	1	37/13	1
Brownlow J.M.	1946	1	0	0	0	0	0	0	0	1	0
Bugg A.A.	1968–1969	4	0	0	0	0	0	0	0	4	0
Burchill M.J.	2000	2/5	1	0	0	0	0	0	0	2/5	1
Burley G.E.	1973–1985	394	6	43	4	35	0	28	0	500	10
Burns M.T.	1938–1951	157	0	11	0	0	0	0	0	168	0
Butcher T.I.	1977–1985	271	16	28	0	29	2	22	3	350	21
Callaghan H.W.	1954	1	0	0	0	0	0	0	0	1	0
Callaghan W.	1952–1954	21	7	1	0	0	0	0	0	22	7
Carberry L.J.	1956–1964	257	0	15	0	8	0	5	0	285	0
Carroll T.R.	1966–1971	115/2	2	2	0	7	1	0	0	124/2	3
Carson T.	1987–1988	1	0	0	0	0	0	0	0	1	0
Casement C.	2005	2/3	0	0	0	0	0	0	0	2/3	0
Chadwick F.W.	1938–1946	40	18	4	5	0	0	0	0	44	23
Chapman L.R.	1994–1995	11/11	1	0	0	1	0	2	0	14/11	1
Cheetham M.M.	1988–1989	1/3	0	0	0	0	0	0/2	0	1/5	0
Clapham J.R.	1998–2002	187/20	10	4/3	1	19/1	4	16/2	1	226/26	16
Clarke F.J.	1969–1972	62/4	15	6	2	3	0	0/1	0	71/5	17
Clarke G.E.	1946–1952	34	1	3	0	0	0	0	0	37	1
Clarke W.A.	1946	3	0	0	0	0	0	0	0	3	0
Clarke W.	2005	1/1	0	0	0	0	0	0	0	1/1	0
Clegg M.J.	2000	3	0	0	0	0	0	0	0	3	0
Cole M.W.	1984–1987	24/14	3	0	0	4/4	3	0/1	0	28/19	6
Collard I.	1969–1974	83/9	5	5/1	0	5/1	1	5/2	0	98/13	6
Collins A.	2002–2005	2/2	0	0	0	1	0	4/4	0	7/6	0
Colrain J.J.	1963–1965	55/1	17	0	0	6	3	0	0	61/1	20
Compton J.F.	1960–1963	111	0	10	0	6	0	4	0	131	0
Connor J.T.	1946	12	4	0	0	0	0	0	0	12	4
Cooper P.D.	1973–1986	447	0	45	0	43	0	40	0	575	0
Cope J.J.	1938	4	0	0	0	0	0	0	0	4	0
Cotterell L.S.	1994	0/2	0	0	0	0/1	0	0	0	0/3	0
Counago P.G.	2001–2004	51/49	31	4/2	0	7	2	7/2	3	69/53	36
Cowie C.	1938	6	0	8	0	0	0	0	0	14	0
Cranson I.	1983–1987	130/1	5	11/1	0	15	0	7	0	163/2	5
Crawford R.	1958–1963										
	1965–1968	320	204	18	5	10	0	6	9	354	218
Creaney G.T.	1996	6	1	0	0	0	0	0	0	6	1
Croft G.	1999–2002	20/9	1	1	0	3/1	0	2/1	0	26/11	1
Crowe A.A.	1953–1954	50	9	5	2	0	0	0	0	55	11
Cundy J.V.	1996–1999	54/4	5	4	0	8	0	2	0	68/4	5
Curran P.J.	1938	7	1	1	0	0	0	0	0	8	1
Currie D.P.	2004–2005	59/13	8	2	0	1	0	0	0	62/13	8
Curtis D.P.	1958–1962	41	17	0	0	1	0	0	0	42	17
Dale W.	1938	43	0	4	0	0	0	0	0	47	0

CAREER RECORDS

Player	Played	LEAGUE A	LEAGUE G	FA CUP A	FA CUP G	FL CUP A	FL CUP G	OTHERS A	OTHERS G	TOTAL A	TOTAL G
Davies A.B.	1938	32	7	3	2	0	0	0	0	35	9
Davin J.J.	1963–1965	77	0	7	0	4	0	0	0	88	0
Davis K.G.	2003–2004	84	0	3	0	2	0	4	0	93	0
D'Avray J.M.	1979–1989	170/41	37	9/2	2	19/4	5	3/7	1	201/54	45
Day A.	1946–1948	63	25	0	0	0	0	0	0	63	25
Deacon D.B.	1950–1959	66	0	9	0	0	0	0	0	75	0
Deehan J.M.	1986–1987	45/4	11	1	0	4/2	1	6/1	2	56/7	14
Dempsey J.	1948	22	5	1	0	0	0	0	0	23	5
De Vos J.R.	2004–2005	88	6	2	0	1	0	0	0	91	6
Diallo D.	2003–2004	39/6	0	0	0	3	0	1	0	43/6	0
Dinning T.	2004	3/4	0	0	0	2	0	0	0	5/4	0
Dobson R.P.	1949–1953	30	5	3	3	0	0	0	0	33	8
Donowa B.L.	1989	17/6	1	2	0	0/2	0	2/1	1	21/9	2
Dougan G.	1962–1963	17	0	1	0	2	0	0	0	20	0
Dozzell J.I.W.	1983–1992 1997	320/20	53	22	12	29/1	3	22	4	393/21	72
Driver A.	1949–1951	86	25	7	1	0	0	1	0	94	26
Durrant L.R.	1993	3/4	0	0	0	0	0	0/1	0	3/5	0
Dyer K.C.	1997–1999	79/9	12	5	0	11	1	5/1	2	100/10	15
Edmonds D.	1991	0/2	0	0	0	0/1	0	0	0	0/3	0
Elliott M.S.	2004	10	0	0	0	0	0	2	0	12	0
Ellis K.E.	1994	1	0	0	0	0	0	0	0	1	0
Elsworthy J.	1949–1964	398	44	27	7	6	0	4	1	435	52
Fearon R.T.	1987–1988	28	0	0	0	1	0	2	0	31	0
Feeney J.M.	1949–1955	214	0	18	0	0	0	0	0	232	0
Fillingham T.	1938	29	1	2	0	0	0	0	0	31	1
Fish M.A.	2005	1	0	0	0	0	0	0	0	1	0
Fletcher C.A.	1938–1945	32	9	4	1	0	0	0	0	36	10
Fletcher L.G.G.	1949–1954	20	0	1	0	0	0	0	0	21	0
Forrest C.L.	1988–1996	263	0	11	0	16	0	14	0	304	0
Forster N.M.	2005	17/3	7	0	0	0	0	0	0	17/3	7
Fox G.R.	1946	11	1	2	0	0	0	0	0	13	1
Friars S.M.	1999–2000	0/1	0	0	0	0	0	0	0	0/1	0
Fuller R.D.	2005	3	2	0	0	0	0	0	0	3	2
Gaardsoe T.	2001–2003	40/1	5	1	1	2/1	1	2/2	0	45/4	7
Garneys T.T.	1951–1958	248	123	25	20	0	0	0	0	273	143
Garrett L.G.	1958	1	0	0	0	0	0	0	0	1	0
Garvan O.	2005	29/2	3	0/1	0	0/1	0	0	0	29/4	3
Gates E.L.	1973–1984	267/29	73	23/3	8	28/1	8	21/6	7	339/39	96
Gayle B.W.	1989–1991	58	4	0/1	0	3	0	0	0	61/1	4
Gaynor J.M.	1951–1952	47	3	5	1	0	0	0	0	52	4
Geddis D.	1976–1978	26/17	5	2/1	1	0/1	0	2/7	0	30/26	6
George F.	2001–2003	24/11	7	0	0	1/1	0	5/4	1	30/16	8
Gernon F.A.J.	1981–1986	76	0	4/1	0	6	0	1	0	87/1	0
Gerrard P.W.	2002–2003	5	0	0	0	0	0	0	0	5	0
Gibbons J.R.	1949	11	3	2	0	0	0	0	0	13	3
Gibson J.	1948	1	0	0	0	0	0	0	0	1	0
Gillespie I.C.	1946	6	1	0	0	0	0	0	0	6	1
Gleghorn N.W.	1985–1987	54/12	11	3/1	0	3/2	0	5/2	2	65/17	13
Goddard P.	1990–1993	59/27	13	6/8	0	7	0	2	0	74/35	13
Grant W.	1954–1956	75	22	3	0	0	0	0	0	78	22
Green D.	1946–1951	52	0	2	0	0	0	0	0	54	0
Gregory D.S.	1988–1994	16/16	2	1	0	3/2	0	3/2	4	23/20	6

THE WHO'S WHO OF IPSWICH TOWN

		LEAGUE		FA CUP		FL CUP		OTHERS		TOTAL	
Player	Played	A	G	A	G	A	G	A	G	A	G
Gregory N.R.	1994–1997	18/27	9	0/1	0	2/3	0	4/3	2	24/34	11
Grew M.S.	1984	6	0	1	0	0	0	0	0	7	0
Gudmundsson N.	1996–1997	2/6	2	0	0	0	0	1/1	1	3/7	3
Guentchev B.L.	1992–1994	39/22	6	6/2	5	6	0	0	0	51/24	11
Hall W.	1960–1962	16	0	1	0	2	0	0	0	19	0
Hallworth J.G.	1985–1987	45	0	1	0	4	0	6	0	56	0
Hamilton B.	1971–1975	142/11	43	11/1	5	11/1	3	22	5	186/13	56
Hammond G.	1970–1973	52/3	2	6	0	4	0	2/2	0	64/5	2
Hancock K.P.	1964–1968	163	0	7	0	10	0	0	0	180	0
Harbey G.K.	1987–1989	53/6	1	2	0	7/1	2	8	0	70/7	3
Harewood M.A.	1999	5/1	1	0	0	0	0	0	0	5/1	1
Harper C.G.	1965–1974	144/4	5	5	1	8/1	0	14	0	171/5	6
Harper D.	1964–1966	70/2	2	6	1	3	0	0	0	79/2	3
Havenga W.S.	1951–1952	19	3	0	0	0	0	0	0	19	3
Hayes H.	1948–1949	9	0	0	0	0	0	0	0	9	0
Haynes D.	2005	6/13	4	1	0	0	0	0	0	7/13	4
Hegan D.	1963–1968	207	34	11	3	12	1	0	0	230	38
Higgins A.R.	1952	2	0	0	0	0	0	0	0	2	0
Hill D.M.	1988–1990	54/7	0	1	0	4	0	5/1	0	64/8	0
Hill M.R.	1969–1972	63/3	18	9	2	2	0	0	0	74/3	20
Hodges L.L.	1998–1999	0/4	0	0	0	0	0	0	0	0/4	0
Holland M.R.	1997–2003	259	38	12	0	23/1	6	17/2	2	311/3	46
Holster M.	1998–1999	1/9	0	0/1	0	0/1	0	0	0	1/11	0
Horlock K.	2004–2005	46/12	0	1	0	1/1	0	1	0	49/13	0
Houghton S.A.	1990	7/1	1	0	0	0	0	0	0	7/1	1
Houghton W.G.	1966–1968	107	3	5	0	5	0	0	0	117	3
Howe S.R.	1996	2/1	0	0	0	1	0	0	0	3/1	0
Hreidarsson H.	2000–2003	101/1	2	6	0	11	0	9	1	127/1	3
Humes A.	1986–1991	107/13	10	4	1	6	0	10	1	127/13	12
Hunt J.R.	1998	2/4	0	0	0	0	0	0	0	2/4	0
Hunt R.R.	1967–1970	16/10	4	1	0	1/1	0	0	0	18/11	4
Hunter A.	1971–1980	280	8	26	0	17	2	31/1	0	354/1	10
Jackson J.K.	1981	1	0	0	0	0	0	0	0	1	0
Jean E.J.	1996	0/1	0	0	0	0	0	0	0	0/1	0
Jefferson D.	1967–1972	163/3	1	6	0	3	0	0	0	172/3	1
Jennings H.W.	1947–1950	102	41	6	1	0	0	0	0	108	42
Johnson D.A.	1997–2001	121/10	55	7	2	13	5	7	0	148/10	62
Johnson D.E.	1972–1975	134/3	35	15	4	8	5	17/1	2	174/4	46
Johnson G.	1988–1994	114/18	11	12/1	2	10/1	2	3/1	1	139/21	16
Johnstone R.G.	1957–1958	35	4	3	0	0	0	0	0	38	4
Jones F.	1938	21	8	2	2	0	0	4	0	27	10
Jones W.J.	1949–1954	33	1	3	0	0	0	0	0	36	1
Juan J.	2005	18/9	5	0/1	0	1	0	0	0	19/10	5
Juryeff I.M.	1988	0/2	0	0	0	0	0	0	0	0/2	0
Karbassiyoon D.	2004	3/2	0	1	0	0	0	0	0	4/2	0
Karic A.	2000–2003	0	0	0	0	0/3	0	0	0	0/3	0
Keeble C.M.	1997–2000	0/1	0	0	0	0	0	0	0	0/1	0
Keeley G.M.	1972–1973	4	0	0	0	0	0	1	0	5	0
Kellard R.S.W.	1965	13	3	2	0	0	0	0	0	15	3
Kennedy J.N.	1997–1999	6/2	0	1	0	0	0	0	0	7/2	0
Kerslake D.	1997	2/5	0	0	0	1/1	0	0	0	3/6	0
Kinsella A.S.	1982–83	7/2	0	1	0	1	0	0	0	9/2	0
Kiwomya C.M.	1988–1994	197/28	51	14	2	14/1	8	5	1	230/29	62

CAREER RECORDS

Player	Played	LEAGUE A	G	FA CUP A	G	FL CUP A	G	OTHERS A	G	TOTAL A	G
Knights D.J.	2004–2005	0/1	0	0	0	0	0	0	0	0/1	0
Kuqi S.	2003–2004	69/10	30	2/1	1	0/2	0	3/1	1	74/14	32
Lambert M.A.	1968–1978	180/30	39	16/5	3	12/5	2	11/4	1	219/44	45
Lang T.	1946	5	1	0	0	0	0	0	0	5	1
Laurel J.A.	1960–1962	4	0	0	0	1	0	1	0	6	0
Lea C.	1964–1968	103/4	2	8	0	8	0	0	0	119/4	2
Leadbetter J.H.	1955–1964	344	43	19	4	8	1	4	1	375	49
Lee A.D.	2005	14	4	0	0	0	0	0	0	14	4
Legg A.	1997	6	1	0	0	1	0	0	0	7	1
Le Pen U.	2001–2003	0/1	0	0/1	0	0	0	0/1	0	0/3	0
Linighan D.	1988–1995	275/2	12	18	1	21	0	11	0	325/2	13
Little J.	1938–1949	146	20	22	5	0	0	0	0	168	25
Logan R.J.	1999–2002	0/3	0	0/1	0	0	0	0	0	0/4	0
Lowe D.A.	1987–1991	121/13	37	3	0	10	2	10/2	3	144/15	42
Lundstrum C.F.	1957–1959	13	1	0	0	0	0	0	0	13	1
McCall S.H.	1978–1986	249/8	7	23/10	1	29	0	20/1	4	321/19	12
McCrory S.M.	1949–1951	97	39	5	1	0	0	0	0	102	40
McDonald D.	2005	4/10	1	0	0	1	0	2/4	2	7/14	3
McEveley J.	2005	17/2	1	0	0	0	0	0	0	17/2	1
McGinn F.	1948	8	2	0	0	0	0	0	0	8	2
McGourty J.	1938	1	0	0	0	0	0	0	0	1	0
McGreal J.	1999–2004	120/3	4	5	0	12	0	10	1	147/3	5
Mackay A.M.	1946	5	0	2	0	0	0	0	0	7	0
MacLuckie G.R.	1953–1957	141	24	11	1	0	0	0	0	152	25
McLuckie J.S.	1938	41	1	16	2	0	0	0	0	57	3
McMillan G.S.	1954–1957	53	0	1	0	0	0	0	0	54	0
McNeil M.	1964–1971	141/5	4	16	0	11	1	0	0	168/5	5
Macrow G.C.	1955–1956	2	0	0	0	0	0	0	0	2	0
Maffey D.	1947	5	1	0	0	0	0	0	0	5	1
Magilton J.	1999–2005	243/30	16	7/2	1	14/1	1	21/4	4	285/37	22
Mahon A.J.	2002–2003	7/4	1	0	0	1	0	0	0	8/4	1
Makin C.G.	2001–2003	78	0	2	0	4	0	7/1	0	91/1	0
Malcolm K.C.	1954–1962	274	2	13	0	1	0	3	0	291	2
Mariner P.	1976–1983	260	96	31	19	20	8	28	12	339	135
Marshall A.J.	2001–2004	53	0	4	0	2	0	6	0	65	0
Marshall I.P.	1993–1996	79/5	32	9	3	4	3	0	0	92/5	38
Mason P.D.	1993–1997	103/10	25	4/3	3	10	4	4	3	121/13	35
Mathie A.	1995–1998	90/19	38	2/2	0	10/3	8	6	1	108/24	47
Meade R.J.	1990	0/1	0	0	0	0	0	0	0	0/1	0
Midgley N.A.	1997	1/3	1	0	0	0	0	0	0	1/3	1
Miller J.T.	1968–1973	38/13	2	1/1	0	2/1	2	2/2	0	43/17	4
Miller T.W.	2001–2004	101/16	30	3/2	3	5/2	2	7/3	2	116/23	37
Mills M.D.	1965–1982	588/3	22	57	5	43/1	2	49	1	737/4	30
Millward H.D.	1955–1962	143	35	10	1	2	0	0	0	155	36
Milton S.C.	1987–1997	217/64	48	12	1	15/8	3	14/2	3	258/74	55
Mitchell A.R.	1947–1949	42	2	4	0	0	0	3	0	49	2
Mitchell D.J.	1966–1968	0/2	0	0	0	0	0	0	0	0/2	0
Mitchell S.A.	2003–2004	0/2	0	1	0	1	0	0	0	2/2	0
Moncur J.F.	1991	5/1	0	0	0	0	0	0	0	5/1	0
Moran D.W.	1961–1963	104	31	7	1	7	3	5	2	123	37
Morgan P.J.	1994	1	0	0	0	0	0	0	0	1	0
Morris P.J.	1967–1973	213/7	13	15	0	8/1	0	13/1	3	249/9	16
Morris T.	1938	1	0	0	0	0	0	0	0	1	0

THE WHO'S WHO OF IPSWICH TOWN

Player	Played	LEAGUE A	LEAGUE G	FA CUP A	FA CUP G	FL CUP A	FL CUP G	OTHERS A	OTHERS G	TOTAL A	TOTAL G
Morrow S.	2002	0	0	0	0	0/1	0	0	0	0/1	0
Mowbray A.M.	1995–2000	125/3	5	9	0	7	1	9	2	150/3	8
Muhren A.J.H.	1978–1981	161	21	19	3	15	2	19	3	214	29
Mulraney A.	1936–1945	28	8	5	2	0	0	3	1	36	11
Murchison R.A.	1950–1954	42	2	6	0	0	0	1	0	49	2
Murray A.	2002	0/1	0	0	0	0	0	0	0	0/1	0
Myles N.T.	1949–1959	223	15	22	3	0	0	0	0	245	18
Nash G.T.	2003–2005	0/1	0	0	0	0	0	0	0	0/1	0
Naylor R.A.	1995–2005	185/84	37	5/5	1	10/10	1	7/6	1	207/105	40
Neilson T.	1948	1	0	0	0	0	0	0	0	1	0
Nelson A.N.	1959–1964	193	0	11	0	7	0	4	0	215	0
Neville C.W.	1989	1	0	0	0	0	0	0	0	1	0
Newman E.I.A.	1952	18	0	6	0	0	0	0	0	24	0
Niven S.T.	1996–2000	2	0	0	0	0	0	0	0	2	0
Norfolk L.R.	1994	1/2	0	0	0	0	0	1	0	2/2	0
O'Brien J.	1949–1950	50	12	4	0	0	0	0	0	54	12
O'Callaghan K.	1979–1984	72/43	4	5/5	0	9/5	1	1/7	0	87/60	5
O'Donnell C.	1986–1988	10/4	0	0	0	2/1	0	5/2	0	17/7	0
O'Mahoney M.A.	1946–1948	58	4	3	0	0	0	1	0	62	4
O'Rourke J.	1967–1969	69	30	1	1	2	0	0	0	72	31
Osborne R.C.	1973–1980	109/15	9	8/4	1	2/1	0	8/2	0	127/22	10
Osman R.C.	1977–1984	294	17	30/2	1	28	3	30/1	0	382/3	21
Overton P.H.	1977	1	0	0	0	0	0	0	0	1	0
Owen A.W.	1958–1961	30	3	3	0	1	0	1	0	35	3
Palmer S.L.	1989–1995	87/24	2	8/3	1	3	0	4/2	0	102/29	3
Parker S.F.	1946–1950	126	43	15	8	0	0	0	0	141	51
Parker T.R.	1946–1956	428	86	37	7	0	0	10	2	475	95
Parkes P.B.N.F.	1990	3	0	0	0	0	0	0	0	3	0
Parkin S.	2005	17/3	5	0	0	0	0	0	0	17/3	5
Parkin T.A.	1977–1986	52/18	0	3/2	0	3/1	0	3/2	0	61/23	0
Parry B.J.	1951–1954	138	0	16	0	0	0	0	0	154	0
Parry O.	1938–1948	104	0	18	0	0	0	0	0	122	0
Paz C.A.	1994	13/4	1	0	0	0	0	0	0	13/4	1
Peddelty J.	1972–1976	44	5	3	0	1	0	2	0	50	5
Pennyfather G.J.	1989–1992	11/4	1	0	0	1/1	0	0/2	0	12/7	1
Peralta S.R.	2001–2002	16/6	3	2	2	1	0	2/2	0	21/8	5
Perrett G.R.	1938–1949	131	4	14	0	0	0	0	0	145	4
Peters J.	2005	4/9	0	0	0	1	0	0	0	5/9	0
Petta R.A.M.	1996–1999	55/15	9	5/1	0	8/2	0	3	0	71/18	9
Petterson A.K.	1992 1995	2	0	0	0	0	0	0	0	2	0
Phillips E.J.	1953–1963	269	161	12	9	7	5	7	6	295	181
Pickett R.A.	1957–1962	140	3	4	0	1	0	3	1	148	4
Pole H.E.	1946–1950	39	13	4	0	0	0	0	0	43	13
Price L.P.	2003–2005	33/1	0	0	0	3	0	0	0	36/1	0
Proudlock A.D.	2005	3/6	0	0	0	0	0	0	0	3/6	0
Pullen J.D.	1999–2003	1	0	0	0	1	0	0	0	2	0
Putney T.A.	1982–1985	94/9	8	9	0	15	1	0	0	118/9	9
Redford I.P.	1988–1990	59/9	8	0	0	6	2	6	2	71/9	12
Reed W.G.	1953–1957	155	43	13	3	0	0	0	0	168	46
Rees D.C.	1948–1958	356	1	29	0	0	0	2	0	387	1
Rees W.D.	1957–1960	90	29	5	3	0	0	0	0	95	32
Reuser M.F.	2000–2004	42/49	14	4/2	1	5/4	2	2/6	2	53/61	19

CAREER RECORDS

Player	Played	LEAGUE A	G	FA CUP A	G	FL CUP A	G	OTHERS A	G	TOTAL A	G
Richards M.L.	2002–2005	97/22	6	4/1	0	4/1	0	4/2	0	109/26	6
Rimmer E.J.	1938	3	0	0	0	0	0	2	0	5	0
Rimmer N.	1985–1987	19/3	3	0	0	1	0	3/1	0	23/4	3
Roberts J.D.	1974–1977	17/1	0	4	0	1	0	0/1	0	22/2	0
Roberts J.N.	1949–1951	73	15	9	2	0	0	0	0	82	17
Robertson J.G.	1969–1971	87	10	8	1	3	1	0	0	98	12
Rodger R.	1938	9	0	2	0	0	0	0	0	11	0
Roy J.R.	1946	15	2	2	0	0	0	0	0	17	2
Rumbold G.	1946–1949	121	11	5	0	0	0	4	0	130	11
Santos G.	2003–2004	28/6	1	0	0	2	0	0	0	30/6	1
Scales J.R.	2000	2	0	0	0	2	0	0	0	4	0
Scowcroft J.B.	1994–2001 2005	166/45	47	9/1	0	21/4	7	7/4	1	203/54	55
Sedgley S.P.	1994–1996	115	15	5	0	10	0	5	1	135	16
Sereni M.	2001–2003	25	0	0	0	2	0	6	0	33	0
Shanahan T.C.	1970	3/1	0	0	0	0	0	0	0	3/1	0
Sharkey P.G.S.	1975–1976	17/1	1	0	0	1	0	0	0	18/1	1
Shufflebottom F.	1938	2	0	2	0	0	0	4	0	8	0
Siddall A.B.	1957–1960	58	6	0	0	1	0	0	0	59	6
Sito L.C.	2005	31/7	0	0/1	0	1	0	0	0	32/8	0
Sivell L.	1969–1983	141	0	19	0	7	0	8	0	175	0
Slater S.I.	1993–1996	61/11	4	6	0	6	0	2/2	0	75/13	4
Smith G.C.	1949	8	0	1	0	0	0	0	0	9	0
Smith J.	1946	2	0	2	0	0	0	0	0	4	0
Smith T.R.	1964–1965	22/1	0	0	0	4	0	0	0	26/1	0
Smythe H.R.	1946–1947	2	0	0	0	0	0	0	0	2	0
Snell V.D.R.	1949–1958	64	2	3	0	0	0	0	0	67	2
Sonner D.J.	1996–1998	28/28	3	1/1	0	6/4	1	0/1	0	35/34	4
Spearitt E.A.	1965–1968	62/10	13	1	0	6	1	0	0	69/10	14
Stacey S.D.	1968	3	0	0	0	0	0	0	0	3	0
Steggles K.P.	1980–1985	49/1	1	4	0	5	1	2	0	60/1	2
Stein E.M.S.	1997	6/1	2	0	0	3/1	1	0	0	9/2	3
Stephenson R.	1960–1964	144	21	8	2	6	2	5	1	163	26
Stevenson W.H.H.	1947	3	0	0	0	0	0	0	0	3	0
Stewart W.M.	2000–2002	65/10	27	4	2	4/2	1	8	7	81/12	37
Stirk J.	1977	6	0	0	0	1	0	1	0	8	0
Stockwell M.T.	1982–2000	464/42	35	28/3	1	42/5	5	21/3	3	555/53	44
Stuart M.R.	1989	5	2	0	0	0	0	0	0	5	2
Sunderland A.	1983–1985	51/7	11	2/1	1	6/1	1	0	0	59/9	13
Supple S.	2005	21/1	0	1	0	0	0	0	0	22/1	0
Swailes C.W.	1995–1997	34/3	1	0	0	3	0	2	0	39/3	1
Talbot B.E.	1973–1978	177	25	23	3	12	1	15	2	227	31
Tanner A.D.	1992–2000	49/24	7	5/2	0	2/2	0	3/1	1	59/29	8
Taricco M.R.	1994–1998	134/3	4	8	0	18	3	7	0	167/3	7
Tennent D.	1952	4	0	0	0	0	0	0	0	4	0
Thetis J.M.	1998–2000	44/3	2	2	0	5	1	2/1	0	53/4	3
Thijssen F.J.	1978–1982	123/2	10	15	2	12/1	0	17	4	167/3	16
Thompson K.J.	1964–1965	11/1	0	1	0	1	0	0	0	13/1	0
Thompson N.	1989–1995	199/7	19	17	1	14/1	1	8	2	238/8	23
Thomsen C.	1994–1996	77/4	7	5	0	8	1	2/1	0	92/5	8
Thorburn J.H.F.	1963–1964	24	0	0	0	0	0	0	0	24	0
Thrower D.A.	1956–1964	27	2	2	0	2	0	0	0	31	2
Tibbott L.	1975–1978	52/2	0	6	0	7	0	5	1	70/2	1

THE WHO'S WHO OF IPSWICH TOWN

Player	Played	LEAGUE A	G	FA CUP A	G	FL CUP A	G	OTHERS A	G	TOTAL A	G
Treacy F.	1963–1965	17/1	5	1	0	1	0	0	0	19/1	5
Trenter R.H.	1951	2	0	0	0	0	0	0	0	2	0
Trotter L.	2005	0/1	0	0	0	0	0	0	0	0/1	0
Turner R.D.	1975–1983	22/26	2	5/1	2	1/2	1	1/4	1	29/33	6
Twamley B.R.	1973–1974	2	0	0	0	0	0	0	0	2	0
Tyler L.V.	1950–1951	73	0	5	0	0	0	0	0	78	0
Uhlenbeek G.R.	1995–1998	77/12	4	4/3	0	5/3	0	7/1	0	93/19	4
Unsworth D.G.	2005	16	1	0	0	0	0	0	0	16	1
Vaughan A.J.	1994–1996	56/11	3	2	0	4/2	0	4	0	66/13	3
Venus M.	1997–2003	144/4	16	4	0	18	3	14	0	180/4	19
Vernazzi P.A.	1998–1999	2	0	0	0	0	0	0	0	2	0
Viljoen C.	1966–1977	303/2	45	28/1	6	20	2	16/2	1	367/5	54
Walls J.P.	1954	1	0	0	0	0	0	0	0	1	0
Walsh R.	1965	6/1	0	1	0	1	0	0	0	8/1	0
Wark J.	1974–1983 1987–1989 1991–1996	533/6	135	55/1	12	42/1	25	40	18	670/8	190
Warne R.	1950–1951	30	11	0	0	0	0	0	0	30	11
Westlake I.J.	2002–2005	94/24	15	3	0	3/2	1	0	0	100/26	16
Whelan P.J.	1991–1994	76/6	2	3/1	0	6/1	0	1	0	86/8	2
Whitton S.P.	1990–1993	80/8	15	8/1	2	7/1	2	4	0	99/10	19
Whymark T.J.	1969–1978	249/12	75	21	2	20	9	32/1	18	322/13	104
Whyte D.A.	1997	2	0	0	0	0	0	0	0	2	0
Wigg R.G.	1967–1969	35/2	14	1	0	3	0	0	0	39/2	14
Williams D.W.	1992–1998	217	2	18	0	24/1	0	4	0	263/1	2
Williams G.J.	2005	12	1	1	0	0	0	0	0	13	1
Williams J.J.	1938	9	0	0	0	0	0	1	0	10	0
Wilnis F.	1999–2005	227/21	6	11	0	10/4	0	13/1	0	261/26	6
Wilson K.J.	1984–1986	94/4	34	10	3	10	8	7	4	121/4	49
Wilson U.J.	1987	5/1	0	0	0	0	0	0	0	5/1	0
Woods C.M.P.	1966–1969	65/17	5	1/1	0	4/1	2	0	0	70/19	7
Woods C.R.	1969–1979	217/50	24	24/4	2	13/3	2	24/3	3	278/60	31
Woods N.S.	1987–1989	15/12	5	0	0	0	0	4	1	19/12	6
Wookey K.W.	1950	15	1	2	0	0	0	0	0	17	1
Wosahlo R.F.	1967 1969	1/1	0	0	0	0	0	0	0	1/1	0
Wright J.M.	1999–2004	147/37	10	8/1	1	15/2	0	10/1	0	180/41	11
Wright R.I.	1995–2001	240	0	13	0	27	0	11	0	291	0
Yallop F.W.	1983–1995	289/27	7	15/3	0	23/2	1	23/4	0	350/36	8
Youds E.P.	1991–1994	38/12	1	5/1	0	1/2	0	0	0	44/15	1
Zondervan R.	1983–1991	270/4	13	11/2	2	24	3	14	2	319/6	20